OTHER TITLES IN THE RELIGIOUS LIFE IN HISTORY SERIES

Charles Hallisey, Series Editor

Understanding Relgious Life, Third Edition
Frederick J. Streng

African Cosmos: An Introduction to Religion in Africa
Noel Q. King

The Buddhist Religion, Fourth Edition
Richard H. Robinson and Willard L. Johnson

The Experience of Buddhism
John S. Strong

Chinese Religion: An Introduction, Fifth Edition
Laurence G. Thompson

The Chinese Way in Religion
Laurence G. Thompson

The Christian Religious Tradition
Stephen Reynolds

The Hindu Religious Tradition
Thomas J. Hopkins

The House of Islam, Third Edition
Kenneth Cragg and R. Marston Speight

Japanese Religion: Unity and Diversity, Third Edition
H. Byron Earhart

The Life of Torah: Readings in the Jewish Religious Experience
Jacob Neusner

The Way of Torah: An Introduction to Judaism, Fifth Edition
Jacob Neusner

Native American Religions: An Introduction
Sam Gill

Native American Traditions: Sources and Interpretations
Sam Gill

Religion in the Japanese Experience

Sources and Interpretations

Second Edition

H. BYRON EARHART
Western Michigan University

Wadsworth Publishing Company
I(T)P® An International Thomson Publishing Company

Belmont, CA • Albany, NY • Bonn • Boston • Cincinnati • Detroit • Johannesburg • London • Madrid
Melbourne • Mexico City • New York • Paris • Singapore • Tokyo • Toronto • Washington

Religion Editor: Peter Adams
Series Editor: Charles Hallisey
Assistant Editor: Clayton Glad
Editorial Assistant: Greg Brueck
Marketing Manager: David Garrison
Project Editor: Karen Garrison
Print Buyer: Barbara Britton
Permissions Editor: Robert Kauser
Advertising Project Manager: Joseph Jodar
Copy Editor: Denise Cook-Clampert
Cover Design: Craig Hanson
Cover Photograph: Itsukushima Shrine, Hiroshima, Japan; ©Travelpix 1988/FPG
International
Compositor: Thompson Type
Printer: Quebecor/Fairfield

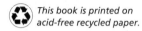
For more information, contact Wadsworth Publishing Company, 10 Davis Drive, Belmont, CA
94002, or electronically at http://www.thomson.com/wadsworth.html

International Thomson Publishing Europe
Berkshire House 168-173
High Holborn
London, WC1V 7AA, England

International Thomson Editores
Campos Eliseos 385, Piso 7
Col. Polanco
11560 México D.F. México

Thomas Nelson Australia
102 Dodds Street
South Melbourne 3205
Victoria, Australia

International Thomson Publishing Asia
221 Henderson Road
#05-10 Henderson Building
Singapore 0315

Nelson Canada
1120 Birchmount Road
Scarborough, Ontario
Canada M1K 5G4

International Thomson Publishing Japan
Hirakawacho Kyowa Building, 3F
2-2-1 Hirakawacho
Chiyoda-ku, Tokyo 102, Japan

International Thomson Publishing GmbH
Königswinterer Strasse 418
53227 Bonn, Germany

International Thomson Publishing
Southern Africa
Building 18, Constantia Park
240 Old Pretoria Road
Halfway House, 1685 South Africa

Library of Congress Cataloging-in-Publication Data

Religion in the Japanese experience : sources and interpretations / H. Byron Earhart. —
2nd ed.
p. cm.—(Religious life in history series)
ISBN 0-534-52461-3
1. Japan—Religion. I. Earhart, H. Byron. II. Series.
BL2202.R445   1997
200′ .952—dc20

96-32328

For
Kenneth, David, and Paul
and for
Michelle, Adrienne, and Bryce

Contents

CHAPTER 3

Buddhism   45

III RELIGION IN RECENT AND MODERN JAPAN

CHAPTER 16

The Dilemma of Organized Religion in Modern Japan   244

CHAPTER 17

The New Religions   268

Foreword

The Religious Life in History series introduces the richness and diversity of religious thought, practice, experience, and institutions as they are found in living traditions throughout the world.

Some of the religious traditions included in the Religious Life in History series are defined by geography and cultural arenas, while others are defined by their development across cultural and geographic boundaries. In all cases, however, the introductions seek to take full account of the variety within each tradition while keeping in sight the traits and patterns that encourage both scholars and members of various religious communities to distinguish a particular religious tradition from others around it. Moreover, as a set of introductions to quite different religious traditions, the series naturally invites comparison between different ways of being religious and encourages critical reflection on religion as a human phenomenon more generally. Thus, besides containing volumes on different relgious traditions, the series also includes a core book on the study of religion that is intended to aid the kinds of comparative inquiry in critical reflection that the series fosters through its introductions to religion, in particular, cultural and historical contexts.

The basic texts in the Religious Life in History series all provide narrative descriptions of a religious tradition, but each also approaches its subject with an interpretive orientation appropriate to its focus. Some traditions lend themselves more to developmental, others more to topical, studies. This lack of a single interpretive stance in the series is itself instructive. It reflects the interpretive choices made by the different authors, choices informed by a deep knowledge of the languages and cultures associated with the religious tradition in question. It also displays the methodological pluralism that characterizes the contemporary study of religion, but perhaps most important, it can serve as a useful reminder that what is considered religiously important in one context may not be so in another; indeed, what is seen as relgious in one culture may not be so regarded elsewhere.

Many of the basic texts in the series have a complementary anthology of reading selections. These include translations of texts used by the participants of a tradition, descriptions of practices and practitioners' experiences, and brief interpretive studies of phenomena important in a given tradition. In addition, all of the basic texts present a list of materials for further readings, including translations and more in-depth examination of specific topics.

The Religious Life in History series was founded more than two decades ago by Frederick J. Streng. While Streng was editor of the series, continuous efforts were made to update the scholarship and to make the presentation of material more effective in each volume. These efforts will continue in the future through the publication of revised editions as well as with the addition of new volumes to the series. But the aim of the series has remained the same since its beginnings: as Frederick Streng said, we hope that readers will find these volumes "introductory" in the most significant sense—as introductions to new perspectives for understanding themselves and others.

Charles Hallisey
Series Editor

Preface

The years that have passed since the appearance of the first edition of this anthology are but a brief span when compared with the several thousand years of Japanese religion. In these years Japanese religion has changed, albeit minimally, while scholarship on the subject has advanced considerably. Unfortunately, space allows us to include in this second edition only a handful of the many works now available.

The general plan of this book is retained from the previous edition, providing descriptions and interpretations of Japanese religion from prehistoric times to the present, viewing as many traditions and aspects as possible. The materials are arranged by individual traditions, overall themes, and historical periods. The major change in this edition is the replacement of older selections with more recent ones.

A new Chapter 4 is devoted to coverage of six Buddhist founders, providing greater depth to the treatment of Buddhism. New selections on two Shinto thinkers and a Neo-Confucian scholar were added to other chapters.

Recent publications on the role of women in Japanese religion have also been included, but rather than create a separate chapter for these materials, they have been integrated in the chapters covering such topics as Shinto, Buddhism, folk religion, and everyday life. Because each selection stands on its own, a professor or reader may create a "women in Japanese religion" unit by studying the appropriate selections together.

As in the first edition, several examples of poetry and literature are excerpted to illustrate the dramatic representation of religious values in a cultural setting. In this edition we have added a piece from the classic *Tale of Genji*, as well as an analysis of Buddhist themes within literature.

The New Religions chapter has been expanded, and includes three additional examples. These three new selections are life histories of members of the New Religions, providing more of an "inside" view of these important contemporary movements. For another example of these movements, a selection on a Christian New Religion has been added to the chapter on Christianity. The modern scene is also highlighted in two social science analyses of religious values in the workplace—in both white-collar and blue-collar settings.

Readers seeking additional information on a subject may go to the source of a reading, or may consult the Annotated Bibliography in *Japanese Religion: Unity and Diversity*, scheduled for publication in a fourth edition next year.

Studying, teaching, and writing about Japanese religion have given me many enjoyable years; I hope the reader's trip through this tradition is interesting and rewarding.

I would like to thank the reviewers for this edition: Harry Krebs, Dickinson College; Herman Ooms, University of California at Los Angeles; and Richard Pilgrim, Syracuse University. Not all people who made this volume possible can be thanked individually, but special acknowledgments go to our departmental secretary, Gwen West, and to Wadsworth's editorial staff.

How to Use This Sourcebook

The selections in this book are gathered into chapters, which in turn are organized into three main parts: following the Introduction, Part I deals with individual religious traditions; Part II emphasizes themes cutting across these traditions; and Part III focuses on religion in recent and modern Japan. Each chapter has its own introduction, and each selection begins with a short treatment of the subject and the chosen excerpt.

This work is designed for use with the overview text, *Japanese Religion: Unity and Diversity*, soon to appear in a fourth edition. A recommended plan to make the most of this sourcebook is to read it together with *Japanese Religion*, utilizing the larger historical and religious picture to place in context the more detailed accounts from the sourcebook.

A set of study questions at the back of *Japanese Religion* sequences interrelated readings from it and the sourcebook, asking the reader to consider major issues of fact and interpretation in these materials.

Japanese religion is too rich and varied to be captured in any one plan or sequence: professors and general readers may develop their own itineraries through Japan's religious panorama. Those who do not wish to survey the entire scene may choose the particular readings of greatest interest. For instance, persons concerned most with a particular tradition, such as Buddhism, may read the chapters devoted to it, and then dip into related selections in other chapters (such as the excerpt on p. 245). Those more interested in a particular historical period, such as early Japan, may read selections on early Shinto and early Buddhism from those chapters, and then move on to the selection on the religious significance of archaeological finds (p. 219). Similarly, the materials on modern Japan can be read together.

Some persons may be drawn more to a particular theme than to a historical period or a specific tradition; they might read the chapter for one or more themes, and then turn to selections from other parts related to that theme. For example, the selections on women can be read together as a unit on the role of women in Japanese religion. (Specifically, these are selections 7, 15, 28, 43, 45, 50, 59, and 63.) To assist the reader in seeing the connections between materials, the introductions preceding each selection contain cross-references to other chapters and selections. For further references, the Annotated Bibliography in *Japanese Religion* will be useful.

CHAPTER ONE

Introduction:
The Nature of
Japanese Religion

Japanese religion comprises an amazing panorama of a wide variety of practices and traditions through several thousand years; even a bird's-eye view of the history of Japanese religion reveals its richness and diversity. Archaeological evidence from prehistoric times points to religious activity regarding fertility and afterlife. In early historic times, influence from China helped stimulate the organization of Shinto out of the earliest tradition; at the same time, Chinese influence brought Buddhism, Confucianism, and Taoism to Japan. Through time, Shinto and Buddhism developed as elaborate organized religions, whereas Confucianism and Taoism penetrated the thought and life of the people. Folk religion existed outside of organized religion, and in the late medieval period and again in modern times, Christianity was introduced to Japan. To top off this already interesting religious scenario, in the past century many new religious movements (usually called New Religions) have arisen.

With such a broad spectrum of traditions to draw on, it is not surprising that the picture of Japanese religion is painted with every imaginable color. The story of prehistoric religion is told by the remains of stone circles, fertility figurines, phallic emblems, and burial sites. From the dim past, Shinto has preserved the mythological origin of Japan and liturgical prayers while continuing to build shrines and celebrate festivals. In Buddhist temples we find scriptures and statues as well as rituals and memorials for the dead. The Confucian tradition is less conspicuous, made known more through the factors of social hierarchy and sense of obligation. Taoism influenced such areas as the calendar, astrology, and beliefs about what is lucky and unlucky. Folk religion operates in the activities of many seasonal celebrations in the home, in unorganized shamanism, and even in folktales. Christianity, although it has never attracted a large percentage of the population, has exerted an important stimulus for educational and social reform. The New Religions[1] in many ways reflect the earlier tradition: they incorporate practices from divination and faith healing to shamanism and seasonal festivals, and their beliefs range from unsystematic folk beliefs to scriptures and elaborate doctrines.

However, the hues of Japanese religion are not strictly confined to these traditions; they spill over into every aspect of the culture and life of its people. For example, the family is equally important, if not more important, as a traditional center of religious activity than the Shinto shrine and Buddhist temple. Artistic and religious themes intermix, and the Japanese view of nature is as much religious as it is aesthetic. Even filial piety and national patriotism are colored by religious devotion. In order to see the whole picture of Japanese religion, then, we must look into many aspects of Japanese culture.

Japanese religion is by no means static; instead, it forms a moving picture, one that proceeds by leaps and bounds rather than in a continuous, straight line. One tradition may dominate the scene while others lie dormant, then another tradition may make a new appearance. Each tradition has a transcendent ideal which is more or less realized within the ambiguities of life, but strange as it may first seem, periods of flourishing institutional strength do not always indicate times when religious ideals are most fully realized. For example, institutional Shinto flourished before and during World War II, but it did not always hold up the highest ideals of Shinto.

How can we understand this kaleidoscope of changing patterns? As with any foreign tradition, the first clue to understanding is the proper attitude. Often we who are associated with the European, or "Western," tradition tend to think that the "Eastern" tradition is one vast unity and that this mysterious or spiritual East is the direct opposite of the rational and materialistic West. However, no single entity can be called Eastern culture or "the East," because a great number of cultures exist between the Middle East and the Far East. In the same fashion, there is no distinctive set of characteristics within the cultures of this area that cannot be found also in Western culture. Hajime Nakamura, one of the foremost Japanese scholars of Buddhism, has stated this point well: "*There are no features of the ways of thinking*

---

1. Throughout this book the term *New Religions* with initial capitals is used to identify the distinctive Japanese new religious movements.

exclusively shared by the East Asians as a whole, unless they are universal traits of human nature in the East and West. Furthermore, if the ways of thinking differ according to the cultural history of each people, then we should expect the cultures formed by these nations to be heterogeneous."[2]

At the outset, we must realize that Japanese religion has a long history and that it possesses its own internal unity. The primary guide, then, is to place Japanese religion within its own historical context and, above all, to understand it within its own basic assumptions. This means we must avoid using the basic assumptions of our own tradition to interpret Japanese religion. For example, in the United States and most Western countries, religion is usually understood as belief in One God and exclusive affiliation to one religious organization; ethical behavior is seen as obedience to God. In sharp contrast, in Japanese religion exclusive affiliation to one religious tradition is rare; the general rule is a plurality of religions, with the same person participating in several religions simultaneously. Some other important features of Japanese religion also contrast with Western religion, as pointed out by Hideo Kishimoto, a distinguished Japanese scholar of religious studies: "The peculiar nature of Japanese religions has brought forth two conspicuous cultural features. One is a distinct separation in the sphere of activities between the religious system and the ethical system. The other is the close relation between religious value and aesthetic value."[3] To apply Western assumptions about religion to Japanese religion, then, would be as confusing as mixing the pieces from two jigsaw puzzles.

In order to understand Japanese religion, we must comprehend it within its own context, in its own historical setting, and through its own activities. The materials in this book are selected and organized to aid this understanding and at the same time to cover as many aspects of Japanese religion as possible: the content of the various traditions, the basic characteristics of the religious heritage as a whole, the changes and ambiguities through the passage of time, and the relationship of religion to other cultural areas. Chapters 2 through 8 examine the major Japanese traditions: Shinto, Buddhism and Buddhist founders, Confucianism, religious Taoism, folk religion, and Christianity. Chapter 9 focuses directly on the syncretism among these traditions. Chapters 10 through 15 treat basic characteristics or persistent themes that constitute the cross section of Japanese religion: the closeness of humans, gods, and nature; the religious significance of the family, living and dead; the

---

2. Hajime Nakamura, *Ways of Thinking of Eastern Peoples* (Honolulu: East-West Center Press, 1964), p. 22.

3. Hideo Kishimoto, "Some Japanese Cultural Traits and Religions," in *The Japanese Mind: Essentials of Japanese Philosophy and Culture,* edited by Charles A. Moore (Honolulu: East-West Center Press, 1967), p. 115.

importance of purification, rituals, and charms; the prominence of local festivals and individual cults; the penetration of religion into everyday life; and the natural bond between religion and state. Chapters 16 and 18 treat the dilemma and future of Japanese religion, and Chapter 17 treats the New Religions. All the chapters suggest the historical changes that religion undergoes and discuss the other areas of life in which religion is active.

Each of the selected readings may be likened to one of the patterns in the kaleido-scope of Japanese religion: the material in every selection is distinct, yet it shares many religious elements with the material in other selections. For example, a selec-tion in the chapter on Shinto not only describes the basic character of Shinto but also reflects a persistent theme such as the closeness of gods, humans, and nature; at the same time, it depicts the situation of early Japanese religion and illustrates the relationship between rice agriculture and religious life. Therefore, each selection should be read not only for its own content but also for its interrelationship with other selections. In many cases the interconnections will be apparent, but cross-references within the introductions make it easier to trace related themes and mate-rials. The patterns of a kaleidoscope are almost endless—that is one reason the instrument is so fascinating; similarly, the aspects of Japanese religion are almost without number. The purpose of these materials is not to exhaust the subject but to provide firsthand experience of some important configurations of Japanese religion.

PART I

Religious Traditions

CHAPTER TWO

Shinto

S hinto grew out of the earliest Japanese traditions and gradually took shape as an organized religion under the influence of Buddhism and Chinese culture. Several factors in the history of Shinto have led people to consider it as the only indigenous or national religion of Japan: Shinto is the only organized religion to arise in Japan, Shinto preserves the most ancient Japanese heritage, and there has been close identification between Shinto, emperor, and state. However, it is well to remember that Shinto, like most religions, includes influences from several other traditions and therefore is not totally Japanese in origin. Additionally, Shinto is not the only national religion, because Buddhism also became identified with state purposes. In fact, some of the central features of Shinto, such as the idea of *kami* (defined in selection 1) and the veneration of nature, are not exclusive to Shinto but penetrate the whole of Japanese culture. (For example, see the selections in Chapter 10.)

Most important in the practice of Shinto are humble respect for the *kami* and voluntary participation in shrine ceremonies (rather than the Western pattern of rational proof for God and exclusive membership in one local institution). Children grew in the religious life of Shinto not through regular Sunday School services or training in catechism but through participation in local festivals and respect for the national tradition. In traditional Japan (especially before the past century of rapid modernization), the countryside was felt to be alive with *kami*, and the children paid their respects to the local *kami,* as they became increasingly aware of the national tradition chronicled in history and idealized in mythology.

Although the prehistoric origins of Shinto make it both the earliest and only native Japanese religious tradition, for much of its history Shinto has been overshadowed by imported traditions, especially Buddhism. In the early centuries of the Common Era,[1] when Buddhism and Chinese culture first entered Japan, a complex interaction took place between the native Japanese tradition and the new traditions. The native heritage influenced the way the imported customs were perceived and accepted, but the elaborate conceptual and institutional forms of Chinese culture and Buddhism overwhelmed the emerging Shinto. Not until medieval times did scholars of Shinto begin to renew their claim that it was the original Japanese faith; by late medieval times Shinto writers developed more elaborate arguments for Japan as the "land of the *kami*" and Shinto as the primary religion of this land.

During the past century, Shinto's fate has undergone two major changes. After the Meiji Restoration of 1868, Shinto shrines were used by the government as part of the official rationale for unifying the people in the new nation-state (see p. 238 and p. 251). This placed Shinto's religious status in an ambiguous position, but at the end of World War II Shinto underwent another momentous change. In 1945 the Allied Occupation forces entered Japan and initiated the disestablishment of shrine Shinto, which placed it on an equal footing with all other religions in Japan. Shinto shrines had already felt the change from a rural agricultural nation to an urban industrial nation, and the defeat in World War II was a severe blow to Shinto, due to its close tie to the war effort. (For a description of attitudes toward Shinto in postwar Tokyo, see p. 255.) Contemporary Shinto leaders are still trying to recover from the disestablishment order.

Although Shinto defines one long Japanese tradition, a number of different facets exist within this tradition. On the most informal level is folk, or popular, Shinto. Folk Shinto refers to the many traditional religious activities surrounding purification, blessing, agriculture, and the home—practices that are not actually a part of institutional Shinto; in this book, such practices are generally treated as part of Japanese folk religion. The simplest form of Shinto organization is the local shrine in villages and smaller divisions of cities. Some major features of these local shrines are the relationship of the *kami* to the Japanese people, the agricultural blessing and protection of local areas by specific *kami,* the periodic celebration of contact with the *kami,* annual (especially seasonal) festivals, and religious observances for stages of life (for example, birth) and special crises (such as sickness).

---

1. Dates in this book will be given according to the Common Era (C.E.) or Before Common Era (B.C.E.).

From ancient times Shinto was also related to the state. In Japanese mythology the *kami* of Shinto heritage are responsible for the creation of the land and the people, and the emperor (as a descendant of the Sun Goddess) is a manifest *kami* who heads both government and worship. Although the emperor performed special rituals on behalf of the nation, and although some larger shrines were rather closely related to the state, this ideal of the unity of state and religion was never fully realized. The common people generally appreciated the legendary origin of Japan from the *kami* and venerated the emperor as a divine or semidivine figure; but their most direct participation in Shinto was through the activities of the local shrine. However, from 1868 to 1945 Shinto was drawn into a much closer relationship to the newly formed nation-state. In contrast to the Tokugawa period (1600–1867), when Buddhism and Neo-Confucianism were more closely tied to government rationale and activities, starting with the Meiji Restoration of 1868 the government relied more on Shinto shrines and notions for supporting the state. The government appealed to the ancient ideal of the unity of state and religion, but had difficulty implementing this ideal within the emerging nation-state. After several experiments the government made a fundamental distinction between the ordinary local shrines, which it called shrine Shinto (*jinja Shinto*), and the sect movements within Shinto (that actively propagated their teachings), which it called sect Shinto (*kyoha Shinto*). Only shrine Shinto could call their buildings "shrines" (*jinja*); shrine Shinto was gradually brought into more formal administrative connection with the state, in terms of such actions as financial aid and designation of shrine priests as government officials. Shrine Shinto was even declared "nonreligious" and officially considered as part of the state, in contrast to sect Shinto, Buddhism, and Christianity, which were treated as religions. By this maneuver the state could provide a guarantee of religious freedom, while at the same time, it used "nonreligious" Shinto notions in the schools and the administrative control of shrines to reinforce nationalism and unify the state.

Sect Shinto was required to use the term *kyokai* (church) for its buildings, since its activities were considered to be religious. Whereas shrine Shinto supposedly had originated out of the natural unity of state and religion, sect Shinto generally developed out of historical founders and independent teachings. Eventually thirteen movements were granted official recognition as members of sect Shinto. Some of the members of sect Shinto may also be considered as new religious movements in their own right; see the example of Tenrikyo (p. 270).

After 1945, the special status of shrine Shinto was abolished, placing it on the same level as other religious organizations; at this time the former groups within sect Shinto (as well as Buddhist and Christian groups) were able to organize freely. Meanwhile, the religious rhythm of local shrines, which depended on such factors as annual festivals and agricultural-seasonal celebrations, continued its own life, especially within the small village shrines.

1
The Centrality of Kami in Shinto

One of the most important aspects of Shinto is belief in the power of the many *kami*. Because the *kami* include mythological divinities, powers of nature, revered human beings and even spirits of the dead, no one English term translates *kami*. In this selection, Holtom provides many examples of *kami* and advises that the best treatment of the word *kami* is to leave it untranslated, thinking of it in the general sense of "sacred."

Even the greatest Japanese scholars have had difficulty in defining the term *kami*, partly because its meaning is lost in antiquity, partly because Shinto has never emphasized rational proof for the existence of *kami* or "theology" as a systematic statement of the nature of *kami*. In religious life, it has been sufficient to recognize the hoary sanctity of the *kami* in the traditional founding of Japan (see p. 13) and humble veneration for the *kami* in one's own neighborhood.

The notion of *kami* is too important in Japanese culture to be confined to Shinto as an organized religion, for the belief in *kami* is directly related to the Japanese appreciation of nature, which is understood as a living, sacred force. This notion of *kami* even interacts with the Buddhist pantheon (see p. 50). The *kami* have always been present in Japan, even before there were shrines dedicated to them. Although Buddhist images were often housed in Shinto shrines, the *kami* were rarely depicted in concrete form. Rather, the shrine was usually considered the place of descent, which the *kami* temporarily visited during the ceremonies that invoked the *kami*'s presence.

THE MEANING OF *KAMI*

D. C. Holtom

In the preceding paragraphs occasion has already been found for introducing the important term, *kami*. It will be necessary to make constant use of it in the ensuing pages and, at this point, in connection with the elucidation of the main characteristics of Old Shinto, its primary significance should be carefully

Reprinted by permission of the publisher from D. C. Holtom, *The National Faith of Japan: A Study in Modern Shinto* (New York: Paragon Book Reprint Corp., 1965).

noted. No other word in the entire range of Japanese vocabulary has a richer or more varied content and no other has presented greater difficulties to the philologist.

The most comprehensive and penetrating account of the meaning of *kami* that has appeared in Japanese literature was given by the great eighteenth century scholar, Motoori Norinaga. Written long before the age of the modern study of folk psychology had dawned, his analysis, in spite of certain insufficiencies, yet may be taken to stand as a remarkable and almost classical definition of the now widely used term, mana.

He says,

"I do not yet understand the meaning of the term, *kami*. Speaking in general, however, it may be said that *kami* signifies, in the first place, the deities of heaven and earth that appear in the ancient records and also the spirits of the shrines where they are worshipped.

"It is hardly necessary to say that it includes human beings. It also includes such objects as birds, beasts, trees, plants, seas, mountains and so forth. In ancient usage, anything whatsoever which was outside the ordinary, which possessed superior power or which was awe-inspiring was called *kami*. Eminence here does not refer merely to the superiority of nobility, goodness or meritous deeds. Evil and mysterious things, if they are extraordinary and dreadful, are called *kami*. It is needless to say that among human beings who are called *kami* the successive generations of sacred emperors are all included. The fact that emperors are called 'distant *kami*' is because, from the standpoint of common people, they are far-separated, majestic and worthy of reverence. In a lesser degree we find, in the present as well as in ancient times, human beings who are *kami*. Although they may not be accepted throughout the whole country, yet in each province, each village and each family there are human beings who are *kami,* each one according to his own proper position. The *kami* of the divine age were for the most part human beings of that time and, because the people of that time were all *kami,* it is called the Age of the Gods (*kami*).

"Furthermore, among things which are not human, the thunder is always called 'sounding-*kami*.' Such things as dragons, the echo, and foxes, inasmuch as they are conspicuous, wonderful and awe-inspiring, are also *kami*. In popular usage the echo is said to be *tengu*[1] and in Chinese writings it is referred to as a mountain goblin. . . .

"In the *Nihongi* and the *Manyoshu* the tiger and the wolf are also spoken of as *kami*. Again there are the cases in which peaches were given the name, August-Thing-Great-*Kamu*-Fruit, and a necklace was called August-Storehouse-shelf-*Kami*. There are further instances in which rocks, stumps of trees and leaves of plants spoke audibly. They were all

---

1. A long-nosed, red-faced, winged goblin.

kami. There are again numerous places in which seas and mountains are called *kami.* This does not have reference to the spirit of the mountain or the sea, but *kami* is used here directly of the particular mountain or sea. This is because they were exceedingly awe-inspiring."

Much similar material could be adduced from Japanese sources. . . . Summarized briefly, it may be said that *kami* is essentially an expression used by the early Japanese people to classify experiences that evoked sentiments of caution and mystery in the presence of the manifestation of the strange and marvelous. Like numerous other concepts discoverable among ancient or primitive people, *kami* is fundamentally a term that distinguishes between a world of superior beings and things which are thought of as filled with mysterious power and a world of common experiences that lie within the control of ordinary human technique. Often the best translation is simply by the word "sacred." In this sense it has an undifferentiated background of everything that is strange, fearful, mysterious, marvelous, uncontrolled, full of power, or beyond human comprehension. The conviction of the reality of the world that is registered was supported by the experience of extraordinary events, such as the frenzy of religious dances, or by outstanding objects that threw the attention into special activity, such as large, or old, or strangely formed trees, high mountains, thunder, lightning, storm and clouds, or by implements of magic, or by uncanny animals, such as foxes, badgers, and manifestations of albinism. These old attitudes exist in the present and strongly influence modern Shinto.

As this sacred, mysterious background became more and more articulated with the progress of experience and thought, descriptive elements were attached to the word *kami,* and the names of the great deities were evolved, as, for example, *Amaterasu-Omikami,* "Heaven-shining-Great-August-*Kami,*" for the Sun Goddess, or *Taka-Mimusubi-no-Kami,* "High-August-Producing-*Kami,*" the name given one of the creation deities or growth principles of the old cosmogonic myth.

In addition to the general sense of sacred as just outlined, the specific meanings of *kami* should be noted. They are: spirits and deities of nature; the spirits of ancestors (especially great ancestors, including emperors, heroes, wise men and saints); superior human beings in actual human society, such as living emperors, high government officials, feudal lords, *etc.;* the government itself; that which is above in space or superior in location or rank (declared, without warrant, by some Japanese scholars to be the primary meaning); "the upper times," *i.e.,* antiquity; God; the hair on the human scalp; paper.

Evidence which cannot be cited here goes to show that the classification of the hair on the human scalp under the *kami* concept had probable origin, not in the very apparent fact that the hair was on the top of the head and hence "superior," but in the association of the hair with a primitive supernaturalism or with the idea of mysterious superhuman force.

Kami in the sense of paper may be a totally unrelated word. It has been suggested, however, that it found its way into the sacred classification because of its unusual importance in the social life.

A phonetic variation of *kami* is *kamu* (or *kabu*), the latter being perhaps the older term. *Kamu* strikingly resembles in both word form and meaning the *tabu* (sometimes written *kabu* or *kapu*) of Polynesia, from which the term taboo is derived. The Ainu *kamui* is also worthy of comparative study in this connection.

Another term, *mi-koto,* is frequently affixed to the descriptive elements of divine names as a substitute for *kami*. This also will be encountered here and there in the pages that follow and its meaning should be explained at this point. The parts signify: *mi* (honorific) and *koto* ("thing" or "person"). The word was originally a title of reverence applied to exalted individuals in the ordinary social life. It is sometimes used of the gods and in such cases is perhaps best translated "deity," as, for example, Susa-no-Wo-no-Mikoto, "The-Impetuous-Male-Deity," the name commonly given the storm god.

Shinto gods and goddesses are sometimes referred to in the literature as the "deities of heaven and earth." As already mentioned, Shinto itself is sometimes called the Way of the Deities of Heaven and Earth. The terminology is an old one and appears in the early writings in the form of a distinction between the so-called *amatsu kami* ("deities of heaven") and the *kunitsu kami* ("deities of earth"). This has caused a bit of perplexity to the commentators. A favored, though problematical interpretation, takes "heavenly deities" in the sense of the original *kami* of the dominant Yamato tribe. They are the gods and goddesses of Takama-ga-Hara. The "earthly deities" are understood to be those which were already being worshipped in the land when the early representatives of the Yamato race entered it. Both terms are interpreted, without good grounds, in a legitimate ancestral sense as ancient chieftains.

In general outline the mythology of old Shinto is closely similar to what is found almost universally among other peoples at like stages of culture. The great deities are the unknown forces of nature formulated in terms of the current social and political patterns. . . . Yamato culture, in the form which eventually became prominent, centered in the adoration of the sun. Dynastic interests were quick to make the most of the uniqueness and majesty deriving from claims for the descent of the Imperial Line from a solar ancestry. By the sixth century of the Western era an imperial solar ancestralism had become the paramount motive in the Yamato state worship. Its influence has widened with the passing centuries until today it constitutes the predominant interest of all Shinto.

Study of the early rituals indicates that the primary interests expressed in the public religious rites were to safeguard the food supply, to ward off calamities of fire, wind, rain, drought, earthquake and pestilence, to obtain numerous offspring and peaceful homes, to secure the prosperity and permanence of the imperial reign, and to effect purgation of ceremonial and moral impurity.

The earliest worship of the *kami* was not necessarily at man-made shrines. Mountains, groves, trees, rivers, springs, rocks, and other natural objects served as primitive sanctuaries. The oldest shrines known to have been constructed by human hands were simple taboo areas formed by the dedication of sacred trees and stones. We do not know when houses first began to be built for the gods. The date is lost in the mist of antiquity. Man-made shrines, copied from the dwellings of chiefs, must have appeared very early in the historical development, however. The records of the oldest existing shrines of the present, that of Omiwa in Yamato and that of the great shrine of Izumo, state that these edifices were first built in the Age of the Gods. By the time of the compilation of the *Engi Shiki* in the tenth century of the Western era the shrines had become sufficiently numerous and diverse to be graded into so-called upper, middle and lower classes. A census given in this document names 2,861 shrines. It is improbable that this figure exhausted the list for the entire country.

2
The Ancient Mythology

The oldest recorded document of Japanese mythology is the *Kojiki,* which is composed in an early form of Japanese. This written mythology does not constitute a sacred scripture like the Christian Bible, but it is important because it helps us recognize early Japanese religious notions that have had lasting influence. Although the *Kojiki* reflects some borrowing from China, it establishes the origin and distinctiveness of the Japanese tradition. The story depicts the creation of the world and the appearance of the mythological deities who created the Japanese islands and the Japanese people, but it contrasts sharply with the biblical account of creation. For example, in the Japanese story the world appears neither by the power of one divinity nor a sudden act but a process whereby the universe emerges amidst many *kami.* The male, Izanagi, and the female, Izanami, provide divine models for procreation and also introduce death into the world. A crowning point of the story is when Ninigi (Piko-po-Ninigi), heir of the Sun Goddess (Ama-Terasu), descends to rule the earth and thereby establishes imperial rule. These episodes constitute the traditional account of the divine origin of Japan and the imperial family.

This mythological tradition is known in outline by every Japanese person, but it is appreciated more as an idealized story of the origin and greatness of Japan than as a description of a historical event. (Compare the ancient poetry p. 171.) Even modern Japanese people would have difficulty with all the specific names of the *kami,* and for the Western reader, too, the important thing is to note the presence of the many *kami* in the universe and their responsibility for simultaneously creating the world and founding the Japanese nation.

THE AGE OF THE *KAMI*

Donald L. Philippi, translator

Chapter 1: The Five Separate Heavenly Deities come into existence.

1   At the time of the beginning of heaven and earth, there came into existence in TAKAMA-NO-PARA a deity named AME-NO-MI-NAKA-NUSI-NO-KAMI; next, TAKA-MI-MUSUBI-NO-KAMI; next, KAMI-MUSUBI-NO-KAMI. These three deities all came into existence as single deities, and their forms were not visible.

2   Next, when the land was young, resembling floating oil and drifting like a jellyfish, there sprouted forth something like reed-shoots. From these came into existence the deity UMASI-ASI-KABI-PIKO-DI-NO-KAMI; next, AME-NO-TOKO-TATI-NO-KAMI. These two deities also came into existence as single deities, and their forms were not visible.

3   The five deities in the above section are the Separate Heavenly Deities.

Chapter 2: The Seven Generations of the Age of the Gods come into existence.

1   Next there came into existence the deity KUNI-NO-TOKO-TATI-NO-KAMI; next, TOYO-KUMO-NO-NO-KAMI. These two deities also came into existence as single deities, and their forms were not visible.

2   Next there came into existence the deity named U-PIDI-NI-NO-KAMI; next, his spouse SU-PIDI-NI-NO-KAMI. Next, TUNO-GUPI-NO-KAMI; next, his spouse IKU-GUPI-NO-KAMI. Next, OPO-TO-NO-DI-NO-KAMI; next, his spouse OPO-TO-NO-BE-NO-KAMI. Next, OMO-DARU-NO-KAMI; next, his spouse AYA-KASIKO-NE-NO-KAMI. Next, IZANAGI-NO-KAMI; next, his spouse IZANAMI-NO-KAMI.

3   The deities in the above section, from KUNI-NO-TOKO-TATI-NO-KAMI through IZANAMI-NO-KAMI, are called collectively the Seven Generations of the Age of the Gods.

Chapter 3: Izanagi and Izanami are commanded to solidify the land. They create Onogoro island.

1   At this time the heavenly deities, all with one command, said to the two deities IZANAGI-NO-MIKOTO and IZANAMI-NO-MIKOTO: "Complete and solidify this drifting land!"

2   Giving them the Heavenly Jeweled Spear, they entrusted the mission to them.

Reprinted by permission of the publisher from Donald L. Philippi, translator, *Kojiki* (Tokyo: University of Tokyo Press, 1968).

3   Thereupon, the two deities stood on the Heavenly Floating Bridge and, lowering the jeweled spear, stirred with it. They stirred the brine with a churning-churning sound, and when they lifted up [the spear] again, the brine dripping down from the tip of the spear piled up and became an island. This was the island ONOGORO.

Chapter 4: Izanagi and Izanami marry and bear their first offspring.

1   Descending from the heavens to this island, they erected a heavenly pillar and a spacious palace.

2   At this time [Izanagi-no-mikoto] asked his spouse IZANAMI-NO-MIKOTO, saying:
"How is your body formed?"

3   She replied, saying:
"My body, formed though it be formed, has one place which is formed insufficiently."

4   Then IZANAGI-NO-MIKOTO said:
"My body, formed though it be formed, has one place which is formed to excess. Therefore, I would like to take that place in my body which is formed to excess and insert it into that place in your body which is formed insufficiently, and [thus] give birth to the land. How would this be?"

5   IZANAMI-NO-MIKOTO replied, saying:
"That will be good."

6   Then IZANAGI-NO-MIKOTO said:
"Then let us, you and me, walk in a circle around this heavenly pillar and meet and have conjugal intercourse."

7   After thus agreeing, [Izanagi-no-mikoto] then said:
"You walk around from the right, and I will walk around from the left and meet you."

8   After having agreed to this, they circled around; then IZANAMI-NO-MIKOTO said first:
"*Ana-ni-yasi,* how good a lad!"

9   Afterwards, IZANAGI-NO-MIKOTO said:
"*Ana-ni-yasi,* how good a maiden!"

10   After each had finished speaking, [Izanagi-no-mikoto] said to his spouse:
"It is not proper that the woman speak first."

11   Nevertheless, they commenced procreation and gave birth to a leech-child. They placed this child into a boat made of reeds and floated it away.

12   Next, they gave birth to the island of APA. This also is not reckoned as one of their children.

Chapter 5: Izanagi and Izanami, learning the reason for their failure, repeat the marriage ritual.

1   Then the two deities consulted together and said:
"The child which we have just borne is not good. It is best to report [this matter] before the heavenly deities."

2   Then they ascended together and sought the will of the heavenly deities. The heavenly deities thereupon performed a grand divination and said:

3   "Because the woman spoke first, [the child] was not good. Descend once more and say it again."

4   Then they descended again and walked once more in a circle around the heavenly pillar as [they had done] before.

5   Then IZANAGI-NO-MIKOTO said first:
"*Ana-ni-yasi,* how good a maiden!"

6   Afterwards, his spouse IZANAMI-NO-MIKOTO said:
"*Ana-ni-yasi,* how good a lad!"

[The story continues with the account of how Izanami died giving birth to fire and descended to the underworld. Her spouse, Izanagi, followed her to the impure underworld, unsuccessfully trying to bring her back to life; this episode is sometimes compared with the Greek story of Orpheus. When Izanagi escaped from the underworld he purified himself, thereby creating many deities, including Ama-Terasu.]

Chapter 12: Izanagi entrusts their missions to the three noble children.

1   At this time IZANAGI-NO-MIKOTO, rejoicing greatly, said:
"I have borne child after child, and finally in the last bearing I have obtained three noble children."

2   Then he removed his necklace, shaking the beads on the string so that they jingled, and, giving it to AMA-TERASU-OPO-MI-KAMI, he entrusted her with her mission, saying:
"You shall rule TAKAMA-NO-PARA."

3   The name of this necklace is MI-KURA-TANA-NO-KAMI.

4   Next he said to TUKU-YOMI-NO-MIKOTO, entrusting him with his mission:
"You shall rule the realms of the night."

5   Next he said to TAKE-PAYA-SUSA-NO-WO-NO-MIKOTO, entrusting him with his mission:
"You shall rule the ocean." . . .

Chapter 38: Piko-po-no-ninigi-no-mikoto is commanded to descend from the heavens and rule the land. Saruta-biko meets him to serve as his guide.

1   Then AMA-TERASU-OPO-MI-KAMI and TAKA-KI-NO-KAMI commanded the heir apparent MASA-KATU-A-KATU-KATI-PAYA-PI-AME-NO-OSI-PO-MIMI-NO-MIKOTO, saying:

2   "Now it is reported that the pacification of the Central Land of the Reed Plains has been finished. Therefore, descend and rule it, as you have been entrusted with it."

3   Then the heir apparent MASA-KATU-A-KATU-KATI-PAYA-PI-AME-NO-OSI-PO-MIMI-NO-MIKOTO replied, saying:

4   "As I was preparing to descend, a child was born; his name is AME-NIGISI-KUNI-NIGISI-AMA-TU-PIKO-PIKO-PO-NO-NINIGI-NO-MIKOTO. This child should descend."

5   This child was born of his union with the daughter of TAKA-KI-NO-KAMI, YORODU-PATA-TOYO-AKI-TU-SI-PIME-NO-MIKOTO, who bore AME-NO-PO-AKARI-NO-MIKOTO; next, PIKO-PO-NO-NINIGI-NO-MIKOTO. (Two deities)

6   Whereupon, in accordance with his words, they imposed the command upon PIKO-PO-NO-NINIGI-NO-MIKOTO:

7   "TOYO-ASI-PARA-NO-MIDU-PO-NO-KUNI has been entrusted to you as the land you are to rule. In accordance with the command, descend from the heavens!"

8   Then, as PIKO-PO-NO-NINIGI-NO-MIKOTO was about to descend from the heavens, there appeared in the myriad heavenly crossroads a deity whose radiance shone above through TAKAMA-NO-PARA and below through the Central Land of the Reed Plains.

9   Then AMA-TERASU-OPO-MI-KAMI and TAKA-KI-NO-KAMI commanded AME-NO-UZUME-NO-KAMI, saying:

10   "Although you are a graceful maiden, you are [the type of] deity who can face and overwhelm [others]. Therefore go alone and inquire: 'Who is here on the path of my offspring descending from the heavens?'"

11   When she inquired, the reply was:
"I am an earthly deity named SARUTA-BIKO-NO-KAMI. I have come out because I have heard that the offspring of the heavenly deities is to descend from the heavens, and I have come forth to wait that I might serve as his guide."

Chapter 39: Piko-po-no-ninigi-no-mikoto descends from the heavens bearing the three items of the sacred regalia and accompanied by various deities. He establishes his palace at Taka-ti-po.

1   Then assigning [their respective] roles to AME-NO-KO-YANE-NO-MIKOTO, PUTO-TAMA-NO-MIKOTO, AME-NO-UZUME-NO-MIKOTO, ISI-KORI-DOME-NO-MIKOTO, and TAMA-NO-YA-NO-MIKOTO, altogether five clan heads, they had them descend from the heavens.

2   Hereupon, she imparted [unto him] the myriad MAGA-TAMA beads and the mirror which had been used to lure, as well as the Sword *Kusanagi;* and also [sent along] TOKO-YO-NO-OMOPI-KANE-NO-KAMI, TA-DIKARA-WO-NO-KAMI, and AME-NO-IPA-TO-WAKE-NO-KAMI, and said:

3   "This mirror—have [it with you] as my spirit, and worship it just as you would worship in my very presence. Next, let OMOPI-KANE-NO-KAMI take the responsibility for the affairs of the presence and carry on the government."

4   These two deities are worshipped at the shrine of ISUZU of the bell-bracelets.

5   Next [was] TOYU-UKE-NO-KAMI; this is the deity who dwells in WATARAPI, the Outer Shrine.

6   Next [was] AME-NO-IPA-TO-WAKE-NO-KAMI, also named KUSI-IPA-MADO-NO-KAMI, also named TOYO-IPA-MADO-NO-KAMI. This deity is the deity of the Gate.

7   Next, TA-DIKARA-WO-NO-KAMI dwells in SANANAGATA.

8   AME-NO-KO-YANE-NO-MIKOTO is the ancestor of the MURAZI of the NAKATOMI.

9   PUTO-TAMA-NO-MIKOTO is the ancestor of the OBITO of the IMUBE.

10   AME-NO-UZUME-NO-MIKOTO is the ancestor of the KIMI of the SARUME.

11   ISI-KORI-DOME-NO-MIKOTO is the ancestor of the MURAZI of the KAGAMI-TUKURI.

12   TAMA-NO-YA-NO-MIKOTO is the ancestor of the MURAZI of the TAMA-NO-YA.

13   Then AMA-TU-PIKO-PO-NO-NINIGI-NO-MIKOTO was commanded to leave the Heavenly Rock-Seat. Pushing through the myriad layers of the heavens' trailing clouds, pushing his way with an awesome pushing, he stood on a flat floating island by the Heavenly Floating Bridge, and descended from the heavens to the peak KUZI-PURU-TAKE of Mount TAKA-TI-PO of PIMUKA in TUKUSI.

14   Then the two deities AME-NO-OSI-PI-NO-MIKOTO and AMA-TU-KUME-NO-MIKOTO took on their backs heavenly stone-quivers, wore at their sides mallet-headed swords, took up heavenly bows of PAZI wood, held heavenly deer[-slaying] arrows, and standing in front of him served him.

15   AME-NO-OSI-PI-NO-MIKOTO—this is the ancestor of the MURAZI of the OPO-TOMO.

16   AMA-TU-KUME-NO-MIKOTO—this is the ancestor of the ATAPE of the
       KUME.
17   At this time he said:
       "This place is opposite the land of KARA; [it is a place to which one]
       comes directly through the Cape of KASASA, a land where the morning sun
       shines directly, a land where the rays of the evening sun are brilliant. This is
       a most excellent place."
18   Thus saying, he rooted his palace-posts firmly in the bedrock below,
       raised high the crossbeams unto TAKAMA-NO-PARA itself, and dwelt [there].

3
Shinto Shrines

Probably in the dim past, Shinto "shrines" were nothing more than natural objects
such as trees and stones that were set apart with straw ropes as specially venerated—that is, sacred—objects. Some such shrines survive even today—for example,
the Nachi Waterfall and Mount Miwa. But typical of Shinto from early times is the
wooden shrine and encompassing grove. The shrine is quite different from a Christian church or Jewish synagogue, since its purpose is not congregational worship,
and originally it differed from the Buddhist temple, since it did not house statues or
representations of divinities. Rather, the Shinto shrine was where men recited ritual
prayers and made offerings to *kami,* who at such times descended temporarily. The
so-called *kami*-body (*shintai*), or object of worship, which might be an old sword or
mirror, was considered technically as the resting place of the *kami* during its temporary descent; however, this *kami*-body was seldom seen by the people and only
rarely by the Shinto priesthood. Depending on how they are counted, there may be
about 100,000 shrines, but most of these are very small structures and unstaffed by
Shinto clergy.

In the following selection, first published in 1938, Holtom refers especially to the
pre–World War II situation. (It should be noted that his reference in the first paragraph to "contemporary Japanese law" refers to the 1930s; the legal situation of
Shinto changed radically after World War II, as can be seen on p. 38.) Nevertheless,
Shinto is very conservative, and several shrines, such as those at Ise and Izumo,
probably preserve ancient building practices harking back to southern Pacific origins,
and the general religious character of the Shinto shrine remains rather constant
throughout the course of history. In general, the shrine and its compound represent
a sacred space set apart from ordinary space. The *torii,* or sacred archway, marks
the entrance into sacred space, and the water basin is provided to purify the person
who prepares himself for closer communion with the *kami* when he offers a prayer
at the shrine. A person might visit the shrine for a personal petition, but more frequently the visit is part of a village celebration.

SHINTO PLACES OF WORSHIP

D. C. Holtom

We turn first to the consideration of the nature of the Shinto places of worship. In contemporary [1938] Japanese law the institutions which are called "shrines" are generally designated *jinja*, from *shin* or *jin*, meaning "deity" (*kami* in pure Japanese) and *sha,* or *ja,* which in this connection is best rendered "house" or "dwelling place." The shrine, or *jinja*, then, is a house or dwelling place in which the deity or deities, worshipped in the local rites, are supposed to live, or where they are believed to take up residence when summoned by appropriate ceremonies. They are the holy places where the *kami* may be found and communicated with. Japanese law permits the use of the term *jinja* only in connection with the traditional institutions of original Shinto wherein the *kami* are enshrined. The institutions of Buddhism and of the existing Shinto sects are denied the right to use the designation. We can preserve the distinction if we speak of the local foundations of State Shinto as shrines, of those of Buddhism as temples (*tera*) and of those of the Shinto sects as churches or chapels (*kyokai*).

Jinja is thus a modern Sino-Japanese legal designation and does not represent the earliest known usage. Older and more widely used terms employed in the literature to indicate the abodes of Shinto deities are *miya* or *omiya, yashiro* or *miyashiro, hokora, hokura,* and *mimuro. Miya* (*mi,* honorific prefix, *ya,* "house") and *omiya* (*o-mi,* double honorific) are the designations most commonly met with. It is not necessary to venture on an extended explanation of this varied terminology here. Suffice it to say that all the terms just listed may properly be taken to mean dwelling place or superior dwelling place in one form or another.

The Shinto shrine may be a small god-house of wood or stone casually met with by the wayside. It may be a Grand Imperial Shrine of Ise or a Great Meiji Shrine of Tokyo, including in its appointments extensive landed holdings and numerous costly buildings along with various objects of ceremony and art, with a total valuation of millions of yen.

The ordinary shrine includes a definite enclosure of land, usually rectangular in shape, surrounded by a sacred fence or wall, one or more buildings where the deities are enshrined and, generally, certain auxiliary structures where special ceremonies are conducted, business transacted, or properties stored. The immediate entrance to the shrine is generally guarded by two stone lions arranged one on either side of the approach. In the case of shrines to the grain-goddess, Inari, the lions give place to the images of foxes, animals to which popular belief attributes the functions of messengers to this deity. Encompassing the shrine proper or adjacent thereto may lie more or less ex-

Reprinted by permission of the publisher from D. C. Holtom, *The National Faith of Japan: A Study in Modern Shinto* (New York: Paragon Book Reprint Corp., 1965).

tended areas devoted to landscape gardening and parkland or utilized as a source of revenue. Associated with the great Meiji Shrine of Tokyo is magnificent equipment providing for all sorts of athletic sports. The shrines, in their diversity of history, of ceremony and of architectural style, present a complicated and almost endless field of study. The most archaic type of shrine is simply a replica of the primitive house of ancient times, consisting of a small structure of natural wood, thatched with reeds or straw, the principal rafters in front and rear projecting through the roof, the total building elevated on piles in a manner that suggests the Swiss lake-dwellings or some of the Indonesian types of house architecture built above water.

Access to the shrine is gained through an opening in the fence or wall at the front, placed exactly in the middle between the left and right extremities, sometimes through similar apertures on either side, rarely, also, at the rear. Openings are guarded by the distinctive Shinto gateway, called the *torii,* a word whose correct etymology is unknown. The literal interpretation of the ideograms with which the term is written, in the sense of "bird-dwelling," offers no help toward the understanding of the proper function of the device. The *torii,* in its most characteristic form, consists of a single, elongated cylinder of wood, ordinarily made from a solid tree trunk, mounted horizontally on two upright posts set one on either side of the approach. A cross-brace is generally attached between the heads of the uprights. *Torii* made of stone or metal, preferably bronze, are not uncommon. The use of curved lines in the design of the horizontal cap-piece, as well as other elaborations, shows a Buddhist influence which orthodox Shinto is attempting to eliminate.

In its original significance the *torii* was not merely a decorative gateway. It was a magical, protective device which guarded the opening in the shrine fence against the entrance of evil and contamination of all sorts. Sometimes the approach to the shrine is made through a first, or outer, *torii,* then through a second, and finally a third. Occasionally one meets with an extended series of *torii* set so close together as to make a veritable tunnel.

On advancing through the *torii* one generally finds immediately before him in the center of the enclosure a building called the *haiden,* meaning the "worship-sanctuary." The name indicates its main use. Before it the people clap their hands and ring a suspended bell to attract the attention of the gods, bow their heads, and occasionally kneel, in brief reverence or prayer, and deposit their offerings in a money chest or on a cloth conveniently placed for the purpose. Within the *haiden* rituals are carried out on stated occasions by the priests in charge. These are for the most part official ceremonies on behalf of the local community or the state, but sometimes, also, purely private rites on behalf of individuals or small groups. Ordinary worshippers do not enter the shrines.

Just beyond the worship-sanctuary is usually placed an inner building called the *honden* or "chief-sanctuary." This is the holy of holies of the shrine where the deities dwell and to which the laity have no access. Two or more deities are sometimes enshrined in a single edifice; sometimes a special sanctum is provided for each deity. The principal function of the *honden* is to shelter a

sacred object called the *shintai* or "god-body." This is sometimes also designated *mitama-shiro* ("spirit-substitute"). An older name is *kamusane,* or *ka-
muzane,* meaning "god-seed," or perhaps, better, "sacred kernel." The *shintai*
is sometimes explained as a symbolic representation of the deity. It is more
generally regarded by priests and people alike as the object in which the enshrined deity takes up residence. The *shintai,* which in and of itself is generally
of small intrinsic value, is regarded with such awe and reverence that the members of the priesthood, themselves, are prohibited under law from viewing or
handling it except by special permit. The popular attitude is well indicated in
the numerous stories of local folklore which tell how those curious and profane people who have dared to steal a peep at the *shintai* have been struck dead
or smitten with blindness for life. Japanese attitudes toward the *shintai* suggest
the relic worship of the European middle ages.

In spite of its sacredness and all the sentiments of awe with which it is
hedged about, it not infrequently happens that judicious questioning of priests
and pilgrims will elucidate the nature of the god-body. Stones, sacred texts,
old scrolls, ancient swords, phallic emblems, strips of consecrated paper cut in
forms that possibly represent the sacred tree, locks of human hair, balls of crys-
tal, jewels (*magatama*), pictures and numerous other like objects appear among
the *shintai.* Under Buddhist influence images of men and deities have found
their way into the holy of holies of Shinto. It has sometimes happened in the
past that when loyal subjects have been deified, objects intimately associated
with their lives, such as head-wear, batons, weapons, writing implements and
clothing have been made into *shintai.* Occasionally an unhoused natural object
is worshipped as the *shintai,* in which case concealment is impossible, of
course. Living trees are most common in this connection. The *shintai* of the
Omiwa shrine of Yamato is a mountain; that of the Yudono shrine on the
slopes of Gassan in Yamagata Prefecture in the north-central part of the Hondo
is a hot-spring. . . .

Shrines which are recognized and counted by the government in its classification are divided into twelve groups. At the head stands the Ise Dai Jingu,
or the Grand Imperial Shrine of Ise, listed in the official statistics as one great
shrine, but really consisting of a group of sixteen shrines, large and small.
Below these are arranged eleven grades which vary from the large government shrines (*kampeisha*) and national shrines (*kokuheisha*) and their sub-classes
down through those of prefecture (*kensha*), district (*gosha*) and village (*sonsha*)
to a large group of more than sixty-one thousand shrines which are designated as being without grade, the so-called *mukakusha,* or "unranked shrines."
Outside of these again lie tens of thousands of little shrines that are not officially counted or recognized in any way. The total number of shrines in
Shinto, large and small, is unknown. The number is legion. Shrines which are
recognized and counted by the government, as given in the latest statistics
available total 110,967. Attached to these are 15,606 priests. No statistics of
adherents of the state shrines are kept by the national government, the assumption evidently being that all Japanese by virtue of nationality are naturally included within the sphere of shrine fealty.

4
Pilgrimage and Devotion at a Shinto Shrine

Worship and devotion in the context of Shinto are usually expressed informally in an experience of gratitude and reverent unity with the *kami*. This contrasts sharply with the Western tendency toward more precise forms: a critical moment of conversion, a statement of faith, and the recitation of creeds. The present document, taken from the fourteenth-century pilgrimage diary of Saka Jubutsu (usually known as Saka), describes the unaffected sincerity and warmth of a pilgrim toward the *kami* when he reaches his goal of the Ise shrines. Saka, the pilgrim who wrote the diary, is a Buddhist priest, and he freely draws on several traditions (including religious Taoism) in interpreting his pilgrimage. (An interesting comparison is the example of Buddhist devotion on p. 65.) Saka's devotion might not be typical for priests, but his tendency to blend several traditions with simple piety toward the *kami* is reflected in popular attitudes toward Shinto.

The Ise shrines, actually two large shrine complexes, form one of the holiest centers of Shinto. Their origin is associated with the enshrinement of the Sun Goddess here in ancient times. The holiness of the shrines is further attested by the traditional practice of having a princess of the imperial line serve as high priestess. These shrines were centers of Shinto scholarship and ritual and have been objects of popular pilgrimage since medieval times.

Remarkable in Saka's account is his increasing sense of awe and reverence as he approaches the shrines. He even experiences the sacredness of the landscape as he nears, and in order to preserve the Shinto purity of the site, he readily observes the rule that prohibits Buddhist priests from drawing too close. Nevertheless, as he approaches one shrine, he realizes the significance of pilgrimage to Ise: by becoming absolutely pure one is able "to become thus one with the Divine." With this realization, he "could not refrain from shedding tears of gratitude." This kind of simple appreciation of the presence of the *kami,* rather than a formal argument for the existence of God, has characterized the Shinto tradition. In contemporary Japan, the same kind of simple piety can be found wherever people pay their respects at Shinto shrines, although it is not as widespread now as it was in the fourteenth century.

A PILGRIMAGE TO ISE

Saka Jubutsu

When on the way to these Shrines one does not feel like an ordinary person any longer but as though reborn in another world. How solemn is the unearthly shadow of the huge groves of ancient pines and chamaecyparis, and

Reprinted by permission of the publisher from A. L. Sadler, translator, *The Ise Daijingu Sankeiki or Diary of a Pilgrim to Ise* (Tokyo: Zaidan Hojin Meiji Seitoku Kinen Gakkai [Meiji Japan Society], 1940).

there is a delicate pathos in the few rare flowers that have withstood the winter frosts so gaily. The cross-beams of the Torii or Shinto gate way is without any curve, symbolizing by its straightness the sincerity of the direct beam of the Divine promise. The shrine-fence is not painted red nor is the Shrine itself roofed with cedar shingles. The eaves, with their rough reed-hatch, recall memories of the ancient days when the roofs were not trimmed. So did they spare expense out of compassion for the hardships of the people. Within the Shrine there are many buildings where the festival rites are performed, constructed just like those in the Imperial Palace. Buddhist monks may go only as far as the Sacred Tree known as the Cryptomeria of the Five Hundred Branches (Ioe-no-sugi). They may not go to the Shrine. This, too, is a ceremonial rule of the Imperial Court. . . .

When I went to worship at the Shrine of the Moon-Deity Tsukiyomi the fallen leaves in the grove covered my traces and the winter powdered the foliage in the court. And the name of Tsukiyomi recalled so vividly the age of the deities that I was inspired to write:

How many long years
Has this ancient shrine-fence stood
Wet with countless dews,
And the Moon of the Gods' Age
Is this selfsame autumn moon.

I fear that my clumsy pen can hardly do justice to the road from Yamada to the Inner Shrine. Sometimes the spray over the hills seems to reflect their reversed silhouettes, sometimes the way is shrouded in cloud so that the countless peaks of the hills are hidden. As we approach the village of Uji the name is welcome to us with its suggestion of nearness to the Capital, and as it lies under the hills at the south-west of the Outer Shrine it is a place where you might imagine people would make cottages to live in retirement. As we went on deep in the shade of the chamaecyparis groves there was not even the smoke of any habitation to be seen, and we felt as though we had suddenly transcended the bounds of this painful world, while the hills with their cloud-capped mystery transported us to the world of Taoist fairyland.

When I entered the second Torii or Shinto Gate Way to worship it was dark under the pines at the foot of the hill and the branches were so thick-matted that one could hardly discern "the Pine of one hundred branches." The cryptomerias within the Shrine precincts were so dense that even the oblique projecting roof-beams could hardly be made out. When I came to reflect on my condition my mind was full of the Ten Evils and I felt shame at so long forsaking the will of Buddha, yet as I wear one of the three monkish robes, I must feel some chagrin at my estrangement from the Way of the Deities.

And particularly is it the deeply-rooted custom of this Shrine that we should bring no Buddhist rosary or offering, or any special petition in our hearts and this is called "Inner Purity." Washing in sea water and keeping the body free from all defilement is called "Outer Purity." And when both these Purities are attained there is then no barrier between our mind and that of the Deity. And if we feel to become thus one with the Divine, what more do we need and what is there to pray for? When I heard that this was the true way of worshipping at the Shrine, I could not refrain from shedding tears of gratitude.

5
Kitabatake Chikafusa: Medieval Shinto Thought

Shinto harks back to prehistoric Japanese traditions, but became organized institutionally and codified in written documents partly in reaction to the introduction of the elaborately systematized Buddhism. For centuries after Buddhism's arrival in Japan, Buddhism dominated the court and much of religious life, with Shinto assuming the role of a borrower and subordinate institution.

Kitabatake Chikafusa (1293–1354) is significant as the writer of *A Chronicle of Gods and Sovereigns,* one of the most important medieval Shinto documents, because he proclaimed Shinto to be the original Japanese tradition. He argued, both politically and religiously, that Japan is the "divine land"—that is, the land of the *kami*—because it was created by the *kami* and is ruled by the emperor who descended from the Sun Goddess (Amaterasu). Kitabatake used Buddhist materials to demonstrate that Japan is in fact at the center of the world. He even claimed that, because Japan's imperial line is unbroken, "Japan differs from all other countries." This medieval argument helped stimulate Shinto to gain a greater role in government and religion; it also stands as a precedent for the argument of Japan's uniqueness or superiority.

A CHRONICLE OF GODS AND SOVEREIGNS

H. Paul Varley, translator

Great Japan is the divine land. The heavenly progenitor founded it, and the sun goddess bequeathed it to her descendants to rule eternally. Only in our country is this true; there are no similar examples in other countries. This is why our country is called the divine land.

Reprinted by permission of the publisher from H. Paul Varley, translator, *A Chronicle of Gods and Sovereigns* Jinno Shotoki *of Kitabatake Chikafusa* (New York: Columbia University Press, 1980). Some notes have been deleted, and the remaining ones renumbered.

During the age of the gods, Japan was known as Toyoashi-hara-no-Chiiho-no-Aki-no-Mizuho-no-kuni. This name was used from the time when heaven and earth were separated, and can be found in the directive that the heavenly progenitor, Kuni-no-Tokotachi-no-mikoto, presented to the male and female deities Izanagi and Izanami. The name also appears in the mandate that the sun goddess, Amaterasu O-mikami, gave to her heavenly grandson, Ninigi. It may therefore be regarded as the original designation for our country.

Another name for Japan is the Land of Eight Great Islands (O-Yashima), which derives from the fact that Izanagi and Izanami created the country in the form of eight islands.

Still another name for Japan is Yamato, taken from a province in the middle of the Land of Eight Great Islands. The eighth deity produced by Izanagi and Izanami was Ame-no-Misora-Toyoakizune-wake, who was designated O-Yamato-Toyoakizu Island. Today this island (Honshu) is divided into forty-eight provinces, the most central of which is Yamato. Because of its centrality, Yamato served for generations after Emperor Jimmu's eastward campaign as the imperial seat; and because Yamato held the imperial seat, its name was applied as well to the rest of Japan. . . .

According to the Buddhist scriptures, there is a mountain called Sumeru,[1] which is surrounded by seven other concentric, golden mountains. Between these golden mountains flows the Sea of Fragrant Waters, and outside them are four great oceans. Within the oceans are four great continents, each of which consists of two lesser parts. The southern continent is called Jambu (or Jambudvipa, a different form of the same name), and is named after the *jambu* tree. At the center of the southern continent is a mountain called Anavatapta, and on its summit is a lake. (Anavatapta is also called Bunetsu. It is none other than the mountain known in non-Buddhist sources as K'un-lun.)[2] Beside this lake is a *jambu* tree seven *yojanas* in circumference and a hundred in height. (One *yojana* equals forty *ri* [in Chinese, *li*]. Six *shaku* make one *bu,* and 360 *bu* make a *ri*. The unit of *yojana* should be calculated on the basis of the *ri*.) Because of its prominence at the center of the southern continent, this tallest of the *jambu* trees has given the name Jambu to the continent.

To the south of Mount Anavatapta are the Himalayas, and to the north are the Pamirs. North of the Pamirs is Tartary, and south of the Himalayas is India. To the northeast of India is China, and to the northwest of India is Persia. The length and breadth of the continent of Jambu is 7,000 *yojanas*: calculated in terms of *ri,* this would come to 280,000 *ri*. From the eastern sea to the western sea is 90,000 *ri*; and from the southern sea to the northern sea is also 90,000 *ri*. India is in the exact center of the continent, and thus is the middle country of Jambu. Its circumference is 90,000 *ri*. China is thought to be a large country, but compared to India it is a remote and small land on the periphery of Jambu.

---

1. Mount Sumeru is at the center of the world and serves as a kind of pillar to support heaven.

2. According to Chinese mythology, K'un-lun is a mountain of great height that stands at the center of the world.

Japan is in the ocean off the continent of Jambu. Great Teacher Dengyo of Mount Hiei and High Priest Gomyo of Nara both wrote that Japan is the "central land." This would make it the land of Camara between the southern and eastern continents. Yet the Kegon Sutra says: "In the ocean to the northeast is a mountain. It is called Diamond (*kongo*) Mountain." This seems to refer to Mount Kongo of Japan, and therefore indicates that our country is situated in the ocean to the northeast of both India and China. As a land apart, it has been independently ruled by a divinely descended line of sovereigns.

Although the creation of heaven and earth, having occurred within the same universe, must have been the same everywhere, there are nonetheless differences in the traditional accounts of creation in India, China, and Japan. . . .

[Kitabatake then describes the beginning of the world according to the Indian tradition.]

Although China is a country that especially esteems the written word and books, there are no positive Chinese records about the creation of the world. The writings of the Confucian school say nothing about the time before a king called Fu Hsi. But in the heterodox Taoist sources we find tales about the original, undifferentiated state of chaos and the beginnings of heaven, earth, and man—tales that resemble the origins of the world during our age of the gods. There is also the legend of a king called P'an Ku,[3] "whose eyes became the sun and the moon and whose hair became the grasses and trees." After P'an Ku, there appeared the sovereigns of heaven, earth, and man, the "five dragons," and many kings, who collectively ruled for tens of thousands of years.

The origin of things in our country, whereby the world was produced by the descendants of the gods on high, bears some resemblance to the creation story of India. A significant difference is that, from the time of the heavenly founder, Kuni-no-Tokotachi-no-mikoto, there has been no disruption in dynastic succession (*keitai*) in Japan. Rather, our country has been uninterruptedly ruled by the sovereigns of a single dynastic line. In India the first sovereign, the people's lord, was selected by the people and was succeeded by his descendants. But in later generations many members of the lord's line perished and even a man of mean origins, if he possessed the military power, could become king—or rise to be ruler of all India.

China is also a country that tends strongly toward disorder. In early times, when life in China was simple and the right way prevailed, men of wisdom were selected to occupy the imperial office. But no single, immutable dynastic line was founded, and whenever the country lapsed into disorder, people mustered their forces and contended for hegemony. Men arose from among the

---

3. The mythical creator of the world.

common people to become emperors, and there were also cases of barbarians who emerged and seized control of the country. In still other cases, hereditary vassals surpassed their lords and ultimately succeeded to the emperorships held by the latter. Since the time of the first ruler, Fu Hsi, there have been thirty-six dynastic changes in China. The resulting disorder has been unspeakable.

In our country alone, the imperial succession has followed in an unbroken line from the time when heaven and earth were divided until the present age. Although, as is inevitable within a single family, the succession has at times been transmitted collaterally . . . , the principle has prevailed that it will invariably return to the direct . . . line. This is entirely the result of the immutable mandate of Amaterasu, and is the reason why Japan differs from all other countries.

The way of the gods (*shinto*) is not readily revealed. Yet if the divine basis of things is not understood, such ignorance will surely give rise to disorder. To rectify the ignorance that is the cause of disorder, I have been motivated to take up my brush. Since my chief aim is to discuss the principles of direct succession . . . to the throne from the age of the gods, I shall omit discussion of matters that are commonly known. I have decided to name what I write "The Chronicle of the Direct Descent of Gods and Sovereigns."

6
Motoori Norinaga: A Shinto View of Aesthetics and Human Nature

Motoori Norinaga (1730–1801) is a leading example of the Kokugaku, or national learning scholars, who arose in the seventeenth and eighteenth centuries, attempting to go behind Buddhist and Confucian interpretations of Japanese culture to discover its distinctively Japanese character and intrinsic worth. Ironically, the inspiration for much of this work came from Confucianism (or Neo-Confucianism) in the sense of returning to the original texts rather than depending on later commentaries.

Among the many ideas Motoori stressed, a leading one was *mono no aware*, a person's "emotional and aesthetic experience." Motoori rejected the moralistic and rationalistic critiques of *Genji Monogatari* (Tale of Genji) drawn from Buddhist and Confucian teachings, insisting that the value of the work is in its emotional and aesthetic power (apart from judgments of "good" and "evil"). Going beyond literature, Motoori rejected also moralistic and rationalistic views of human nature. The modern scholar Shigeru Matsumoto writes that Motoori insisted "the *mono no aware* experience of man is in essence based upon the reality of the human heart, or human nature itself, which he sees as essentially feminine rather than masculine." In his rejection of the stoic ideal of warrior manhood and in his view of the essentially "feminine" heart of all people, Motoori was far ahead of his time. He also studied the nature of *kami* and the "ancient way" of Shinto in his exploration of a distinctively Japanese tradition.

THE CONCEPT OF *MONO NO AWARE*

Shigeru Matsumoto

Mono no aware is the key concept representing the essence of Norinaga's thought as formed in the second phase of his life. At the same time as he was studying Confucian texts, he was also developing this important idea through his private study of ancient Japanese literature, particularly of *Genji monogatari*. *Mono no aware* is important not simply as an aesthetic concept basic to his theory of literature, but also as a central idea in his view of human nature. Although the last and finest presentation of the concept is given in his *Genji monogatari tama no ogushi* (The small jeweled comb, a study of *The tale of Genji*), written in his old age, we can already see it germinating in his first essay, *Ashiwake obune* around 1757, and it finds almost complete expression in *Shibun yoryo* and *Isonokami sasamegoto,* both written in 1763 at the age of thirty-three.

Mono no aware is a subtle term, which is very difficult to render into another language. It consists of three words: *mono* ("thing" in a broad sense), *no* (a possessive particle), and *aware* (usually translated as "sadness" or "pity"). As is often the case, however, a literal translation, such as "sadness of things," not only fails to convey its real meaning, but is also misleading. Our problem here is what Norinaga means by it. Because the term refers to a rather subtle notion, Norinaga's exposition itself is not very systematic. But here I will try to approach its meaning and implication by distinguishing three aspects: the basic meaning of *mono no aware;* the significance of *mono no aware* for literature; *mono no aware* and human nature. And on each of these, I would like to let Norinaga speak for himself as far as possible.

According to Norinaga, the key word is *aware,* to which *mono* is added to supply a somewhat broader connotation, as in *monogatari* (story), *monomi* (sight-seeing), *monomode* (visit to shrines), and so forth. In *Isonokami sasamegoto,* he expounds the word *aware,* on the basis of his philological studies, as follows: "*Aware* is in essence an expression for deep feeling in the heart. In later periods, this word has been used to refer merely to a sad feeling, but that is only one facet of the term . . . *Aware* was originally an exclamation, expressing any heartfelt sentiment. It belonged to the same category as *ana* and *aya* [both exclamations]." Then, after quoting a number of poems in illustration, he says: "Although people usually conceive *aware* as simply meaning sadness, this is not quite right. Rather, any deep emotion, whether happy, amused, joyous, sad, or yearning, can be referred to as *aware*. Hence we see many instances in which *aware* denotes something interesting or amusing."

Norinaga does not fail to mention the historical change in usage, which, he holds, was based on subtle human psychology. "Among the various things

Reprinted by permission of the publisher from Shigeru Matsumoto, *Motoori Norinaga 1730–1801* (Cambridge: Harvard University Press, 1970). The notes have been deleted.

that move a man's heart, something amusing or cheerful will move it rather lightly, whereas something sad or something yearned for stirs the heart especially deeply. So these latter feelings have been particularly identified with *aware,* so that *aware* is now commonly understood simply as sadness. This can be compared to the term *hana,* which denotes all kinds of flowers and yet is also used to refer particularly to cherry blossom as against plum and other kinds."

Thus, according to Norinaga, *aware* is above all a word of exclamation or a word for expressing any of the deep emotions that man experiences in regard to things or events. Norinaga also stresses the spontaneous and irresistible nature of such emotion or *aware.* He says in *Shibun yoryo:* "The things by which man is deeply moved are diverse, some being good and others being evil, but man's heart itself is so spontaneously and irresistibly moved that it is beyond his control and can be moved even by evil things. However much a man tries not to be stirred by something which he regards as evil, his heart is naturally and irresistibly moved."

It should be noticed that Norinaga has a special psychological insight into the nature of man's emotional orientation toward such exterior objects. That is, Norinaga sees that the object in such a context can have no neutral connotation when it involves some moving or affecting significance for the subject. According to Norinaga, "for the subject to be affected" is not separable from "for the object to be affecting." He calls this significance of the object *mono no kokoro* (the heart of the thing) or *koto no kokoro* (the heart of the event). For Norinaga, "to be aware of the heart of a thing" (*mono no kokoro o shiru*) is identical with "to be sensitive to *mono no aware*" (*mono no aware o shiru*). In his own words:

> For instance, if a man, viewing beautiful cherry-blossoms in full bloom, appreciates them as beautiful, he is aware of *mono no kokoro* or the heart of the thing [the moving significance of the cherry blossoms]. Being aware of the beauty of the blossoms, he is moved by it. That is, he is sensitive to *mono no aware.* In contrast, if a man, whatever beautiful flowers he sees, does not feel them to be beautiful, he is not aware of *mono no kokoro.* Such a man is never moved by the beauty of the flowers. That is to say, he is not sensitive to *mono no aware.*

Norinaga gives another instance as follows:

> When a man, seeing some other person deeply grieving for some serious trouble, sympathizes in the grief, he does so because he knows that the event is distressing. That is, he is aware of *koto no kokoro* or the heart of the event [the affecting significance of the sad event]. Being aware of the heart of the event to be grieved for, he feels sympathy for that grief within his own heart, so that he is emotionally moved. This is *mono no aware . . .* On the other hand, a man who is not sensitive to *mono no aware* and so not aware of the heart of the sad event, has no sympathy for the other's grief, however acutely he perceives it, so that his heart is not moved at all.

Thus we can see that *mono no aware* experience involves some intuitive and aesthetic understanding of the "heart" of an object, which implies a certain sympathy for or even empathy toward the object. In short, *mono no aware* as Norinaga conceives it may be understood as man's emotional and aesthetic experience on being aware of the stimulating or affecting significance of the object with which he is involved.

Next, let us examine the implications of *mono no aware* in relation to literature. According to Norinaga, the purpose of literature is to express what man feels deeply in his heart, that is to say, to give expression to his *mono no aware* experience, and nothing else. Already in *Ashiwake obune*, Norinaga, in answer to the question whether poetry should be of political utility, had replied: "No. The essence of poetry is not to assist government, nor even to cultivate oneself. It is simply to express what one feels in one's heart. Some poems may be helpful to government or to moral instruction, but others can have a harmful effect upon a country or on private life. It depends on the poem; each is composed according to the author's heart."

In *Shibun yoryo*, discussing the essential significance of *Genji monogatari*, Norinaga more decidedly remarks: "This novel sets out exclusively to describe *mono no aware* in many guises and to make the reader conscious of it. The reader in turn should be concerned only with feeling *mono no aware* in the novel. And this is also the essence of the poetic art. There is no significance in novels and poems apart from *mono no aware*."

The importance of this view is best understood within the sociocultural context in which it was proposed. In medieval Japan there was a common notion, based on Buddhist teaching, that the author of *Genji monogatari*, Murasaki Shikibu, went to hell for writing such a lewd novel and corrupting so many people. Confucians in the early Edo period, too, usually disapproved of the novel as lustful. On the other hand, some critics did try to rescue *Genji monogatari* from this stigma by propounding the view that, although it was superficially erotic, it had actually been written to uphold moral principles or *kanzen choaku* (encouraging good and castigating evil). This problem did not concern *Genji monogatari* alone; literature in general was subject to moralistic or political interpretations under the influence of Confucian and Buddhist thought. . . .

. . . It was Norinaga, with his idea of *mono no aware*, who most decisively insisted upon the intrinsic value of literature independent of moral or political interests.

In *Shibun yoryo* Norinaga criticizes the previous commentaries on *Genji monogatari*, saying: "The traditional commentaries, following the moralistic discussion in Confucian and Buddhist books, tend to wrench the novel into the shape of a piece of moral instruction. They comment on what the novel speaks of as good, as if it were evil, and explain passages of the novel as lessons to various ends. They have thus often misled readers and missed the author's real intention." Norinaga even says that such distorted interpretations are "devils," harmful to the novel. According to him, the value standard implied in *Genji monogatari,* and in all literature, is *mono no aware*. The concepts of "good" and "bad," as applied to literature, derive from whether or not a work is in harmony with the deepest feelings of man. They are essentially different from the concepts of "good and evil" in Confucian or Buddhist teachings. "These teachings," says Norinaga, "are in essence meant to encourage good, to suppress evil in human nature, and to lead evil to good. Consequently, they often strictly admonish man against evil and, in so doing, tend to be contrary to human nature." In contrast, literature is not concerned with "good and evil" in the Confucian or Buddhist sense, but simply with *mono no aware.*

Norinaga refers to the hero of *Genji monogatari,* Hikaru Genji, for an illustration of his point. Genji is described as leading a life full of love affairs and adulteries with many women, including even an empress; this empress eventually had a child by Genji, who was taken to be the emperor's son and even succeeded him. Despite all these "evil" acts, Norinaga argues, "Prince Genji lived his whole life in peace and comfort, with overflowing prosperity, to such an extent that he received the honorific title of father of the emperor. And not only could he do anything he desired, but his children also flourished. Who, seeing this, would make up his mind to refrain from sensuality?" For Norinaga it is therefore clear that the meaning of the novel does not lie in moral instruction. Murasaki Shikibu described Genji most beautifully, "by concentrating upon him all the desirable qualities conceivable," simply because she intended to make readers feel *mono no aware* as deeply as possible. . . .

Norinaga's view of the essence of literature is basically related to his understanding of human nature—the third and most critical aspect of his concept of *mono no aware.* According to Norinaga, the *mono no aware* experience of man is in essence based upon the reality of the human heart, or human nature itself, which he sees as essentially feminine rather than masculine. He says in *Shibun yoryo:* "In general, the real heart of a human being is effeminate and weak like a woman or a child. To be manly, resolute, and wise is a mere superficial appearance. As far as the depth of man's real heart is concerned, the wisest men do not differ from a woman or a child. The difference between them lies merely in that the former conceal the real heart for shame, whereas the latter do not."

This notion of the human heart or human nature as feminine was already present in, and even basic to, Norinaga's thought in *Ashiwake obune.* It is particularly evident in his vivid description of the differences between father and mother in their attitudes to the death of a beloved child. Norinaga writes:

> Although father and mother must grieve equally for their child, the father appears to be little affected, whereas the mother is overwhelmed with grief and weeps distractedly. Why is there this difference? It is because the mother cannot restrain her real heart and simply expresses it as it is, while the father, lest people should think him effeminate, restrains himself from shedding a single tear, and by rigid self-control so conceals his great grief that he keeps up the appearance of manful resignation to fate. In my view, the mother's reaction appears frantic and even indecent, but this represents the reality of the human heart. The father, on the other hand, is appar-

ently manly, resolute, and composed, but this does not represent his real heart. If he were really so from his heart, he would be like the trees and stones.

Norinaga further argues that even the bravery of warriors was only an aspect of superficial virility, veiling the real human heart. He says:

> For instance, it is customary that a loyal samurai warrior on the battlefield should be willing to sacrifice his life manfully for the sake of his lord and his country. But when he is dying, does he not feel yearning toward the wife and children he left at home? Does he not wish to see his old parents once again? Can even a man rough as a devil avoid feeling sad, when he is dying? These feelings in the last moments are natural human feelings, shared by thousands and millions of people, without distinction between sages and ordinary men.

Thus, according to Norinaga, differences between men and women, between warriors and nonwarriors, and even between sages and ordinary men, are only superficial in view of the fact that the real depth of the human heart is all "effeminate and weak." *Mono no aware* is the experience which is deeply rooted in, and derives from, these feminine depths of human nature. And literature expresses these depths in terms of *mono no aware.* . . .

Norinaga's emphasis upon feminine qualities as against the masculine is thus noteworthy. The first two aspects of *mono no aware* are in harmony with this last point. We have seen that *mono no aware* is man's emotional, aesthetic, and intuitive experience rather than experience primarily based on will or reasoning. Also, the *mono no aware* experience is more associated with man's "expressive" motivations and orientations than with his "instrumental" ones. It seems that in every point *mono no aware* involves a feminine, rather than masculine, tone.

The significance of Norinaga's idea of *mono no aware* will be more evident, when it is considered in its sociocultural and historical setting. The period was one in which women were generally regarded as inferior to men, not only in social status but also in natural qualities. There was a common saying at that time that a woman should obey her parents in childhood, her husband in adulthood, and her children in her old age. Marriage was a matter for the family, arranged mainly to ensure the continuity of the family lineage, and a wife was always expected to submit selflessly to her husband and his parents. When she was childless, it was often an excuse for her husband to take a concubine or to divorce her, although the adoption of a son or daughter was more common. Confucianism was the most influential ideological system to support the established family and social order and its values. A Confucian teaching well known at that time rationalizes the customary notion of man's superiority to women in metaphysical terms, saying that "a man is *yang* and noble, and a woman is *yin* and base, just as heaven is *yang* and noble, and the earth is *yin* and low." Kaibara Ekken (1630–1714), like many other Confucian scholars, insisted that "women are by nature weak, irresolute, lacking intelligence, and mostly wicked; they cannot follow the right way." In this social and cultural situation, love between a man and a woman was not normally approved as natural, but was rather to be avoided or kept secret. As a strict Confucian moral principle insists, "boys and girls are not supposed to be seated together after the age of seven." It was no wonder in that period that love novels like *Genji monogatari* were criticized as immoral, or interpreted in rather distorted ways.

It was against this sociocultural background that Norinaga proposed the idea of *mono no aware*. He emphatically affirmed the value of feminine qualities like emotion, tenderness, weakness, effeminacy, and so on, which were generally looked down upon as mean, and inferior to masculine qualities like resolution, formality, strength, and manliness. He not only affirmed femininity against masculinity, but, purifying it in terms of the symbol *mono no aware*, exalted it as true and essential to human nature, relegating masculinity to the status of something superficial and secondary.

7
The Role of Women in Shinto

Women at large Shinto shrines today are conspicuous in appearance, but relatively inconspicuous and unimportant in their actual religious roles. The modern visitor to large shrines cannot help but notice a number of young women, often the daughters of shrine priests, because of the striking sight they present with their contrasting colors of long black hair, pure white blouses, and bright red skirts. However, it is the male priests who perform all the major actions in Shinto ceremonies, and young women only assist with minor duties, such as playing musical instruments and dancing, or pouring sake (rice wine). More often these young women, called *miko,* perform a variety of clerical tasks, such as selling amulets, postcards, and publications at booths outside the main shrine, and handling other nonritual tasks.

The relatively minor role of women in contemporary Shinto does not give any indication of the long and varied history of women's roles within Shinto. In prehistoric and protohistoric Japan women actually were more important than men both in the religious and the political realm, but by early historical times the fortunes of women were reversed, with men assuming the dominant role both in government and religion.[1]

The following selection describes the earlier and more important religious life of women in Shinto, and traces the changing role of women in later periods, discussing some of the reasons that account for such change. In contemporary Shinto women do not play a central role, but the prehistoric and protohistoric precedent for women having special access to religious power is reflected in the female shamans within folk religion and the female founders of New Religions, both of which we will discuss later (see p. 129 and p. 270).

---

1. For Okano's treatment of the role of women in Shinto from the viewpoint of sexism, see Haruko Okano, "Women and Sexism in Shinto," *The Japan Christian Review* 59 (1993): 27–31.

SUMMARY: WOMAN AND
THE SHINTO RELIGION

Haruko Okano

The national religion of Japan, called *Shinto* (the "Way of the Gods") to distinguish it from *Butsudo* (Buddhism, the "Way of Buddha"), is a collective term for several different forms of religion. Besides the primary form, primitive Shinto, there are Shrine Shinto, the orthodox form which also included the Shinto of the Imperial family, popular Shinto, the religion of the people, and finally Sect Shinto, a set of independent systems. The present study examines the position of woman in all these four forms.

Woman appears in Shinto as a female deity, a virgin, empress and ruler, priestess, cult dancer, founder of sects and as a "shaman" outside the organised system of Shintoism. These female figures have in common a special relationship with the deity, based largely on the experience of the state of ecstasy. They have always been, and are still, called *Mikos,* literally "children of God." This term means a mediator between the gods and men, and is used to designate not only the lower orders of priestesses in Shinto shrines and women unconnected with any shrine claiming religious and magical powers, but women in general, who because of their charism have played an important part in religious life from primitive times to the present day.

The task of this study is to examine the various roles of women from the points of view of religious history, religious phenomenology, religious sociology, and religious typology. The position of the woman in the religious system of Shinto depends on the changes in the system itself and on a variety of sociological factors. Thus the work begins with a historical account of woman's role, as regards which the history of Japan can be divided into three periods:

1. Primitive Shinto, from early history to the organisation of Shinto, c. end of 2nd to 7th century AD.

2. Organised Shinto, from the Taika Reform to the Meiji Restoration, 7th century AD to 1867.

3. Shinto after the Meiji Restoration, 1868 to the present day.

The first period, when government was still closely connected with religious practice, can with some justification be called the Golden Age as far as woman's role is concerned. Not only creative power, closely related to the concept of the fertility goddess, but also the power of charism, on the whole central and indispensable to a shamanist society, were attributed more or less indiscriminately to all women in Japan. They were worshipped as deities, as

Reprinted by permission of the publisher from Haruko Okano, *Die Stellung der Frau im Shinto* (Wiesbaden: Otto Harrassowitz, 1976).

consorts of the gods, as chieftains or empresses, as priestesses or other such numinous figures. At this point one may pose the question as to whether ancient Japanese society did in fact rank women higher than men, and there have been many speculations on the likelihood of a matriarchal society and on whether the priestesses were superior to the priests, since many of the old chronicles and many traditional customs offer proof of a certain gynecocratic tendency. But according to other sources society was predominantly patriarchal and men were involved in the most important religious rites.

I do not think there is one single answer to this question, and a much more important problem is the relationship between men and women in society, where this can be proved from history. In the earliest stage rulership implied priesthood, and as the social structures themselves were composed of men and women, so power in the ruling classes was distributed between men and women in rather an interesting way. The woman was in direct contact with the deity and announced the divine will to mankind. The realisation of this will on earth was entrusted to the man. Thus priesthood was embodied in a man and woman relationship (usually brother and sister). This man + woman system is first found in the clan systems (*Uji*), the territorial administrations of the provinces (*Kuni*) and in the centralised government of the Yamato Empire.

However, in time this man + woman system underwent changes. The more dependent everyday life was on the mystical, magic elements in religion, the more important was woman's role. A proof of this is that many of the *Mikos* were deified and that the ancient chronicles speak of female rulers such as Himiko and priestesses such as Tamayori-hime. As, however, the rights and privileges of the various petty rulers were gradually absorbed by the Imperial family and a centralised empire formed, politics assumed an increasingly rational character, although it was supposed to be determined ultimately by divine will. Thus began the formal and conceptual rift between politics and religion, as a result of which women retired more and more from this form of society, as in the case of cult princess *Saio*. At this stage the woman was only the emperor's representative in the religious sphere, and the same process could be observed in the independent provinces.

The second period of Shinto history began with the Taika Reform which brought about the change from the old form of government to a centralised absolute monarchy. In order to achieve political unity in the state, the power of the earlier provincial lords fell to the emperor. This meant that the individual cults of the local gods of the clans (*Ujigami*) had to be organised into one central system. Thus such local deities, originally worshipped only by certain clans, took on an official and national character. The "Divine Cult Office" (the *Jingi-kan*) was set up to organise religious life and to see to the administration of the shrines. In this sense the religious cult had now become the rationalised concern of the bureaucrats instead of being the spontaneous act of a naturally religious person. In former times individuals endowed with charism had summoned the gods and these had taken possession of certain chosen persons. But in State Shinto fulfilling the rite correctly meant that the gods could only appear at a certain time and in a certain place. For this reason, the rites had to be performed by official priests, and the bureaucrats of the *Jingi-kan,* the "Divine Cult Office," sometimes assisted by other court dignitaries, male or female, officiated at ceremonies in the shrines at the Imperial court and at other shrines of major importance, while the rites at local shrines were the responsibility of the provincial governors (the *Kokushi*) and priests such as the *Kannushi, Negi* and *Hafuri.* These official priests were as a rule men, but in many old shrines the tradition of having a priestess persisted until the tenth century AD. After this time priestesses were very rare, but at Ise, the Imperial ancestral shrine, the body of priests was led by a priestess up until the Middle Ages.

Three factors are responsible for the decline in priestesses at most shrines: 1) since the descent of the divinity could now be calculated "mechanically" as it were, women were no longer really necessary in the priesthood, 2) the Chinese legal system, recently introduced to Japan and on which the priesthood was based, was strictly male-orientated, 3) Buddhism strengthened the notion of the uncleanness of woman, due to her biological and psychological make-up.

The newly created bureaucratic state took over the rites and the priesthood and organised them, thus rendering them static; but charismatic figures, mostly women, continued to be active among the people, outside the system of organised Shinto. We may find them in secularised types such as dancers, puppeteers or courtesans, or even as pillars of popular Shinto, true to its name the belief of the people.

Each new step in the modernisation of the cultural, political or economic fields ousted women further from significant positions in the priesthood, because their religious authority, often inherited, was based on superstitious religious notions among the people.

The third period, beginning with the Meiji Restoration, also considerably affected the position of women. The newly restored Imperial dynasty, with its new national awareness, strove to establish pure Shinto as the national religion, and abolished such mystical elements of Shinto as the concept of inherited charism and also the practising of magic rites. Woman could no longer be a member of the official priesthood.

Since the Second World War, however, women have once again been accepted into the priesthood. No distinction is made between them and their male colleagues and both men and women fulfil the same functions. It must be admitted, though, that women are generally seen as substitutes for male priests. Thus women have achieved a new position in the Shinto religion by renouncing their specific femininity, which was their traditional function and role within the religious community.

While the traditional functions of women within organised religion may have all but vanished, the *Mikos,* female sorcerers, are once again active among the people. They will tell fortunes and prophesy, for a consideration, and also function as medicine-women. The great number of female founders of sects should also be mentioned. Their new teachings on religion and values and their faith-healing claims appeal to the mass of the people. Religious communities founded by such women existed even before the Meiji dynasty. This particular type of charismatic women, seeing themselves as mediators between gods and men and, filled with prophetic awareness, founding universal religious communities, is a new phenomenon in Japanese religious history, but it is interesting to note that such "new" religions show in their community life old elements of primitive magic and base their authority on the tradition of the "classical" religions.

8

The Disestablishment of State Shinto, and the Emperor's "Renunciation of Divinity"

In medieval times, Shinto was dominated by Buddhism, but in late medieval times, Shinto attempted to restrengthen her own tradition. The major political changes of 1868 favored Shinto, and from that time until 1945, Shinto was increasingly treated as a state religion, which Holtom called State Shinto. During this period most Shinto shrines and Shinto priests came to be considered state institutions and state officials. Attendance at shrines amounted to more than a simple religious act; because it was a patriotic obligation, it was considered to be the duty of every Japanese as a citizen of the state. Schools taught an ethical system based on the mythological origin of the Japanese people and absolute loyalty to the state as embodied in the person of the emperor. It should be remembered that Shinto was only one of several elements that were used to support this all-embracing nationalism. (For greater detail, see Chapter 15, especially Selection 54.) On one hand, for many people, Shinto meant the annual festivals, seasonal celebrations, observances in the home, and veneration of the *kami*—living within a world blessed by the *kami*. On the other hand, especially as an institution and a social force, state Shinto was used to support ultranationalism and militarism before and during World War II.

At the end of World War II, the Allied military leaders and many Japanese intellectuals felt that Shinto had become a tool of the ultranationalists and the military rather than a religion of the people. Therefore, the Allied occupation forces in Japan required the disestablishment of Shinto and stated this requirement in a document, which is the first part of this selection. Shinto (including sect Shinto) would be allowed to exist as a religion on the same legal basis as other religious organizations in Japan. The general restrictions were spelled out more in terms of the state—to prevent the state from giving special privileges to any religious group.

Since 1945, various problems have arisen regarding the interpretation and implementation of this document. These issues have never been completely resolved, and continue to pose difficulties for Shinto today. Shinto authorities claim that the directive was a foreign intervention into the Japanese tradition, creating an artificial division of state and religion that had never existed in Japan. Controversy arises particularly around such concrete issues as the religious status of the emperor and whether his annual ritual ceremonies are only a private matter or (according to Shinto authorities) are actually state ceremonies; whether the funeral for an emperor and the enthronement of a new emperor are state ceremonies or religious rituals; whether the national shrine for war dead (Yasukuni Shrine in Tokyo) is only a religious institution or (according to Shinto authorities) is also a national monument; whether rites at the Ise Shrine and the periodic rebuilding are only religious ceremonies or (according to Shrine authorities) also involve state concern. Within the present Japanese constitution, all of these issues are treated as private religious concerns, but state funds were used for the funeral of Emperor Hirohito (also known as the Showa emperor) in 1989 and the enthronement of his son as Emperor Akihito.

The second part of this selection is, in effect, Emperor Hirohito's answer to the directive on disestablishment. Although the status of the emperor is at stake, he begins with a reference to the highly revered Emperor Meiji, who was seen as the architect of modern Japan. This is the beginning of an appeal for the people to band together in the love of their country to overcome defeat and rebuild the nation. This speech, broadcast over the radio on New Year's Day, 1946, brought the emperor into closer contact with his subjects than ever before; the placing of the emperor on the same level of humanity with his subjects in "mutual trust and affection" is also quite new. The denial of a mythical support for the emperor and his status as a manifest god, although a departure from prewar indoctrination and a surprise for the lesser educated, was an unvoiced understanding among educated people.

The postwar decline of popular interest in Shinto was not solely due to the disestablishment order or the emperor's radio speech. Shinto's involvement in the war machine, followed by the sudden defeat in 1945, were also contributing factors. (See p. 255 for attitudes toward Shinto in postwar Japan.)

ABOLITION OF STATE SHINTO
Abolition of Governmental Sponsorship, Support, Perpetuation, Control, and Dissemination of State Shinto (Kokka Shinto, Jinja Shinto)

SCAPIN 448 (CIE) 15 Dec 45 (AG 000.3)

1. In order to free the Japanese people from direct or indirect compulsion to believe or profess to believe in a religion or cult officially designated by the state, and

---

Reprinted by permission of the publisher from William P. Woodard, *The Allied Occupation of Japan and Japanese Religions* (Leiden: E. J. Brill, 1972). Some notes have been deleted.

In order to lift from the Japanese people the burden of compulsory financial support of an ideology which has contributed to their war guilt, defeat, suffering, privation, and present deplorable condition, and

In order to prevent a recurrence of the perversion of Shinto theory and beliefs into militaristic and ultranationalistic propaganda designed to delude the Japanese people and lead them into wars of aggression, and

In order to assist the Japanese people in a rededication of their national life to building a new Japan based upon ideals of perpetual peace and democracy,

It is hereby directed that:

a. The sponsorship, support, perpetuation, control and dissemination of Shinto by the Japanese national, prefectural, and local governments, or by public officials, subordinates, and employees acting in their official capacity are prohibited and will cease immediately.

b. All financial support from public funds and all official affiliation with Shinto and Shinto shrines are prohibited and will cease immediately.

   (1) While no financial support from public funds will be extended to shrines located on public reservations or parks, this prohibition will not be construed to preclude the Japanese Government from continuing to support the areas on which such shrines are located.

   (2) Private financial support of all Shinto shrines which have been previously supported in whole or in part by public funds will be permitted, provided such private support is entirely voluntary and is in no way derived from forced or involuntary contributions.

c. All propagation and dissemination of militaristic and ultra-nationalistic ideology in Shinto doctrines, practices, rites, ceremonies, or observances, as well as in the doctrines, practices, rites, ceremonies, and observances of any other religion, faith, sect, creed, or philosophy, are prohibited and will cease immediately.

d. The Religious Functions Order relating to the Grand Shrine of Ise and the Religious Functions Order relating to State and other Shrines will be annulled.

e. The Shrine Board (*Jingi-in*) of the Ministry of Home Affairs will be abolished, and its present functions, duties, and administrative obligations will not be assumed by any other governmental or tax-supported agency.

f. All public educational institutions whose primary function is either the investigation and dissemination of Shinto or the training of a Shinto priesthood will be abolished and their physical properties diverted to other uses. Their present functions, duties and administrative obligations will not be assumed by any other governmental or tax-supported agency.

g. Private educational institutions for the investigation and dissemination of Shinto and for the training of priesthood for Shinto will be permitted and will operate with the same privileges and be subject to the same controls and restrictions as any other private educational institution having no affiliation with the government; in no case, however, will they receive support from public funds, and in no case will they propagate and disseminate militaristic and ultra-nationalistic ideology.

h.   The dissemination of Shinto doctrines in any form and by any means in any educational institution supported wholly or in part by public funds is prohibited and will cease immediately.

(1) All teachers' manuals and textbooks now in use in any educational institution supported wholly or in part by public funds will be censored, and all Shinto doctrine will be deleted. No teachers' manual or textbook which is published in the future for use in such institutions will contain any Shinto doctrine.

(2) No visits to Shinto shrines and no rites, practices or ceremonies associated with Shinto will be conducted or sponsored by any educational institution supported wholly or in part by public funds.

i.   Circulation by the government of "The Fundamental Principles of the National Structure" (*Kokutai no Hongi*), "The Way of the Subject" (*Shinmin no Michi*), and all similar official volumes, commentaries, interpretations, or instructions on Shinto is prohibited.

j.   The use in official writings of the terms "Greater East Asia War" (*Dai Toa Senso*), "The Whole World under One Roof" (*Hakko Ichi-u*), and all other terms whose connotation in Japanese is inextricably connected with State Shinto, militarism, and ultranationalism is prohibited and will cease immediately.

k.   God-shelves (*Kamidana*) and all other physical symbols of State Shinto in any office, school, institution, organization, or structure supported wholly or in part by public funds are prohibited and will be removed immediately.

l.   No official, subordinate, employee, student, citizen, or resident of Japan will be discriminated against because of his failure to profess and believe in or participate in any practice, rite, ceremony, or observance of State Shinto or of any other religion.

m.   No official of the national, prefectural, or local government, acting in his public capacity, will visit any shrine to report his assumption of office, to report on conditions of government or to participate as a representative of government in any ceremony or observance.

2.   a.   The purpose of this directive is to separate religion from the state, to prevent misuse of religion for political ends, and to put all religions, faiths, and creeds upon exactly the same basis, entitled to precisely the same opportunities and protection. It forbids affiliation with the government and the propagation and dissemination of militaristic and ultra-nationalistic ideology not only to Shinto but to the followers of all religions, faiths, sects creeds, or philosophies.

b.   The provisions of this directive will apply with equal force to all rites, practices, ceremonies, observances, beliefs, teachings, mythology, legends, philosophy, shrines, and physical symbols associated with Shinto.

c.   The term State Shinto within the meaning of this directive will refer to that branch of Shinto (*Kokka Shinto* or *Jinja Shinto*) which by official acts of the Japanese Government has been differentiated from the religion of Sect Shinto (*Shuha Shinto* or *Kyoha Shinto*) and has been classified a non-religious cult commonly known as State Shinto, National Shinto, or Shrine Shinto.

   d. The term Sect Shinto (*Shuha Shinto* or *Kyoha Shinto*) will refer to that branch of Shinto (composed of 13 recognized sects) which by popular belief, legal commentary, and the official acts of the Japanese Government has been recognized to be a religion.

   e. Pursuant to the terms of Article I of the Basic Directive on "Removal of Restrictions on Political, Civil, and Religious Liberties" issued on 4 October 1945 by the Supreme Commander for the Allied Powers in which the Japanese people were assured complete religious freedom,

      (1) Sect Shinto will enjoy the same protection as any other religion.

      (2) Shrine Shinto, after having been divorced from the state and divested of its militaristic and ultranationalistic elements, will be recognized as a religion if its adherents so desire and will be granted the same protection as any other religion in so far as it may in fact be the philosophy or religion of Japanese individuals.

   f. Militaristic and ultra-nationalistic ideology, as used in this directive, embraces those teachings, beliefs, and theories which advocate or justify a mission on the part of Japan to extend its rule over other nations and peoples by reason of:

      (1) The doctrine that the Emperor of Japan is superior to the heads of other states because of ancestry, descent, or special origin.

      (2) The doctrine that the people of Japan are superior to the people of other lands because of ancestry, descent, or special origin.

      (3) The doctrine that the islands of Japan are superior to other lands because of divine or special origin.

      (4) Any other doctrine which tends to delude the Japanese people into embarking upon wars of aggression or to glorify the use of force as an instrument for the settlement of disputes with other peoples.

3. The Imperial Japanese Government will submit a comprehensive report to this Headquarters not later than 15 March 1946 describing in detail all action taken to comply with all provisions of this directive.

4. All officials, subordinates, and employees of the Japanese national, prefectural, and local governments, all teachers and education officials, and all citizens and residents of Japan will be held personally accountable for compliance with the spirit as well as the letter of all provisions of this directive.

THE IMPERIAL RESCRIPT OF
JANUARY 1, 1946

In greeting the New Year, We recall to mind that Emperor Meiji proclaimed, as the basis of our national policy, the Five Clauses of the Charter Oath at the beginning of the Meiji Era. The Charter Oath signified:—

1. Deliberative assemblies shall be established and all measures of government decided in accordance with public opinion.
2. All classes, high and low, shall unite in vigorously carrying on the affairs of State.
3. All common people, no less than the civil and military officials, shall be allowed to fulfill their just desires, so that there may not be any discontent among them.
4. All the absurd usages of old shall be broken through, and equity and justice to be found in the workings of nature shall serve as the basis of action.
5. Wisdom and knowledge shall be sought throughout the world for the purpose of promoting the welfare of the Empire.

The proclamation is evident in significance and high in its ideals. We wish to make this oath anew and restore the country to stand on its own feet again. We have to reaffirm the principles embodied in the Charter, and proceed unflinchingly towards elimination of misguided practices of the past, and keeping in close touch with the desires of the people, we will construct a new Japan through thoroughly being pacific, the officials and the people alike, attaining rich culture, and advancing the standard of living of the people.

The devastation of war inflicted upon our cities, the miseries of the destitute, the stagnation of trade, shortage of food, and the great and growing number of the unemployed are indeed heart-rending. But if the nation is firmly united in its resolve to face the present ordeal and to seek civilization consistently in peace, a bright future will undoubtedly be ours, not only for our country, but for the whole humanity.

Love of the family and love of the country are especially strong in this country. With more of this devotion should we now work towards love of mankind.

We feel deeply concerned to note that consequent upon the protracted war ending in our defeat, our people are liable to grow restless and to fall into the Slough of Despond. Radical tendencies in excess are gradually spreading and the sense of morality tends to lose its hold on the people, with the result that there are signs of confusion of thoughts.

We stand by the people and We wish always to share with them in their moments of joys and sorrows. The ties between Us and Our people have always stood upon mutual trust and affection. They do not depend upon mere legends and myths. They are not predicated on the false conception that the

Emperor is divine, and that the Japanese people are superior to other races and fated to rule the world.

Our Government should make every effort to alleviate their trials and tribulations. At the same time, We trust that the people will rise to the occasion, and will strive courageously for the solution of their outstanding difficulties, and for the development of industry and culture. Acting upon a consciousness of solidarity and of mutual aid and broad tolerance in their civic life, they will prove themselves worthy of their best tradition. By their supreme endeavours in that direction, they will be able to render their substantial contribution to the welfare and advancement of mankind.

The resolution for the year should be made at the beginning of the year. We expect Our people to join Us in all exertions looking to accomplishment of this great undertaking with an indomitable spirit.

CHAPTER THREE

Buddhism

Buddhism arose in India and was transmitted through China and Korea to Japan. On one hand, Buddhism in Japan still displays Indian religious concepts and artistic images, and it is expressed in Chinese forms, such as the scriptures in Chinese translation; on the other hand, Buddhism became thoroughly nationalized in Japan, and it shares most of the persistent themes of the Japanese religious tradition.

Buddhism came to Japan as a foreign religion, but it tended to blend with the native tradition rather than to try to oust the indigenous tradition and "convert" the people. The Buddhist divinities of India and China and the *kami* of Japan were more often seen as complementing one another than as competing with each other. In fact, Buddhist art and ritual were so impressive that they were borrowed and used in Shinto shrines too.

Buddhism as a philosophical and metaphysical system is a match to any other heritage, but Buddhism usually enters the religious life of the people through more direct means, such as the regular practices of the family and memorial rites in the home. Although Buddhism's visible structure appears as temples and monastic institutions, the influence of Buddhism as a way of life is also expressed less explicitly—almost invisibly—in noninstitutional forms such as literature, where Buddhism's worldview is presupposed and represented dramatically rather than in doctrinal terms.

Buddhism, like any religious tradition, can be seen as an "existential" message, an attempt to define the human condition and answer the question of the meaning of human existence. The cardinal teachings of Buddhism include the need for all human beings to overcome the illusion that life can be lived by the senses; to be concerned not just with their own condition but have compassion for all forms of life; and to realize the impermanence of life is to awaken to a higher awareness of life. This insight is a clue to the power of Buddhism, which is able to drive out adversity and lead the person to a full life. The awakening can be sought through individual meditation, as in Zen; more often, however, the quest for this power is pursued through regular devotions such as those described on p. 65.

Buddhism entered Japan as a highly organized religion, and many of the doctrinal and ecclesiastical forms of Japanese Buddhism are direct descendants of Chinese and Indian forms of Buddhism. The numerous religious and philosophical writings of Buddhism, often Indian materials in Chinese translation, found their way to Japan; usually a specific branch of Buddhism was organized around the study of several related texts and accompanying practices. As time passed and Buddhism became increasingly naturalized in its Japanese setting, new Buddhist branches arose both through the introduction of Chinese patterns and through the development of more distinctively Japanese patterns (such as Nichiren Buddhism). Some major founding figures of Japanese Buddhism will be treated in Chapter 4.

Buddhism has made extensive contributions to Japanese culture in many areas, such as providing a rationale for the nation and enriching artistic life. Buddhism features both a deep, diverse philosophical tradition and a number of impressive rituals. Once Buddhism became widely accepted on a popular level, its most important religious function has been the celebration of funeral and memorial masses. In fact, in the Tokugawa period (1600–1867), when Buddhism practically became an arm of the government, families were required to belong to a parish Buddhist temple and to have their parish temple perform rites for the dead. To this day, a small Buddhist altar for memorializing family ancestors is a prominent feature in many homes, even in homes in which there is no Shinto altar (kamidana) (see p. 255). Buddhist funerals are no longer required by law, but they still are the general rule. However, the continuation of this custom is not necessarily evidence of respect for Buddhism; rather, it reflects strong family tradition. The kind of Buddhist temple most familiar to the average Japanese person is the local parish temple. There are also the rather large headquarters of every denomination, and some temples are important for the granting of special petitions or answering of prayers.

Japanese Buddhism was very much a part of feudal structures until the Meiji Restoration of 1868, when Buddhism was rejected as an arm of the government and government patronage turned toward Shinto. Nevertheless, Buddhist temples have not completely outlived their feudal past. Although Shinto is linked most closely to World War II, Buddhism was close behind Shinto in nationalistic support of the war effort. In addition, Buddhism has been criticized in the past century as a carryover from feudal times whose main concern is for the souls of the dead. A number of Buddhist priests and scholars are aware of the validity of these criticisms and are attempting to renew and revitalize Buddhism. Also, some of the New Religions are really lay movements of Buddhism, which attempt to overcome the formalism of Buddhist temples and priests.

9
The Formal Entry of Buddhism into Japan

This selection from an eighth-century national chronicle, *Nihongi,* records an important court event of the middle of the sixth century. The ruler of a Korean territory, Paekche, offered tribute to the Japanese court to gain a political ally. For our purposes, the most significant aspect is the tribute itself—Buddhism. Although Buddhist elements were brought to Japan by Korean individuals in previous centuries, this event marks the formal introduction of Buddhism.

In this case, Buddhism means especially images, ritual decorations, and scriptures. This tradition is praised as hailing from distant India and as having the endorsement of China, a classical culture for both Korea and Japan. The power and wisdom of this great tradition are infinite.

The Japanese emperor's delight at this tribute is better understood by contrasting it with the native tradition, which lacked both statuary and scriptures. Also, the emperor approached Buddhism as a possible means of attaining religious power. At first, the Japanese court was unable to appreciate the profound philosophy of Buddhism; in fact, even the nobility could not read these scriptures (most of which were Chinese translations of Indian texts). After a brief setback, it became clear that Buddhism was not a threat to the harmony of the native *kami* but was an effective complement to the *kami*. This treatment of Buddhism as a source of power is the manner in which Buddhism often found its place in the religious life of the people.

BUDDHISM: TRIBUTE FROM KOREA

W. G. Aston, translator

Winter, 10th month. King Syong-myong of Pekche (also called King Syong) sent Kwi-si of the Western Division, and the Tal-sol, Nu-ri Sa-chhi-hye, with a present to the Emperor of an image of Shaka Butsu in gold and copper, several flags and umbrellas, and a number of volumes of "Sutras." Separately he presented a memorial in which he lauded the merit of diffusing abroad religious worship, saying:—"This doctrine is amongst all doctrines the most excellent. But it is hard to explain, and hard to comprehend. Even the Duke of Chow and Confucius had not attained to a knowledge of it. This doctrine can create religious merit and retribution without measure and without bounds, and so lead on to a full appreciation of the highest wisdom. Imagine a man in possession of treasures to his heart's content, so that he might satisfy all his wishes in proportion as he used them. Thus it is with the treasure of this wonderful doctrine. Every prayer is fulfilled and naught is wanting. Moreover, from distant India it has extended hither to the three Han, where there are none who do not receive it with reverence as it is preached to them.

Thy servant, therefore, Myong, King of Pekche, has humbly despatched his retainer, Nu-ri Sa-chhi, to transmit it to the Imperial Country, and to diffuse it abroad throughout the home provinces, so as to fulfil the recorded saying of Buddha: 'My law shall spread to the East.' "

This day the Emperor, having heard to the end, leaped for joy, and gave command to the Envoys, saying:—"Never from former days until now have we had the opportunity of listening to so wonderful a doctrine. We are unable, however, to decide of ourselves." Accordingly he inquired of his Ministers one after another, saying:—"The countenance of this Buddha which has been presented by the Western frontier State is of a severe dignity, such as we have never at all seen before. Ought it to be worshipped or not?" Soga no Oho-omi, Iname no Sukune, addressed the Emperor, saying:—"All the Western frontier lands without exception do it worship. Shall Akitsu Yamato alone refuse to do so?" Okoshi, Mononobe no Oho-muraji, and Kamako, Nakatomi no Muraji, addressed the Emperor jointly, saying:—"Those who have ruled the Empire in this our State have always made it their care to worship in Spring, Summer, Autumn and Winter the 180 Gods of Heaven and Earth, and the Gods of the Land and of Grain. If just at this time we were to worship in their stead foreign Deities, it may be feared that we should incur the wrath of our National Gods."

The Emperor said:—"Let it be given to Iname no Sukune, who has shown his willingness to take it, and, as an experiment, make him worship it."

Reprinted by permission of the publisher from W. G. Aston, translator, *Nihongi: Chronicles of Japan from the Earliest Times to A.D. 697* (London: George Allen & Unwin Ltd., 1956).

The Oho-omi knelt down and received it with joy. He enthroned it in his house at Oharida, where he diligently carried out the rites of retirement from the world, and on that score purified his house at Muku-hara and made it a Temple. After this a pestilence was rife in the Land, from which the people died prematurely. As time went on it became worse and worse, and there was no remedy. Okoshi, Mononobe no Ohomuraji, and Kamako, Nakatomi no Muraji, addressed the Emperor jointly, saying:—"It was because thy servants' advice on a former day was not approved that the people are dying thus of disease. If thou dost now retrace thy steps before matters have gone too far, joy will surely be the result! It will be well promptly to fling it away, and diligently to seek happiness in the future."

The Emperor said:—"Let it be done as you advise." Accordingly officials took the image of Buddha and abandoned it to the current of the Canal of Naniha. They also set fire to the Temple, and burnt it so that nothing was left. Hereupon, there being in the Heavens neither clouds nor wind, a sudden conflagration consumed the Great Hall (of the Palace).

This year Pekche abandoned Han-syong and Phyong-yang. Silla took advantage of this to make an entrance and to settle in Han-syong. These are the present Silla towns of U-to-pang and Ni-mi-pang [these names of places are unclear].

14th year, Spring, 1st month, 12th day. Pekche sent Kwa-ya Chha-chyu, Tok-sol of the Higher Division, the Han-sol, Nye-se-ton, and others to ask for troops.

15th day. The Pekche Envoys, Mok-hyop-keum-ton, Tok-sol of the Middle Division, and Kahachi Be no Asapita took their departure.

Summer, 5th month, 7th day. The following report was received from the province of Kahachi:—"From within the sea at Chinu, in the district of Idzumi, there is heard a voice of Buddhist chants, which re-echoes like the sound of thunder, and a glory shines like the radiance of the sun." In his heart the Emperor wondered at this, and sent Unate no Atahe [here we have only Atahe, and the personal name is not given, probably owing to the error of some copyist] to go upon the sea and investigate the matter.

This month Unate no Atahe went upon the sea, and the result was that he discovered a log of camphor-wood shining brightly as it floated on the surface. At length he took it, and presented it to the Emperor, who gave orders to an artist to make of it two images of Buddha. These are the radiant camphor-wood images now in the Temple of Yoshino.

10

Harmony Between the Buddhist Pantheon and Shinto Kami

As seen in the previous selection, the entry of Buddhism into Japan was marked by a brief conflict between Buddhas and *kami,* but this gave way to a general sense of harmony between the two groups of divinities. This harmony came to be expressed in terms of the Buddhist notion of incarnation (or reincarnation): the members of the Buddhist pantheon were the concrete manifestation of the hidden *kami.* This theory was very effective in both Shinto shrines and Buddhist temples for reconciling the unseen *kami* with the Buddhist statues. In the experience of the people, there is practically an identity between such Buddhas and *kami.* One of the chief characteristics of Japanese Buddhism is this close blending with native tradition.

One good example of the Buddhist idea of reincarnation is the case of Prince Shotoku, often regarded as the founding father of Buddhism in Japan. (See the support of Buddhism in the so-called "Constitution" attributed to him on p. 235.) Prince Shotoku is treated as the reincarnation of either a Chinese Buddhist priest or of a *bodhisattva* (a kind of Buddhist saint). Although Prince Shotoku is not a *kami* in the official mythology, in Japan a great person is often treated as a *kami* (see also p. 167). As time passed, many *kami* were treated as hidden counterparts of Buddhist divinities in the form of statues, and the mutual influence between Shinto and Buddhism was considerable.

JAPANESE BUDDHISM AND THE BUDDHIST
PHILOSOPHY OF ASSIMILATION

Alicia Matsunaga

Buddha and Kami

For centuries the Japanese have preserved and protected the priceless treasures they received from the continent at the dawn of their civilization. As early as the eighth century special treasure houses were constructed to house these precious objects and there they have remained intact until the present day. This concern was not merely limited to dead artifacts, but encompassed living skills and arts as well. For instance, the court music of T'ang China once adapted to Japanese tastes, has survived up to modern times while it has been long forgotten on the continent. In such a way Japan became a storehouse of

Reprinted by permission of the publisher from Alicia Matsunaga, *The Buddhist Philosophy of Assimilation* (Tokyo: Monumenta Nipponica, Sophia University, 1969).

the past, a place where treasures long obliterated in their native lands can be viewed and appreciated.

If we were to select one general classification for the majority of Japan's inherited treasures, it would be Buddhism, since in Japan, as in many other lands, Buddhism served as the vehicle of higher civilization. Buddhist philosophy, technology and art forms found their way from India, Central Asia, China and Korea to Japan where they were not only preserved but also added their influence to the course of Japanese thought.

What is known today as "Japanese Buddhism" is the unique living product of these diverse origins and their combination with native elements. Any study that attempts to ignore these historical antecedents or explain the essence of Japanese Buddhist thought without giving them due consideration is in effect an attempt to study the branches of a tree while ignoring its life-giving trunk. Many existing works have created considerable confusion about the nature and historical continuity of Japanese Buddhism with the result that its basic tenets are still very much misunderstood, particularly in the West.

If we were to select a single representative area where the mixed origins of Japanese Buddhism are most obviously evident, then the Buddhist pantheon would provide the best example. Here we can find deities of Indian, Chinese and Central Asian origin venerated beside the indigenous divinities who inhabited Japan prior to the introduction of Buddhism. In examining this phenomenon certain questions naturally arise such as: How was this process of assimilation carried out? Does it have a counterpart in other lands influenced by Buddhism? Is there a *Buddhist* philosophy of assimilation? And finally, does the Japanese form of assimilation markedly differ from that found in other lands?

In Japanese Buddhism we can find two important related terms specifically dealing with the problem of assimilation: the first is *shimbutsu-shugo* (unification of gods and Buddhas) and the second is the *honji-suijaku* (true nature—trace manifestation) theory. The former is a broad term encompassing all efforts to unite the indigenous faith with Buddhism, a process beginning with the inception of Buddhism in Japan and generally dealing with exterior phenomena brought together without systematization. On the other hand, the *honji-suijaku* theory is the culminating philosophy arising out of this initial exterior unification and although it can also be classified under the general category of *shimbutsu-shugo,* it represents a systematic Buddhist philosophy of assimilation.

In popular parlance, the *honji-suijaku* theory is described as the philosophy by which the native Japanese gods are believed to be manifestations of Buddhas or bodhisattvas in order to save sentient beings and lead them to Enlightenment. Since the terminology is Japanese and the deities involved appear to be native to Japan, modern Japanese have no hesitation in believing the theory originated in their land. . . .

It is our purpose here to demonstrate how the Japanese theory of *honji-suijaku* is merely an expression of the ancient Buddhist philosophy of assimilation that commenced with the first dawning of Buddhist thought to serve as an essential handmaiden of Buddhist doctrine in every new land the religion entered. In Japan with the rich heritage of Indian and Chinese thought, the philosophy of assimilation was systematized and given practical application, yet the components for this systematization and application were already present in Chinese Buddhism. Finally, even in the applied Japanese theory, which was not so systematical, we find that Indian deities appear both as the *honji* (true nature) as well as the *suijaku* (trace manifestation) of various Buddhas and bodhisattvas. These facts alone make it apparent that the *honji-suijaku* theory is not an isolated phenomenon that can be studied within the framework of Japanese thought or folk beliefs alone.

The practice of absorbing native gods and various other rites into Buddhism began in India. The popularity of the practice is attested by the fact that many of these Indian elements were exported all the way to China, Korea and Japan. In order to study the Japanese theory of assimilation we must first of all discover what is the *Buddhist* philosophy of assimilation. To do this, we must begin with the tenets of Early Buddhism or the Buddhism practiced in India during the life of the historical Buddha and by his disciples directly after his death. It was in the framework of this early philosophy that the Buddhist theory of assimilation had its origin. . . .

The Elevation of Japanese Buddhist Saints

The earliest forms of what we might term *honji-suijaku* application did not apply to the relationship between the Japanese gods and Buddhas but rather to the relationship between Buddhas proper and the Buddhas or bodhisattvas. We can find the first evidence of such application appearing in the late Nara and early Heian period in regard to Shotoku Taishi.

Immediately after the death of Prince Shotoku in 622 he began to be regarded as a deified legendary figure in popular thought. In view of his own active belief and support of Buddhism, it was natural that a Buddhist effort would be made to elevate him to the position of a saint, and this was best accomplished by considering him to be some form of a Buddha or bodhisattva. Since Prince Shotoku had never belonged to any particular sect of Buddhism, he was in a sense the common property of all. He also was considered as a national heritage, since he had played such an important role in introducing Chinese culture and civilization to Japan.

It is uncertain exactly when Shotoku Taishi first became regarded as the manifestation of a bodhisattva, although we can estimate that it probably occurred at the end of the Nara period. The earliest account of such an incident can be found in the *To-daimajo-toseiden,* which relates the following story that supposedly took place in China:

> The Buddhist monk Ei-ei went to the Daimyoji Temple and saluted the Great Elder [Ganjin], telling him the reason for his visit. He said, "Buddhism came from the East to arrive in Japan and although there was Buddhism, there was no person to teach it. Formerly in Japan, Shotoku Taishi lived and said: 'After two hundred years the Buddhist doctrine will arise

in Japan.' Now may you [Ganjin] follow this tradition and go to the East
to instruct the people." So the Great Elder answered, "I have heard before
that after Nangaku Zenji died he would be born as a prince of Japan to
make Buddhism flourish and enlighten sentient beings."

This is one of the earliest correlations between Shotoku Taishi and Nangaku
Zenji, second patriarch of the Chinese T'ien T'ai sect. In Ninchu's biography
of Saicho, the *Eizandaishiden,* a similar story is related:

> In the Sui Dynasty there lived Shi (Szu) Zenji on Mt. Nangaku. This
> monk always hoped and said "after my death I will certainly be born in
> the East—Japan, to introduce Buddhism." Later Prince Shotoku was born
> in Japan . . . All the contemporary people say that Prince Shotoku is the
> *goshin* of Shi Zenji.

Here Prince Shotoku clearly appears as the "after-body" (*goshin*) of Nangaku.
This theory was set forth by Saicho, founder of the Japanese Tendai sect, and
his support of the belief that Shotoku was an after-body of Eshi made the
Prince into one of the Tendai saints during the Heian period. After the death
of Saicho, his disciples Kojo, Ennin, and Chisho further propagated the belief.
This opinion was not merely confined to the Tendai sect, however, for we can
find that even Kukai believed it.

From the middle Heian period throughout the Kamakura, the belief in
Shotoku Taishi so increased that he was transformed from merely the "after-
body" or manifestation to a *honji.* In this case, his own manifestations became
such personages as Emperor Shomu, Kukai, and Rigen Daishi. On the other
hand, the *honji* of Shotoku also developed, becoming not only Eshi in China,
but also figures such as Dainichi Nyorai (Vairocana) and Kannon (Avalokites-
vara). Such belief was further popularized with the compilation of the *Taishi-
wasan* and *Taishi-koshiki* of later periods.

This belief in Shotoku Taishi can be considered as one of the first practical
applications of the *honji-suijaku* theory in Japan; however, since it was not
characteristic of the application of the theory in its early stages to the Japanese
gods, it appears that the incident represented predominant Chinese influence.
We have already mentioned a similar occurrence in the life of En no Gyoja, so
the thought was not uncommon.

The Elevation of the Indigenous Gods

As we have seen in previous chapters, the first endeavors to create harmony
between the native cult and Buddhism occurred almost immediately after the
inception of the new religion and progressed with its growing popularity. This
movement of harmonization falls into the general classification of *shimbutsu-
shugo,* a trend representing practical accomplishments rather than any form of
purposeful philosophy or systematization. Besides the previously mentioned
reasons for the success and development of *shimbutsu-shugo* we can summarize
some of the obvious factors as the following:

1. The Japanese indigenous faith as the religion of the Japanese race served the social and regional interests of the people, while Buddhism met the needs of the individual seeking personal spiritual salvation. Thus each belief had different characteristics.

2. Both religions had an interest in magical or mystical ritual.

3. Both were supported by the upper classes. (A factor that at times also became a source of friction when it became a matter of institutionalized vested interests.)

4. The early Shinto prosperity rituals were simple in content, while the Buddhists had an elaborate liturgy which appealed to the aesthetic tastes of the Japanese people. As the indigenous cult developed under the influence of Chinese culture, it was possible to incorporate forms of Buddhist liturgy into the Shinto rituals, particularly those advocating the protection of the nation and the needs of the individuals.

All of these reasons which augmented the growth and development of *shimbutsu-shugo* were sources of motivation leading to the gradual development of the *honji-suijaku* theory, as well as reasons for the Buddhists to take a favorable view of the native deities.

11
A Buddhist Scripture: The Lotus Sutra

The complete Buddhist canon in its Chinese version consists of hundreds of volumes containing thousands of separate writings: some are sayings attributed to the historical Buddha, while others are commentaries, or independent works, many of which were composed in China, Korea, and Japan. One of the important Buddhist scriptures in the spread of Buddhism from India across China to Japan is the *Lotus Sutra*. Although the average person does not read the Chinese version of this scripture, he or she is probably familiar with its memorable stories and key teachings.

The *Lotus Sutra* expresses several basic themes of Mahayana, the form of Buddhism that found greatest acceptance in China and Japan. Mahayana (the Great Vehicle) criticized non-Mahayana Buddhism as being self-centered and lacking in altruism. Mahayana therefore used the disparaging term Hinayana (Inferior or Small Vehicle) to refer to those Buddhists with whom they did not agree. Mahayana Buddhism emphasizes that everyone, monk and layperson alike, can attain enlightenment or "become a Buddha"; the *Lotus Sutra* teaches laypeople the simple techniques that guarantee *anuttara-samyak-sambodhi* (true enlightenment or perfect understanding).

According to the *Lotus Sutra,* the Buddha appeared on earth once more to reveal the true meaning of his teaching. From the top of a mountain he taught Shariputra and other disciples the message of Mahayana, which is also called the single Buddha vehicle. The parable of the burning house conveys in story form the Mahayana message that "expedient means" such as Hinayana were used in earlier times to persuade children (all people) to leave the burning house (this world), but their father (the Buddha) wants to ultimately reward them with the best carriage or vehicle (Mahayana). In other words, although there may seem to be different paths and different goals, actually this variety is nothing more than "expedient means." The truth of the *Lotus Sutra* is the only real truth; other teachings have been given to conform to the lesser abilities of different people.

The essence of Mahayana Buddhism's message is that even the lowliest people, by virtue of even the humblest acts of devotion, are eventually able to achieve the highest enlightenment and rank with the Buddhas themselves. The Buddha says that to follow his teaching (or "Law"), acts of devotion such as offering incense and flowers are more important than intellectual reasoning.

This enfolding compassion for the common person helped make the *Lotus Sutra* a religious classic for all people. Indeed, for some Buddhists, anyone can draw on the power of this scripture simply by reciting a phrase of praise to the title of the scripture (Namu Myoho Rengekyo). The *Lotus Sutra* is the chief scripture for the Tendai and Nichiren sects and also some New Religions such as Soka Gakkai, but it has been revered by most Japanese people, whether or not they were affiliated with these sects.

ENLIGHTENMENT IS POSSIBLE FOR ALL PEOPLE

Burton Watson, translator

The Buddha said to Shariputra, "A wonderful Law such as this is preached by the Buddhas, the Thus Come Ones, at certain times. But like the blooming of the udumbara, such times come very seldom. Shariputra, you and the others must believe me. The words that the Buddhas preach are not empty or false.

"Shariputra, the Buddhas preach the Law in accordance with what is appropriate, but the meaning is difficult to understand. Why is this? Because we employ countless expedient means, discussing causes and conditions and using words of simile and parable to expound the teachings. This Law is not something that can be understood through pondering or analysis. Only those who are Buddhas can understand it. Why is this? Because the Buddhas, the World-Honored Ones, appear in the world for one great reason alone. Shariputra, what does it mean to say that the Buddhas, the World-Honored Ones, appear in the world for one great reason alone?

"The Buddhas, the World-Honored Ones, wish to open the door of Buddha wisdom to all living beings, to allow them to attain purity. That is why they appear in the world. They wish to show the Buddha wisdom to living

Reprinted by permission of the publisher from Burton Watson, translator, *The Lotus Sutra* (New York: Columbia University Press, 1993). Some notes have been deleted.

beings, and therefore they appear in the world. They wish to cause living beings to awaken to the Buddha wisdom, and therefore they appear in the world. They wish to induce living beings to enter the path of Buddha wisdom, and therefore they appear in the world. Shariputra, this is the one great reason for which the Buddhas appear in the world." . . .

"Shariputra, the Thus Come Ones have only a single Buddha vehicle which they employ in order to preach the Law to living beings. They do not have any other vehicle, a second one or a third one. Shariputra, the Law preached by all the Buddhas of the ten directions is the same as this.

"Shariputra, the Buddhas of the past used countless numbers of expedient means, various causes and conditions, and words of simile and parable in order to expound the doctrines for the sake of living beings. These doctrines are all for the sake of the one Buddha vehicle. These living beings, by listening to the doctrines of the Buddhas, are all eventually able to attain wisdom embracing all species." . . .

At that time the Buddha said to Shariputra, "Did I not tell you earlier that when the Buddhas, the World-Honored Ones, cite various causes and conditions and use similes, parables, and other expressions, employing expedient means to preach the Law, it is all for the sake of anuttara-samyak-sambodhi? Whatever is preached is all for the sake of converting the bodhisattvas.

"Moreover, Shariputra, I too will now make use of similes and parables to further clarify this doctrine. For through similes and parables those who are wise can obtain understanding.

"Shariputra, suppose that in a certain town in a certain country there was a very rich man. He was far along in years and his wealth was beyond measure. He had many fields, houses and menservants. His own house was big and rambling, but it had only one gate. A great many people—a hundred, two hundred, perhaps as many as five hundred—lived in the house. The halls and rooms were old and decaying, the walls crumbling, the pillars rotten at their base, and the beams and rafters crooked and aslant.

"At that time a fire suddenly broke out on all sides, spreading through the rooms of the house. The sons of the rich man, ten, twenty, perhaps thirty, were inside the house. When the rich man saw the huge flames leaping up on every side, he was greatly alarmed and fearful and thought to himself, I can escape to safety through the flaming gate, but my sons are inside the burning house enjoying themselves and playing games, unaware, unknowing, without alarm or fear. The fire is closing in on them, suffering and pain threaten them, yet their minds have no sense of loathing or peril and they do not think of trying to escape!

"Shariputra, this rich man thought to himself, I have strength in my body and arms. I can wrap them in a robe or place them on a bench and carry them out of the house. And then again he thought, This house has only one gate, and moreover it is narrow and small. My sons are very young, they have no understanding, and they love their games, being so engrossed in them that they are likely to be burned in the fire. I must explain to them why I am fearful and alarmed. The house is already in flames and I must get them out quickly and not let them be burned up in the fire!

"Having thought in this way, he followed his plan and called to all his sons, saying, 'You must come out at once!' But though the father was moved by pity and gave good words of instruction, the sons were absorbed in their games and unwilling to heed him. They had no alarm, no fright, and in the end no mind to leave the house. Moreover, they did not understand what the fire was, what the house was, what danger was. They merely raced about this way and that in play and looked at their father without heeding him.

"At that time the rich man had this thought: The house is already in flames from this huge fire. If I and my sons do not get out at once, we are certain to be burned. I must now invent some expedient means that will make it possible for the children to escape harm.

"The father understood his sons and knew what various toys and curious objects each child customarily liked and what would delight them. And so he said to them, 'The kind of playthings you like are rare and hard to find. If you do not take them when you can, you will surely regret it later. For example, things like these goat-carts, deer-carts, and ox-carts. They are outside the gate now where you can play with them. So you must come out of this burning house at once. Then whatever ones you want, I will give them all to you!'

"At that time, when the sons heard their father telling them about these rare playthings, because such things were just what they had wanted, each felt emboldened in heart and, pushing and shoving one another, they all came wildly dashing out of the burning house.

"At this time the rich man, seeing that his sons had gotten out safely and all were seated on the open ground at the crossroads and were no longer in danger, was greatly relieved and his mind danced for joy. At that time each of the sons said to his father, 'The playthings you promised us earlier, the goat-carts and deer-carts and ox-carts—please give them to us now!'

"Shariputra, at that time the rich man gave to each of his sons a large carriage of uniform size and quality. The carriages were tall and spacious and adorned with numerous jewels. A railing ran all around them and bells hung from all four sides. A canopy was stretched over the top, which was also decorated with an assortment of precious jewels. Ropes of jewels twined around, a fringe of flowers hung down, and layers of cushions were spread inside, on which were placed vermilion pillows. Each carriage was drawn by a white ox, pure and clean in hide, handsome in form and of great strength, capable of pulling the carriage smoothly and properly at a pace fast as the wind. In addition, there were many grooms and servants to attend and guard the carriage.

"What was the reason for this? This rich man's wealth was limitless and he had many kinds of storehouses that were all filled and overflowing. And he thought to himself, There is no end to my possessions. It would not be right if I were to give my sons small carriages of inferior make. These little boys are all my sons and I love them without partiality. I have countless numbers of large carriages adorned with seven kinds of gems. I should be fair-minded and give one to each of my sons. I should not show any discrimination. Why? Because even if I distributed these possessions of mine to every person in the whole country I would still not exhaust them, much less could I do so by giving them to my sons!

"At that time each of the sons mounted his large carriage, gaining something he had never had before, something he had originally never expected. Shariputra, what do you think of this? When this rich man impartially handed out to his sons these big carriages adorned with rare jewels, was he guilty of falsehood or not?"

Shariputra said, "No, World-Honored One. This rich man simply made it possible for his sons to escape the peril of fire and preserve their lives. He did not commit a falsehood. Why do I say this? Because if they were able to preserve their lives, then they had already obtained a plaything of sorts. And how much more so when, through an expedient means, they are rescued from that burning house! World-Honored One, even if the rich man had not given them the tiniest carriage, he would still not be guilty of falsehood. Why? Because this rich man had earlier made up his mind that he would employ an expedient means to cause his sons to escape. Using a device of this kind was no act of falsehood. How much less so, then, when the rich man knew that his wealth was limitless and he intended to enrich and benefit his sons by giving each of them a large carriage."

The Buddha said to Shariputra, "Very good, very good. It is just as you have said. And Shariputra, the Thus Come One is like this. That is, he is a father to all the world. His fears, cares and anxieties, ignorance and misunderstanding, have long come to an end, leaving no residue. He has fully succeeded in acquiring measureless insight, power and freedom from fear and gaining great supernatural powers and the power of wisdom. He is endowed with expedient means and the paramita of wisdom, his great pity and great compassion are constant and unflagging; at all times he seeks what is good and will bring benefit to all.

"He is born into the threefold world, a burning house, rotten and old, in order to save living beings from the fires of birth, old age, sickness and death, care, suffering, stupidity, misunderstanding, and the three poisons; to teach and convert them and enable them to attain anuttara-samyak-sambodhi.

"He sees living beings seared and consumed by birth, old age, sickness and death, care and suffering, sees them undergo many kinds of pain because of the five desires and the desire for wealth and profit. Again, because of their greed and attachment and striving they undergo numerous pains in their present existence, and later they undergo the pain of being reborn in hell or as beasts or hungry spirits. Even if they are reborn in the heavenly realm or the realm of human beings, they undergo the pain of poverty and want, the pain of parting from loved ones, the pain of encountering those they detest—all these many different kinds of pain.

"Yet living beings, drowned in the midst of all this, delight and amuse themselves, unaware, unknowing, without alarm or fear. They feel no sense of loathing and make no attempt to escape. In this burning house which is the threefold world, they race about to east and west, and though they encounter great pain, they are not distressed by it.

"Shariputra, when the Buddha sees this, then he thinks to himself, I am the father of living beings and I should rescue them from their sufferings and give them the joy of the measureless and boundless Buddha wisdom so that they may find their enjoyment in that." . . .

At that time the World-Honored One addressed Bodhisattva Medicine King, and through him the eighty thousand great men, saying: "Medicine King, do you see in this great assembly the immeasurable number of heavenly beings, dragon kings, yakshas, gandharvas, asuras, garudas, kimnaras, mahoragas, human and nonhuman beings, as well as monks, nuns, laymen and laywomen, those who seek to become voice-hearers, who seek to become pratyekabuddhas, or who seek the Buddha way? Upon these various kinds of beings who in the presence of the Buddha listen to one verse or one phrase of the Lotus Sutra of the Wonderful Law and for a moment think of it with joy I will bestow on all of them a prophecy that they will attain anuttara-samyak-sambodhi."

The Buddha said to Medicine King: "In addition, if after the Thus Come One has passed into extinction there should be someone who listens to the Lotus Sutra of the Wonderful Law, even one verse or one phrase, and for a moment thinks of it with joy, I will likewise bestow on him a prophecy that he will attain anuttara-samyak-sambodhi. Again if there are persons who embrace, read, recite, expound and copy the Lotus Sutra of the Wonderful Law, even only one verse, and look upon this sutra with the same reverence as they would the Buddha, presenting various offerings of flowers, incense, necklaces, powdered incense, paste incense, incense for burning, silken canopies, streamers and banners, clothing and music, and pressing their palms together in reverence, then, Medicine King, you should understand that such persons have already offered alms to a hundred thousand million Buddhas and in the place of the Buddhas have fulfilled their great vow, and because they take pity on living beings they have been born in this human world.

"Medicine King, if someone should ask what living beings will be able to attain Buddhahood in a latter-day existence, then you should show him that all these people in a latter-day existence are certain to attain Buddhahood. Why? Because if good men and good women embrace, read, recite, expound and copy the Lotus Sutra, even one phrase of it, offer various kinds of alms to the sutra, flowers, incense, necklaces, powdered incense, paste incense, incense for burning, silken canopies, streamers and banners, clothing and music, and press their palms together in reverence, then these persons will be looked up to and honored by all the world. Alms will be offered to them such as would be offered to the Thus Come One. You should understand that these persons are great bodhisattvas who have succeeded in attaining anuttara-samyak-sambodhi. Pitying living beings, they have vowed to be born among them where they may broadly expound and make distinctions regarding the Lotus Sutra of the Wonderful Law. How much more so is this true, then, of those who can embrace the entire sutra and offer various types of alms to it!

"Medicine King, you should understand that these persons voluntarily relinquish the reward due them for their pure deeds and, in the time after I have passed into extinction, because they pity living beings, they are born in this evil world so they may broadly expound this sutra. If one of these good men or good women in the time after I have passed into extinction is able to secretly expound the Lotus Sutra to one person, even one phrase of it, then you should know that he or she is the envoy of the Thus Come One. He has been dispatched by the Thus Come One and carries out the Thus Come One's work. And how much more so those who in the midst of the great assembly broadly expound the sutra for others!"

12
Buddhist Themes in Medieval Literature

What we call Buddhism can be located in many sites or places: in the founding figure of the Buddha, in scriptures and commentaries by and about the founder and his message, in the institutions such as temples and monasteries that preserve this message, and in rituals that implement and celebrate the way of the Buddha. This is Buddhism as an organized religion.

The present article approaches Buddhism in a different manner, seeing it more as an integral part of Japanese culture than as an organized religion apart from culture; in fact, the author argues that Buddhism in this cultural expression is the defining characteristic of medieval Japan. By providing both elites and common people with "a coherent explanation of the world and of human experience," Buddhism afforded everyone not only salvation but also an explanation of the world, a "map of reality," a kind of theodicy.

The gist of this Buddhist map is an understanding of all life and the universe as governed by six "courses," or modes of being, through which all beings pass, propelled by karmic reward or retribution. This idea had its origins in India and was an important contribution of Buddhism to all of East Asia; it is expressed in various Buddhist scriptures, especially the *Lotus Sutra,* and it also came to be the theme of much of Japanese literature, from the Heian period *Tale of Genji* through medieval works such as the *Nihon Ryoiki,* and on into contemporary Japanese literature.

THE ARC OF JAPAN'S MEDIEVAL EXPERIENCE

William R. LaFleur

What is most needed in our knowledge of medieval Japan [is] a reconstruction of the basic intellectual and religious *shape* of that epoch. This is to say that all the bits of seemingly esoteric information and the lines of seemingly arcane discussions were not esoteric or arcane to the medieval Japanese, and we will

Reprinted by permission of the publisher from William R. LaFleur, *The Karma of Words: Buddhism and the Literary Arts in Medieval Japan* (Berkeley: University of California Press, 1983). Some paragraphs have been rearranged, and the notes have been deleted.

really understand that era and its texts only if we see these disparate things as parts of a framework. This framework was one of interrelated problems and concepts shared jointly by all literate Japanese and possibly a portion of the illiterate population as well.

In other words, when medieval Japan is described in terms of its intellectual shape and suppositions, it can be seen to form what today is often called an *episteme*. It was a period during which there was a general consensus concerning what kinds of problems needed discussion, what kinds of texts and traditional practices constituted authority worthy of citation and appeal, and what kinds of things constituted the symbols central to the culture and to the transmission of information within it. This means that we are able to come to an approximate definition of medieval Japan in intellectual terms. I would suggest that we can best account for the vast array of materials in this period by defining *medieval* Japan as that epoch during which the basic intellectual problems, the most authoritative texts and resources, and the central symbols were all Buddhist. This is not to say that Buddhist problems, texts, and symbols were the sole ones of the era; it is merely to claim that they held intellectual hegemony during that period of time. I would further suggest that through a careful analysis of materials at our disposal we can not only observe and describe the inception of this epoch but can also see that, at a point in time many centuries later, Buddhist problems, texts, and symbols ceased to hold the central place they once occupied. Although they continue to exist and even have a certain vitality in the twentieth century, they now live alongside serious competitors in the intellectual and cultural arena.

Buddhism gained ascendency in medieval Japan largely because it successfully put forward a coherent explanation of the world and of human experience; it was the single most satisfying and comprehensive explanation available to the Japanese people at the time. This is to deny neither that Buddhism was espoused by persons who had great social and political power nor that it provided justifications for their power and prestige. Moreover, this is not to disembody it or overlook the impressive technological and artistic side of the Buddhism that came to Japan from China and Korea—its magnificent architecture, paintings, icons, vestments, illuminated scrolls, and choreographed ritual. It is merely to call attention to the cognitive dimension and to observe that Buddhism provided not only salvation but also explanation. That is, as a religion in a medieval context, it was considerably more comprehensive, than religion in modern settings. In many ways, Buddhism performed in medieval Japan much of the role now customarily assigned to science. It did so by giving to the epoch a basic map of reality, one that provided cognitive satisfaction not only to learned monks in monasteries but also to unlettered peasants in the countryside. This chapter attempts to reconstruct that map of reality as it seems to have been universally accepted throughout Japan's medieval era.

I shall argue that Buddhism's cognitive framework was characterized by both simplicity and comprehensiveness. It functioned quite effectively as what Max Weber called a *theodicy;* that is, it made the world and the vast variety of individual destinies rational and acceptable—something needed perhaps equally by princes and peasants. In addition, it provided a relatively simple framework within which a vast amount of varied and complex data could be located and described. The basic portrait of the universe in terms of a taxonomy called the *rokudo,* or "six courses," was universally accepted by all the schools of Buddhism and included the belief that karmic reward or retribution for anterior acts pushed every kind of being up and down the ladder of the universe.

Ironically, however, though Buddhism's portrait of the universe was cognitively satisfying, it was not necessarily personally reassuring. Medieval Japan was a context in which virtually everyone believed in multiple lives and the system of karmic causality; but most people, while believing in it, found it distressing at best and terrifying at worst. So they sought personal salvation in one way or another from the causal sequence. In many ways Buddhism gave an explanation but also presented a problem. The reconstruction essayed in this chapter will therefore move in two stages: first, an overview of the formation of the medieval paradigm as shown by close analysis of a basic Buddhist text; and second, a survey of a number of specifically Buddhist remedies for the personal anxieties aroused by the paradigm. The relationship of these things to the literary arts of the era will also be a continuous concern here.

What I shall describe as the taxonomy of medieval Japan is what the Chinese called the *liu-tao* and the Japanese the rokudo. It was a pervasive idea in East Asia although its origins were in India. Thus, it is present in the sutras of Indian origin, the most important commentaries in Chinese, and the basic Buddhist texts by the Japanese themselves. It is found in the *Saddharma-pundarika sutra,* which the Japanese called the *Hokke-kyo* (usually rendered as *Lotus Sutra* in English), the *Ta-ch'eng ch'i-hsin-lun (Daijo-kishin-ron),* the *Mo-ho chih-kuan (Makashikan),* the *Wu-men kuan (Mumon-kan),* the *Ojo-yo-shu,* the *Shobo-genzo,* and the *Tanni-sho,* to name only a few of the important texts of this era. Its use and acceptance cut across the various differences of doctrine and practice among the schools, and it is, therefore, appropriate to view it as having been universally accepted. In all these works the depiction of the universe as constituted by six basic modes of being and by a karmic causality that pushes all beings through the taxonomy is simply assumed to be true and immediately evident. The idea was reinforced with every mention, a cognitive scheme so basic and pervasive that it found its way into virtually every major literary work. The notion of karma and transmigration appears not only in overtly Buddhist works, such as the *Shaseki-shu* or those groups of lyrics specifically devoted to Buddhism, but also in all the major collections of verse, in all the *monogatari,* and in all the major dramas of the period. For nō, it is an essential part of its histrionic mechanics and meaning. It pervades the literature and art of medieval Japan. According to Watsuji Tetsuro:

> Belief in transmigration through the six courses was made into a view of things that made complete common sense, so that it lay at the basis of ordinary observations of life. Through it the whole of people's lives was explained as demonstrations of the principle of karmic rewards and punishments. And it is not too much to say that the literary arts of medieval Japan were completely and uncritically under its sway.

An interesting and perhaps coy reference to the rokudo is already in a *Man'yo-shu* poem by Otomo Tabito (665–731); this poem is included in a section of thirteen of his poems celebrating the pleasures of drinking:

Getting my pleasures
This way in my present life
May make me turn
Into an insect or a bird
In the life to come.

That the poet does not seem to experience any great anxiety over his karmic fate possibly reflects the early date of the poem.

The rokudo taxonomy was not, of course, indigenous to Japan. It has been integral to the Buddhism the Japanese absorbed from the Chinese and Koreans. Through it, the process of transmigration was concretely imagined. It consisted of a classification of all beings into six types: gods, mankind, asuras, animals, hungry ghosts, and the creatures of hell. Slight variations in the order were possible, but that it was a hierarchy of value was always implicit. Perhaps only two of the rubrics need definition: asura (*ashura*) are titans whose killings in the past have given them a warlike and ever-warring nature; and hungry ghosts (*gaki*) are beings with literally insatiable cravings and desires (they are often represented as having enormous stomachs and needle-thin throats). The six were usually ranked as follows:

gods	(*kami*)
humans	(*ningen*)
asuras	(*ashura*)
animals	(*chikusho*)
hungry ghosts	(*gaki*)
creatures of hell	(*jigoku*)

As a system for classifying the beings of the universe, this includes and combines types seen every day with types seen scarcely, if ever. Thus it gives to the unseen an aura of greater presence and positivity. In some ways it bears a similarity to the taxonomy widely accepted in medieval Europe. There is, however, at least one decisive difference, and it is due to the Indian notion of transmigration. Each of the six is not only a rubric but also a route. Each being in the universe is involved in an ongoing journey and, against the backdrop of nearly infinite cosmic time, is only temporarily located in its present slot. Death will result in rebirth, and rebirth always poses the possibility of either progress or slippage to another location in the taxonomy. In strict interpretations, everything depends on the life lived now and the karma engendered in the present. The system thus makes each person individually responsible for his or her own future. Injustice is an impossibility. . . .

The best way to observe the Japanese fascination with this new way of viewing the world in terms of karma and transmigration is through an early

Heian work, the *Nihonkoku genpo zen'aku ryoi-ki,* usually abbreviated *Nihon ryoi-ki* [authored by the Buddhist monk Kyokai]. It is prized by historians as a rich vein of information about the late Nara and early Heian periods and by students of literature as the first of the *setsuwa,* a very large and remarkable genre of legendary literature in Japan. The analysis of this work undertaken here, however, will be in order to demonstrate that the *Nihon ryoi-ki* can serve in a remarkable way as an aperture through which to view the formation of the medieval episteme in Japan. It is a uniquely valuable text because through it we can witness the transition from the archaic to the medieval paradigm. This is because it presents, according to Taketori Masao, "the basic world view of Buddhism." . . . Although it had precedents in China, Kyokai's work stands as a unique creation, a work that related Buddhist teachings to earlier Japanese experience while at the same time arguing for the wholesale adoption of the Buddhist paradigm of reality.

The *Nihon ryoi-ki* is a watershed work. In arguing as it does for the Buddhist ideas of karma and transmigration, it reflects a time when these ideas were still novel, unacceptable, or unintelligible to large portions of the populace in Japan. In this way it contrasts sharply with all the great literature of medieval Japan—the *Tale of Genji,* the great military romances, subsequent legendary literature such as the *Konjaku-monogatari,* the poetic anthologies beginning with the *Kokin-shu,* as well as the private collections of both clergy and laymen, histories such as the *Gukan-sho,* and the classical drama of nō. The critical difference is that in all of these works the taxonomy of rokudo and the operations of karma are simply presumed to be true, universally applicable, and intelligible. The *Nihon ryoi-ki* makes no such presumption. It assumes that they are not well known and therefore require demonstration and argument. This is why, I think, it represents the introit to a new era of epistemic possibilities in Japan and is probably the key work for understanding the arc of the Japanese medieval experience.

A portion of the introduction to the *Nihon ryoi-ki* will illustrate how Kyokai's excitement at the inception of a new epoch comes out directly in the text.

> Here at the temple called Yakushi-ji in Nara, I, Kyokai, am a monk. I see human society very clearly and notice able people who are doing evil things. Some have a greed and eagerness for profit that is mightier than the magnet that pulls iron out of the mountain. They covet what others have and yet hang on to everything that is their own with a tight-fistedness more than that of the miller who squeezed even a chestnut shell trying to get something out of it. Some cheat Buddhist temples; they will certainly be reborn as calves and pay off by work what they have now taken. Some slander Buddhist monks; they will meet with disaster while still in their present lives. Others, however, follow the Buddhist path and discipline themselves; they are rewarded already in this life. Others have deep faith, practice what is good, and enjoy happiness here and now. Good or evil deeds make their own reward or retribution the way a shape

in the sunlight makes its own shadow. Pain and pleasure are produced by such actions in the same way that a sound in the valley produces its own echo. Those who see and hear such things immediately think of them as marvels but forget that they are real events in our own world. The person with reason to be ashamed finds that his heart is pounding wildly and looks for some way to make a hasty exit. If we did not have such illustrations of what is good and what is evil, what could we use to straighten out those whose lives are crooked and how could we differentiate the evil from the good? And, without these examples of the workings of the law of karma, with what could we rectify the evil-minded and pursue the path of the good?

Long ago in China the *Ming-pao chi* (*The Record of Invisible Karma*) was written and in the great T'ang dynasty the *Po-jo yen-chi* (*The Record of Wonders Connected with the Vajra-Prajnaparamita-sutra*) was composed. Why is it that we stand in awe before records compiled in other countries but do not believe in and marvel at the strange things that happen on our own soil? Having with my own eyes seen such things happen right here, I cannot be indolent and indifferent. I have spent a good deal of time sitting and thinking about this, but now it is time for me to break my silence. Therefore, I have here compiled the rather limited number of such stories that has reached my ears; I have entitled my work the *Nihonkoku genpo zen'aku ryoi-ki* [*An Account of Wondrous Cases of Manifest Rewards and Retribution for Good and Evil in Japan*].

13
The Buddhist Temple as a Center of Devotion

Buddhist temples differ from the American church or synagogue, which serves as the meeting place for a congregation at weekly services. Local parish temples usually house the ashes of family ancestors and provide funeral and memorial services for parish families. The parish as a whole will participate in several annual festivals, the precise character of which varies with the denomination and the Buddhist divinity enshrined in the local temple.

The present selection describes a more individual function of the Buddhist temple—as a center of devotion. The account is fictional, taken from the novel *The Buddha Tree* (the author Niwa was himself a priest before taking up literature). This novel treats the problem of love and desire within the confines of a Buddhist temple (Butsuoji) of the True Pure Land Sect. Soshu is the chief priest of the temple, devout in his religion and suffering from the remorse of an immoral relationship with his mother-in-law, Mineyo, who is less conscientious than he is. The excerpts portray three episodes from the novel.

The first extract depicts an interesting contrast between Soshu and Mineyo in their simultaneous performance of morning prayers in the temple's main altar and in the family altar. Soshu is even more convicted of his sin by the penetrating presence of Saint Shinran (founder of the Jodo Shinshu, or True Pure Land Sect) and Amida (the major focus of worship and faith in True Pure Land Buddhism), whereas Mineyo naively feels self-righteous in her punctual repetitions—without realizing the meaning of the words—of the prayer for repentance. (Shoju is an older priest assisting Soshu.)

The second extract is an evening conversation in the temple between Soshu and Tachi, a parish member who is also a union leader and staunch communist. Soshu does not try to counter Tachi's arguments for materialism; this is not necessary because Tachi finally explains how the pursuit of materialism led to his conversion once more to Buddhist faith. Soshu is impressed with Tachi's rational argument, and Tachi is equally impressed with Soshu's honesty about his uncertainty concerning salvation.

The third extract finds Soshu once more in the evening prayers, but this time in preparation for an evening service in which Soshu vows to confess his sins to his own parish. In this crisis of courage, Soshu recites the *nenbutsu* (or *nembutsu*), the prayer of sinners seeking compassionate help from Amida. This prayer might be simply mechanical repetition, but with Soshu it is a complete emptying of the heart and an earnest petition for the aid of Amida. All three of these episodes are fictional, but the content of devotion is not. In fact, the artistic context renders dramatically the dynamics of Buddhist devotion.

DEVOTION TO AMIDA AND REPENTANCE

Fumio Niwa

[Up to this point in the novel we have learned of Soshu's affair with his mother-in-law, and his increasingly heightened sense of repentance, which he expresses in his daily temple devotions to Shinran and Amida. On the other hand, Mineyo feels no repentance about her immoral affair and therefore performs her devotions mechanically. It was the custom for the temple priest to recite the daily prayers before the temple altar at the same time that the senior woman of the priestly family (Mineyo, in the absence of Soshu's wife) recited prayers before the smaller family altar in the residential section of the temple. In this episode the setting for Soshu is the temple altar, for Mineyo, the family altar; the time is the same for both settings.]

The gilded pillars flickered with the reflected light of row after row of candles. From behind a thin line of incense-smoke St. Shinran looked Soshu calmly in the face; from above, the bronze Kamakura-style Amida, blackened by the smoke of incense, gazed down at him with its glittering, all-seeing eyes, de-

Reprinted by permission of the publisher from Fumio Niwa, *The Buddha Tree,* translated by Kenneth Strong (London: Peter Owen, 1966).

manding insistently to know what had made his wife desert him and abandon their child. . . . From those eyes there was no escape; their light pierced into the obscurest regions of Soshu's heart. Shoju was aware this morning of an intense sincerity in his superior's prayers, a heart-felt quality which they usually lacked. The sutra readings which Soshu and Shoju used at these brief morning and evening services were simple and straightforward; they did not include any gathas, for instance. These gathas, which appear in the Chinese translations of the sutras, are rhymed songs or poems, with from four to seven words in each line. Their function is to tell a congregation which sutra it is that is being read. At Butsuoji, it was the custom to use only the Amida Sutra. The old priest struck the great gong before him as Soshu intoned the ancient text.

In the house, as the two men were beginning morning prayers in the temple, Mineyo took their place at the family shrine. The dark, twelve-mat room containing the shrine was sometimes called the "altar-room"; the altar itself, normally hidden behind the doors of the closet where it was kept, was about six feet wide, a perfect replica on a smaller scale of the great altar in the temple. Mineyo arranged the rice offerings on their little tables—which looked like a child's toy meal set—lit the hanging oil-lamp with a candle, and burnt some incense.

Sitting on the floor in front of the altar, Mineyo began to read the Shoshinge. The book was torn and curled at the corners from long years of use. Mineyo read fast. It had never occurred to her to ask what the words on the page meant, nor did she know that the Shoshin-nenbutsu-ge scripture, to give it its full name, had been written by Shinran himself as the conclusion of the section on "Conduct" in his book, *Doctrine, Works, Faith and Attainment*. For Mineyo, the morning and evening offerings and scripture reading were merely a duty that had to be fulfilled as part of the inevitable routine of life in a temple. After thirty years of daily reading, she practically knew the Shoshinge by heart.

> Let the sinner with his burden call upon Amida: it is all that is needful.
> For He will save me, even me, with His loving mercy; though my eyes are darkened by lust so that I can no more behold Him, yet with love unwearying He will lighten my way for ever.

The words were to be intoned: Mineyo did not understand what they meant. In thirty years she had never dreamt of trying to apply them to herself. It was enough if she could finish each morning's duty in good time. The fact that she had never once missed a morning seemed to her proof of the depth of her faith; and being convinced of her own saintliness, she convinced others of it too. . . .

[As the story unfolds Soshu is driven almost to despair in his attempt to withdraw from the passionate entanglement with his mother-in-law. For the first time he really questions whether faith in Amida will deliver people from their selfish desires and ambitions. At this point enters Tachi, a professed communist, who comes to the

Buddhist priest Soshu for assurance that salvation is available to humans through Amida. But as the discussion continues, it is Soshu who asks Tachi if salvation is possible.]

The *Doctrine, Works, Faith and Attainment* contains the whole of Shinran's thought. Tachi had borrowed an annotated edition of the volumes on Doctrine and Works; no doubt he wanted to go on now to the volume dealing with Paradise and Incarnation. A priest or specialist in religion would read the books as a matter of course, but for a layman it was another matter, and Tachi's interest in the work was the measure of how different he was from the ordinary Buddhist. Soshu had long felt inferior to Tachi, and never more so than now; he had begun to be afraid of him. In a mind so convinced of materialism as Tachi's, how could there be any room for spiritual ideas like those of Buddhism? Shinran had never depended on the abstract ideas of Buddhist philosophy. All through his life he believed man was made to call on Buddha and awaken to Him. By this single act of awakening to Buddha, a man would know the meaning of his life, and where and when he would die. Soshu remembered a verse from the Shozomatsu-wasan: "Even those who cannot read may have true faith; but every word of him who boasts of his learning is vain." Shinran had not offered an intellectual explanation of human destiny; instead, he had penetrated to the ultimate source of life itself, and had been overwhelmed with awe at the majesty of what he found there. That the Buddha-Vow should dwell in men who were yet in bondage to the flesh—he wept in gratitude for such boundless mercy, so far beyond all human understanding. Knowing himself to be no saint but an ordinary sinful man, he had experienced in his own person the saving compassion of Amida, and with deep thankfulness had accepted the Vow, sinner as he was. This was a natural stage in all our lives, he believed. "When a man feels in his heart a desire to call upon the name of Buddha," this is the first motion in him of the divine mercy. All men have within them both a Buddha-nature, and that which is its enemy—the arrogant human intellect. When in times of danger we call on the name of Buddha, what makes us utter that involuntary cry, Shinran believed, is none other than the grace of Amida working within us. At such a time we have only to repeat that call, in simple faith; all questioning, all reasoning is vain.

Soshu wanted to find out how much of this teaching Tachi could understand and accept. In the meantime, he could not rid himself of the feeling that Tachi and himself were on opposite sides. . . .

. . . Tachi began to fill a pipe. "I was brought up in a religious atmosphere all right. Both my parents were very pious and strict. I had to learn by heart the *Monrui,* the *Shoshinge* and the Pure Land hymns; but it was only parroting what they taught me—there was never any question of thinking for myself about what the scriptures meant, or applying them to my own life. I was copying what mother and father did, that's all. I always had a vague feeling of awe, though, in front of the shrine at home, ever since I was small. Then when I grew up and had to go to work in the porcelain factory because we were so poor, I forgot all about Buddhism and didn't give a thought to it for years. A passion for social science took hold of me then."

Soshu merely nodded, not wanting to interrupt.

"You know what I mean by 'social science,' no doubt." Tachi had spent several short periods in prison, Soshu remembered.

"Marxism still rejects religion, you see, even if churches have now been recognised in the Soviet Union. When I was in prison, though—it's the way these things happen, I suppose—I found myself beginning to believe that there really might be such a thing as religious truth. I never told my wife about this; but when I came out she soon noticed how interested I was in the shrine all of a sudden. She certainly was surprised, and then relieved, I think, to see me so religious for a change." The faint ironic smile with which he spoke these last words gave way suddenly to a look of intense concentration. He turned his face away from Soshu. "Marx says in his critique of Hegel, 'Religious misery is in one mouth the expression of real misery, and in another is a protest against real misery. Religion is the moan of the oppressed creature, the sentiment of a heartless world, as it is the spirit of spiritless conditions. It is the opium of the people. The abolition of religion, as the illusory happiness of the people, is the demand for their real happiness. The demand to abandon the illusions about their condition is a demand to abandon a condition which requires illusions. The criticism of religion therefore contains potentially the criticism of the Vale of Tears whose aureole is religion.' There was a time when I believed every word of it." . . .

"Gods, Buddha-spirits, and what have you—they're all the same, products of human consciousness." Such directness shocked Soshu, but he let Tachi continue. "Man made the gods in his own image. That's why they look like men and have so many human qualities," he went on, looking almost angry. "All that about God creating the world and everything in it—it's mythical nonsense, as far as I'm concerned, and I don't believe a word of it."

Soshu managed a smile.

"That's an elementary question. I know—not the sort of thing I should trouble you with, Father. But we shan't get anywhere if I don't make my position clear at the start." Tachi smiled slightly, too—though the subject was hardly anything to smile about, nor did he consciously intend any irony. "Man made the gods in his own image—not the other way about," he repeated.

"It's natural, I suppose, for a Communist to want to reject anything that smacks of the irrational, or 'mystical nonsense,' as you call it."

"I'm a hundred per cent materialist still—I believe emotion and consciousness and spirit are products of matter, and matter alone."

"But what about the 'religious truth' you were talking of a moment ago?"

"It's the product of consciousness," Tachi said with finality, as if he were knocking religion down like a ninepin, "and consciousness is simply the functioning of matter in the form of the human body."

"And what's the connection between this religious truth and the social doctrines you believe in?"

"None—none whatever."

"Then what about 'Man shall not live by bread alone' and the high ideal of man that that implies?"

"When I talk of religious truth, what's happening is that I'm being conscious of my consciousness—making my mind take a look at itself, if you like. Forget about Shinran for a moment—it's all very well for people who already have faith to start right away on him and his teaching, but for unbelievers, if you don't begin by getting clear what religious truth is all about, none of his doctrines will mean a thing, no matter how profound and wonderful they may be."

"I quite agree—go on."

Tachi paused for a moment to order the thoughts that kept flooding into his mind. He had stopped smoking.

"There's no telling how far human knowledge is going. We've got the hydrogen bomb, and even space travel is within reach now. All this is just consciousness developed to a very high level. As science has advanced, so knowledge has covered more fields and got more and more exact; which means that we are in a position to deal more and more effectively with our environment—with the whole external world, that is. But religious truth has nothing to do with this outer world—so it isn't of the slightest use."

Soshu listened intently.

"Religious truth is concerned only with our consciousness, not with our knowledge of the external world. A being capable of consciousness is conscious of himself—consciousness becoming self-conscious, you might call it—and that's where religious truth begins to operate." . . .

"If religious truth has to do with the self-consciousness of consciousness, as I think it does, it obviously depends on consciousness working in a very special way, and can't be measured by the ordinary workings of the mind, because it's outside them altogether. That's the most fundamental thing about it. When we start thinking about prayer to God or Buddha with our ordinary mental processes, we get tied up in doubts and inconsistencies. Even talk about doing away with idols and images is absurd when you come to think of it— images make it possible for consciousness to operate *inwardly* in the way I spoke of, and to use the processes of ordinary consciousness to condemn them or do away with them is to destroy the basis of religion. . . . I don't have any use for these 'new religions,' and the material benefits some of them make such a noise about. They don't know what religion is. Religious truth and scientific truth are quite different—they deal with different worlds, religion with the inner world and science with the outer. People say, what about psychology then, but psychology treats the mind as science treats an object—the method is the same. The mind it talks about is not the mind alive, any more than the reflection of an eye in a mirror is the real eye itself. It's a mind objectified, solidified—dead."

"Shinran says in the Ichimaikishomon, 'A man shall cast aside learning, and all show of wisdom, and become as the nuns that have entered the Way,'" recited Soshu, half to himself. "And again in the Yuishinsho, 'He who longs for the Pure Land must no longer strive to seem wise or virtuous; let him harbour no secret thoughts, and make no show of pity.' He was saying the same thing as you, I think—that religious experience can't even begin to be assessed by ordinary mental processes."

"I don't think he meant that a man with a brilliant intellect couldn't be saved. He was simply warning us not to think of spiritual things in physical terms. The first thing is to realise that as far as insight into religious truth is concerned, ordinary knowledge and ordinary intellectual processes are not of the slightest use."

"Ordinary knowledge" meant the reflection of external phenomena in the mind, phenomena being the object and mind the subject; relativity as between subject and object was an inevitable condition of such knowledge. Religious knowledge could only be reached by the mind contemplating itself, a form of activity transcending the subject-object opposition. Tachi held religious truth arrived at in this way to be absolute and unconditional. . . .

Soshu remembered a verse from the Jinen Honi: "It is not the will or choice of the seeker, but the holy power of Amida, that causes us to have faith in the prayer with which we call upon His Name, and seeks to turn us to Himself. This working of His mercy, I have learned, is called Jinen. The meaning of the Vow is that Amida has promised to lead us to supreme Buddhahood. This final Buddhahood or Nirvana is Being with form; and that is why it is called Jinen. When we describe it as having form, then it is no longer the supreme state that we are speaking of. It was Amida, I have heard, who first taught us that Nirvana is without form." . . .

Paradise is described in the vaguest terms, such as "the land which is real and yet not real," which "exists and yet does not exist," and so on. What was important is not whether or not it existed, thought Soshu, but whether one could or could not reach it. Where true faith was, there was Paradise already; where faith was lacking, Paradise could never be. The question was, did one believe in Paradise or not? Paradise, it was said, was in the peace that comes from faith in Buddha and in the calling on his name. It was invisible to the eye of reason, but could be known, the preachers said, by an instinct that lay hidden behind man's faculty of reasoning. If one asked who first became consciously aware of this instinct, the answer the preachers gave was—Amida; and it was through his Original Vow that all men learn of its presence in themselves. Such was the teaching; but nowadays people responded more readily to a rational explanation such as Tachi's.

"This is really where my problem begins," said Tachi with a smile, relaxed again now. "I've worked for the Union all these years, and can't remember ever having done anything I'd want to apologize for, as far as the Union's concerned anyway. When it comes to really personal problems, though, what you might call the spiritual side of me, I suppose—it's another story, and not a pleasant one. I've never liked to play second fiddle—always wanted to be at the top; and if I'm Chairman of the Union, it's not just pure disinterested zeal, but conceit, too. I'm twice as conceited as the next man, and more. I managed to hide it from other people, somehow, but a man can't fool himself. There was a time when I talked a lot about a life of unselfish service. It was only talk—self-deception, as I soon found out. Prison taught me something, and I'm grateful."

"By 'something,' do you mean spiritual peace, or salvation?"

"Yes. At first I thought I'd go mad when they locked me up, from the loneliness. The *nenbutsu* was almost part of me, of course, I'd been so used to hearing and repeating it since I was a baby; but I never had any real faith. Then it happened, in prison. Suddenly, without thinking, I found myself repeating 'Namu Amida Butsu' . . . In that moment I knew I had a Buddhanature. It was Mind becoming conscious of itself—"

"Tell me, do you think salvation is really possible?"

"I wanted to ask *you* that question, Father."

"But I don't know . . . I don't know . . ." As he spoke the words, Soshu seemed to hear a drumming in his ears, as of lust and greed and all sin transmuted into sound—the cry of a wounded beast on a moor. . . . He would hear it forever . . . now it was the dull roaring of the sea, a sea of evil in which he was condemned to drown, beyond all forgiveness.

"What assurance can there be of salvation . . ." His voice was sad.

Tachi's expression showed that he was moved. "You are honest, Father . . ." he said.

"I know all we have to do is to forget self and trust Him for everything—but I—I've a long way to go yet before I get that far . . . I haven't thought deeply enough about Shinran's teaching."

Mineyo and the maid must have gone to bed while they were talking. Silence filled the house. . . .

[The novel reaches a climax as Soshu's repentance forces him to consider confessing his immoral love affair before his assembled parish. Mineyo threatens him not to take this radical step, and Soshu is sustained only by his faith in Amida. The prayer "Namu Amida Butsu" is the watchword of True Pure Land Buddhism, whereby the believer acknowledges his helplessness and places absolute trust in the mercy of Amida. In this brief excerpt Soshu is once more before the temple altar, steeling himself for his meeting with the parishioners. The outcome of this personal dilemma is not divulged here, so as not to spoil the novel for those who wish to read it themselves.]

Candles were already burning in the sanctuary. After pausing in the recess to bow before the portraits of the Seven Patriarchs of the Pure Land Sect, Soshu passed on to the sanctuary, where the old priest was already sitting, his head bent low over the sutra-table. According to custom, he first lit a stick of incense and stood with clasped hands in front of the statue of Amida, then turned to repeat the same act of reverence before the portrait of Shinran. Memories of his long priesthood at Butsuoji came crowding in heavily upon his mind, jostling the unspoken prayers.

Finally he sat down facing the statue, clasped his hands once more, and began to murmur the *nenbutsu*. The old priest joined in, but in a louder, more urgent tone, as though with the words he were expelling some tangible inner impurity. . . .

Then he stopped. Shoju followed suit instantly, so that their two voices died away in unison on the last syllable of the prayer. "Namu Amida Butsu-u- u . . ." The old priest struck the sutra-bell as Soshu raised the book of scripture to his forehead in the gesture of devotion to the Holy Law—and caught his breath, for Soshu was still murmuring *nenbutsu* . . . oblivious of the sutra-book in his hand, of the bell, of the service he was there to conduct, he was repeating still the prayer of St. Honen and St. Shinran. "Namu Amida Butsu . . . Namu Amida Butsu . . . Namu Amida Butsu . . ." The old priest was sitting at right angles to Soshu, not two yards away. In the younger man's face he could read the desperate intensity of his absorption in the words of the prayer; and was filled with a feverish, constricting sorrow, for he had glimpsed the conflict within. Knowing nothing of what was in Soshu's mind, sensing only the agony the struggle was costing him, he wondered what he could be going to propose to the meeting that night. During the day there had been no sign of anything unusual. But now the old man shivered; without looking, he knew that Soshu was weeping, no longer aware of his presence. Father Soshu weeping . . . he remembered how strained his face had looked recently. . . .

There had been other things: the hurried settling of odds and ends of temple business, the handing over to Shoju of the parishioner's death register. And he was murmuring *nenbutsu* still, his head bent over clasped hands. . . . The old man wished he could have slipped away from the sanctuary and left him to his solitude.

Behind his praying lips Mineyo's words were echoing in Soshu's mind, taunting him with his weakness: "if you did confess, I'd leave you, I promise— you'd have gone too far away from me then. *But it won't happen—you know it won't* . . ." Abruptly, the stream of murmured *nenbutsu* stopped. It was time, then, for the service? Soshu turned to look at the old priest; he was sitting with bowed head and closed eyes, no longer praying, but quietly waiting for Soshu to begin.

14
The Organization of Buddhism and the Family

Buddhism, like any world religion, can be viewed as a number of different things: as the extension of its founder (the Buddha), as a body of scriptures or set of teachings, as a variety of philosophical ideas or religious doctrines, and as a program of ritual performances. Buddhism can also be seen as an institution, and, in fact, from the time of its Indian origins saw itself in terms of the "three treasures": Buddha, *dharma* (teaching), and *sangha* (monastic institution).

However, in the setting of Japanese Buddhism the notion of the monastic institution (*sangha*) is relatively weak, as is seen in the fact that monastic discipline (*vinaya* in Sanskrit, *ritsu* in Japanese) was never central to Buddhist practice in Japan. Rather than looking at Buddhist sects and temples in Japan only as an elaboration of (or deviation from) the Indian *sangha,* it is also useful to consider them as expressions of the family or household (*ie*) system that was so pervasive throughout Japanese society. Seen in this light, "Social organization within Buddhist sects themselves became markedly patterned after the *ie* system." Even the local temple (*tera*) can be seen as modeled after the Japanese family or household system. From the priest's point of view, *tera* is an *ie,* or his residence, his family, or his household. Just as the *tera* is an *ie* or household for priests living in local temples, so are Buddhist sects a kind of federation of various *ie.* This approach to temples and sects shows how thoroughly *Japanese* the religion of Buddhism has become—in other words, it has been transformed into *Japanese* Buddhism. This demonstrates the significance of the family, not only as the basis for religious activities in folk religion, but also as an organizing principle for Buddhist institutions.

BUDDHIST SECTS AND THE FAMILY SYSTEM IN JAPAN

Kiyomi Morioka

Introduction

The *ie,* or traditional family (or household), system was the pervasive pattern of Japanese social organization, not only familial, but also commercial . . . , industrial . . . , artistic . . . , and religious. To some extent, it still remains so. Hence, the *ie* system must be seriously taken into consideration in any scholarly discussion of Japanese social structure.

Buddhism was originally a religion calculated to free people from secular bonds, including that of the familial tie. But, as it became firmly established among the Japanese populace, its practices became closely associated with ceremonies in honor of the dead and of ancestors. Ancestors are not necessarily one's own biological forebearers, but predecessors in the household line. Ceremonies in honor of deceased family members and ancestors are an essential obligation of descendants, a means to secure ancestral assurance for household prosperity and good fortunes. As a result of this accommodation, Buddhist practices now precisely meet the religious needs of the traditional stem family in Japan. But Buddhism in Japan did not merely tolerate special interpretation on the part of laymen or make concessions in its tenets. Social organization within Buddhist sects themselves became markedly patterned after the *ie* system. . . . This aspect of Japanese Buddhism . . . has been relatively neglected, even by Japanese scholars.

Reprinted by permission of the publisher from Kiyomi Morioka, "Buddhist Sects and the Family System in Japan," in *Religion in Changing Japanese Society* (Tokyo: University of Tokyo, 1975).

The Temple, or the Sociological Unit of Buddhism

Every Buddhist sect has a clergy and laity, its priests and parishioners, but as individuals they are not the sect's main components. Rather, the local temples to which priests and people affiliate are the primary components of a Buddhist sect. Therefore, our attention will be directed first of all to the temple.

The *tera* or *jiin* of Japan, usually translated into English as "temple," has several connotations:

1. The *tera* as a set of structures in a Buddhist compound. As such, it comprises various Buddhist halls and a rectory.

2. The *tera* as a juridical person or an incorporated body. As such, the *tera* comprises property and persons: the above-mentioned Buddhist structures, Buddhist statues enshrined in halls, priests living in a rectory and taking care of altars, and parishioners who apply for the priests' services and are responsible for the upkeep of buildings. In this sense, the *tera* is the primary element of a sect. This second meaning has gained both clarity and importance as the result of modern religious laws that applied the concept of a juridical person to local religious bodies and to their national federation as well. In pre-modern periods, before the Meiji Restoration in 1868, this connotation was left rather vague and obscure.

3. The third connotation centers on persons, namely, the *tera* as a residence group of clerics. It is a group of priests and apprentices living together in a single Buddhist compound and taking care of altars in the halls. This connotation was clear even in pre-modern times and continues to be important as the core of the juridical-person concept outlined above.

From the priest's viewpoint, *tera* has all three connotations simultaneously. It is his residence (the first meaning), his family or household (the third meaning), and the business incorporation of his household (the second meaning). To go back to the term *ie* (pronounced ee-ye and translated "household" or "house"), the *tera* (unlike the Christian minister's church) is the priest's *ie*, for *ie* in identical fashion has three connotations: residence, household as a social group, and house as a semi-legal entity.

A number of lines of evidence substantiate my conceptualization. For example, in the pre-Meiji periods Buddhist priests did not publicly carry a family name, but used their temple name as a substitute for it. Later, in the opening years of Meiji, the national government ordered them to take their temple name as their family name, for as long as they stayed in that temple. To take another example, as the *ie* continues to exist for generations, so the temple is expected to exist from generation to generation. Just as a son of the house head, commonly the eldest son, succeeds to the family headship, so is the position of the head priest of a temple taken over by his first disciple. The relationship of a teacher-priest to his disciples is that of a man to his adopted sons. Therefore, succession to the headship and continuance of the institution through succession are concepts shared in common by both the *ie* and the *tera*.

Buddhism as an Organized Religion

If we regard a *tera* as an *ie* for priests living there, the sect to which the *tera* belongs may be considered to be a sort of federation of *ie*. Now, what organizational form does this federation take in the case of a Buddhist sect?

Temples are ranked within a sect; at the top is the main temple (*honzan*), headquarters of a sect, and below it are subordinate temples (*matsuji*). Their relation neatly parallels that of a main household (*honke*) to its branch or subordinate households (*bunke* or *makke*) in the secular world. Of course there are some differences. First of all, the majority of those who founded branch houses in a *dozoku* were actual junior sons of the main households, whereas the founder of a subordinate temple was only very rarely actual kindred to the head priest of the central temple; instead such priest-founders were only his disciples or fictive sons. Moreover, the relationship between a main household and its branches in the secular world is personal, face-to-face and intimately informal, whereas that in Buddhism is by and large formal and impersonal both because of the absence of a kinship tie and because of the social and geographical distance that separates branches from the central temple. These are minor and inevitable discrepancies, but it is clear that there is a strong resemblance or basic pattern common to the secular and the Buddhist organizations.

15
The Role of Nuns in Japanese Buddhism

The presence of women in contemporary Shinto and Buddhism presents an interesting set of contrasts. As mentioned earlier (see p. 34), young women are conspicuous at Shinto shrines even though they do not play an active part in actual ceremonies. In Buddhist temples and monasteries females are conspicuous by their absence; nuns and nunneries represent a tiny fraction of Buddhist institutions and the Buddhist priesthood as a whole. However, one interesting parallel between women in Shinto and nuns in Buddhism is that in earlier times their numbers and roles were much more important.[1]

This selection's author points out that the first ordained Buddhist in Japan was a nun, and the first Buddhist temple in Japan was headed by a nun. In ancient times such nuns were from the imperial or noble families; the Heian period *Tale of Genji* portrays episodes of women retiring from the world to lead a nun's life.

This selection gives a brief historical background before describing some of the daily activities of "life in a Zen nunnery." In contrast to the contemporary *miko* in Shinto, Buddhist nuns lead a complex and rich religious life within their own institu-

---

1. For a treatment of the role of women in Buddhism from the viewpoint of sexism, see Aiko Ogoshi, "Women and Sexism in Japanese Buddhism," *The Japan Christian Review* 59 (1993): 19–25.

tions. Although their numbers are so small that they are hardly noticeable within Buddhism as a whole, the author argues that nuns "represent a vital stream in Japanese society and culture," and that "nuns can serve as a model for all women who seek liberation."

SOTO ZEN NUNS IN MODERN JAPAN

Keeping and Creating Tradition

Paula K. R. Arai

In the fall of 1987, as a travelling scholar of Buddhism, I sojourned to India. At this time I met Kito Shunko, an elderly Soto Zen nun returning to India for a final pilgrimage to the Mahabodhi Temple in Bodh Gaya. As we walked around the Bodhi Tree her face glowed with the wisdom of enlightenment. Compassion emanated forth from her every motion. Her laughter resounded with the peace found in understanding life and death. I knew after our first conversation under the bodhi tree that I wanted to learn as much as possible about her way of life. She was a living model of all that I had been studying. This nun embodied harmony in its richest form. What teachings have helped her gain such wisdom? How did she train to be so compassionate? Where is the spring of her ebullient laughter?

As we walked along the Nirange river where Sakyamuni once walked, a brilliantly pink sun rose into the sky. She wove stories of the years she spent in India building the Japanese Temple in Bodh Gaya with poetry by the Zen master Eihei Dogen Zenji (1200–1253) and information about a nunnery, Aichi Senmon Nisodo, in Nagoya, Japan. We laughed heartily as the image of meeting again in this nunnery worlds away flashed through our minds.

Nuns in Perspective

Nuns have been a vital and important facet of Buddhism since the original Sangha was formed during Sakyamuni Buddha's lifetime (c. 566–486 BCE). To date, however, nearly all scholarly research has focused primarily on the male monastic experience and history within the tradition. Recently, however, there has been increasing attention to nuns within the Buddhist tradition.

The first ordained Buddhist in Japan was a nun named Zenshin-ni. She took the tonsure in 584 CE. Shortly thereafter, two women, Zenzo-ni and Ezen-ni, became her disciples. In 588, they again made history by being the

Reprinted by permission of the publisher from Paula K. R. Arai, "Soto Zen Nuns in Modern Japan: Keeping and Creating Tradition," in *Religion and Society in Modern Japan,* edited by Mark R. Mullins, Shimazono Susumu, and Paul L. Swanson (Berkeley: Asian Humanities Press, 1993). The notes and Japanese characters have been deleted.

first Japanese to go abroad to study. They undertook the strenuous voyage to China in pursuit of a deeper understanding of the monastic regulations. Another landmark in Japanese Buddhism is that the first Buddhist temple in Japan was an *amadera* [a temple headed by a nun], Sakurai-ji, founded in 590. Although these monumental moments in the development of Japanese Buddhist history illustrate the fact that nuns were a significant force in the introduction of Buddhism to Japan, their vital contribution has been relegated to rare footnotes and scarce publications.

My exploration into the world of Japanese Buddhist nuns concentrates upon the Soto sect of Zen, for it is the largest and most organized sect of nuns in Japan. Presently there are about 1,000 Soto nuns, followed by approximately 400 Jodo-shu nuns, and around 300 Rinzai Zen nuns. The Soto-shu has the highest number of nunneries, three (Aichi Senmon Nisodo, Niigata Senmon Nisodo, and Toyama Senmon Nisodo), compared to the Jodo-shu, which has one (Yoshi-mizu Gakuen of Chion-in). The other sects do not have a special school for the sole purpose of training nuns.

My study of Soto Zen Buddhist nuns focuses on the foremost Soto nunnery in Japan, Aichi Senmon Nisodo. This nunnery, the first autonomous school established for nuns, was founded in 1903 by four nuns during the Meiji years of rapid modernization. Since then Japan has spiraled to the peak of technological accomplishment. The quality of life at the nunnery, however, remains a living kernel of the traditional arts and values of Japanese culture.

The current abbess of Aichi Senmon Nisodo, Aoyama Shundo, is a woman widely respected within the tradition by virtue of her spiritual excellence and her being among the first women to be granted an education at the Soto sect's Komazawa University. Her reputation extends into the broader Japanese society through her numerous books and articles written for the laity on topics including tea and zen and spiritual development. The international scholarly community is familiar with her work in religious dialogue. Therefore, under the leadership of Aoyama Sensei, Aichi Senmon Nisodo is a vital resource for exploring the various facets of the dynamic life of nuns in Japan.

Life in a Zen Nunnery

Through Kito Sensei's introduction, I spent four months in training at the nunnery, from 1 September to 23 December 1989. My academic background in Japanese Buddhism, personal religious orientation, and Japanese cultural heritage (my mother is a native Japanese) enabled me to segue into the rhythm of life within the cloistered walls of the nunnery with a minimum of discordance. This phase of participant observation was a rare opportunity to examine at first hand the nuns' daily pattern of study and meditative discipline.

The daily schedule of the nunnery is similar to that of any standard Zen monastery, for they all use as their base Dogen's *Eiheishingi*. Dogen wrote these regulations in a thorough and meticulous fashion. It is designed to teach the disciples to act in accordance with the Dharma in each and every activity—to treat all life with respect, to purify the mind of illusions of self and other, good and bad, desire and dislike. The ideal behind this method is to make the regulations and ideals of the Sangha an internalized mode of living, rather than an external set of regulations to be obeyed. No actual system, of course, is as perfect as the ideal that can be articulated on paper. Nonetheless, the training at the nunnery seeks to free one from the delusions, desire, and ignorance that plague most sentient beings. Although modifications of some of the regulations have been permitted due to the changes in technology since Dogen's time, the rhythm of life at the nunnery retains the spirit of Dogen's ideal.

4:00 a.m.	*shinrei,* wake up
4:15	*zazen*
5:00	*choka-fugin,* morning sutra chanting
6:15	*seiso,* daily morning cleaning of nunnery
7:30	breakfast
8:00–12:00	time for classes, *samu* (working together—gardening, cleaning, preparation for events), or private study
12:00	lunch
12:30–3:00	classes, *samu,* or private study
3:00	tea
4:00	*banka,* evening sutra chanting
4:30	*hatto soji,* clean Worship Hall
5:30	*yakuseki,* dinner, which consists of the day's leftovers
6:00–8:00	private study in one's own room
8:15	*yaza,* nightly *zazen*
9:00	*kaichin,* lights out

The key to finding peace in the midst of the strenuous schedule at the nunnery is to accept the fact that the present moment is important. What must be done, must be done. One just does what is necessary. To rebel against this reality only causes one to suffer. To contemplate "maybe" or "later" only means that one must fight against these wishes *and* keep pace with the others. Yet, to accept the task before you and to do it with your whole heart leads to joy and freedom. These are words that many acquainted with Zen practice are familiar with. I was, too. But in the midst of it, I found out just how true they are. When it is cold, it is cold. When your right knee hurts, it hurts. When the morning wake-up bell rings, you wake up. When the bell in the *zendo* is struck, you stand up. When the gong is struck, you go to eat. When the *samu* drum is beaten you go to work. It is as simple as that.

Preserving the traditional schedule, this nunnery allows the nuns to bathe, shave their heads, and do laundry on days that contain either a 4 or a 9. At times when the heat and humidity of Nagoya persisted, I dreamt of pouring the water for the flowers over my own wilting head. At these moments I felt the tenacity of tradition. Yet, it is precisely because the nuns do not waver on these details that they are genuine living bearers of the Zen tradition.

CHAPTER FOUR

Buddhist Founders

uddhism, like other world religions such as Christianity and Islam, presents an
amazing diversity of forms and expressions throughout its chronological span
and geographical range. Buddhism in Japan is only one chapter in the worldwide history of this tradition, but even within this more narrowly defined time and space, it is
by no means monolithic or uniform. Indeed, just as it is difficult to characterize Buddhism generally, it is not easy to simply describe this religion in its Japanese setting.

Two different ways of approaching this subject are apparent in the contrasting terms
used to label it. The phrase "Buddhism *in Japan*" emphasizes the continuity of Buddhism from its Indian origins and the Buddha's message through its Chinese and
Korean forms and finally to its Japanese forms. The phrase "*Japanese* Buddhism"
highlights the originality and distinctively Japanese character of the way Buddhism
was accepted and transformed in Japan. Which is the best approach to this subject?
Rather than choosing either "Buddhism in Japan" or "Japanese Buddhism," we will
more fully appreciate the complexity and diversity of this tradition by combining the
two approaches. In fact, Japanese Buddhists hold both that their heritage is a faithful transmission of earlier Buddhism, and that the founders of Japanese Buddhist
groups were highly creative and quite Japanese in the way they transformed Buddhism. Because in this book we are concerned primarily with Japanese religion, we

will focus more on transformation than on transmission—Japanese Buddhism rather than Buddhism in Japan—but we must recognize that these are two inseparable aspects of the same religion.

In Japan as in all the countries and cultures where Buddhism has flourished, it has attracted some of the greatest minds and most powerful personalities. The selections in this chapter are taken from the writings of several prominent founders of major Buddhist movements in Japan—founders who built on previous Buddhist precedents as well as developed new patterns of thought and practice.

Perhaps the most common feature shared by these founders is their claim of locating the authentic Buddhism and establishing it in Japan for the benefit of the Japanese people and nation. However, somewhat like the blind men describing the elephant, these figures identified a rich variety of authentically Buddhist forms. Some of the differences among them are due to the fact that each founder focused on a limited set of sutras, commentaries, and practices for his presentation of Buddhism. Other differences are due to the tensions that can be found within any tradition—for example, concern with monastic discipline rather than lay practice, emphasis on meditation rather than devotion, or viewing the ritual and mystical possibilities of a tradition rather than its practical everyday benefits.

Whatever their differences, these founders were religious geniuses in the sense of discovering (or rediscovering) Buddhist means of training the mind and body for the highest religious fulfillment. Each of them had their own way of viewing Buddhism's goal of *nirvana,* or enlightenment, and their own set of practices leading to it. As an example, take two different strands of Buddhism: devotion to Amida leads to rebirth in a pure land or paradise; meditation leads to enlightenment or awakening. Even within one particular strand of Buddhist development—devotion or meditation—there were sharp disagreements. These Buddhists were highly competitive with one another, and were not bashful about criticizing predecessors or contemporaries. Each founder—or his disciples—claimed to have the highest knowledge or wisdom about Buddhism, not just intellectual information, but the means to know the truth and the ability to realize the goal of Buddhism. These were not simply abstract arguments, for each founder (or his disciples) mobilized followers and established institutions to continue his set of beliefs and practices.

Studying these founders and their ideals, as well as their criticisms of other Buddhist positions, gives us some idea of the variety and richness of Buddhism within Japanese religion, and reminds us of the diversity within any religious tradition or subtradition. The material in the following selections is not necessarily the popular fare of everyday Buddhist practice; in fact, some of these works have been read and known mainly by Buddhist priests and scholars. The average person in Japan today has little or no knowledge of most of these historical teachings, which is the case in most religions—for instance, in Europe and North America, few Presbyterians read the writings of their founding father John Calvin, and few Roman Catholics read the works of the great theologian Thomas Aquinas. In Japan many people whose families are members of parish Buddhist temples, and whose homes have Buddhist altars, do not even know the Buddhist sect of their parish temple. Nevertheless, whether or not they are widely read and known today, these Buddhist founders were the original leaders of important Buddhist institutions and were major innovators in Japanese religious history. They continue to be important representatives of the religious genius in Japanese history.[1]

16
Dengyo Daishi and Tendai Buddhism

Although Dengyo Daishi (767–822) and his contemporary Kobo Daishi went to China on the same diplomatic mission, each in search of authentic Buddhism, Dengyo returned to Japan ahead of Kobo. Dengyo Daishi was attracted to many forms of Buddhism, especially the Chinese T'ien-t'ai and its emphasis on the *Lotus Sutra,* but he brought back a variety of Buddhist practices. Dengyo (also called Saicho) stressed the Mahayana teaching in its T'ien-t'ai (or Tendai) form of enlightenment for all humans, or enlightenment as an innate possibility for all. He was concerned as well with establishing the authenticity of monastic Buddhism in Japan, including proper study and meditation, with the dual purpose of preserving Buddhism and enhancing the nation.

This document written in 818 focuses mainly on one aspect of Buddhist practice, the necessity for monks' lengthy seclusion and appropriate study to assure suitable training, which would lead to their Tendai ordination. The goal of this petition was to gain governmental approval of this ordination. Although such a rigorous program of twelve years of training at a mountain monastery may seem far removed from the ordinary layperson, Dengyo summarizes clearly the intention of this program: to "uphold the Buddha's Dharma [Law or Teaching], benefit the nation, draw sentient beings to the true teaching, and encourage future students to do good." By ensuring the transmission of the proper Buddhism under the supervision of the state, in the long run the country and its people would be drawn to the true teaching. The following is Dengyo Daishi's proposal for the ordination of monks.

---

1. See *Shapers of Japanese Buddhism*, edited by Yusen Kashiwahara and Koyu Sonoda, translated by Gaynor Sekimori (Tokyo: Kosei Publishing Co., 1994), for a work giving longer treatments of major Buddhist founders (such as those found in this chapter), and brief descriptions of other Buddhist figures.

REGULATIONS TO ENCOURAGE TENDAI
YEARLY ORDINAND STUDENTS

Dengyo Daishi
Paul Groner, translator

1. (At any one time) there will be twelve intermediate students. . . . Their period of study will be set at six years. Since the number of students will decrease by two each year, two more should be added (each year). In order to test the intermediate students, the teachers will all gather in the study hall and examine the students on their reading of the *Lotus Sutra* and the *Chin kuang ming ching (Suvar naprabhasasutra)*. If they pass, it will be fully recorded in the register; on the day they fulfill the requirements, the authorities shall be informed. If they pass after six years, they will be added to the ranks of those who have fulfilled the requirements. If they do not pass, they will not be added to the ranks of those who have fulfilled the requirements. If anyone withdraws, his name and the name of the person replacing him will be recorded and reported to the authorities.

2. All intermediate students will provide their own food and clothing. However, if there is someone who is of excellent mind, ability and health, but who lacks sufficient clothing and food, then this hall . . . will issue him a certificate permitting him to go and beg in the nine directions.

3. If an intermediate student's character is not in accord with the Dharma and he breaks the rules, then the authorities shall be informed and he will be replaced, as is specified in the regulations.

4. Intermediate students will receive the full precepts the same year that they are initiated. Once they have received the full precepts, they will not leave the confines of the mountain for twelve years and will devote themselves to their studies and practices. For the first six years, they will learn mainly through lectures. Secondary emphasis will be placed on contemplation and the practice (of meditation). Each day two thirds of their studies will concern Buddhism and one third will concern other subjects. Extensive lecturing will be their training; preaching the Dharma will be their discipline. During the last six years, contemplation and the practice (of meditation) will be stressed. Secondary emphasis will be placed on lectures. Those in the (Tendai) Meditation Course will thoroughly practice the four types of meditation. Those in the Esoteric Course will thoroughly practice chanting and meditation on the *sanbu* [the three divisions of the Taizokai—the Buddha, Lotus, and Diamond].

5. Tendai yearly (ordinand) students and any others who wish to practice in the One-vehicle Meditation Hall will not have their names removed from their original temple's register. Their names will be entered in (the register of one of) the temples of Omi which receives a sufficient stipend of food. That

Reprinted by permission of the publisher from Paul Groner, *Saicho: The Establishment of the Japanese Tendai School* (Berkeley: Berkeley Buddhist Studies Series, 1984). The notes and Japanese characters have been deleted.

temple will send them food. Robes, however, for the summer and winter will be obtained by going out and begging in different places in accordance with Mahayana teachings. Thus they will be able to clothe themselves and will not backslide in their practice. From now on, they will strictly adhere to these customs. They will make thatched huts their abodes and use bamboo leaves as their seats. They will disregard their own needs and respect the Dharma. Thus will the Dharma long endure, and the nation be protected.

6. With the exception of yearly ordinands from other schools, any monk who has been initiated and received the full precepts, and who comes of his own accord and wishes to remain on the mountain for twelve years to practice the two courses, will note the name of his temple and teacher, obtain a certificate from the hall on Mount Hiei and deposit it with the governmental authorities. When he has spent twelve full years on the mountain, he will be granted the rank of *hosshi* (Dharma Teacher) along with the yearly ordinand students of this school. If he does not follow the rules of the school, he will be sent back to his former temple.

7. After a student has completed twelve years on the mountain, studying and practicing in accordance with the regulations, he will be granted the rank of *daihosshi* (Great Dharma Teacher). If his studies are incomplete, but he still has spent a full twelve years on the mountain without leaving, then he will be granted the rank *hosshi*. If a student of the School does not follow the rules or stay in the mountain halls, or if he remains on the mountain but repeatedly breaks the rules, or if the number of years (spent on the mountain) is not sufficient, his name will be permanently removed from the Tendai School's official registers and he will be sent back to his former temple.

8. Two lay administrators will be appointed to the Tendai School's Hall. They will take turns supervising the order, and also be responsible for prohibiting theft, liquor, and women (on the mountain). They will uphold the Buddha's Dharma and protect the nation.

The above eight articles uphold the Buddha's Dharma, benefit the nation, draw sentient beings to the true teaching, and encourage future students to do good.

I humbly ask for His Majesty's judgment.

The twenty-seventh day of the eighth month of the ninth year in the Konin era (818).

Submitted by Saicho [Dengyo Daishi], the monk who formerly went to China in search of the Dharma.

17
Kobo Daishi and Shingon (Esoteric) Buddhism

Esoteric Buddhism was only one of the many aspects of Chinese Buddhism that intrigued Dengyo Daishi, but the scriptures and rituals of esoteric Buddhism were the center of attention for Kobo Daishi (774–835). In China Kobo studied mainly Chenyen Buddhism; *Chenyen* is Chinese for "true word," (Sanskrit *mantra*), the secret or esoteric formula. *Chenyen* is pronounced "Shingon" in Japanese. Although Tendai eventually adopted many esoteric practices, Shingon has been the first and foremost tradition of esoteric Buddhism. This form of Buddhism is a highly icono-graphic tradition known today primarily in its Tibetan forms.

As defined by Kobo Daishi, the doctrine revealed by the historical Buddha (Shakyamuni Buddha or Nirmanakaya Buddha) is exoteric; it is a simplified Buddhism adapted to a particular time and place. This is contrasted with esoteric Buddhism, set forth by the cosmic Buddha (Dharmakaya or Mahavairocana), the secret and ultimate truth. Kobo underwent the initiatory ritual called *abhisheka,* learned the Sanskrit sacred words or *mantras,* and also received instruction in yogic practices. This is what the Dharma, or Buddhist teaching, meant to Kobo Daishi in his hierarchical view of Buddhism, because it was the highest development of Buddhism in India and China.

In this document from 806 Kobo (also called Kukai) is reporting back to the emperor on his activities in China, describing how he came to acquire the teachings and practices of esoteric Buddhism, which he praises as the essence of the Buddhas and the speediest path to enlightenment. Kobo stresses that his mission to China to study and bring back Buddhist materials was in compliance with the emperor's command. He also emphasizes the mutual benefit that accrues to Buddhism and the throne. Like the virtue of the emperor, "the Buddha, who is analogous to the sun, will rise higher and higher"; in turn, the emperor is likened to the Buddha: "His Majesty is like a father of the people and an incarnation of the Buddha." Kobo Daishi focused on esoteric Buddhism, but he saw a close tie between the state and Buddhism. This selection is the gist of Kobo Daishi's report on his mission to China.

A MEMORIAL PRESENTING
A LIST OF NEWLY IMPORTED SUTRAS
AND OTHER ITEMS
Kobo Daishi
Yoshito S. Hakeda, translator

The report of Kukai [Kobo Daishi], a monk who studied the Dharma in T'ang China:

In the twenty-third year of Enryaku (804), I, Kukai, as one of a number of students sent to study abroad by imperial order, sailed far away to a port tens of thousands of *ri* distant. In the last month of the same year, we arrived at Ch'ang-an. On the tenth day of the second month of the following year, in obedience to an imperial edict, I took up residence at the Hsi-ming Temple.

Reprinted by permission of the publisher from Yoshito S. Hakeda, *Kukai: Major Works* (New York: Columbia University Press, 1972). Some notes have been deleted.

Thereafter, I visited Buddhist temples everywhere, calling on Buddhist teachers. I was fortunate enough to meet the acharya [master] of *abhiseka,* whose Buddhist name was Hui-kuo, of the Ch'ing-lung Temple. I regarded him as my main preceptor. This great priest was the disciple chosen to transmit the Dharma of the Master of the Tripitaka of Broad Wisdom, Pu-k'ung, of the Ta-hsing-shan Temple. He was well versed in the sutras and in the rules of discipline and had a thorough knowledge of the Esoteric Buddhist teachings. He was a defender of the Dharma and was esteemed the teacher of the nation. This great teacher eagerly desired to spread Buddhism and was deeply concerned about uprooting the sufferings of people.

This master granted me the privilege of receiving the Esoteric Buddhist precepts and permitted me to enter the altar of *abhiseka*. Three times I was bathed in the *abhiseka* in order to receive the mantras and once to inherit the mastership. I learned directly from him whatever was left untaught and heard reverently from him whatever was new to me. I was fortunate enough, thanks to the compassion of the great master, a national teacher of distinguished merit, to learn the great twofold Dharma[1] and the yogic practices which use various sacred objects of concentration. This Dharma is the gist of the Buddhas and the quickest path by which to attain enlightenment. This teaching is as useful to the nation as walls are to a city, and as fertile soil is to the people. Thus, it is known that unfortunate ones are deprived of a chance even to hear the name of this teaching mentioned; the heavily defiled ones are unable to approach it. In India the Tripitaka Master Subhakarasimha renounced his throne in order to practice it; in China the Emperor Hsuan-tsung (r. 713–55) forgot the savor of other things in the excess of his appreciation and admiration for it. Henceforth, in China, each successive emperor and his three highest ministers devoted themselves to it one after another; the four classes of believers[2] and tens of thousands of people respectfully started to learn it. The Esoteric Buddhist school has hence been called a dominant force. The Exoteric teachings were overwhelmed and paralyzed by it, being as imperfect as a pearl of which one half is missing.

When a pair of phoenixes are seen flying in harmony, people secretly look forward to the appearance of a sage king such as Yao or Shun. Whether the Dharma appears or remains concealed in the world depends upon the trend of the times. I have now imported the teachings of the Diamond Vehicle (Vajrayana) contained in more than one hundred texts and in the dual mandalas, the pictorial presentations of the sacred assembly that is extensive as the sea. I have crossed the sea abounding with whales, though the billows were high and the ship drifted about in storms, and have returned safely to the domain of His Majesty. This is due to the effect of His Majesty's influence.

---

1. The teachings of Esoteric Buddhism in terms of the Diamond and Matrix Realms.

2. Monks, nuns, laymen, and laywomen.

The highest virtue of His Imperial Majesty is like that of heaven; [the name of] the Buddha, who is analogous to the sun, will rise higher and higher.[3] His Majesty is like a father of the people and an incarnation of the Buddha. Out of compassion for his people, he dips his feet in water;[4] he calls together those who are committed to the Buddha and bestows robes upon them. That newly translated sutras have recently arrived from afar may be due to the fact that the emperor had newly ascended the throne, the pivot which regulates the movements of the cosmos. Or it may be because of the way the emperor graciously nurtures the seagirt world that paintings of the oceanlike assembly [mandalas] have come here across the sea. There seems to be a mysterious coincidence here; who but a sage knows why?

Though I, Kukai, may deserve to be punished by death because I did not arrive punctually, yet I am secretly delighted with my good luck that I am alive and that I have imported the Dharma that is difficult to obtain. I can hardly bear the feelings of fear and joy which alternate in my heart. I respectfully submit this memorial to the throne and entrust it to Takashina Mahito Tonari of the senior sixth rank, upper grade, judge and senior secretary of Dazaifu. Also attached to it is a list of newly imported sutras and other items. Dishonoring by my haste the dignity of His Majesty, I am increasingly struck with a sense of awe.

Most respectfully,

Monk Kukai

Twenty-second Day of the Tenth Month,

Daido 1 (806)

18

Honen and Pure Land Buddhism

Today scholars contrast Honen's Buddhism with that of Dengyo Daishi and Kobo Daishi in a number of ways. As an example, Tendai and Shingon Buddhism were established in mountain headquarters and were closely related to the aristocracy and nobility; Honen's Pure Land Buddhism was established in the plains and cities and directed more to the common people. However, Honen (1133–1212) focused on the sharp religious distinctions he drew between earlier sects and his style of Buddhism. He boldly stated that his practice of the *nembutsu,* recitation of the name of Amida, is superior to the meditation of Tendai and the ritual practices of Shingon. The *nembutsu's* superiority is attested in Amida's Original Vow, and is assured of bringing all people—monks and laity, men and women—to rebirth in the Pure Land. (In the text, Ojo is rebirth in the Pure Land.)

Although there were important forerunners to Honen who advocated devotion to Amida and practice of the *nembutsu,* they used the *nembutsu* as one among

---

3. The implication is that under the patronage of the emperor, the name of Mahavairocana Buddha, the Great Sun Buddha, will be greatly enhanced.

4. To share the sufferings of farmers who toil in the rice paddies.

many Buddhist techniques and they did not found institutions. For Honen, who developed his own sect, the *nembutsu* was not just an additional practice, but an all-sufficient means. Honen confidently announced, "I throw aside those practices not included in Amida's Vow . . . and devote myself exclusively to the practice of that mightily effective discipline of the *Nembutsu,* with earnest prayer for birth into the Pure Land." Honen's emphasis was on the purity and simplicity of devotion, not the "pedantic airs" of intellectuals or the elaborate rituals and meditation of earlier Japanese Buddhism.

One excerpt in this selection is a general statement of faith, and the other is a personal letter. "The One-Sheet Document" from 1212 was handed down as Honen's final testament, a concise interpretation of the *nembutsu* as "the method of final salvation." This document praises the simplicity of the faith of the ignorant rather than the intellectual knowledge of Buddhism. The earlier written "Letter to Tsukinowa's Wife" is noteworthy for two features: first, it is written to a woman, clearly demonstrating that the Pure Land was equally available to females; second, it stresses the simplification of Buddhism to faith or trust in Amida rather than lengthy monasticism or abstract doctrine or elaborate rituals.

HONEN'S ADVICE ON THE
REPETITION OF THE *NEMBUTSU*

Harper Havelock Coates and
Ryugaku Ishizuka, translators

Honen's Parting Message—"The One-Sheet Document"

As Honen was drawing near to the end, Seikwambo said to him, "I have for many years been indebted to you for instruction and counsel in the way of faith in the *Nembutsu.* But now will you not write me something with your own hand, that you think will be good for me, that I may preserve it as a memento." At this he took up his pen and wrote as follows: "The method of final salvation that I have propounded is neither a sort of meditation, such as has been practiced by many scholars in China and Japan, nor is it a repetition of the Buddha's name by those who have studied and understood the deep meaning of it. It is nothing but the mere repetition of the 'Namu Amida Butsu,' without a doubt of His mercy, whereby one may be born into the Land of Perfect Bliss. The mere repetition with firm faith includes all the practical details, such as the three-fold preparation of mind and the four practical rules. If I as an individual had any doctrine more profound than this, I should miss the mercy of the two Honorable Ones, Amida and Shaka, and be left out of the

Reprinted by permission of the publisher from Harper Havelock Coates and Ryugaku Ishizuka, *Honen the Buddhist Saint* (Kyoto: Chionin, 1925). The notes have been deleted.

Vow of the Amida Buddha. Those who believe this, though they clearly understand all the teachings Shaka taught throughout his whole life, should behave themselves like simple-minded folk, who know not a single letter, or like ignorant nuns or monks whose faith is implicitly simple. Thus without pedantic airs, they should fervently practice the repetition of the name of Amida, and that alone."

The foregoing is without question Honen's autograph, and a truly worthy model for all men in these later degenerate times, and it is still in circulation, known as the *Ichimai Kishomon*, "One-Sheet Document."

Honen's Letter to Tsukinowa's Wife

The legal wife of Kanezane Tsukinowa, the ex-Regent, influenced by the profound faith of her husband, herself came to believe, and she asked Honen some questions regarding the *Nembutsu Ojo*, to which he replied as follows: "I have the honour of addressing you regarding your inquiry about the *Nembutsu*. I am delighted to know that you are invoking the sacred name. Indeed the practice of the *Nembutsu* is the best of all for bringing us to *Ojo*, because it is the discipline prescribed in Amida's Original Vow. The discipline required in the Shingon, and the meditation of the Tendai, are indeed excellent, but they are not in the Vow. This *Nembutsu* is the very thing that Shaka himself entrusted to his disciple Ananda. As to all other forms of religious practice belonging to either the meditative or non-meditative classes, however excellent they may be in themselves, the great Master did not specially entrust them to Ananda to be handed down to posterity. Moreover the *Nembutsu* has the endorsation of all the Buddhas of the six quarters; and, while the discipline of the exoteric and esoteric schools, whether in relation to the phenomenal or noumenal worlds, are indeed most excellent, the Buddhas do not give them their final approval. And so, although there are many kinds of religious exercise, the *Nembutsu* far excels them all in its way of attaining *Ojo*. Now there are some people who are unacquainted with the way of birth into the Pure Land, who say, that because the *Nembutsu* is so easy, it is all right for those who are incapable of keeping up the practices required in the Shingon, and the meditation of the Tendai sects, but such a cavil is absurd. What I mean is, that I throw aside those practices not included in Amida's Vow, nor prescribed by Shakamuni, nor having the endorsement of the Buddhas of all quarters of the universe, and now only throw myself upon the Original Vow of Amida, according to the authoritative teaching of Shakamuni, and in harmony with what the many Buddhas of the six quarters have definitely approved. I give up my own foolish plans of salvation, and devote myself exclusively to the practice of that mightily effective discipline of the *Nembutsu,* with earnest prayer for birth into the Pure Land. This is the reason why the *Sozu* of the Eshin-in Temple in his work *Ojoyoshu* makes the *Nembutsu* the most fundamental of all. And so you should now cease from all other religious practices, apply yourself to the *Nembutsu* alone, and in this it is all-important to do it with undivided attention. Zendo, who himself attained to that perfect insight *(samadhi)* which apprehends the truth, clearly expounds the full meaning of this in his Commentary on the Meditation Sutra, and in the Two-volumed Sutra the Buddha (Shaka) says, "Give yourself with undivided mind to the repetition of the name of the Buddha who is in Himself endless life. And by 'undivided mind' he means to present a contrast to a mind which is broken up into two or three sections, each pursuing its own separate object, and to exhort to the laying aside of everything but this one thing only. In the prayers which you offer for your loved ones, you will find that the *Nembutsu* is the one most conducive to happiness. In the *Ojoyoshu*, it says that the *Nembutsu* is superior to all other works. Also Dengyo Daishi, when telling how to put an end to the misfortunes which result from the seven evils, exhorts to the practice of the *Nembutsu*. Is there indeed anything anywhere that is superior to it for bringing happiness in the present or the future life? You ought by all means to give yourself up to it alone." *(The preceding is the gist of the letter.)* Through the friendly counsel here given, the lady engaged in the practice of the *Nembutsu* with one heart and mind.

19
Shinran and the True Pure Land Sect

Shinran (1173–1262) himself did not establish a new Buddhist movement, but his followers consider Shinran as the founder of the True Pure Land Sect. Just as Honen built upon and elaborated the precedents of faith in Amida and practice of the *nembutsu,* so Shinran went beyond Honen to advance this Pure Land tradition. Shinran apparently considered himself as carrying to a logical conclusion the position Honen advocated: if the *nembutsu* and rebirth in the Pure Land were open to all people, then Shinran saw no real distinction between monks ("the Path of Sages") and laity, men and women. Thus he married and spread his Buddhist faith as a married priest, setting a precedent for later Japanese Buddhism.

For Shinran, religious fulfillment depended not on one's social class or status (even a celibate monk), or one's actions (even endless repetitions of the *nembutsu*), but on complete trust in Amida. Shinran stressed that shinjin, or "faith" in Amida, and a single wholehearted repetition was sufficient; the important thing was not to rely on one's own power ("self-power"), but on the power of Amida ("Other Power"). For this reason he argued that it is easier for a wicked person to be reborn in paradise, because the wicked person recognizes his or her own worthlessness and will rely completely on Amida's power.

This selection is excerpted from the thirteenth-century *Tannisho,* a collection of Shinran's sayings compiled by his disciple Yuien. The full title is *Tannisho. A Primer: A Record of the Words of Shinran Set Down in Lamentation over Departure from His Teaching.* In these sayings we see Shinran's complete, absolute trust in Amida's vow, which will enable the believer to "realize birth into the Pure Land." He also is completely trusting in his teacher Honen, and uses this notion of total dependence on Other Power to demonstrate his argument that the evil person is more likely to have this dependence than a good person.

TANNISHO

Shinran

Dennis Hirota, translator

"Saved by the inconceivable working of Amida's Vow, I shall realize birth into the Pure Land": the moment you entrust yourself thus, so that the mind set upon saying the Name arises within you, you are brought to share in the benefit of being grasped by Amida, never to be abandoned.

Know that the Primal Vow of Amida makes no distinction between people young and old, good and evil; only the entrusting of yourself to it is essential. For it was made to save the person in whom karmic evil is deep-rooted and whose blind passions abound.

Thus, entrusting yourself to the Primal Vow requires no performance of good, for no act can hold greater virtue than saying the Name. Nor is there need to despair of the evil you commit, for no act is so evil that it obstructs the working of Amida's Primal Vow.

Thus were his words.

Each of you has crossed the borders of more than ten provinces to come to see me, undeterred by concern for your bodily safety, solely to inquire about the way to birth in the land of bliss. But if you imagine in me some special knowledge of a way to birth other than the nembutsu or a familiarity with writings that teach it, you are greatly mistaken. If that is the case, you would do better to visit the many eminent scholars in Nara or on Mount Hiei and inquire fully of them about the essentials for birth. I simply accept and entrust myself to what a good teacher told me, "Just say the Name and be saved by Amida"; nothing else is involved.

I have no idea whether the nembutsu is truly the seed for my being born in the Pure Land or whether it is the karmic act for which I must fall into hell. Should I have been deceived by Honen Shonin and, saying the Name, plunge utterly into hell, even then I would have no regrets. The person who could have attained Buddhahood by endeavoring in other practices might regret that he had been deceived if he said the nembutsu and so fell into hell. But I am one for whom any practice is difficult to accomplish, so hell is to be my home whatever I do.

If Amida's Primal Vow is true and real, Sakyamuni's teaching cannot be lies. If the Buddha's teaching is true and real, Shan-tao's commentaries cannot be lies. If Shan-tao's commentaries are true and real, can what Honen said be a lie? If what Honen said is true and real, then surely my words cannot be empty.

Reprinted by permission of the publisher from Dennis Hirota, translator, *Tannisho. A Primer: A Record of the Words of Shinran* (Kyoto: Ryukoku University, 1982).

Such, in essence, is the shinjin[1] of the foolish person that I am. Beyond this, whether you entrust yourself, taking up the nembutsu, or whether you abandon it, is your own, individual decision.

Thus were his words.

Even a good person can attain birth in the Pure Land, so it goes without saying that an evil person will.

Though such is the truth, people commonly say, "Even an evil person attains birth, so naturally a good person will." This statement may seem well-founded at first, but it runs counter to the meaning of the Other Power established through the Primal Vow. For a person who relies on the good that he does through his self-power fails to entrust himself wholeheartedly to Other Power and therefore is not in accord with Amida's Primal Vow. But when he abandons his attachment to self-power and entrusts himself totally to Other Power, he will realize birth in the Pure Land.

It is impossible for us, filled as we are with blind passions, to free ourselves from birth-and-death through any practice whatever. Sorrowing at this, Amida made the Vow, the essential intent of which is the attainment of Buddhahood by the person who is evil. Hence the evil person who entrusts himself to Other Power is precisely the one who possesses the true cause for birth.

Accordingly he said, "Even the virtuous man is born in the Pure Land, so without question is the man who is evil."

In the matter of compassion, the Path of Sages and the Pure Land path differ. Compassion in the Path of Sages is to pity, sympathize with, and care for beings. But the desire to save others from suffering is vastly difficult to fulfill.

Compassion in the Pure Land path lies in saying the Name, quickly attaining Buddhahood, and freely benefiting sentient beings with a heart of great love and great compassion. In our present lives, it is hard to carry out the desire to aid others however much love and tenderness we may feel; hence such compassion always falls short of fulfillment. Only the saying of the Name manifests the heart of great compassion that is replete and thoroughgoing.

Thus were his words.

Disputes have arisen, with companions in the singlehearted practice of the nembutsu claiming this practicer as their own disciple and numbering that one among someone else's. Such contention is totally senseless.

I have not a single disciple. For if I were to guide someone to the nembutsu through my own devices and efforts, then he would be my disciple, but

---

1. *Shinjin* usually is translated as "faith," but the Shin Buddhism Translation Series prefers to leave the term untranslated, explaining it as follows: "*Shinjin*: The realization of Other Power in which human calculation is negated through the working of Amida Buddha." See Yoshifumi Ueda, editor, *Letters of Shinran* (Kyoto: Hongwanji International Center, 1978), p. 83.—ED.

to call a person "my disciple" when he says the Name solely through the working of Amida would be preposterous.

One adheres to a teacher when brought by one's karmic conditions to join him, leaves a teacher when brought by karmic conditions to leave. In spite of this, some assert that even though a person may say the Name, if he has turned from one teacher to follow another, he cannot attain birth. This is absurd. Are those who say this threatening to take back the shinjin given by Amida as if it were their own property? Let there be an end to all such claims.

If one is in accord with the reality of jinen, one will surely awaken to the benevolence of the Buddha and of one's teachers and respond with gratitude.

Thus were his words.

The person of the nembutsu treads the great path free of all obstacles. For the gods of heaven and the deities of earth bow in homage to a practicer of shinjin, and those of the world of demons or of non-Buddhist ways never hinder him; moreover, the evil he does cannot bring forth its karmic results, nor can any good act equal in virtue his saying of the Name.

Thus were his words.

20
Nichiren and Nichiren Buddhism

Nichiren (1222–1282) shares with figures such as Honen the conviction that Buddhism should be open to all people and that the power of Buddhism should be easily accessible through a simple technique. However, Nichiren disagreed sharply with Honen's religious message, condemning him for advocating faith in Amida and the practice of reciting the *nembutsu*. For Nichiren the power of Buddhism was in the recitation of *Nam-myoho-renge-kyo*, which is the title of the *Lotus Sutra*; he believed devotion should be reserved for the actual Buddha (Shakyamuni), the one who revealed the *Lotus Sutra*, rather than the lesser divinities such as Amida.

Nichiren is famous for his open criticism not only of other religious leaders such as Honen, but also of secular authorities for failing to eliminate other forms of Buddhism. Nichiren saw the need for the state to establish the true Buddhism based on the *Lotus Sutra*, and risked his life to insist on this point. Nichiren has been called a Buddhist prophet, but he saw himself as a *bodhisattva* (enlightened being) because of his work in advocating the true Buddhism. In fact, he viewed the *Lotus Sutra* at the heart of converting all of Japan, and becoming the center of Buddhism for the three countries of India, China, and Japan. This vision of a universal Buddhism is an important historical precedent for many New Religions based on faith in the *Lotus Sutra*.

The first excerpt is from a public document, the second from a personal letter. *Rissho Ankoku Ron,* literally "Establishment of the Legitimate Teaching for the Protection of the Country," was submitted by Nichiren to the government in 1260; its harsh criticism of other Buddhists and government rulers led to Nichiren's being sent into exile. The general purpose of the document was to lay blame for a series of disasters on the erroneous Buddhist teaching of Honen, to predict future disasters if the teachings of the *Lotus Sutra* were not followed, and to advocate the practice of reciting the title of the *Lotus Sutra.* In the 1272 letter "Earthly Desires Are Enlightenment," Nichiren gives advice to a samurai who maintained faith in the *Lotus Sutra* and trust in Nichiren's teaching even after Nichiren was sent into exile by the government. He encourages this samurai and his wife to continue practicing their faith even in the face of persecution, so that they may "behold the faces of Shakyamuni . . . and all the other Buddhas."

NICHIREN'S ADVICE FOR PRACTICE OF
NAM-MYOHO-RENGE-KYO

Nichiren
Burton Watson, translator

Rissho Ankoku Ron

In the reign of Emperor Gotoba there was a priest named Honen who wrote a work entitled the *Senchaku Shu*. He contradicted the sacred teachings of Shakyamuni and brought confusion to people in every direction. The *Senchaku Shu* states: "The Chinese priest Tao-ch'o distinguished between the *Shodo* or Sacred Way teachings and the *Jodo* or Pure Land teachings and urged men to abandon the former and immediately embrace the latter. First of all, there are two kinds of Sacred Way teachings, [the Mahayana and the Hinayana]. Judging from this, we may assume that the esoteric Mahayana doctrines of Shingon and the true Mahayana teachings of the Lotus Sutra are both included in the Sacred Way. If that is so, then the present-day sects of Shingon, Zen, Tendai, Kegon, Sanron, Hosso, Jiron, and Shoron—all these eight schools are included in the Sacred Way that is to be abandoned. . . .

. . . Honen says: "If one wishes to escape quickly from the sufferings of birth and death, one should confront these two superior teachings and then proceed to put aside the teachings of the Sacred Way and choose those of the Pure Land. And if one wishes to follow the teachings of the Pure Land, one should confront the correct and sundry practices and then proceed to abandon all those that are incorrect and devote one's entire attention to those that are correct."

When we examine these passages, we see that Honen quotes the erroneous explanations of T'an-luan, Tao-ch'o, and Shan-tao, and establishes the

Reprinted by permission of the publisher from Burton Watson, translator, and Philip B. Yampolsky, editor, *Selected Writings of Nichiren* (New York: Columbia University Press, 1990). The notes have been deleted; the bracketed remarks are from the original.

categories he calls Sacred Way and Pure Land, Difficult-to-Practice Way and Easy-to-Practice Way. . . . And on top of that, he groups together all the sage monks of the three countries of India, China, and Japan as well as the students of Buddhism of the ten directions, and calls them a "band of robbers," causing the people to insult them!

In doing so, he turns his back on the passages in the three Pure Land sutras, the sutras of his own sect, which contain Amida's vow to save everyone "except those who commit the five cardinal sins or slander the True Law." At the same time, he shows that he fails to understand the warning contained in the second volume of the Lotus Sutra, the most important sutra expounded in the five preaching periods of the Buddha's life, which reads: "One who refuses to take faith in this sutra and instead slanders it. . . . After he dies, he will fall into the hell of incessant suffering."

And now we have come to this later age, when men are no longer sages. Each enters his own dark road, and all alike forget the direct way. How pitiful, that no one cures them of their blindness! How painful, to see them vainly lending encouragement to these false beliefs! And as a result, everyone from the ruler of the nation down to the humblest peasant believes that there are no true sutras outside the three Pure Land sutras, and no Buddhas other than the Buddha Amida with his two attendants.

Once there were men like Dengyo, Gishin, Jikaku and Chisho who journeyed ten thousand leagues across the waves to acquire the sacred teachings, or visited all the mountains and rivers of Japan to acquire Buddhist statues which they held in reverence. In some cases they built holy temples on the peaks of high mountains in which to preserve those scriptures and statues; in other cases they constructed sacred halls in the bottoms of deep valleys where such objects could be worshiped and honored. As a result, the Buddhas Shakyamuni and Yakushi shone side by side, casting their influence upon present and future ages, while the Bodhisattvas Kokuzo and Jizo brought benefit to the living and the dead. The rulers of the nation contributed counties or villages so that the lamps might continue to burn bright before the images, while the stewards of the great estates offered their fields and gardens [to provide for the upkeep of the temples].

But because of this book by Honen, this *Senchaku Shu,* the Lord Buddha Shakyamuni is forgotten and all honor is paid to Amida, the Buddha of the Western Land. The Lord Buddha's transmission of the Law is ignored, and Yakushi, the Buddha of the Eastern Region, is neglected. All attention is paid to the three works in four volumes of the Pure Land scriptures, and all the other wonderful teachings that Shakyamuni proclaimed throughout the five periods of his preaching life are cast aside. If temples are not dedicated to Amida, then people no longer have any desire to support them or pay honor to the Buddhas enshrined there; if monks do not chant the Nembutsu, then people quickly forget all about giving those monks alms. As a result, the halls of the Buddha fall into ruin, scarcely a wisp of smoke rises above their mossy tiles; and the monks' quarters stand empty and dilapidated, the dew deep on the grasses in their courtyards. And in spite of such conditions, no one gives a thought to protecting the Law or to restoring the temples. Hence the sage monks who once presided over the temples leave and do not return, and the benevolent deities who guarded the Buddhist teachings depart and no longer appear. This has all come about because of this *Senchaku Shu* of Honen. How pitiful to think that, in the space of a few decades, hundreds, thousands, tens of thousands of people have been deluded by these devilish teachings and in so many cases confused as to the true teachings of Buddhism. If people favor perverse doctrines and forget what is correct, can the benevolent deities be anything but angry? If people cast aside doctrines that are all-encompassing and take up those that are incomplete, can the world escape the plots of demons? Rather than offering up ten thousand prayers for remedy, it would be better simply to outlaw this one evil doctrine that is the source of all the trouble!

Earthly Desires Are Enlightenment

The teaching that I, Nichiren, am now propagating may seem limited, but it is actually most profound. This is because it goes deeper than the teachings expounded by T'ien-t'ai and Dengyo. It reveals the three important matters contained in the *Juryo* chapter of the essential teaching. To practice only the seven characters of Nam-myoho-renge-kyo may appear limited, yet since this Law is the master of all Buddhas of the past, present, and future, the teacher of all bodhisattvas in the ten directions, and the guide that enables all beings to attain Buddhahood, its practice is incomparably profound.

The sutra states, "The wisdom of all Buddhas is infinitely profound and immeasurable." "All Buddhas" means every Buddha throughout the ten directions in every age of the past, present, and future. It represents every single Buddha and bodhisattva of any sutra or sect whatsoever, including both Dainichi Buddha of the Shingon sect and Amida Buddha of the Jodo sect, every Buddha of the past, the future, or the present, including even Shakyamuni Buddha himself.

Next, what is meant by the "wisdom" of all Buddhas? It is the true aspect of all phenomena, the Dharma entity of the ten factors that leads all beings to Buddhahood. What then is the dharma entity? It is nothing other than Nam-myoho-renge-kyo. T'ien-t'ai states, "The profound principle of the 'true aspect' is the originally inherent Law of Myoho-renge-kyo." The true aspect of all phenomena indicates the two Buddhas Shakyamuni and Taho [seated together in the Treasure Tower]. Taho represents all phenomena and Shakyamuni, the true aspect. The two Buddhas also indicate the two principles of truth as object . . . and the subjective wisdom to grasp it. . . . Taho Buddha signifies the truth as object and Shakyamuni the subjective wisdom. Although these are two, they are fused into one in the Buddha's enlightenment.

These teachings are of prime importance. They mean that earthly desires are enlightenment and that the sufferings of birth and death are nirvana. When one chants Nam-myoho-renge-kyo even during the sexual union of man and woman, then earthly desires are enlightenment and the sufferings of birth and death are nirvana. Sufferings are nirvana only when one realizes that life throughout its cycle of birth and death is neither born nor destroyed. The *Fugen* Sutra states, "Even without extinguishing earthly desires or denying the five desires, they can purify all of their senses and eradicate all of their misdeeds." It is stated in the *Maka Shikan* that "the ignorance and dust of desires are enlightenment and the sufferings of birth and death are nirvana." The *Juryo* chapter of the Lotus Sutra says, "This is my constant thought: how can I cause all living beings to gain entry to the highest Way and quickly attain Buddhahood?" And the *Hoben* chapter states, "The aspect of this world [as it manifests the Law] abides eternally." The Dharma body is none other than Nam-myoho-renge-kyo. . . .

As a votary of the Lotus Sutra, you suffered severe persecutions, yet still you came to my assistance. In the *Hosshi* chapter the Buddha states, "I will send monks and nuns and laymen and laywomen [to make offerings to the teacher of the Lotus Sutra and hear his preaching of the Law]." If you are not one of these laymen, then to whom else could the passage possibly refer? You have not only heard the Law, but have taken faith in it and since then have followed it without turning aside. How wondrous! How extraordinary! Then how can there be any doubt that I, Nichiren, am the teacher of the Lotus Sutra? I have fulfilled the words of the Buddha: "He is the envoy of the Buddha, sent to carry out the Buddha's work." I have propagated the five characters of the daimoku which were entrusted to Bodhisattva Jogyo when the two Buddhas sat together within the Treasure Tower. Does this not indicate that I am an envoy of Bodhisattva Jogyo? Moreover, following me as a votary of the Lotus Sutra, you also tell others of this Law. What else could this be but the transmission of the Mystic Law?

Carry through with your faith in the Lotus Sutra. You cannot strike fire from flint if you stop halfway. Bring forth the great power of faith and establish your reputation among all the people of Kamakura and the rest of Japan as "Shijo Kingo of the Hokke sect." Even a bad reputation will spread far and wide. A good reputation will spread even farther, particularly if it is a reputation for devotion to the Lotus Sutra.

Explain all this to your wife, and work together like the sun and moon, a pair of eyes, or the two wings of a bird. With the sun and the moon, how can you fall into the paths of darkness? With a pair of eyes, how can you fail to behold the faces of Shakyamuni, Taho, and all the other Buddhas of the ten directions? With a pair of wings, you will surely be able to fly in an instant to the treasure land of Tranquil Light. I will write in more detail on another occasion.

2 1
Dogen and Zen Buddhism

Dogen Kigen (1200–1253), like other Japanese Buddhist founders, continued and elaborated the Buddhist tradition originating in India and developed in China; he is also similar to these founders in making his own contribution to this tradition. Like Dengyo Daishi, Dogen also was deeply interested in the monastic rule, and wrote about the proper behavior of a good monk. Some consider Dogen as the most original thinker or philosopher Japan has produced. Dogen followed a long line of Buddhist meditation techniques, but developed his own style and interpretation of meditation.

There are many forms of Buddhist meditation; even within Zen Buddhism, there are sharp differences. For example, Rinzai Zen favors the use of *koan*, "Zen riddles" or "public cases," in meditation, but Dogen and Soto Zen believe the use of *koan* will lead one off the path to Buddha. For Dogen, enlightenment is achieved through sitting in meditation (*zazen*), gaining the deepest insight we can about the self. The notion of "self" here is not just "person," nor is it simply a psychological notion, but a combination of body and mind. For Dogen, the attained enlightenment may seem to end, but it should be prolonged.

The excerpts in this selection are taken from several sections of Dogen's main work, *Shobo genzo* ("Eye Storehouse of the True Law"), which took more than two decades to write and was still incomplete at his death in 1253. In this writing Dogen tried to convey his own understanding of Buddhism and the special technique of *zazen*, letting go of one's body and mind, and thus attaining enlightenment.

SHOBO GENZO

Dogen
From *Sources of Japanese Tradition*

Realizing the Solution

[Against the notion that enlightenment is a single, momentary experience]

To study the way of the Buddha is to study your own self. To study your own self is to forget yourself. To forget yourself is to have the objective world prevail in you. To have the objective world prevail in you, is to let go of your "own" body and mind as well as the body and mind of "others." The enlightenment

Reprinted by permission of the publisher from *Sources of Japanese Tradition*, edited by Ryusaku Tsunoda, Wm. Theodore de Bary, and Donald Keene (New York: Columbia University Press, 1958). The notes have been deleted, and the bracketed remarks are from the original.

thus attained may seem to come to an end, but though it appears to have stopped this momentary enlightenment should be prolonged and prolonged.

[Against the notion that the objective world is merely a projection of one's own mind]

When you go out on a boat and look around, you feel as if the shore were moving. But if you fix your eyes on the rim of the boat, you become aware that the boat is moving. It is exactly the same when you try to know the objective world while still in a state of confusion in regard to your own body and mind; you are under the misapprehension that your own mind, your own nature, is something real and enduring [while the external world is transitory]. Only when you sit straight and look into yourself, does it become clear that [you yourself are changing and] the objective world has a reality apart from you.

[The fullness of enlightenment]

Our attainment of enlightenment is something like the reflection of the moon in water. The moon does not get wet, nor is the water cleft apart. Though the light of the moon is vast and immense, it finds a home in water only a foot long and an inch wide. The whole moon and the whole sky find room enough in a single dewdrop, a single drop of water. And just as the moon does not cleave the water apart, so enlightenment does not tear man apart. Just as a dewdrop or drop of water offers no resistance to the moon in heaven, so man offers no obstacle to the full penetration of enlightenment. Height is always the measure of depth. [The higher the object, the deeper will seem its reflection in the water.]

When your body and mind are not yet filled with enlightenment, you may feel that you are enlightened enough. But when enlightenment fills your whole body and mind, then you may be aware that something is still lacking. It is like taking a boat out into a vast expanse of water. When you look in all directions, that expanse looks round all around and nothing more. But the ocean is not merely round or square; its virtues are truly inexhaustible, like the Dragon's palace with its innumerable reflecting jewels. Only as far as our eyesight can reach does the ocean appear to be round. It is the same with the real world; inside and out it has numerous features, but we can see only as far as our spiritual eyesight reaches. Once we learn the true features of the real world, it is more than round, more than square. Its virtues are illimitable, as is the vastness of the ocean and the immensity of the mountain. There are worlds on all four sides of us, and not on all sides only, but underneath as well and even in the little dewdrop.

Sitting and the Koan

In the pursuit of the Way [Buddhism] the prime essential is sitting (*zazen*). . . . By reflecting upon various "public-cases" (*koan*) and dialogues of the patriarchs, one may perhaps get the sense of them but it will only result in one's being led astray from the way of the Buddha, our founder. Just to pass the time in sitting straight, without any thought of acquisition, without any sense of achieving enlightenment—this is the way of the Founder. It is true that our predecessors recommended both the *koan* and sitting, but it was the sitting that they particularly insisted upon. There have been some who attained enlightenment through the test of the *koan,* but the true cause of their enlightenment was the merit and effectiveness of sitting. Truly the merit lies in the sitting.

The Importance of Sitting

When I stayed at the Zen lodge in T'ien-t'ung [China], the venerable Ching used to stay up sitting until the small hours of the morning and then after only a little rest would rise early to start sitting again. In the meditation hall he went on sitting with the other elders, without letting up for even a single night. Meanwhile many of the monks went off to sleep. The elder would go around among them and hit the sleepers with his fist or a slipper, yelling at them to wake up. If their sleepiness persisted, he would go out to the hallway and ring the bell to summon the monks to a room apart, where he would lecture to them by the light of a candle.

"What use is there in your assembling together in the hall only to go to sleep? Is this all that you left the world and joined holy orders for? Even among laymen, whether they be emperors, princes, or officials, are there any who live a life of ease? The ruler must fulfill the duties of the sovereign, his ministers must serve with loyalty and devotion, and commoners must work to reclaim land and till the soil—no one lives a life of ease. To escape from such burdens and idly while away the time in a monastery—what does this accomplish? Great is the problem of life and death; fleeting indeed is our transitory existence. Upon these truths both the scriptural and meditation schools agree. What sort of illness awaits us tonight, what sort of death tomorrow? While we have life, not to practice Buddha's Law but to spend the time in sleep is the height of foolishness. Because of such foolishness Buddhism today is in a state of decline. When it was at its zenith monks devoted themselves to the practice of sitting in meditation (*zazen*), but nowadays sitting is not generally insisted upon and consequently Buddhism is losing ground.". . .

Upon another occasion his attendants said to him, "The monks are getting overtired or falling ill, and some are thinking of leaving the monastery, all because they are required to sit too long in meditation. Shouldn't the length of the sitting period be shortened?" The master became highly indignant. "That would be quite wrong. A monk who is not really devoted to the religious life may very well fall asleep in a half hour or an hour. But one truly devoted to it who has resolved to persevere in his religious discipline will eventually come to enjoy the practice of sitting, no matter how long it lasts. When I was young I used to visit the heads of various monasteries, and one of them explained to me, 'Formerly I used to hit sleeping monks so hard that my fist just about broke. Now I am old and weak, so I can't hit them hard enough. Therefore it is difficult to produce good monks. In many monasteries today the superiors do not emphasize sitting strongly enough, and so Buddhism is declining. The more you hit them the better,' he advised me."

Body and Mind

Is the Way [of liberation] achieved through the mind or through the body? The doctrinal schools speak of the identity of mind and body, and so when they speak of attaining the Way through the body, they explain it in terms of this identity. Nevertheless this leaves one uncertain as to what "attainment by the body" truly means. From the point of view of our school, attainment of the Way is indeed achieved through the body as well as the mind. So long as one hopes to grasp the Truth only through the mind, one will not attain it even in a thousand existences or in eons of time. Only when one lets go of the mind and ceases to seek an intellectual apprehension of the Truth is liberation attainable. Enlightenment of the mind through the sense of sight and comprehension of the Truth through the sense of hearing are truly bodily attainments. To do away with mental deliberation and cognition, and simply to go on sitting, is the method by which the Way is made an intimate part of our lives. Thus attainment of the Way becomes truly attainment through the body. That is why I put exclusive emphasis upon sitting.

CHAPTER FIVE

Confucianism

Shinto and Buddhism are the major organized religions in Japan; the influence of Confucianism and religious Taoism have been more subtle and diffuse. Neither Confucianism nor Taoism has ever constituted a full religious organization with priests, scriptures, regular worship services, and other ecclesiastical aspects. In general, Confucianism entered the stream of social ethics and government rationale, whereas Taoism pervaded the realm of everyday religious observances such as astrology and fortunetelling. Some Japanese scholars and popular lecturers advocated Confucianism as a system of thought and code of ethics, occasionally in conjunction with other teachings (see p. 163). Most Japanese people, however, implicitly felt the Confucian rationale in their social conduct and in their support of the government.

Confucianism entered Japan on the tidal wave of Chinese culture and soon became a pillar of governmental order, as seen in Confucianism's support of the emperor (see p. 235). As time passed, Confucianism changed not only in terms of the transformation of Neo-Confucianism in China but also in terms of its relationship to Japanese circumstances. Especially in Tokugawa times Neo-Confucianism played a major role in providing the set of ideas, or ideology, that supported the rationale for the government. The role of Confucian or Neo-Confucian thought has varied from official governmental policy to the informal values supporting the family and education. It is ironic that in modern Japan Confucianism became a bulwark of Japanese nationalism and even an ideological tool for controlling Japan's colonial possessions.

22

Neo-Confucianism in Tokugawa Japan

Although Confucianism arrived in Japan very early, about the same time as Buddhism, this early form was mixed with other teachings and was less important than the dominant tradition of Buddhism. The form of Confucianism that later became influential in Japan was the new stream of Confucian thought developed in China, particularly by Chu Hsi (or Zhu Xi, 1130–1200), and studied within Zen Buddhist monasteries. By Tokugawa times Neo-Confucian thinkers moved beyond the boundaries of the monastery to advise rulers and spread popular teachings.

This selection surveys the course of Confucianism and Neo-Confucianism in Japan, cautioning us that Neo-Confucian scholars in Tokugawa times exaggerated both the role of Neo-Confucianism as an "orthodox" ideology and its tie with the government. Nevertheless, interest in Neo-Confucian thought was widespread in Tokugawa Japan because Confucianism afforded solutions to the problems facing the shogunal governments throughout the Tokugawa period.

NEO-CONFUCIANISM AND
TOKUGAWA DISCOURSE

Peter Nosco

The intellectual history of the Tokugawa period has been intimately identified from start to finish with the orthodox Neo-Confucian mode of thought, by which I mean the thought of the philosopher Chu Hsi (1130–1200) in China and of those later followers and interpreters in China, Korea, and Japan who regarded themselves as part of an elaborate and complex intellectual lineage which they traced directly to the master. . . . [This essay] is concerned as much with the broad range of responses and reactions to Neo-Confucianism in the Tokugawa era, and what might arguably be regarded as responses to those very responses, as it is with Tokugawa Neo-Confucianism per se. This question of the relationship between Neo-Confucianism and Tokugawa discourse is by no means a simple one, and just as the work of recent decades has served to refine our understanding of Neo-Confucianism and Tokugawa thought, [recent essays] challenge numerous commonly held assumptions on the subject, calling attention to responses to Neo-Confucianism in heretofore uncharted regions of the vast map of Tokugawa thought. . . .

Reprinted by permission of the publisher from Peter Nosco, "Introduction: Neo-Confucianism and Tokugawa Discourse," in *Confucianism and Tokugawa Culture*, edited by Peter Nosco (Princeton: Princeton University Press, 1984). The notes and most of the Chinese and Japanese terms have been deleted.

Early Japanese chronicles state that Confucianism was introduced to Japan in A.D. 285 during the reign of Emperor Ojin when Wani of Paekche brought copies from his native Korea of the *Analects* of Confucius and the *Thousand Character Classic,* a Confucian primer. Though the actual date of this event may have been a century or more later, it is equally likely that Confucian teachings were known by at least some of those immigrants from the continent who were reaching Japanese shores in increasing numbers at this time. The Confucianism to which the Japanese were first exposed already represented more than the humble, ethical teachings of Confucius and his followers. Over the centuries, those teachings had been overlaid and, to a certain extent, obscured by a complex set of correlative doctrines that combined to form an entire cosmology and were drawn from the Taoist and Yin-yang schools that had influenced ethico-religious practice in China. However, for a variety of reasons Confucianism was eclipsed both in China and Japan by the doctrines of Buddhism which, particularly in Japan, were linked first to an aestheticism that enchanted courtly circles and later to a popular appeal that captured the faith of a broad audience.

Confucianism appears to have left its mark on Japanese society with its concern for hierarchical relationships and its emphasis on harmony within the home as the basis for harmony in the state, but equally plausible is the argument that in most instances Confucianism merely reinforced and justified social practices that had their antecedents in the pre-Confucian era. Prior to the Tokugawa, most Japanese were attracted more to the superstitious overlays of Confucian rites and practices than to the philosophical and ethical nucleus. Chinese diviners were thus routinely consulted over such matters as building homes, selecting auspicious dates for travel or marriage and other similar activities, but Confucian advice on how to run the state or on how to regulate the affairs of man was largely ignored.

Aware of similar tendencies in China, and concerned over the relative strength of Buddhism, Chu Hsi transformed Confucianism and reinvigorated it as an intellectual discipline. He rejected the exegetical practices of his predecessors in the T'ang (618–907) dynasty and stressed the importance of studying the Way of the Sages as expressed in the Four Books: the *Analects,* the *Mencius,* the *Great Learning,* and the *Mean.* In order to structure his thought, he developed a qualified monistic ontology that interpreted reality in terms of a singular natural principle; and in order to guide the individual he counseled the methods of first the investigation of things, by which he meant the contemplation of one's physical environment with the aim of understanding the role of principle in it, and second the exercise of seriousness and reverence.

The joy of the Chu Hsi mode of thought was that it was both scholarly and spiritual: while it emphasized the quasi-scientific examination of the external world, it nonetheless provided for the development of the individual mind, recognizing the spiritual dimensions of such development. In this latter respect, Chu Hsi drew fruitfully from the teachings of Ch'an (Zen) Buddhism, but by transforming both the ends and the means, he made of it a genuinely Confucian doctrine. Regrettably, Chu Hsi's emphasis on seriousness at times lapsed, at the hands of his successors, into a humorless and dour tone far removed from those expectations that had inspired Neo-Confucianism in its earliest stages.

The Chu Hsi mode of thought was introduced to Japan in the early thirteenth century, perhaps as early as 1200, the year of Chu Hsi's death. For the most part, the philosophy was institutionally housed for nearly four centuries within Zen monasteries where it was regarded as a stimulating mental exercise that if properly directed, might point one toward the same truths as Zen. During these centuries, Zen enjoyed the patronage of the succession of military elites who ruled Japan, and since there were numerous similarities between the two modes of thought, Zen advocates were quick to assert that such Chu Hsi contemplative practices as "holding fast to seriousness and sitting quietly" were less developed stages of what they knew as "sitting in meditation" *(zazen)*.

Chu Hsi's philosophy enjoyed a brief period of favor at the imperial court in the early fourteenth century during the reigns of Emperors Hanazono (r. 1308–1318) and Godaigo (r. 1318–1339), and emperors and shoguns alike summoned scholars to lecture on Confucian topics at intervals throughout the medieval period. Several thousand students, many of them Zen monks, attended the nonecclesiastical Ashikaga Academy where they studied a Neo-Confucian curriculum. Nonetheless, Neo-Confucianism did not achieve independent status during these centuries and remained in the shadow of its Buddhist patron. However, since the Chu Hsi philosophy originally arose as a rational alternative to Buddhism, the possibility of a rupture between these two modes of thought always existed, and it was out of that rupture that the Chu Hsi philosophy came into its own in Japan. The rupture began with the introduction of texts representative of new developments within Neo-Confucianism which the Japanese obtained during their invasion of Korea in the 1590s, and it was more or less complete by the time the first Tokugawa shogun, Tokugawa Ieyasu (1542–1616), appointed the leading Chu Hsi advocate to his retinue in 1605.

The rapidity with which the major themes of medieval Japanese discourse are replaced by the new themes of Tokugawa discourse is impressive; yet one must acknowledge that the transformation is no less rapid or striking than the concurrent political transformation. During the space of little more than half a century, the Japanese polity was transformed through the efforts of three great empire builders—Oda Nobunaga (1534–1582), Toyotomi Hideyoshi (1536–1598), and Tokugawa Ieyasu—from a loose confederation of semiautonomous fiefdoms into the more centralized feudal system that distinguishes the Tokugawa as Japan's early-modern state. Where the predominant concerns of the medieval period had dealt with such Buddhist themes as human suffering in the world, and the quest for personal salvation or enlightenment, the discourse of the Tokugawa was concerned more with the achievement and maintenance of a stable and harmonious society, placing the responsibility for maintaining that delicate equilibrium at the heart of both man and the cosmos squarely on the shoulders of man. Seventeenth-century discourse was characterized by the presence of a well-developed humanistic political discourse absent in the thought of the sixteenth century, and this discourse drew fruitfully from the assumptions and vocabulary of Neo-Confucianism for its descriptions of man and his society.

Our understanding of the nature of this transformation has changed as a result of recent research. Where it had once been assumed that the Neo-Confucianism present in early-seventeenth-century Japan was virtually identical to the original formulation of Chu Hsi, it is now understood that the pioneers of Neo-Confucian thought in Tokugawa Japan drew as much from Yi dynasty (1392–1909) Korean interpretations and Ming dynasty (1368–1644) Chinese interpretations of the Chu Hsi orthodoxy as they did from the original teachings of Chu Hsi; and where it had once been thought that Neo-Confucianism enjoyed a near-hegemonic role in the formulation of this new discourse, Herman Ooms makes [it] apparent . . . that Neo-Confucianism was just one, though still a most important, ingredient in it.

Neo-Confucianism appears at the very start of the Tokugawa era as one of several modes of thought which are of use to the bakufu for its political purposes. While its long incubation during the medieval period did not result in the appearance of any Japanese Neo-Confucians of stature, the interval was sufficient for the thought to prepare for its larger role. Thanks to the official recognition that Neo-Confucianism would receive during the first Tokugawa century, however qualified that recognition may have been, Neo-Confucian thought would rapidly gain broader acceptance in Japanese society and culture, both politically and intellectually. This is hardly surprising in view of the fact that Confucianism had traditionally been directed toward precisely those issues which were now of immediate concern at all levels of Tokugawa society. Nonetheless, no single intellectual tradition would be privileged in Tokugawa Japan with exclusive government support, as had been and remained the case in China.

What is perhaps surprising is the extent to which Neo-Confucianism appears in tandem with Shinto and Buddhist elements in the new discourse. As Herman Ooms suggests, . . . the Tokugawa bakufu was never at a loss for ideologues prepared to propagate affirmative teachings on man and society. Where Neo-Confucianism was prepared to provide arguments constructed from principles linking the terrestrial order to the cosmic, traditional Shinto, particularly its Yoshida denomination, was equipped to provide that element of mythification so useful in obfuscating the historical wellsprings of Tokugawa power.

In the Buddhist camp as well, one finds articulate spokesmen who, while not directly under the influence of Confucian thought, nonetheless addressed those same concerns of social order and ethical life toward which Neo-Confucianism had been directed. Such attempts on the part of leading Buddhists to assert that Buddhism might service the nation's interests were, of course, nothing new in the Japanese tradition, but the terms of the argument were different. Where Buddhism in past centuries had sought to expand its social and political role, in the Tokugawa it would seek to preserve its hard-won gains against new and more formidable challenges. . . .

Of course, Neo-Confucianism was well equipped to contribute to the legitimizing function of the new discourse. Confucianism had traditionally served this function in China, but Japanese elites had long been accustomed to justifying their status more on the grounds of pedigree and precedent than merit or humanity. Yet once the validity of Neo-Confucian assumptions was acknowledged in the early Tokugawa, there arose the problem of reconciling Neo-Confucian norms with Japanese reality. . . . For example, in a Confucian-inspired history of Japan, Hayashi Razan's (1583–1657) son, Hayashi Gaho (1618–1680), cast Tokugawa Ieyasu in the classic guise of the newly anointed recipient of the mandate of heaven, equipping him both morally and spiritually for the task of humane rulership. However, the obverse side of this issue—that heaven might withdraw its mandate from an inhumane regime—was of necessity skirted by all Tokugawa Confucian thinkers until the very last years of the Tokugawa.

Likewise, Chu Hsi's notion of the Way of the ruler, the Way of the minister, the Way of the parent, the Way of the child, and so on, divided the social system into constituent functions in such a way as to affirm the enduring stability and continuity of the status quo. This highly segmented way of interpreting society reappears in several guises in Tokugawa thought and may also be an indication of Neo-Confucianism's success in Tokugawa Japan. It was, after all, what Toyotomi Hideyoshi had attempted to do through legislation by disarming the peasants, removing samurai from villages, and "freezing" all individuals and their descendants into component, class-defined functions. Nonetheless, the economic realities of Tokugawa Japan propelled the (in Confucian eyes) despised merchant class into a position with considerable social leverage.

What is clear, however, is that Neo-Confucianism alone did not service these legitimizing functions for the Tokugawa bakufu, nor did it function with the degree of official orthodoxy that has heretofore been assumed of it. Whence, then, this concern with orthodoxy? Not surprisingly, the concern would appear to have originated among those who stood most directly to benefit from the official endorsement of their thought. For example, . . . it was the descendants of Hayashi Razan who skillfully fabricated the impression of a monopolistic orthodoxy allegedly enjoyed by the premier Tokugawa Neo-Confucian, Hayashi Razan. . . . It was not until the mid-seventeenth century that the issue of orthodoxy itself arose, and it may not have been until precisely this time that Neo-Confucianism began to enjoy a degree of acceptance that can be said even to approximate its status as orthodoxy in China. Yet, by this time, responses to Neo-Confucianism were already incipient, confirming the extraordinary degree of pluralism and intellectual diversity that characterized late-seventeenth-century thought in Japan. As Maruyama Masao observed in making something of a correction to his earlier thesis, "The diffusion of Neo-Confucianism as an ideology and the School of Ancient Learning's challenge to it developed almost contemporaneously. Moreover, if one asks not just about *scholarly* Confucianism but about the basic thought categories of Confucianism that constituted the *Aspektstruktur* of Tokugawa society, then one can argue that they tenaciously retained a currency until the very last instant of the Tokugawa regime."

It is remarkable how quickly, deeply, and widely interest in Neo-Confucianism spread in Tokugawa Japan. The Japanese, like the Koreans some centuries earlier, appear to have taken Confucian thought seriously, almost passionately, and even if the degree of official interest in Neo-Confucianism may have been exaggerated, it would appear likely that the bakufu's interest in Confucian thought, and the attendant prestige which such interest bestowed, contributed to the currency of Confucian thought in Japan. Confucianism was, after all, able to provide answers to the differing questions of various shogunal governments from the start of the Tokugawa period until its end.

23
Neo-Confucian "Orthodoxy" and Hayashi Razan

Confucianism is one of the significant Chinese contributions to Japanese culture (and to a number of other Asian cultures). In the history of cultural exchange, however, it is seldom the case that what is borrowed is the same as that which is lent; Confucianism in China is not the same as Confucianism in Japan (or in other countries). The present selection, while acknowledging the major role of Confucianism (especially Neo-Confucianism) in Tokugawa Japan, attempts to remove misconceptions that exaggerate and distort its actual function, and to place it within its historical and cultural context.

Although in China Neo-Confucianism did constitute a kind of "orthodoxy" supported by the state, in Japan there was no comparable state-supported orthodoxy (although some Neo-Confucian scholars have advanced this notion). Nor was the Neo-Confucianism of Tokugawa times a "monolithic body of thought." Rather, there were various influences upon this tradition as it came to Japan. While Neo-Confucianism played its role in shaping Tokugawa political thought, it had to share this role with both Shinto and Buddhism. The author focuses on the life and thought of the Neo-Confucian scholar Hayashi Razan, whose writings are excerpted in the next selection.

NEO-CONFUCIAN ORTHODOXY
AND THE HAYASHI HOUSE

Herman Ooms

. . . For a very long time it has been assumed that early Tokugawa political thought was simply a transplant of a monolithic body of thought from (Sung) China, that it was thus identical to early Neo-Confucianism. This view overlooked, however, developments in Neo-Confucianism between the Sung and the late Ming periods. . . . Variety and pluralism characterized Japanese Neo-Confucianism from the beginning: scholars chose from among a number of Ming Chinese and Korean interpretations. This revision has recently been incorporated into the writings of a group of American scholars. . . . In concluding that early Tokugawa Neo-Confucianism was not monolithic, these scholars, working from the vast Chinese perspective, quite naturally also tend to emphasize continuities along lines found in the Chinese and Korean experience.

The accuracy of this analysis in its general lines and as it pertains to Neo-Confucianism is beyond dispute. Since the writing of history, however, is a matter of perspective, it is also understandable that this analysis cannot give due weight to the question of early Tokugawa ideology, that is, to the conversion of thought constructs into a servicable ideology. Moreover, since most research on early Tokugawa thought . . . has concentrated on Neo-Confucianism, the impression has been created that political thought at that period comprised only Neo-Confucianism.

This research, since it did not focus sufficiently on the process by which an ideology is put into place, has also tended to assume too readily that Neo-Confucianism occupied in Japan a position although not precisely identical but nevertheless closely analogous to the one it held in China as an officially sponsored "state" ideology. This assumption ignores the fact that in Japan, as elsewhere—including China—orthodoxies are always established through political struggles: a discourse on power that achieves the status of orthodoxy is itself a successful exercise in power.

The analysis that follows indicates that Hayashi Razan was primarily responsible for making all later generations believe that political thought in early Tokugawa Japan was Neo-Confucian, and that the bakufu was its active sponsor. In order to understand how this projection of orthodoxy served Hayashi interests, it is necessary to review briefly Razan's career and examine the position he sought to secure within the bakufu.

At age fourteen Razan, the son of a ronin family, left Kenninji, a Zen temple in Kyoto that he had joined two years earlier and where he otherwise would soon have been ordained. In 1605, at age twenty-two, he entered

Reprinted by permission of the publisher from Herman Ooms, *Tokugawa Ideology* (Princeton: Princeton University Press, 1985). The notes have been deleted.

Ieyasu's service, not as a Confucian scholar or Buddhist priest but as an exceptionally learned young man who impressed his interviewers with his broad knowledge of Chinese scholarship; a knowledge which he had picked up from a number of teachers and from any book that he could get his hands on.

At Kenninji, Razan studied under scholars who belonged to the Kiyohara tradition, since Heian times one of the few houses that studied Confucianism. In more recent times, this house used a mixture of traditional Confucian and Neo-Confucian texts. Through one of his former teachers he made ambitious but fruitless attempts to become a disciple of Kiyohara Hidekata, one of the most famous official court scholars. Razan, no doubt, believed that Hidekata, whose functions brought him in contact with Ieyasu, Toyotomi Hideyori, the kanpaku, and the emperor, could provide him with the right connections to start his career. Razan failed, however, and instead sought introductions to Fujiwara Seika, who accepted him as his disciple in 1604.

Razan was employed by the bakufu from 1605 until his death in 1657—fifty-two years—during which he outlived the first three shoguns as well as his great rivals in the bakufu bureaucracy, the monks Suden and Tenkai. When Tenkai died at age one hundred seven in 1643, Razan replaced him as policy advisor. Razan's career was not that of a Confucian scholar. Rather he used his career to establish himself as one, notwithstanding the fact that in 1607 Ieyasu ordered him to shave his head and adopt a monk's name. . . .

During the Ieyasu and Hidetada years, Razan must have been a frustrated functionary, an ambitious clerk/librarian whose talents were rarely called upon for lecturing, and whose future as either a scholar or a bureaucrat was not very bright. In 1610–1611 he was allowed to draft some official documents related to foreign trade and also the three-point loyalty oath Ieyasu exacted from the daimyo, but from then on until Iemitsu's succession, his duties seem to have been insignificant. In 1611 he complained to Seika that he felt like a fraud. He was not allowed to teach, he wrote, what Seika had prepared him for (the Chinese classics), but instead received assignments on works such as the *Azuma kagami* (a history of the Kamakura bakufu); and yet he could not change his situation because he had to support his parents and felt obliged to his friends. . . .

In 1614, Razan requested Ieyasu's support to open a school in Kyoto, where he intended to put up Seika as a teacher, but this plan to enhance his scholarly position failed. Ieyasu, busy with preparations for his Osaka campaign, had no time to pay attention to Razan's wishes. Moreover, Ieyasu seems to have lacked a basic interest in matters of great concern to Razan. Ieyasu certainly did not take either to Razan's virulent anti-Buddhism or to his love of Neo-Confucianism. Among the many books that were printed under Ieyasu's patronage—printing presses had just been introduced to Japan—there were a number of works on Buddhism, military science, history, or traditional Confucianism (only two), but not a single one on Neo-Confucianism. . . .

In 1630, one of Razan's dreams came true. Iemitsu granted him, probably as a gesture of gratitude for twenty-five years of service to the bakufu, a plot of land on which to build a school. This grant, however, did not signify bakufu sponsorship of Neo-Confucianism as its official ideology. The bakufu did not even finance the school's Confucian temple (built in 1632), which was a gift from the lord of Owari, who had a similar temple in his own domain in Nagoya. The following year the first Confucian ceremony took place (without a bakufu delegation). . . .

It is clear that the Hayashi College, located in the vicinity of the shogunal palace grounds, was of no importance whatsoever to the bakufu. Yet when scholars discuss Tokugawa ideology, they always mention Neo-Confucianism and the Hayashi College as proof of the bakufu's concern with these matters. They overlook the frequent shogunal visits to the remote mountain place of Nikko, the astonishing outlay of funds for the building of Ieyasu's mausoleum there, and the building of Kan'eiji, the center of the Ieyasu cult in Edo. It seems that scholars have seen what Hayshi Razan wanted them to see and ignored what he wanted them to ignore.

In 1644, Razan was empowered to decide on a change of era names, a function that until then had been the prerogative of traditional Confucian court scholars . . . ; he also started work that year on a compilation of Japanese history. His first task as a Neo-Confucian scholar to the bakufu came only in 1656, one year before his death, when he lectured on the *Great Learning* to the fifteen-year-old Ietsuna.

The trajectory of Razan's career indicates that Neo-Confucianism was never perceived by the early Tokugawa shoguns as a tradition deserving specific support. Neo-Confucianism, in the first half century of Tokugawa rule, cannot in any responsible way be spoken of as an officially espoused "state ideology" or orthodoxy, no matter how one qualifies the term. Razan, often portrayed as the bakufu's ideologue, functioned more as the sacristan than as the theologian of the system. . . . Consisting mainly of private notes or occasional compositions, Razan's writings never reached a wide audience during his own lifetime. The bulk of his writings was not printed until after his death, when Razan's two sons published his complete works. To conclude from this, however, that Neo-Confucian teachings were not being studied or taught would be erroneous. They were—but not with bakufu support.

Indeed, toward the end of Razan's life, and in the years following his death, the Hayashi house had to deal with serious competitors in the field of Chinese learning. By that time other scholars, like Kumazawa Banzan and Yamaga Soko, had not only made names for themselves; they also were better paid than Razan. . . . Moreover, just before Iemitsu died, he seems to have been on the verge of inviting Banzan and Soko into the bakufu. . . .

It was in the 1650s and 1660s that "orthodoxy" became important. The issue, however, was created not by the bakufu but by the Hayashi scholars, who saw their opportunity to become purveyors of official teachings—a position they had long coveted—threatened by others. Their aim and motivation was not to promote correct knowledge, but to secure the power to produce official knowledge.

Ultimately, the Hayashi house had great responsibility for creating the emblematic links between Ieyasu, the bakufu, Seika, Neo-Confucianism, and

Razan. The Hayashi helped establish the fiction of a Neo-Confucian, bakufu-supported orthodoxy, which not only informed the text of Matsudaira Sadanobu's Ban on Heterodoxy in 1790, but still dominates much of today's scholarship. They, and not the bakufu leadership, were eager to have Neo-Confucianism clearly marked as a separate tradition under their own aegis. . . .

The use of orthodoxy as political leverage did not mean, even for these few men, exclusive reliance on Neo-Confucianism. Although most learned men of the time had reservations of various degrees of intensity about Buddhism, many did appropriate Shinto teachings into their political thinking, as did the supporters of orthodoxy.

24
Hayashi Razan: Neo-Confucianism in Support of the Government and the Social Order

This selection is taken from the writings of Hayashi Razan (1583–1657), a major architect of Neo-Confucian thought and much of government policy during Tokugawa times. The major point of the first excerpt is to justify the authority of the Tokugawa government and the social order dictated by it. The strategy in Razan's writing is to establish the cosmic pattern of the "natural order and social order," and then to show that the Tokugawa government and social classes are in conformity with this cosmic order. Therefore, humans should conform to political rule and to set social relationships.

Razan first recognizes the cosmic Principle and the Supreme Ultimate behind it. When set into motion, the Supreme Ultimate created *yang* and *yin,* the Five Elements (wood, fire, earth, metal, and water), and eventually humans. Having grounded all of life in a cosmic pattern of "the work of heaven and earth," Razan argues that the Five Constant Virtues—human-heartedness, righteousness, propriety, wisdom, and good faith—"are given by heaven," and that the Confucian "five relationships" between humans are the "supreme way" continuing from ancient times. The conclusion to this chain of reasoning is that there is a hierarchical pattern to the universe—"Heaven is above and earth is below"—thus it is natural that there is a hierarchical pattern to human relationships. The most important human relationship is between ruler and subject, but the entire social order of the four classes and the five relationships is determined by this hierarchical pattern.

In the second excerpt Razan argues that the Principle is the same for Shinto and Confucianism, but its application is different. He states that Shinto and Confucianism must unite against the doctrine of Buddhism in establishing a stable government and society.

RULING AND LIVING IN CONFORMITY
WITH THE ORDER OF HEAVEN AND EARTH

Hayashi Razan
David John Lu, translator

Natural Order and Social Order

The Principle (*ri,* or in Chinese *li*) which existed constantly before and after heaven and earth came into being is called the Supreme Ultimate. When this Supreme Ultimate was in motion, it created the *yang,* and when it was quiescent, it created the *yin.* The *yin* and *yang* were originally of the same substance but were divided into two complementary forces.[1] They were further divided into the Five Elements which are wood, fire, earth, metal and water. When the Five Elements were further divided, they became all things under heaven. When these Five Elements were brought together to take shapes, people were also born.

All creatures existing between heaven and earth were shaped by the Five Elements. However, because of the difference in the Ether, there emerged plants, animals and men. . . .

A concrete object comes into being because of the work of heaven and earth. All creatures, plants, animals and inanimate objects owe their existence to the will of heaven and earth. Thus not a single object lacks within it the principles of heaven. . . .

Therefore the Five Constant Virtues of human-heartedness, righteousness, propriety, wisdom, and good faith are given by heaven and exist on account of the principles of heaven. . . .

The five relationships governing the ruler and the subject, father and son, husband and wife, older brother and younger brother, and friend and friend have been in existence from olden days to the present time. There has been no change in these basic relations, and they are thus called the supreme way. In judging the worth of a person, one needs only to use these five relationships as the criteria, and teachings which try to implement the ideals of these five relationships are those of the sage and of the wise men. . . .

Heaven is above and earth is below. This is the order of heaven and earth. If we can understand the meaning of the order existing between heaven and earth, we can also perceive that in everything there is an order separating those who are above and those who are below. When we extend this understanding between heaven and earth, we cannot allow disorder in the relations between

Reprinted by permission of the publisher from David John Lu, *Sources of Japanese History,* vol. I (New York: McGraw Hill, 1974). The notes and most of the Chinese and Japanese terms have been deleted.

1. Here Razan is commenting on the cosmological significance of *yin* and *yang;* for a reference to *yin* and *yang* in a social setting see pp. 32–34.—ED.

the ruler and the subject, and between those who are above and those who are below. The separation into four classes of samurai, farmers, artisans and merchants, like the five relationships, is part of the principles of heaven and is the Way which was taught by the Sage (Confucius). . . .

To know the way of heaven is to respect heaven and to secure humble submission from earth, for heaven is high above and earth is low below. There is a differentiation between the above and the below. Likewise among the people, rulers are to be respected and subjects are to submit humbly. Only when this differentiation between those who are above and those who are below is made clear, can there be law and propriety. In this way, people's minds can be satisfied. . . . The more the rulers are respected, and the more the subjects submit humbly, and the more the differentiation is made clear-cut, the easier it is to govern a country. Among the rulers, there are the Emperor, the *shogun,* and the *daimyo,* and even among them there is also differentiation. . . .

On the Unity of Shinto and Confucianism

Our country is the country of gods. Shinto is the same as the Way of the King. However, the rise of Buddhism made the people abandon the Way of the King and Shinto. Someone may ask how Shinto and Confucianism can be differentiated. I respond by saying that according to my observation the Principle (*ri*) is the same, but only its application differs. . . .

In comparing the books on the age of gods in the *Nihonshoki* (Chronicles of Japan) with Master Chou's (Chou Tun-yi, 1017–1073) *T'ai-chi T'ushuo* (Diagram of the Supreme Ultimate Explained), I have yet to find any discrepancy in substantive matters. The Way of the King transforms itself into Shinto and Shinto transforms itself into the Way. What I mean by the term "Way" is the Way of Confucianism, and it is not the so-called alien doctrine. The alien doctrine is Buddhism.

25
Confucianism and Nationalism in Modern Japan

Confucianism is a great achievement of Chinese culture and a positive contribution to the countries that received Chinese influence. Like other great philosophical and religious systems, however, it has also come to be used as an ideological tool to reinforce questionable programs. In modern Japan, Confucianism was one of several means used to support nationalism and militarism.

The Confucian notions of social harmony and respect for one's superiors were translated to mean that the Japanese people should unite in unquestioning loyalty to the political state and its aims. Following the ideal of social harmony would eliminate problems between management and labor, problems thought to be caused by the poisoning influence of Western individualism. In early Japan, Confucianism had reinforced the status of the emperor, and in modern times, the Confucian notion of loyalty was used to stimulate absolute loyalty to the state through the symbol of the emperor. As can be seen on page 236, this ideal was promoted through the educational system.

The present selection describes how Confucianism became a popular rationale for fanatical support of nationalism, militarism, and patriotism. Some people became convinced by this brand of Confucianism that Japan's problems were due to the introduction of Western culture, which had weakened Japan's distinctive heritage. The solution was to reject Western culture and to reaffirm Oriental culture—meaning Confucianism and absolute loyalty to the state. As a system of social philosophy, Confucianism usually emphasized filial piety to one's parents and continuing the family line. In this context, both the monastic life of Buddhism and loss of life in military service were contrary to Confucian philosophy because they disrupted family order. In the nationalistic context, though, the soldier's sacrifice of his life during combat was seen as the supreme expression of Confucianism, since absolute loyalty was now interpreted as owed to the state, rather than to the family.

It is one of the curious ironies of history that Confucianism was invoked to bolster fanatical militarism and patriotism against China, the birthplace of Confucius and Confucianism, a fact that should remind us that Confucianism was not responsible for Japanese nationalism, in the sense that it created something that was not already there. At the same time, we can see why Confucianism in modern Japan tended to support the status quo, even when that status quo was questionable. Confucianism entered the religious life of the people, providing a bridge between the hazy areas of national identity and religious commitment, and although it is easy for us to see the inherent weakness of this bridge, the same problem of how to build nationalism faces every modern country. (Compare also Chapter 15.)

THE NATIONALISATION OF CONFUCIANISM IN JAPAN

Warren W. Smith, Jr.

After 1933, the trends apparent in the development of Confucianism in Japan from 1918 to 1933 became accelerated, but the most prominent of these was the growing identification of Confucianism with the Japanese spirit, the Imperial way, and the Japanese *kokutai* (national polity). The term "Japanese spirit" in particular became a favorite after 1933 for speakers who wished to contrast Japanese civilization and ideals with those of the rest of the world. Often this was done in order to justify the motives of Japanese expansion, for it was claimed that Japan had a mission to perform in protecting and develop-

Reprinted by permission of the author and publisher from Warren W. Smith, Jr., *Confucianism in Modern Japan: A Study of Conservatism in Japanese Intellectual History* (Tokyo: The Hokuseido Press, 1959).

ing spiritual civilization in Asia which was threatened by the egoistical and materialistic culture of the West.

Ever since the Imperial Restoration in 1868, individual Confucianists and Confucian organizations had insisted on the dichotomy between the spiritual civilization of the East and the material civilization of the West. The latter was invariably felt to be inferior, and this point of view followed logically from the premises of Confucian philosophy in which man was considered to have a fundamental moral nature whose development constituted the primary aim of civilization.

Similar in this respect to Catholic philosophy in the West, Confucianism claimed that when preoccupation with material life led man to forget his moral nature, he was no longer fulfilling the purpose of his existence.[1] Closely related to this was the Confucian attitude towards Marxism as basically a product of the materialistic emphasis in the West. . . .

. . . From the isolated statements on Confucianism found in popular literature and educational books during the period from 1934 to 1945, it is clear that Confucianism came to have a valuable appeal in the ideological program of Japanese nationalists.

The rise of one new and apparently influential Confucian organization during this period needs to be mentioned, for statements by its members and interested individuals indicate how Confucian attitudes towards spiritual culture could serve to bolster the Japanese spirit.

The founding ceremonies of the Nippon Jukyo Senyokai (Japanese Society for the Promotion of Confucianism) were held in Tokyo on January 27, 1934 at the Tokyo Kaikan. About seven hundred people participated, including the Prime Minister, Saito Makoto, the Home Affairs Minister, Yamamoto Tatsuo, the Minister of Education, Hatoyama Ichiro, the head of the House of Peers, Prince Konoe Fumimaro, and the head of the Lower House, Akita Kiyoshi.

These men all made congratulatory statements in which they spoke of the value of Confucianism for stabilizing the people's thoughts and restoring traditional morality from the excess of Western materialism. But most significant of all was the address by Kato Masanosuke (b. 1854).

Kato, an influential politician and member of the House of Peers, was head of the Daito Bunka Gakuin (Academy of Oriental Culture). This was a cultural and educational institution formed in 1923 as a part of the Daito Bunka Kyokai (Society of Oriental Culture) for the purpose of combating dangerous

---

1. Among the many passages in the Confucian classics which display this is one by Mencius:

The Minister of Agriculture taught the people to sow and reap, cultivating the five grains. When the five grains were brought to maturity, the people all obtained a subsistence. But men possess a moral nature; and if they are well-fed, warmly clad, and comfortably lodged, without being taught at the same time, they become almost like the beasts. This was a subject of anxious solicitude to the sage Shun, and he appointed Hsieh to be the minister of Instruction to teach the relations of humanity. James Legge, *The Confucian Classics*, second edition, revised (Oxford: Clarendon Press, 1895), II, 251.

thoughts and strengthening Japanese civilization. The Daito Bunka Gakuin had for over ten years supported Confucianism as part of its own program of reviving the Japanese spirit. Kato and others had finally felt that in view of the times, it was necessary actively to spread Confucian ideas in society, and therefore they had organized the Nippon Jukyo Senyokai.

With this as a background, Kato's opening address takes on importance as representing the aims and attitudes of the new organization. He spoke in a particularly disparaging way of the materialistic civilization of the West and blamed it for many of Japan's ills.

> In the short space of forty or fifty years, threatened by the people of Europe and America, we realized great [material] progress which, needless to say, was felicitous for the nation. But what I feel is most deplorable is that together with the advance of material culture, every type of evil that should have been avoided was introduced. This was so-called individualism and utilitarianism. The result of revering individualism was that our traditional national principles were relegated to a secondary place; and the result of being infatuated with utilitarianism was that fame and profit occupied the foremost position, while justice and humanity were discarded. Without reflection, we have amplified the mad condition in which we have nothing but fame and profit in mind.
>
> Capitalists exploiting the flesh and blood of laborers while laborers unite and strike in opposition; landlords and tenants each wishing their own harvest to be large, with tenant disputes arising constantly; politicians taking advantage of their positions and yearning for unfair profits; the problem of the sale of doctor's degrees at the Nagasaki Medical College; the problem of the buying and selling of Tokyo school principalships; and the problem of Communist influence at Kyoto University and Nagano elementary school; all these are the poison of following material culture.

Kato then asked his audience to consider how the Emperor Meiji had dealt with a similar situation when materialism was sweeping Japan in 1886. He had published the *Seiyuki,* and ordered the creation of a special course in Japanese and Chinese studies at Tokyo Imperial University. Kato felt that the Nippon Jukyo Senyokai in 1934 could play a similar role in strengthening the spiritual culture of Japan, and copies of the *Seiyuki* were distributed to everyone in the audience. The address ended with Kato asserting that any help given to advance the aims of the Nippon Jukyo Senyokai would be felicitous for Japan.

Many letters of congratulation and encouragement poured into the offices of the Nippon Jukyo Senyokai, and typical of the kind of messages sent was one by Major General Horiuchi Bunjiro entitled "Confucianism and Chinese studies, a great critical problem."

General Horiuchi said that Confucianism was the basis of Oriental spiritual culture, which had no equivalent in Western material culture. At the present time, however, Confucianism existed primarily only in Japan, where it was most prominently displayed in the virtues of loyalty and filial piety. The examples of bravery by war heroes such as Commander Hirose Takeo (1868–1905) in the Russo-Japanese war and the Bakudan Sanyushi[2] in the fighting around Shanghai in 1932 were the result of loyalty and filial piety.

To appreciate Confucianism, though, one had to master *kangaku* (Chinese studies) which had been used to express the Japanese spirit. Therefore *kangaku* was really a Japanese thing, and General Horiuchi felt it might more accurately be termed *Nihongaku* (Japanese studies). In any case, a study of Confucianism was especially needed in Japan in order to help her carry out her mission of cooperating with and guiding China and Manchuria. Japan had the great task of making a peaceful Orient, and the strength of Confucianism and Chinese studies could be re-exported to China for this purpose. This of course meant that in general, English would be unnecessary, and General Horiuchi hoped the Prime Minister and educational authorities would consider this basic problem.

2. The Bakudan Sanyushi were three Japanese soldiers who acted as human torpedoes in storming a Chinese position during the fighting between the Chinese and Japanese at Shanghai in February, 1932. They carried a torpedo into a Chinese barbed-wire entanglement and blew themselves up in accomplishing their mission. This heroic deed had a great effect on Japanese public opinion. For a description of the incident and its repercussions in Japan, see A. Morgan Young, *Imperial Japan, 1926–38,* (London: George Allen and Unwin Ltd., 1938), 141–142.

CHAPTER SIX

Religious Taoism

Taoism in Japan is similar to Confucianism in that it was part of the dominant Chinese influence on Japanese culture, but never enjoyed the status of an organized religion. Taoism's actual influence in Japan is even more difficult to trace than Confucianism's, because the latter had a more obvious identity in the *Analects* of Confucius and in other Confucian (and Neo-Confucian) writings so influential on political and social systems. By contrast, Taoist writings such as the *Tao te ching* were important in Japan, but they did not come to form a clearly identifiable body of materials or become the basis for a major school of thought.

What is known as Taoism or "religious Taoism" in Japan is a more nebulous set of Chinese beliefs, symbols, and practices that includes but is not limited to "Taoism" as known in China. Various Chinese notions and practices, especially those associated with the calendar, astrology, and divination, became so much a part of Japanese culture and religion that most Japanese people long ago forgot their Chinese origins. The Chinese calendar was adopted in early Japan and soon was taken for granted in planning festivals and regulating personal life. (For example, see the astrological advice of a medieval writer on p. 158.) In ancient times the Onmyoryo, literally the bureau of *yin-yang* (or bureau of divination), conducted divination for the court based on Chinese notions of astrology and the interaction of *yin* and *yang;* from medieval times such notions of lucky and unlucky intervals and directions became part of popular culture and religion. The average person today still feels such influence through the calendar (important for distinguishing "good" and "bad" days for weddings, funerals, and other important occasions), and through the ever-popular fortunetellers.

The Koshin cult discussed next is one of the rare examples of an obvious "Taoistic" influence, although even in its Chinese form it was already mixed with Buddhist elements. In Japanese religion, too, the Chinese influence known as Taoism or religious Taoism has always been mixed with other traditions and practices.

26
Religious Taoism in a Japanese Cult

By the sixth century A.D., when Taoist influence entered Japan with other Chinese culture, Taoism meant not simply Taoist literature but also the welter of beliefs and practices known generally as religious Taoism. One of the most clearly identifiable Taoist customs to make a lasting impression on the Japanese scene was the Koshin cult described in this selection.

The Koshin cult arose in China under the influence of ancient indigenous religious practices mixed with Buddhist and mainly Taoist elements. This selection is an interesting interpretation because the author analyzes both the theoretical and the practical aspects of the cult and then shows how it became such an integral part of Japanese life that its foreign origin was largely forgotten. The notion that mythological "worms" dwell within the body provides the rationale for holding regular meetings to honor these messengers to the gods. These meetings are characterized by nocturnal vigils and abstinence from sexual relations.

This document illustrates several important features of Japanese religion. It points up not only the contribution of religious Taoism but also the highly syncretistic character of Japanese religion. It shows how once-aristocratic importations filtered down to the level of popular life. In addition, it shows how cults of the *ko* type formed an important aspect of annual and devotional religious customs. (The word *ko* means religious association or pilgrim association and is not related to the word *Koshin*; although this *ko* happens to focus on a Taoist divinity, there were many *ko* organized around other religious traditions, and some *ko* were secular in nature.)

KOSHIN; AN EXAMPLE OF
TAOIST IDEAS IN JAPAN

E. Dale Saunders

In many ways Japan is a kind of storehouse. In the domain of the arts, the Shosoin[1] at Nara contains objects from various parts of the continent, representing the cosmopolitan character of VIII century aristocratic taste. In the field of religion as well, Japanese beliefs bear the imprint of foreign influences, conserving sometimes concepts which have long since disappeared in the country of their origin. Such is the case of the belief connected with the koshin, or monkey day, the subject of this paper. The present aim, therefore, is to set forth, first, a resume of the underlying koshin concept as it appeared in Chinese Taoist thought and, second, its transference to Japan and its evolution in that country from an historical and cultural standpoint.

The Chinese idea which seems to be the basis of the koshin practice is this. There exist in man's body three Worms, called the *san chu* (or *san shi*). The first, known as the old Blue (Ch. *ch'ung-ko*), lives in the head and causes blindness, deafness, baldness, loss of teeth, stuffy nose and bad breath. The second, the white Maid (Ch. *po-lo*), lives in the breast and is the cause of heart palpitations, asthma, and melancholia. Last of all, the bloody Corpse (Ch. hiue-shih?), dwells in the loins and causes intestinal cramps, drying of the bones, fading of the skin, rheumatism in the legs, aching of the wrists, weakening of the mind and will. Because of him, one is hungry but cannot eat, lacks vitality and is confused. One text adds that this worm is especially addicted to sexual intercourse.

These three parasitical worms are vindictive creatures, disposed to spy on the men in whose bodies they dwell, but which they look upon as a prison. They may gain their freedom only at the death of their host. On the koshin day, which occurs six times each year, they report to Heaven concerning the transgressions of their man, and his life is accordingly shortened by the director of destiny—300 days for the greater transgressions, three for the lesser. Moreover, it was specifically believed that on the koshin night, the Worms took advantage of man's slumber to make good their escape to Heaven and it was hence thought undesirable indeed to sleep either during the koshin day or on that night.

Interestingly enough these basic ideas present in Japan a contamination with a variety of concepts. Already in China, Buddhism had adopted to a cer-

Reprinted by permission of the publisher from E. Dale Saunders, "Koshin: An Example of Taoist Ideas in Japan," in *Proceedings of the IXth International Congress for the History of Religions, 1958* (Tokyo: Maruzen Company Ltd., 1960). Also by permission of the Science Council of Japan.

1. *Shosoin,* an imperial storehouse dating from the eighth century.—ED.

tain extent koshin celebrations, and two non-Taoist divinities were associated with the observance of the monkey day. . . .

There is a further association between the koshin god in Japan and the Shinto divinity Sarutahiko no kami. Sarutahiko is known as the god of the crossways, and for this reason koshin stones (*koshin-to*) are often found even today by the wayside and are there worshipped as a protective divinity of travellers. This identification between koshin and Sarutahiko is difficult to explain conclusively. Perhaps it was due to the homophonous koshin, meaning both "monkey day" and "god of happiness," this latter denomination being synonymous with Sarutahiko. Or perhaps the existence of *"saru,"* meaning monkey, as a part of the god's name was sufficient to establish a connexion. Actually the koshin image is often shown accompanied by three monkeys covering their eyes, ears and mouth. These three acts are symbolic of the Japanese words "not seeing," "not hearing," "not speaking" in which the homonym *saru* occurs meaning monkey and at the same time being a negative verbal suffix. The use of these monkeys as images would seem to come from the fact that monkey (*shin*) is one of the elements of the koshin compound. . . .

A third association may be seen by the relation of the koshin divinity with the bodhisattva Myoken. Myoken controls longevity and *karma* and supposedly reports to the powers of the lower world. . . .

As a result of these associations, koshin, at least as it exists in Japan, may best be thought of as an example of what Professor Kubo . . . calls "acculturation arising from the introduction of Taoism into Japan."

The early introduction of Taoist concepts like the koshin—and the practice of *kata-tagae* (directional taboos)—is doubtless to be laid to the count of the masters of Yin and Yang (*ommyo-ji*). In the Heian period, the study of the Way of Yin and Yang (*ommyo-do*) assumed considerable importance. There was even a government bureau called the *ommyo-ryo,* which was one of the departments of state. *Ommyo-ji* were appointed in the capital as well as in the provincial centers and they became, in fact, official soothsayers. It is probably largely through them that Taoist concepts were introduced to Japan.

Although tradition has it that the koshin was early celebrated under Mommu at the Shitennoji (701), there is some doubt that such was really the case. However, it is certain that the koshin was celebrated by the beginning of the IX century at least. Ennin, in his diary under 838 (11 month, 26 day) refers indirectly to this observance when he says of the Chinese practice: "In the evening the people do not sleep—just like the koshin of the first month in Japan." In 834 and 836 the *Shoku-Nihongi* mentions that banquets were held on the koshin day but no note is made of the sleepless night that was later to become so characteristic of this day. It may consequently be assumed that koshin practices of some kind existed by the end of the VIII century, and by the beginning of the ninth there were doubtless people who observed the koshin day by staying up all night. Just who these people were is not known, but very probably they were mostly nobles and priests, for koshin observances during the Heian period appear to have been essentially aristocratic. Koshin celebrations at this time, it is known, took place in the palace where attendants arranged special mats and screens for the occasion. Cakes and wine were served and poems were composed during the night. As dawn approached it was the custom for the Emperor to give presents to the participating nobles, who in turn offered their best wishes to him. Sometimes *koto* and *biwa* were played for entertainment; games like dice and *go* were the order of the day. It appears that the time for the beginning of these past times was not set; perhaps they commenced around ten-thirty in the evening and continued until near dawn. . . .

The celebration of the koshin throughout the Heian and Kamakura periods remained an aristocratic cult and, like Buddhism, it was not until the end of the Muromachi period that it became a popular practice. Of this important period, there are few detailed texts, and it is actually the Edo period which not only furnishes abundant documentation on the subject of koshin but which forms as well the immediate basis of the modern cult. . . .

Unlike the aristocratic pursuits of the Heian nobles, modern koshin (i.e., from the end of the Muromachi period on) is characterized by much more simple patterns. In villages, gatherings were held, commonly in the home of the village head: at this time a purificatory bath was taken, offerings made to the gods, and sometimes sutras were recited. After a banquet stories were told to pass the hours until dawn, although the length of time spent in these past times differs from place to place.

This gathering of people (*ko*) is one of the characteristics of modern koshin. The *ko* may be organized on the basis of people from the same land or of the same family, or even of a mixture of the two. Moreover, they may be composed of men, of women, of men and women, or even of children. The celebration of this *ko* is often largely Buddhist in nature in view of the above mentioned relation with such divinities as Taishaku-ten and Shomen Kongo. But from the Edo period on there may be noticed a kind of Shinto koshin in association with Sarutahiko no kami. Here, instead of the recitation of sutras, *norito* are read and a meal of fish is prepared. Of course, in the Buddhist koshin (Shomen Kongo) no animal food is eaten. . . .

Actually the koshin divinity is thought of in a variety of ways. He is the protector of the harvest, children, horses, roads, he is a long life divinity, and many others. Even in the same locality people may think of the koshin deity differently. Of course, in agricultural areas he is largely a god of the harvest. In such communities there is a saying "the more one eats the better the harvest" and as a consequence abundant banquets are given on that day. In this connection, Koshin-san is also thought of as the "busy" god and, particularly in the form of the many-armed Shomen Kongo, he can help with the harvest.

Curiously enough in the Edo period, the belief sprang up that children born (sometimes conceived) on the koshin night were predestined to become thieves. This is traditionally explained by the fact that the famous thief Ishikawa Goemon was thought to have been conceived and/or born on a koshin day. His life was made the theme of a *joruri*,[2] and echos of this belief

---

2. *Joruri*, a kind of ballad-drama.—ED.

occur again and again in popular Tokugawa literature. For example, [the character] Kozo says: "Alas, evil as it may be, I am born a thief. And it is useless to let my conscience bother me. I may resist my desire to steal (with one hand) but the other hand gives in. When I see gold I enter, no matter how strong the chain may be. . . ." And Yosobe answers: "Your tale brings to mind my very own son. Because he was born on the koshin night, I was so worried I took him to the priest, who proclaimed that the baby had a streak of the thief in his face," and so forth. Not only were children born on koshin days thought to become thieves, but they were believed to be afflicted in varying degrees with naughtiness and stupidity as well.

Such beliefs were obviously closely connected with the interdiction against sexual activities on the koshin night, and a number of earthy satyrical verses exist from the Edo period to show this popular attitude. Moreover, the monkey figure used to represent the koshin would seem to show sexual overtones. The divinity is often shown in conjunction with a pair of monkeys, one holding a *gohei*[3] while the other holds a peach which, in Japan as in China, is a feminine sexual symbol. . . .

To summarize. The koshin celebration present from the Heian period until the present day is celebrated six times a year on the day when, according to the Chinese sexagesimal cycle, the sign of the monkey is united with that of metal. Originally based on the religious, if not the philosophical, Taoist belief in the three Worms who report to Heaven on man's transgressions, the koshin practice was transmitted to Japan through the *ommyo-ji* certainly by the VIII century, and by the IX there are literary references to this observance. An aristocratic practice, largely Chinese in nature during the Heian and Kamakura periods, by the beginning of the Edo period, the koshin celebration had become popularized and concomitantly Japanized, with both Shinto and Buddhist elements. During the Edo period, koshin was to become firmly entrenched as a popular belief, and multiple references to it are to be found in the literature of the day. Consequently, the koshin celebration as it existed from the Tokugawa period to the present may properly be thought of as being Japanese for the most part, although it is undeniable that the beliefs rest on a basis of ancient Taoist concepts early transmitted to Japan. Today, koshin is most actively observed in the country areas, especially in the Tohoku and central Kanto regions, the obvious exceptions being the Daikyoji, devoted to Taishaku-ten, and the Kiho-in, . . . Tokyo, as well as the famous koshin shrine (*koshindo*) of the Shitenno temple in Osaka.

---

3. *Gohei*, a Shinto ritual wand, a stick with paper streamers.—ED.

CHAPTER SEVEN

Folk Religion

Japanese religion has never been as tightly controlled and centralized as religion in the West. Denominational patterns in Buddhism and Protestant Christianity may seem familiar, but what is more important is the fact that religious life for the Japanese was not so exclusively centered around ecclesiastical matters. While every family tended to be related to one Shinto shrine by geographical location and affiliated to one Buddhist temple by family tradition, many religious activities took place outside the temple and shrine without the benefit of professional religious leaders.

Many popular beliefs existed independently of organized religion, and many aspects of seasonal celebrations were not controlled by Shinto and Buddhism. The family and the home were centers of religious life, a theme that is taken up in Chapter 11. Folk religion is not simply an addition to organized religion but is a vital part of the religious life of the people.

Most folk religion in Japan is handed down orally and in the annual festivals. Usually this pattern of folk religion varies considerably with such factors as the local situation and the economic activities of the area. For example, farmers usually carry out some celebrations for transplanting and harvest, whereas fishermen observe their own ceremonies for safety and big catches. Urbanization and industrialization are causing much folk religion to disappear, but throughout Japan there are attempts to preserve the local color associated with all folk customs.

27
Rites of Passage in the Life Cycle

In almost all religious traditions, rites of passage guide a person through life—from "cradle to grave"—providing the ritual transition from one stage of life to the next. In traditional religious life, the three most frequently found rites of passage are birth, marriage, and death, but of course each tradition has had its own way of celebrating passage into life itself, entry into child-bearing and creation of life, and eventually leaving this life and world for possibly another world and a new life. Each tradition also has its own way of defining the additional junctures where passage occurs.

The author of the following selection describes some of the distinctive Japanese rites for birth, marriage, and death; he also mentions other Japanese rites of passage—the "Three, Five, and Seven Years of Age" celebrations, "Years of Peril and Years of Jubilation," and the memorial rites that occur after death. Such rituals are very important, both within folk religion and in relationship to the organized religions of Buddhism and Shinto, because by participating in these rituals and observing their performance by others, people become aware of the nature of religion.

This scholar reminds us that rites of passage are not isolated and separate events, but can be seen "as a homogeneous whole," giving "expression to a discernible belief structure." This overall pattern of events in the life cycle is one way of viewing the unity of folk religion.

RITES OF PASSAGE

Hitoshi Miyake

The stages through which one passes in the course of life are formally introduced by certain rites of passage. The chief rites of this nature in Japan are those described below.

1. Birth (*tanjō*). An infant is born, according to Japanese folk belief, when it is granted a soul by the deity in charge of birth. One week later, in the evening (called *shichiya* or "seventh night"), the child is named and introduced to his relatives. On the thirtieth day after the birth, the taboos are lifted, and the body is taken to the local shrine where the parents introduce him to the tutelary *kami* of the area and offer their own worship. At the child's first doll festival (*hina matsuri* or *tango no sekku*, depending on the sex) and again when the first birthday arrives, there is a special family celebration.

2. Three, Five, and Seven Years of Age (*shichi go san*). 15 November is a gala day for children of three, five, and seven. On this day five-year-old boys

Reprinted by permission of the publisher from Hitoshi Miyake, "Folk Religion," in *Japanese Religion* (Tokyo: Kodansha International, 1972).

and girls of three and seven are taken to the local shrine to pray that the *kami* will watch over them as they grow. From this time the children are recognized as being under the care of this guardian deity.

3. Coming of Age (*seijin shiki*). During the feudal period, boys were regarded as coming to maturity sometime between the ages of thirteen and nineteen. The rites that attended this recognition were given the name *genpuku,* meaning "first clothes," i.e., the clothes of manhood. At this time the sons of high-ranking samurai were given, in an official ceremony, a new name and a special cap symbolic of their new status, while from their families, in a separate rite, they received a new loincloth. This latter part of the "first clothes" rites was called *fundoshi iwai* ("loincloth celebration"). Sons of lesser samurai and commoners received only the loincloth in a family and kinship group ceremony. For girls, the sign of maturity was the first menstruation. At the ceremony that followed, the daughter, regardless of class, was presented by her family and kinship group with a *koshimaki* or underskirt. At the present time the coming of age rite is a civic ceremony held on 15 January for those of both sexes who will become twenty during the calendar year. After this ceremony they are considered adults and may legally marry even without parental consent.

4. Marriage (*konrei*). The rituals connected with marriage in present-day Japan include more than the wedding ceremony. The first is the rite of engagement, confirmed by betrothal gifts from fiance to fiancee. Then comes the wedding rite in which the couple make an implicit pledge, through the ritual exchange of nuptial cups in the presence of a *kami,* to be husband and wife to one another. This ceremony is usually followed by a banquet in which the newlyweds are introduced to relatives and friends as man and wife and the mutual ties of all concerned are ratified through toasts of sake.

5. Years of Peril (*yakudoshi*) and Years of Jubilation (*toshi iwai*). According to the almanac, for each person, depending on the date of his birth, there are certain years in which he is threatened by evil influences and must take careful precautions. Among them the one year that is particularly ominous for men is the forty-second year of life, for women the thirty-third. This is called the *daiyaku,* the year of great peril. During these hazardous years, one is well advised to take an active part in shrine festivals and make use of amulets and spells to ward off evil. On the other hand, the sixty-first year of life, marking as it does a new beginning on the sexagenary calendrical cycle, and again the seventieth year, traditionally regarded as a rare attainment, are both years to be celebrated.

6. Mortuary Rites (*tomurai*). Japanese folk belief has it that death occurs as a result of the soul's departure from the body. When death is imminent, therefore, people cry out to the soul of the dying person, beseeching it to remain with the body. But once it is certain the person is dead, a bowl of cooked rice is placed by his pillow to sustain him in the spirit world, and a sword (or other edged tool such as a razor) is provided for him to protect himself against malevolent spirits. The night before the funeral those closest to the deceased stay up all night with the corpse. The next morning the body is cleaned with

warm water, dressed in white, and placed in a coffin. Buddhist priests then conduct the funeral service, which includes words of counsel to the deceased (*indo*), after which the family, relatives, and neighbors accompany the dead person either to the cemetery or the crematorium.

One week after death, the day being called *shonanuka* ("seventh day"), a priest gives the deceased a posthumous name—a name for use in the spirit world. The bereaved family is in mourning for forty-nine days. On the forty-ninth day, a ceremony is held in honor of the dead person, and from this time the taboos are lifted. Subsequently, requiem masses on behalf of the deceased are held at the first Feast of the Dead (*bon*) and on the first, third, seventh, thirty-third, and in some districts the forty-ninth anniversaries of the person's death. With the conclusion of these requiem masses, the last of which is called *tomurai age* ("completion of the obsequies"), the spirit of the dead person is believed to lose its individuality and become one with the ancestral *kami*. It is also believed that the ancestral spirit, led by the *kami* in charge of birth, may be reincarnated in a newborn child.

Considered as a homogeneous whole, these rites of passage give expression to a discernible belief structure. Life begins with the receiving of a soul, and under the care and protection of *kami* and spirits, this soul develops and advances as the person, passing from stage to stage, grows to maturity. At death the soul leaves the body, but when honored by surviving family members with the proper rituals, it continues to rise in status, at first being no more than an ancestral spirit but eventually becoming a *kami*.

Also noteworthy is the symmetrical relation between the rites associated with birth and the process of growth, on the one hand, and those associated with death and requiem masses on the other. One thinks, for example, of the parallel between the seventh night after birth (*shichiya*) and the seventh day after death (*shonanuka*), each involving the bestowal of a name. The lifting of birth taboos can be balanced against the termination of death taboos, the celebration of the first birthday against the requiem mass held one year after death, the periodic rituals of the third, fifth, and seventh years of life against the series of requiem masses, the coming of age ceremony against the completion of the obsequies, etc. From this symmetry it may be inferred that in the thinking of many Japanese people, the souls of the living and the souls of the dead go through much the same process of development.

28
Shamanistic Practices in Japan

In Japanese folk religion are practitioners who perform various religious services without being formally part of the institutional religions of Shinto or Buddhism. The blind mediums, always female, known as *itako* or *ichiko* are good examples of these popular practitioners. Some scholars call these *itako* or *ichiko* shamans, but the Japanese scholar Hori did not use this term, because a shaman is usually characterized by a trance or "ecstatic state," and the *itako* do not experience this kind of state. Blacker follows Hori's avoidance of the shaman label, preferring to write about "shamanistic practices." Whatever label is applied to them, these practitioners present a fascinating example of folk religion.

In a folk setting there is always emphasis upon oral tradition and local variation, rather than on written tradition and uniformity (through institutional regulations). Nevertheless, by tracing the careers of a number of these mediums, Blacker is able to show a common pattern of practice. During a lengthy period of apprenticeship—a combination of religious training and ascetic practices carried out under the supervision of an older medium—the young girl is prepared for the initiation ceremony that will qualify her to serve as a medium in her own right.

Such mediums have played a major role in mediating between the present world and the other world. Although the number of *itako* is declining, their practice is an important precedent for understanding the dynamics of interaction between the everyday life, and what lies beyond.

THE BLIND MEDIUM

Carmen Blacker

The blind mediums known as *itako* or *ichiko* are not considered by some authorities, notably Hori, to be true shamans. They exhibit none of the symptoms of "arctic hysteria," the neurotic oddity and proneness to dreams and haunting that we saw to be the prelude to the sacred life among the living goddesses. They experience no call from the other side, neither in dreams nor in sudden possessions. Nor do they show any true power-giving relationship with a tutelary deity. The deity to whom they are formally "wedded" at their ceremony of initiation seldom comes to their aid thereafter with the supernatural gifts we saw to be the strength of the living goddesses. Nor are they capable any longer of achieving a truly ecstatic state. What passes for a trance among them is seen on shrewd inspection to be mere imitation. . . .

First let us examine the motive of the *itako* for entering her sacred calling. A girl is impelled to become an *itako* purely and simply because she is blind. Either she is born blind, or she becomes blind in infancy as a result of sickness or malnutrition. A number of occupations have been traditionally reserved for blind people in Japan, among which massage and lute-playing are prominent examples. In the north the profession of medium has also for some time been in the hands of such people.

The blind *itako* is not forced into her calling, as are the living goddesses, by an irresistible command from the other side. Her motive is voluntary and purely practical. By becoming a medium she will become a viable member of

Reprinted by permission of the publisher from Carmen Blacker, *The Catalpa Bow* (London: George Allen & Unwin, 1975). The notes have been deleted.

her community rather than a burden. It is in order to save her from the stigma of uselessness that her parents apprentice her to an older, already established *itako,* in whose house she may receive the necessary training.

It is her parents rather than she herself who make this decision, since she is seldom more than twelve or thirteen years old at the time. A firm belief prevails throughout the district that she must start her apprenticeship before the onset of menstruation. Sexual desire, it is alleged, is a hindrance to the practice of the necessary austerities and to the proper accomplishment of the initiation ritual. With a young girl the god will "take" her without difficulty. With a girl trained over the age of puberty he may well be reluctant, and many attempts may be required before success is attained. Nor can an adult-initiated medium be trusted to transmit reliably the utterances of *kami* and ghosts. The rumour soon gets round that *yoku ataranai,* her transmissions are unreliable, and soon she has no clients. Hence the early age at which she is usually apprenticed to her teacher.

For the period of her apprenticeship she commonly lives in the house of her teacher. There she stays for the two, three or even five years that may be necessary for her training, acting as maid of all work in the intervals between her lessons. During this period she must undergo an ascetic regime, the severity of which varies according to the district and the individual teacher.

Hasegawa Sowa, for example, an *itako* from the Tsugaru district of Aomori prefecture, aged sixty-five when interviewed, told Sakurai that her daily routine throughout the year of her training had been as follows. She got up before dawn and performed her morning cold water austerity. There followed a short service of chanting before the family altar, and after breakfast the morning lesson. Here she would have to repeat phrase by phrase after her teacher a number of sutras, ballads, *norito* and the psalms known as *wasan.* Over and over again she repeated these chants until she had them effortlessly by heart. The texts included the *Hannya Shingyo,* the Kannon Sutra, the Jizo Sutra and the *Jizo wasan.* After lunch she had to go over with the other two pupils in the house the phrases she had learnt in the morning. After supper there was more practice until the evening cold water austerity and bed. The teacher had been very strict, she recalled, and would scold her unmercifully if her memory was bad. If she was wilting with tiredness, the teacher would direct at her a short sharp yell which startled her so much that she often burst into tears. So unhappy was she that she once ran away.

In Yamagata prefecture a similarly strict regime was the rule in the early 1930s. Suzuki Tsuyako, born in 1923, recalled a severe daily *mizugori* at crack of dawn, twelve buckets of cold water from the river to be poured over each shoulder. In winter this austerity was excruciating; the cold was so intense that often she nearly lost consciousness and only kept herself from fainting by focusing all her power and concentration on reciting the *Hannya Shingyo.* She had nothing to eat until midday. All the morning was spent in repeating, phrase by phrase after her teacher, various kinds of sacred text, including *norito* and invocations to Inari, Kojin and the deities of the nearby mountains Gassan and Yudonosan. Her memory was bad, and her teacher often scolded her until she cried.

Once the initiation ritual drew near, however, the austerities increased ferociously in intensity. For the week immediately preceding the rite, the girl was subjected to appallingly severe *gyo,* calculated to reduce the body to a pitch of exhaustion verging on total breakdown.

Suzuki Tsuyako, for example, described the ordeals which she underwent in 1935 at the age of twelve. The intensification of her *gyo* started a hundred days before her initiation, when every morning at 2 a.m., the spiritually powerful hour of the ox, she had to get up, grope her way to the river bank and pour twelve buckets of cold water over each shoulder. She then had to walk to the local Inari shrine, light candles and chant the *Hannya Shingyo.* Blind as she was and unaffected by the darkness, she nevertheless found the precincts of the shrine at that hour of the morning terrifyingly uncanny. During this period neither she nor her family ate meat or strong-smelling vegetables.

For the week immediately before her initiation the austerities were further intensified to an almost incredible pitch of severity. She had first to observe the *sandachi* of Three Abstentions. No cereals must pass her lips, no salt, nor any cooked foods. Nor, if the austerities took place in winter, must she ever go near a stove or any other form of heating.

Every day she had to pour over her shoulders no less than a thousand buckets of cold water, each one counted on the beads of a rosary. At the same time she must recite a thousand *Hannya Shingyos* and twenty-one Kannon Sutras. This appalling austerity lasted from crack of dawn until late at night, so that throughout the week she was allowed next to no sleep. The first two days of this fearful regime, she recalled, were almost unbearable. The intense cold, the sleeplessness and the semi-starvation brought her to the point of breakdown. Her joints ached so agonisingly that she could scarcely walk or lift the buckets over her head. But on the third day her pain suddenly vanished. She felt herself flooded with an extraordinary access of strength and enthusiasm such that she felt capable of enduring any ordeal in order to accomplish the final initiation. . . .

In Miyagi prefecture the picture is much the same. The three abstentions are observed for three weeks before the initiation, with the water austerity night and morning. The night before the ceremony is due to take place—and a favourite time for the event is the "great cold" just before New Year—must be spent in the continuous performance of the cold water exercise. It is alleged that in some districts the number of buckets poured over the head and shoulders during the night reaches the almost unbelievable figure of 33,333.

Sleeplessness, semi-starvation and intense cold is thus the picture for the whole north-eastern district. Such strains would normally, in a profane context, reduce the body to the point of breakdown. In almost all the accounts before us, however, we read that just when the girl was on the verge of collapse, she felt herself flooded by a new access of strength which transformed her outlook on life. For the rest of the period a wave of enthusiastic determination to continue until the moment of her initiation made her impervious to pain and fatigue. . . .

Very similar descriptions come from Yamagata and Miyagi prefectures. The curtained, cordoned and darkened room; the sacks of rice, the loud continuous chanting, the tremors, shivers and convulsive shaking which overtake the girl, culminating in a dead faint. When she recovers consciousness in the adjoining room, she is told by her teacher that the deity Nittensama, or Fudo Myoo, has satisfactorily taken possession of her and will henceforth act as her tutelary deity. The same lavish wedding feast follows, with red rice, whole fish, as much sake as can be afforded, and the girl in a red wedding dress to indicate her spiritual marriage with the deity.

Here we have a rite of unmistakably initiatory character. A preliminary ordeal of an excruciating kind involving fasting, cold water and repetitive chanting; a rite in which tension is raised to the point at which the candidate faints dead away. Dying to her old self, she is reborn in the dazzling garb of the bride of the deity implanted in her at the moment of death and with whom she will henceforth stand in a close tutelary relationship. . . .

Once a girl is fully initiated and possessed of her instruments of power, what tasks is she expected to perform? In all districts of the north-east her duties fall into two broad categories: *kamioroshi* or bringing down *kami,* and *hotokeoroshi* or *kuchiyose,* summoning ghosts. She is expected to deliver utterances from both kinds of spirit on the problems which beset the human community.

The ritual and treatment which she offers to each kind of spirit tends to differ in different areas. An elderly *itako,* for example, who was called in for the evening to the house in Tanabu in which I was staying in 1958, declared herself equally capable of summoning either *kami* or ghosts, but not both on the same day. Always she had to sleep before making the transition from one to the other. Both types of spirit, she declared, were helpful in solving human problems, though ghosts were slightly better in advising on the personal difficulties of their surviving families.

The methods she employed to invoke each kind of spirit were nevertheless very similar. Whether she was summoning the family ancestors that evening, or the local *kami* the following morning, she banged repeatedly on a fan-shaped drum, rubbed her black rosary and recited sutras and invocations, many of which seemed to be identical. In the summoning of ghosts, however, and the delivery of their messages, she always used a special vocabulary of taboo words. . . . These were the only names, she declared, to which the dead spirits would respond.

Further south in Miyagi prefecture, however, the calling of *kami* takes a different form altogether from the invocation of dead spirits.

The *kami* are called by means of ritual performed in the local shrine, apparently very similar to the one we tried to reconstruct for the ancient *miko.* It is performed at crucial seasons in the calendar when supernatural advice about the future is particularly welcome. At New Year, for example, at the time of the rice planting and at harvest time, the god is petitioned to reveal what are the prospects for the village in the way of storms, monsoon rains, sickness and fires, as well as of the rice harvest itself. The ritual is so similar, both to the ancient model and to those performed with the assistance of an ascetic which we shall deal with in the chapter on village oracles, that it would be repetitive to describe it in detail here. Suffice to say that in Miyagi prefecture and in Yamagata as well, the blind medium is the intermediary for a seasonal call to the local deity for his advice and help.

More important and more time-consuming than the calling of *kami* is the task of *kuchiyose,* or the calling of dead spirits.

Sakurai in his account of the *ogamisan* of the Rikuzen district gives us an extremely full and interesting description of the manner in which ghosts are summoned. Unlike the rest of the north-eastern area, two distinct processes are here observed. One relates to "new ghosts," the spirits of those who have died within the last hundred days. The other relates to "old ghosts," whose death took place before this period.

The calling of new ghosts should properly be performed during the period of forty-nine days after the funeral. In some districts it is incumbent to perform the rite on the third or fifth days after the coffin has left the house, in others on the day immediately afterwards. Always it is performed in the house of the bereaved family, where the *ogamisan* is expected to reside for the duration of the ceremony.

The structure of the ritual is an interesting one. The first step is always to summon myriads of *kami,* ranging from superior deities with names down to anonymous village and household divinities. Always, before a ghost can be invoked, these *kami* must be summoned to the scene of the seance. They act as wardens or guardians of the ritual, in a manner which recalls the practice in spiritualist circles in the west, whereby the medium's control must be summoned before any "ostensible communicator" can be induced to speak.

Before a newly dead spirit can be reached, however, another preliminary step must take place. This is the summoning of the Ancestor of the family, a ghost at least fifty years old who acts as the *michibiki* or guide. This Ancestor must make seven utterances in response to a fixed order of seven questions relating to the condition and abode of the new ghost. Where is the spirit now, is it satisfied with the offerings supplied, is it happy?

At last the new ghost itself comes through and addresses each of its relations in turn. To parents, children, brothers, sisters, grandchildren, uncles, aunts, it speaks just as it might have done when still alive, save that it always addresses them by means of the taboo words. Everyone present sobs and cries during these utterances, and the atmosphere is said to be indescribably uncanny. In a large family, where the ghost has many relatives to address, this stage of the rite may well go on for eight or nine hours. A "new calling" which starts at nine o'clock in the morning may well continue until nightfall.

The next stage is therefore a short rest, enabling the *ogamisan,* who has been talking continuously all this while, to refresh herself with a little tea. The final step is of the nature of an envoi. The new ghost is despatched to its own world, and the Ancestor is requested to show it the way back. Finally the myriad *kami* summoned at the beginning of the rite and who have been present all the while are in their turn sent back to their own abode. . . .

We infer that the decline of the truly shamanic medium in the north came about when the profession became the monopoly of the blind; when it was not so much a religious call that propelled a woman into the occupation of spirit medium, as the need to find one more gainful occupation for the increasing numbers of blind girls. Hori is therefore right when he declares that the blind *itako* as they survive today are not shamanic persons. Equally surely, however, their practice betrays that they perpetuate, without inspiration or supernatural gift, practices which go back to antiquity. They have replaced women who fulfilled more closely the requirements of shamanic inspiration; whose call to the life was a truly religious one, through dreams or possession, and who achieved for the deliverance of the spiritual messages a genuine state of dissociated trance.

29
Japanese Folktales

Folktales are an important part of the Japanese cultural heritage, a popular mixing of religious beliefs and historical events with local color and pride in antiquity. As handed down in Japan, folktales represent a dimension of culture not so prominent in the West; these tales are not really "believed in," as with religious scriptures, yet they are treasured much more than fairy tales are in the West.

The Japanese are very proud of their long national heritage, and are equally jealous of the distinctiveness of local traditions. For example, if there is a Saint Kobo's Well in the district it will be pointed out to a visitor. Even a local historian who knows that Saint Kobo (the founder of the Buddhist Shingon sect) could not have visited the village might still take pride in the antiquity of this legend. What is crucial is not so much what actually happened long ago but how the local people relate themselves to the memorable personages and events of Japanese history.

Some of the brief tales printed here are specifically religious, such as "Saint Kobo's Well," "The Serpent Suitor," and "Human Sacrifice to the River God." In fact, these stories might be called folk legends, because they tell of the religious significance of local institutions, particularly the local shrines. The main point of "The Revengeful Spirit of Masakado" is how prior historical events still affect us today; this is most true of the curse of the dead and family ties. The tale of Benkei recounts superhuman aspects of the life of this famous warrior, who is one of the most important topics for art and plays.

FOLK LEGENDS OF JAPAN

Saint Kobo's Well

There is a spring by the name of St. Kobo's Well in the village of Muramatsu, Ninohe-gun. The following story concerning this well is told in this district. A girl was once weaving alone at her home. An old man, staggering, came by there and asked her for a cup of water. She walked over the hill more than a

---

All of the tales in selection 29 have been reprinted from *Folk Legends of Japan*, by Richard M. Dorson, with permission of the publisher, Charles E. Tuttle Co., Inc.

thousand yards away and brought back water for the visitor. The old man was pleased with her kindness and said that he would make her free from painful labor. After saying this, he struck the ground with his cane. While he was striking, water sprang forth from the point struck by his cane. That spring was called St. Kobo's Well.

The old man who could do such a miraculous deed was thought to be St. Kobo, however poor and weak he might look.

The Revengeful Spirit of Masakado

Masakado fought against Hidesato at Nakano-ga-hara in Musashi Province in the third year of Tenkei [940]. He was shot in the shoulder by Taira Sadamori and grappled down by Fujiwara Chiharu, and his head was cut off.

Therefore Masakado's spirit remained on the field of Nakano and caused suffering to the people of the vicinity in many ways. In the eastern districts of Japan, Masakado's spirit effected various miracles, but to the people who had some blood connection with Hidesato, his spirit caused fierce spells. Especially in the Sano family it was forbidden to go to the Kanda Myojin Shrine, because the Sano were the descendants of Hidesato. The Sano house at Ogawa-machi in Kanda was very near the Kanda Myojin, so on the festival day at this shrine the gate of the house was not opened to anyone; on ordinary days every person of the Sano house was forbidden to walk in front of the shrine.

During the Anei era [1770–80], a samurai named Kanda Oribe lived at Kobinatadai-machi. This man was a descendant of Masakado and wore his crest. His close companion Sano Goemon lived at Yushima. One day Sano dropped in at Kanda's on his way back from his official duties, as they were intimate friends. They had a good time together, and after a while Kanda said: "I shall take you to a fine place." And he took Sano to a *yujoya*[1] named Kashiwaya, near Agaki Shrine.

At the time Sano had been wearing ceremonial dress. But it was ridiculous to go to a *yujoya* dressed thus, so Kanda lent Sano an informal cloak with the Masakado crest on it.

While they were making merry at the *yujoya*, Sano's face suddenly turned pale, sweat poured from his brow, and he fainted in agony. In a moment the circumstances were entirely changed. In confusion, they called for doctors and medicine. Kanda hired a sedan and sent Sano to his home.

Kanda was so anxious about his friend that he hurried over early next morning to see him. However, Sano came briskly out of his room and said: "Last night I shivered and fainted. After shivering and fainting I fell unconscious until they took off that cloak of yours I was wearing. When I went into bed, I immediately recovered. And now I feel just as well as usual. This probably happened because I borrowed your cloak with your crest on it. Maybe Masakado's spirit put a spell on me."

---

1. *Yujoya*, a brothel.—ED.

So Kanda was also convinced of the power of his ancestor's spell, and he apologized to Sano for his carelessness.

The Serpent Suitor

Once there lived a village headman named Shiohara in Aikawa-mura, Ono-gun. He had a lovely daughter. Every night a nobleman visited the daughter, but she knew neither his name nor whence he came. She asked him his name, but he never told her about himself. At length, the girl asked her nurse what to do. The nurse said: "When he comes next time, prick a needle with a thread through his skirt, and follow after him as the thread will lead you. Then you will find his home."

The next day the girl put a needle in the suitor's skirt. When he departed, the girl and the nurse followed him as the thread led them. They passed through steep hills and valleys and came to the foot of Mt. Uba, where there was a big rock cave. As the thread led inside, the girl timidly entered the cave. She heard a groaning voice from the interior. The nurse lighted a torch and also went into the cave. She peered within and saw a giant serpent, bigger than one could possibly imagine. It was groaning and writhing in agony. She looked at the serpent carefully, and she noticed that the needle which the girl had put in her lover's skirt was thrust into the serpent's throat.

The girl was frightened and ran out of the cave, while the nurse fainted and died on the spot. The serpent also died soon. The nurse was enshrined in Uba-dake Shrine at the foot of Mt. Uba, and the cave of the serpent is also worshiped. . . .

If a man enters this cave with something made of metal, or if many people go into the cave at the same time, the spirit of the cave becomes offended and causes a storm.

Relics of Benkei

There is a hill called Benkei-mori in Nagami, Honjo-mura, Yatsuka-gun. A small shrine formerly called Benkichi's Shrine, which is now in the precinct of Nagami Shrine, stands there. According to a document kept in the shrine, the woman named Benkichi was the daughter of a samurai in the province of Kii [now Wakayama-ken]. She was born on May 5, in the third year of Taiji [1129]. For some reason she came to Nagami in Honjo-mura in the third year of Kyuan [1147] and stayed there. After three years she met a *tengu*[2] on a mountain path and conceived a child. In the thirteenth month she gave birth to Benkei.

When Benkei was seventeen years old his mother died. He enshrined her as the goddess Benkichi and left this place. These things are written in detail in Benkei's letter, which is said to have been presented to the shrine by Benkei. Near Benkei-mori there is a well. Tradition says that Benkei took his first bath with water from this well.

---

2. *Tengu*, a mountain goblin.—ED.

A small island called Benkei-jima is in the sea off the coast of Nohara in Honjo-mura. Trees grow very thick on its mountains. According to tradition, Benkei was a very naughty boy and in his ninth year he was abandoned on this island. Benkei played the game of fox and geese with the *tengu*. While they were playing, the *tengu* taught Benkei many tactics. The stone base which they used for the game was later carried by boat to another place. But the boat was overthrown by a sudden storm and the stone base sank into the sea.

This island is connected to the mainland by a narrow sand path. It is said that Benkei made this path, by dropping little stones which he carried in his sleeves and skirt, for the purpose of escaping from the island. There is also a place called Benkei's Smithy at Shinjo in the same village, where Benkei is said to have had his sword forged.

Human Sacrifice to the River God

An old wise-woman came from Miyanome in Ayaori-mura and settled at Yazaki in Matsuzaki-mura, Kamihei-gun. She had a daughter whom she cared for lovingly. The girl grew up and was married to a man who came to live with them. The young couple loved each other, but the mother disliked the son-in-law and wanted to get rid of him.

In those days the dam which supplied the villagers with water from the Saru-ga-ishi River would give way several times every year, and people were troubled by floods. It happened again that the dam broke when the villagers were in need of water. Thrown into confusion, they gathered together and talked the matter over. At last they decided to consult the wise-woman. She, on her part, thought this a good opportunity to destroy her son-in-law. Accordingly, she told the people to catch a person who would be dressed in white and riding a gray horse to Tsukumoshi-mura the next morning, and to throw him into the river as a sacrifice. The villagers assembled at the dam and waited from midnight on for a person in white dress to come by on horseback.

Early next morning the old woman's son-in-law, unaware of impending disaster, dressed himself in white, as he had been told to do by the mother, and rode off on his gray horse. When he came to the dam, many villagers stood in his way to catch him. The son-in-law was surprised and asked them: "Why are you all here?"

The villagers were surprised in their turn to see that the person was none other than the wise-woman's son-in-law, whom they all knew well. When the son-in-law heard about the matter he said: "If it is the god's word, I must obey. I will drown myself in the bottom of the river and sacrifice myself for the sake of the villagers. But a human sacrifice cannot be made by one person. A couple, man and woman, are needed to satisfy the god. I will have my wife die with me."

Just then the wise-woman's daughter, who knew of the mother's evil plot, rushed to the scene, riding on a gray horse and dressed in white. The husband and wife rode into the river together and sank down to the bottom. The old wise-woman regretted that her plan had miscarried. She also jumped into the water, weeping.

All at once the sky darkened and a fierce thunderstorm lashed the heavens. For three days and nights it rained ceaselessly, and the river overflowed its banks. After the flood had subsided, the people noticed a big stone that they had never seen before. The villagers used this stone as the foundation in re-constructing the dam. This stone was called the Wise-woman's Stone.

The son-in-law and his wife were deified as gods of the dam [*seki-gami*]. There is also a shrine called Bonari Myojin where the old wise-woman died.

CHAPTER EIGHT

Christianity

C hristianity has always had a difficult time in Japan. It arrived rather late in
Japanese history, after the major religious traditions had already interacted to
form a distinctive Japanese religious heritage. In addition, Christianity sharply contrasted with the Japanese heritage. The career of the Christian church in Japan generally can be characterized by two features: first, Christianity has emphasized its
distinctiveness and uniqueness, resisting mixture with the Japanese tradition; second, no more than a small percentage of the population has assumed church membership, so that Christian influence in Japan has often been outside the church and
has never been dominant.

Christianity was present in Japan for about one hundred years (1550–1650) before
being completely proscribed, and then it reentered Japan in the last half of the nineteenth century. The Jesuits who introduced Catholicism in the mid-sixteenth century
faced great obstacles in their missionary efforts, but they gradually won sincere converts. Some descendants of these first Japanese Christians secretly maintained their
faith in spite of persecution and contacted Roman Catholic priests who entered
Japan in the 1860s.

For over a century, Catholic and Protestant missions from the entire Western world
have been active in Japan. In fact, one of the problems facing Christianity in Japan
has been the extreme proliferation of institutions and denominations arising out of

European and American experience but not necessarily suitable for the Japanese experience. At several times, there has been optimism for mass conversion to Christianity—during the enthusiasm for Western culture in the 1870s and during the disorientation after World War II, for example—but in both cases the optimism was unfounded. Christianity is respected in various ways—in recognition of Jesus as a religious leader, in the reading of the Bible, and in praise of Christianity's role in education and social reform. However, Japanese Christian churches still are a minor influence in the country's religious life when compared with Shinto shrines and Buddhist temples. (One interesting aspect of Christianity adopted by the Japanese is the popular celebration of Christmas, described on pp. 308–312.)

Because Christianity has attracted such a small number of Japanese members over a considerable time span, we might conclude that Japan is simply unsuited to the Christian message. It can also be argued that Christianity's lack of success stems from a failure to fully integrate Christianity into Japanese culture and religion. The New Religion called Makuya is an interesting and controversial example of the attempt to graft a pentecostal form of Christianity onto Japan's religious tradition. Makuya may be evidence of how it is possible for Christianity to shed its foreign image and become a "Japanese religion."

30
The Introduction of Roman Catholicism into Japan

The first form of Christianity to appear in Japan was Roman Catholicism, and the first missionaries were members of the Jesuit order. The earliest period of Christianity in Japan, from the arrival of St. Francis Xavier in 1549 until its total and severe persecution about a hundred years later, has been called "the Christian century." This century is a fascinating case study of the interaction of European and Japanese culture, government, and religion. Westerners, especially Christians, question how initially some Japanese accepted this religion, and how finally it was totally rejected. The relative success and later the complete elimination of Christianity is much more than a story of religious contact, however; it is also a story of competing cultures and governments.

This selection outlines the complex factors in the meeting of European missionaries with Japanese officials and potential converts. The author deals with some of the differences between Japanese thought and Catholic conceptions, and also shows that the governmental conflict with Catholics was akin to the rulers' earlier struggle with some Buddhist institutions. In the long run the Christian century was most important historically for the policies it helped forge in the subsequent period.

THE CHRISTIAN CENTURY: ACCEPTANCE
AND REJECTION OF CATHOLICISM

George Elison

The "Christian Century" of Japan extends from 1549 to 1639, from the arrival of Saint Francis Xavier to the Tokugawa interdiction of all traffic with Catholic lands. The century falls short of a hundred years, the religion failed in its evangelical aims. Paradoxically, the significance of this *entr'acte* is not in the triumph of Christianity but in the effect of its defeat. The Christian intrusion left few Christian traces; it was but the exotic element in an already gaudy period of Japanese history. But upon the "Christian Century" follow more than two centuries of Sakoku, the Closed Country. The Christian aberration would be a mere interlude were it not for its causal relation to the Sakoku policy. The total rejection of Christianity helps to define an era.

Christianity was introduced into Japan at a time when that country's medieval order was in its final convulsions. The missionaries viewed a tumbling body politic. But beneath the surface of a country rent by war developed institutional changes which gave form to Japanese history's Early Modern period. The broad terms which define this concept of comparative history for Europe apply as well to Japan: secularization of the tenor of life and rationalization of political authority. In the Japanese interpretation, the ethos and the doctrine of Christianity clashed with these.

Japanese thought held no preconception corresponding to the Christian predicate. The Japanese critic found the notion of an omnipotent personal deity specious, its consequence disastrous. The foreign religion could be accused of otherworldliness; for the Christians removed the justification of human action from the social sphere to an extraterrestrial locus. The Christian dictate of a supernal loyalty pre-empted loyalty to a secular sovereign. Philosophy, ethics, and politics rejected the Christian claim that the One God existed and acted to determine the moral order.

These judgments the artificers of Early Modern Japan took into account and applied to the fabric of policy. The negative verdict was prosecuted unremittingly under the Tokugawa Bakufu: the stigmatization of all internal traces of Christianity is one of the most prominent motifs in the history of the shogunate's establishment and initial development. This measure could not be effective unless external Christian influences were denied entry. And contacts with the outside world were cut.

Tokugawa Japan is a culture under isolation. The brief Azuchi-Momoyama age, which preceded it, appears flamboyantly cosmopolitan by contrast. But the anti-Christian verdict had already been weighed, passed, and partially im-

---

Reprinted by permission of the publisher from George Elison, *Deus Destroyed* (Cambridge: Harvard University Press, 1973). The notes have been deleted.

plemented by the immediate predecessors of the Tokugawa. Direct antecedents of the shogunate's policy are found along the course which Toyotomi Hideyoshi (in his own fashion a champion of external contacts and foreign ventures) set in reorganizing Japan. And the seeming friend of the foreigners, Oda Nobunaga, in his steps against Buddhist sects first set in motion the machinery which his successors were to operate so efficiently against the Christians. To check centrifugal tendencies was the common interest of the hegemons; and they worked to eliminate potential poles of disaffection. The required corollaries of their labors were the suppression of Christianity and the land's nearly total seclusion. The dictates of internal policy were the principal causes of Christianity's doom.

The acceptance of Christianity in Japan was a peculiar phenomenon of the disjointed polity of Sengoku, the Country at War, and the factors which had made it possible were nullified in the Tokugawa realm of political equilibrium and an established intellectual orthodoxy. The rejection of Christianity was a necessary characteristic of this Japanese version of the state as a work of art, whose dynamic tensions were held in bounds by the cordons of Sakoku. The political organism of the Tokugawa—the *bakuhan* [shogunate and domain] system—was in many ways a remarkable structure. Its most notable aspect was, of course, its endurance as a regime of peace for over two hundred years. But the stability was posited upon a subtle arrangement of countervailing forces. The structure's architects were primarily intent, at the time when they formulated the Sakoku policy, that nothing should disturb the balance of what yet seemed a perilously organized realm. They viewed with the gravest suspicion the Christians' loyalty to foreign masters, and refused to distinguish between spiritual and temporal allegiance. Indeed, in the case of certain daimyo of Sengoku Japan, that distinction is difficult to draw even today. One of them, Omura Sumitada, had even ceded the authority over Nagasaki and the neighboring portion of his domain to the Jesuit Order.

The Tokugawa policy-makers extended the principle of distrust into a sweeping generality. The causes of Sakoku were complex, but a nurtured stage of alarm at Christianity as the external threat was prime matter in the policy's justification. And Sakoku became the sum total of the shogunate's approach to foreign affairs.

The conclusive proscription in the final Sakoku Edict of 1639 of all vessels of the Christian contagion was forced by the shock of the Shimabara Uprising of 1637–38. Although even hostile sources attribute the origins of the outbreak to the harsh taxation levied by a lord who was inordinately greedy, the rising did possess an incontrovertibly Christian taint. The peasants were spurred on by quasi-messianic hopes. . . . In their inspection of the emblems of the Shimabara Uprising, the leaders of the newly established Tokugawa regime could review the other major crisis in the securing of their dominance over Japan. When quelling the vestigial challenge of Toyotomi Hideyori's party in the Osaka Campaigns of 1614 and 1615, they saw the ranks of their adversaries swelled by Christian ronin [masterless samurai] with "so many crosses,

Jesus and *Santiagos* on the flags, tents, and other martial insignia which the Japanese use in their encampments, that this must needs have made Ieyasu sick to his stomach."

The Tokugawa indeed felt that Christianity was a disease which infected their subjects with disloyalty. Their effort to extirpate Christianity inspired certain of the measures of social control which were such significant features of their system. Forced registry of all the land's people in Buddhist temples made of Buddhism an instrument applied to the elimination of religious heterodoxy. Groups of collective responsibility—the five-family neighborhood associations . . . —were utilized to arrest the Christian peril. The suspiciousness of the Tokugawa officials, and the thoroughness of their control measures, reached a hysterical pitch akin to that of their Spanish contemporaries (or of those petty bureaucrats of modern Germany) who were bent on enforcing "racial purity." Entry into almost any sort of service occupation involved the prior attestation that the person was not a Christian. For instance, a whore's initial contract required such a formula; for officialdom was most concerned that the lady's customers not be contaminated.

31
Fabian Fucan: A Japanese Critique of Roman Catholicism

In the unfolding of the Christian century there were a number of complex factors and important figures. The life of the Japanese man named Fabian Fucan (1565?–1621) provides us a window to the personal process of bringing these factors and figures together, a process that resulted in his decision to join the religion and later to leave it. Fabian had studied Buddhism as a young man before converting to Christianity at an early age, and he later wrote a Christian critique of Buddhism; but after twenty years as a Christian he rejected Christianity and wrote a critique of it from the viewpoint of the religions of Japan.

In Fabian's 1620 critique of Christianity, *Deus Destroyed,* Christianity is called "the cult of Deus" because the Jesuit missionaries used the Latin term *deus* to refer to God. In the translated excerpt from *Deus Destroyed,* Fabian explains in the preface his personal background. Then he describes a Christian teaching, and after stating "To counter, I reply," he gives his critique of this teaching. This description and critique gives us some idea of the Japanese perception of Catholic Christianity and religious reasons for rejecting it.

DEUS DESTROYED

Fabian Fucan
George Elison, translator

Preface

What is the cult of Deus? What are the scriptures on which this cult's adherents rely, and the terminology they use? Who is the main deity they worship, and what do they say about his Causal State? What are the principles they teach? Because the followers of the Buddhas do not inquire into these matters, they are not able to strike down and defeat this sect. Because the priestly attendants of the gods are not familiar with these matters, they are not able to vanquish this cult's adherents and chase them from the land. And therefore the cursed doctrine has grown day by day; wickedness has flourished many months—how many years have passed thus!

I joined this creed at an early age; diligently, I studied its teachings and pursued its practices. Due to my stupidity, however, I was long unable to realize that this was a perverse and cursed faith. Thus fruitlessly I spent twenty years and more! Then one day I clearly perceived that the words of the adherents of Deus were very clever and appeared very near reason—but in their teaching there was little truth. So I left their company. Some fifteen years have passed since: every morning I have lamented my desertion of the Great Holy True Law [Buddhism]; every evening I have grieved over my adherence to the crooked path of the barbarians. All that effort to no effect! But I had a friend who remonstrated with me, saying: " 'If you have made a mistake, do not be afraid of admitting the fact and amending your ways.' Here, this is the Confucians' golden rule of life—act on it! Before, you learned all about the cursed faith of Deus; take pen in hand now, commit your knowledge to writing, and counter their teachings. Not only will you thereby gain the merit of destroying wickedness and demonstrating truth; you will also supply a guide toward new knowledge."

All right. Though I am not a clever man, I shall by all means try to act on this advice. I shall gather the important points about the teachings of the Deus sect and shall skip what is not essential; my aim is to write concisely. Thus shall I mount my attack; and I shall call my volume DEUS DESTROYED.

In the sixth year of Genna, *kanoe saru,*
on the sixteenth day of the first month,
a Zen recluse in my hermitage,
at random I write this Preface.

Reprinted by permission of the publisher from George Elison, *Deus Destroyed* (Cambridge: Harvard University Press, 1973). The notes have been deleted.

For those initially entering the Deus sect
there is a seven-step gate to the doctrine.
And the sum of the FIRST STEP is as follows——

In the myriad phenomena of heaven and earth, we recognize an all-powerful creator; in the unaltering change of the seasons, we recognize his regulating hand. To use an analogy: When we see a splendid palace, we realize that there existed a skilled craftsman who built it; when we see that house laws exist within a family and the family is governed according to their intention, we realize that the family must certainly have a household head. Such realization is the universal rule. Therefore, since there was a time when heaven did not exist and earth did not exist and nothing existed and all was a lonely void, then the fact that heaven and earth emerged, that the sun, the moon, and the stars with boundless brilliance shed their light in the heavens, rising in the east and setting in the west in unaltered sequence, that the thousand grasses and the myriad trees grow on earth, sprouting fresh buds and shedding old leaves exactly in the appointed season—this fact would be inconceivable without the existence of an all-powerful creator. This all-powerful creator we call Deus.

To counter, I reply:
What is so amazing about all this? What schools fail to discuss this? It is stated:

> There was something before heaven and earth:
> The shapeless original emptiness;
> It acts as the lord of the myriad phenomena,
> It does not wane in accord with the four seasons.

And also:

> Heaven does not speak;
> Yet the four seasons run their course thereby,
> The hundred creatures, each after its kind,
> Are born thereby.

Moreover, Buddhists discuss this in terms of the process of origination, continuation, destruction, and void; and in Shinto the Age of the Gods is divided between the Seven Gods of Heaven and the Five Gods of Earth. And the first of the Seven Gods of Heaven are the Three: Kuni-tokotachi no Mikoto, Kuni-sazuchi no Mikoto, and Toyokunnu no Mikoto; they are the ones who opened up heaven and earth. The lord who always rises to the land's government: this is the meaning of the worshipful name Kuni-tokotachi no Mikoto. Why then do the adherents of Deus press their tedious claims with the pretence that they alone know the lord who opened up heaven and earth? Idle verbosity without substance, and most annoying!

The adherents of Deus claim:
Deus is *infinitus*—without beginning or end. He is *spiritualis substantia*—true substance without material shape. He is *omnipotens*—all is in his power. He is *sapientissimus*—the wellspring of wisdom without superior. He is *justissimus*—the wellspring of universal law. He is *misericordissimus*—the wellspring of uni-

versal mercy and universal compassion. Aside from all this, he is the wellspring of all good and all quality. Since the Buddhas and the gods all are merely human beings, they do not possess the above-mentioned qualities. Since they are subject to the process of birth and death, how can they be said to be the creators of heaven and earth?

To counter, I reply:

To regard the Buddhas and the gods as merely human is but the wicked view of ignorant men, a supposition truly befitting the adherents of Deus. The Buddhas all possess the Three Bodies: the Law Body, the Recompensed Body, and the Accommodated Body. The Tathagata in the Accommodated-Transformed Body did undergo the Eight Stages of Earthly Life, for the sake of salvation of all sentient beings and as a means of bestowing grace. However, the Tathagata in the Law Body is the Buddha of Eternal Existence and Eternal Constancy in kalpas boundless and without beginning: he is the True Buddha of the Law Body of Thusness. He therefore transcends all attempts to define him; one does not speak of "good" or "evil" in him. And so the scriptures also say:

> Constant dwells the Tathagata;
> There is in him no change.

Only the deluded and unenlightened consider him merely human. And those who say that the gods also are merely human likewise are ignorant.

The August Gods in their origins are manifestations of the Buddhas under the figures of Japanese deities.[1] For instance, Tenman Daijizai Tenjin in his original state is the all-merciful all-compassionate Kanzeon; but when in subdued brilliance he became part of this world of dust, he appeared in the person of the Grand Minister Kan Shojo and left his evidence for posterity at Kitano; he is celebrated as the God Protector of the Hundred Kings. Where the god of shrine or mausoleum to whom this principle does not apply?! But let us go further, let us take up the example of Kuni-tokotachi no Mikoto. How could you ever say he is a mere human, he who was a god before even one human existed, before heaven and earth were opened up! Don't dare say it, don't dare say it! Accept as understood the things you can understand, admit you do not fathom the things you can not fathom. Even the Sage Confucius spoke about the gods as follows:

> They cause the men of the world
> To fast and be purified and wear
> Their finest clothing:
> Thereby to carry out religious ritual.
> In mighty overflow, they are above
> And on the right
> And on the left as well.

[We skip the second through the fifth steps.]

---

1. See page 50 for an interpretation of *kami* as manifestations of Buddhas.—ED.

Sixth Step

The adherents of Deus claim:

The above-mentioned entry of Deus into this world occurred after some five thousand years had passed from the time when heaven and earth were opened up. His birth took place during the reign of an emperor named Caesar, in a village called Belem, in the country of Judea. His mother's name was Santa Maria, and Joseph was the name of his father. But both Santa Maria and Joseph were *virgem,* by which is meant to say that throughout their lives they did not have marital relations; and in these circumstances he was conceived and born.

But how did all this come about? How are we to understand this entry of Deus into the world? Well, first of all, this Santa Maria not only possessed the virtue of lifelong chastity but also, because she was endowed with the various good qualities and all the virtuous accomplishments, she paid zealous attention to devotional pursuits and to the recitation of prayers. One day at dusk, as she had composed her mind toward the open window of spiritual contemplation, an *anjo* [angel] suddenly appeared before her. And he knelt down, his hands upraised and joined, and uttered: *Ave, gratia plena. Dominus tecum.* The meaning of these words is: "Hail Maria, full of Deus's grace. The Lord is with you." And from that moment she conceived and after the ten months were fulfilled she gave birth in the aforesaid Belem, at deepest midnight, in a stable. And angels descended from the heavens, playing music, and a wonderful fragrance pervaded the four directions. And marvellous signs were seen at this time, to testify that Deus had entered this world.

Now the name of the Lord who was thus born is Jesus Christus. For thirty-three years he remained on this earth, to teach the way of goodness to all sentient beings. But because he claimed that he was Deus a group of people called Jews on hearing this said it was deviltry. And, swaying their judges, they heaped blows and tortures upon him, and then they suspended him upon a stake known as the *cruz* [cross]. And thus he crushed sin and gave effect to good for mankind, and by this merit he accomplished atonement for the sin of Adam and Eve. And thus in his thirty-third year he summoned forth death. But on the third day he rose again from the dead, and after forty days he ascended into Heaven. Some one thousand and six hundred years have passed since.

To counter, I reply:

So it took all of five thousand years after heaven and earth were opened up for Deus to enter this world! Was the atonement so late in coming because heaven and earth are so far apart? Were so many years expended along the way on this distant route? Or were all those years spent on fuss and preparation for the journey? Since atonement was not accomplished for five thousand years all the human beings in the world had to fall into hell—a measureless, countless number! All those people falling down to hell! Really, it must have been like a torrent of rain. And him who watched this and did not even feel sad, who for five thousand years was not disposed to find a way to redeem sentient beings—are we to call him the all-merciful, all-compassionate Lord? One simple look at this will make it clear that all the teachings of the adherents of Deus are fraud.

And what they say about the total number of years is also extremely dubious. Five thousand years from the opening up of heaven and earth until the coming of Jesus Christus added to the one thousand and six hundred years since his coming make a sum of six thousand and six hundred years. In balancing this number of years against that recorded in the Japanese and Chinese histories one finds the number exceedingly short. But perhaps the heaven and earth of the adherents of Deus are somewhere outside this heaven and this earth, and came into existence at a later date. Perhaps there is yet another, a separate heaven and earth. Dubious, dubious!

So Jesus Christus was born with lifelong virgins, the virtuous Joseph and Santa Maria, as father and mother. What sort of ideal virtue is this? "Man and wife have separate functions." The universal norm of moral law is that one and all shall enter into marital relations. Actually, to counter the universal norm is evil; and evil may be defined as the departure from the Way. If marital relations were not completely the standard of moral law in the world, then what else could we expect but the extinction of the human seed in every province and district, down into the last village! So it is obvious now that the standard Way is virtuous and all outside it not virtuous.

So Jesus Christus assumed the name of Lord of Heaven and Earth and because of this the group of Jews, saying that this was deviltry, sued him before their judges, suspended him upon a stake, and took his life. Now this, to be sure, is both plausible and proper! *The Odes* say:

> To hack an axe-haft
> an axe
> hacks;
> the pattern's near.

And now, before our very eyes here in Japan, you adherents of Deus are preaching a doctrine wicked and contrary to the Way of the Sages; and therefore the wise ruler has decided to stamp out your doctrine, and the people also hate it and inform on it and denounce its followers, so that they are beheaded or crucified or burnt at the stake. The methods of government of the wise men of former and of latter days agree perfectly, like the halves of a tally joined. But the doctrine you adherents of Deus preach is a perverse faith; I shall unmask it later, point by point.

Well, then: What you say about the resurrection and ascent to Heaven sounds quite splendid; but in a faith perverse from its very roots everything must be devilish illusion, magical trickery.

The right and wrong of enlightenment, right or wrong, is all resolved as right. The right and wrong of delusion, right or wrong, is all resolved as wrong. The right and wrong of true doctrine, right or wrong, is all resolved as truth. The right and wrong of deviltry, right or wrong, is all resolved as devilish. There is no ground for indecision about this!

32
The Plea for an Authentic Japanese Christianity

The relative success and then persecution and elimination of Christianity during the Christian century obviously were closely related to the governmental policy first favoring and then officially rejecting this foreign religion. However, even in modern times, beginning in the late 1800s when the government allowed Christian missionaries freedom to seek Japanese converts, less than 1 percent of the population has become Christian.

One of the problems that has plagued Christianity, especially Protestantism, in modern Japan is the proliferation of European and American church organizations. The difficulty is not simply the number of denominations, but the fact that each denomination tended to force the identity of the Japanese Christian into the mold of a particular denominational tradition. As Uchimura Kanzo points out so well in the following excerpt, most Christian denominations arise out of and express the national character of people or even the regional character within a nation, as with Cumberland Presbyterianism. But because no Japanese Christian was born and raised in the Cumberland region of Kentucky, his or her social, political, economic, and artistic sensitivities are not nurtured by the same factors that influence the Cumberland resident. In short, Uchimura says that it is hypocritical for a Japanese Christian to ape the mannerisms of Kentucky; someone who has been brought up in Japan cannot "jump out of his skin" and become a Cumberland Presbyterian.

Uchimura advocates that Japanese Christians must express their Christianity in distinctively Japanese fashion, through the forms of Japanese culture. For this reason he talks about the "two J's," Japan and Jesus. The Japanese person who is truly committed to Jesus as a religious leader will be able to express his commitment through Japanese culture. Uchimura presents a high ideal for Protestant Christianity in Japan, an ideal that is still pursued but seems not yet to have been widely attained.

JAPANESE CHRISTIANITY

Uchimura Kanzo
From *Sources of Japanese Tradition*

I am blamed by missionaries for upholding Japanese Christianity. They say that Christianity is a universal religion, and to uphold Japanese Christianity is to make a universal religion a national religion. Very true. But do not these very missionaries uphold sectional or denominational forms of Christianity

Reprinted by permission of the publisher from *Sources of Japanese Tradition*, edited by Ryusaku Tsunoda, Wm. Theodore de Bary, and Donald Keene (New York: Columbia University Press, 1958), paperback edition, Vol. 2, pp. 348–350.

which are not very different from national Christianity? Are they sure that their Methodism, Presbyterianism, Episcopalianism, Congregationalism, Lutheranism, and hundred other Christian isms—they say that in Christiandom there are above six hundred different kinds of Christianity—are they sure that all these myriad kinds of Christianity are each of them a universal religion? Why blame me for upholding Japanese Christianity while every one of them upholds his or her own Christianity? If it is not a mistake to uphold any one of these six hundred different forms of Christianity, why is it wrong for me to uphold my Japanese Christianity? Please explain.

Then, too, are these missionary-critics sure that there is no national Christianity in Europe and America? Is not Episcopalianism essentially an English Christianity, Presbyterianism a Scotch Christianity, Lutheranism a German Christianity, and so forth? Why, for instance, call a universal religion "Cumberland Presbyterianism"? If it is not wrong to apply the name of a district in the state of Kentucky to Christianity, why is it wrong for me to apply the name of my country to the same? I think I have as much right to call my Christianity Japanese as thousands of Christians in Cumberland Valley have a right to call their Christianity by the name of the valley they live in.

When a Japanese truly and independently believes in Christ, he is a Japanese Christian, and his Christianity is Japanese Christianity. It is all very simple. A Japanese Christian does not arrogate the whole Christianity to himself, neither does he create a new Christianity by becoming a Christian. He is a Japanese, and he is a Christian; therefore he is a Japanese Christian. A Japanese by becoming a Christian does not cease to be a Japanese. On the contrary, he becomes more Japanese by becoming a Christian. A Japanese who becomes an American or an Englishman, or an amorphous universal man, is neither a true Japanese nor a true Christian. Paul, a Christian apostle, remained an Hebrew of the Hebrews till the end of his life. Savonarola was an Italian Christian, Luther was a German Christian, and Knox was a Scotch Christian. They were not characterless universal men, but distinctly national, therefore distinctly human, and distinctly Christian. . . .

I have seen no more sorrowful figures than Japanese who imitate their American or European missionary-teachers by being converted to the faith of the latter. Closely examined, these converted "universal Christians" may turn out to be no more than denationalized Japanese, whose universality is no more than Americanism or Anglicanism adopted to cover up their lost nationality.

"Two J's"

I love two J's and no third; one is Jesus, and the other is Japan.

I do not know which I love more, Jesus or Japan.

I am hated by my countrymen for Jesus' sake as *yaso*, and I am disliked by foreign missionaries for Japan's sake as national and narrow.

No matter; I may lose all my friends, but I cannot lose Jesus and Japan.

For Jesus' sake, I cannot own any other God than His Father as my God and Father; and for Japan's sake, I cannot accept any faith which comes in the name of foreigners. Come starvation; come death; I cannot disown Jesus and Japan; I am emphatically a Japanese Christian, though I know missionaries in general do not like that name.

Jesus and Japan; my faith is not a circle with one center; it is an ellipse with two centers. My heart and mind revolve around the two dear names. And I know that one strengthens the other; Jesus strengthens and purifies my love for Japan; and Japan clarifies and objectivises my love for Jesus. Were it not for the two, I would become a mere dreamer, a fanatic, an amorphous universal man.

Jesus makes me a world-man, a friend of humanity; Japan makes me a lover of my country, and through it binds me firmly to the terrestrial globe. I am neither too narrow nor too broad by loving the two at the same time.

O Jesus, thou art the Sun of my soul, the saviour dear; I have given my all to thee!

O Japan,

Land of lands, for thee we give,
Our hearts, our pray'rs, our service free;
For thee thy sons shall nobly live,
And at thy need shall die for thee.
     J. G. WHITTIER

To Be Inscribed Upon My Tomb

I for Japan;
Japan for the World;
The World for Christ;
And All for God.

33
A New Religion as the Japanese Way of Christianity

Christianity in Japan contrasts sharply with Japanese New Religions. Although many Christian missionaries have been active in Japan for more than a century, the total number of Christians is less than a million, while several New Religions have memberships in the millions; and while Christianity is still perceived as a foreign religion, the New Religions are seen as thoroughly Japanese. Indeed, the fact that only a few Japanese New Religions developed out of Christianity is an indication that Christianity has not become a part of Japanese culture.

Makuya is an exception to the rule that Japanese New Religions are not derived from Christianity. Actually Makuya is an offshoot of the Mukyokai ("non-church") movement, whose members are highly intellectual and mainly upper-class Christians. As the author characterizes the two groups, "the Mukyokai grafted a puritan form of Christianity onto the *samurai* tradition," whereas "the Makuya movement . . . grafted a pentecostal form of Christianity onto the popular religious tradition of

Japan." The Makuya movement emphasizes Bible study (as does Mukyokai), and especially healing, speaking in tongues, and miracles. It has appealed to less-educated, lower-class people. Makuya may be seen as a form of Christianity that is thoroughly Japanese or a New Religion that is thoroughly Christian—"the Japanese way of Christianity." (For more materials on New Religions see Chapter 17.)

THE MAKUYA CHRISTIANITY

Carlo Caldarola

Some twenty-five years ago [about 1950] a small group of Mukyokai Christians with pentecostal leanings became dissatisfied with the professorial tone of the Bible meetings and left to form a sect of their own to provide them with deeper emotional satisfaction.

The founder of this new movement was Teshima Ikuro. Born in a small town of South Japan, son of a school teacher who later converted to Christianity under his son's influence, Teshima was the second of four children, and he grew up convinced that his mother did not love him as much as she did the other children. Because of Ikuro's poor performance in school, his father decided to make him a merchant, a decision which so disappointed Ikuro that he wanted to kill himself. At the age of 14 he happened to come across one of Kagawa's essays, which drew him into the study of Christianity and the Bible; at 15, he was baptized into the Protestant Church of Japan. A friend introduced him to the Mukyokai movement, which he joined as a disciple of Tsukamoto Toraji; later he formed his own Bible group and taught for several years.

At his father's behest, Teshima had attended the Nagasaki Business College, and subsequently operated several businesses with considerable success before and during World War II.

In 1947, the incident occurred which changed his life completely. An Occupation official decided to raze a grammar school in Teshima's neighborhood, and when Teshima organized and led a protest movement, the official ordered his arrest and imprisonment. Fearing for his life, Teshima fled to Mount Aso, where he hid in a cave for a month, praying and meditating. His concentration within the rugged and solitary setting led him to experience the mysterious presence of God and to hear His voice calling him to a higher mission. Nerving himself to return home, he dissolved his business enterprises and devoted himself wholeheartedly to his ministry. At first, he was not very successful, as people had a tendency to doze off during his lectures. But at the end of a summer Bible Conference in his old setting by Mount Aso, Teshima suddenly began to pray aloud with great fervor, calling on God to send him

Reprinted by permission of the publisher from Carlo Caldarola, *Christianity: The Japanese Way* (Leiden: E. J. Brill, 1979). The notes have been deleted.

the power of His spirit. The audience was greatly affected, and many people wept or cried out in spiritual and emotional excitement.

This was the turning point in Teshima's ministry for his Bible classes retained the tremendous emotional involvement of his original spiritual experience. However, he became greatly dissatisfied with Mukyokai Christianity, which he found too cold, abstract, and speculative a setting for bringing people into true contact with God. Though he agreed that the Mukyokai movement had indeed disengaged Japanese Christianity from the western Church, he felt that it had stopped at the cross and had neglected the Resurrection and the Pentecost. He therefore undertook to form his own offshoot of Mukyokai Christianity emphasizing the presence of the Holy Spirit through healing and speaking in tongues. He called this new movement the "Original Gospel Movement" (*Genshi Fukuin Undo*) or more popularly *Makuya* (Tabernacle of Christ) to indicate its goal of bringing the living Christ to the people. . . .

THE MAKUYA MOVEMENT

As an offshoot of the Mukyokai movement, the Makuya reject all institutionalized forms of Christianity, including constitutions, creeds, clergy, sacraments, and liturgy; there are no membership rolls, statistics, or church buildings. The movement is centered around Bible study groups which currently number some 500 throughout the country, with a total membership of approximately 60,000. Groups meet in private homes (usually the leaders') or rented halls, and their internal structure is based on the familiar teacher-disciple relationship.

Apart from these general features, however, the Makuya differs significantly from the Mukyokai movement. The Makuya appeals primarily to people of lesser education and lower social status; its membership is composed of unskilled or semiskilled labor, lower white-collar workers, and small businessmen. University graduates, professionals, primary and high school teachers constitute only two or three per cent of the adherents.

In contrast to the absolute individualism and group autonomy of the Mukyokai, the Makuya movement displays a certain degree of centralization. During his twenty years of charismatic leadership, Teshima was both the driving force behind the Makuya and the only controlling power within it. He personally trained all of its Bible teachers in Greek, Hebrew, and Biblical exegesis for at least three months in his own home, and then appointed them to lead various groups, transferring them from place to place as the need arose. Since Teshima's death in 1973, there has been no official successor as the Makuya's non-church principles prohibit any form of institutionalized succession. A joint leadership of all the Bible teachers has been established in order to transact the movement's major items of business. Theoretically, each of the approximately 300 *sensei* has equal rights and responsibilities, but in practice those who are full-time evangelists and reside in Tokyo have the most responsibility and power. Mrs. Teshima is the most powerful, and virtually nothing is decided without consulting her. Though she is not a charismatic leader or a preacher, she is regarded as the living memory of Teshima and his personality and charisma are perceived to be still operative in the movement through her. Many Makuya feel this leadership situation to be only temporary but no one cares to speculate about the future.

The leadership vacuum among the Makuya may last indefinitely, or a new charismatic leader may emerge from among the Bible teachers. Following a pattern which recurs frequently among the new religions, Teshima's son Jacob, who is now studying in New York, may decide to take up the mantle of leadership. Whatever the outcome, the Makuya are firmly set against becoming as individualistic as the Mukyokai or as formalized as the institutional churches.

Teshima's mansion in Tokyo remains the Makuya headquarters, locus for their meetings and for publication of their national monthly *Seimei no Hikari* (Light of Life) and weekly *Shukan Genshi Fukuin* (Weekly Original Gospel) periodicals. Bible teachers are now trained in two steps: introductory training in Bible studies is done by a specially-appointed Makuya teacher, following which the trainees go to Israel for one to three years in order to familiarize themselves with Hebrew and the monuments of the Holy Land.

Makuya teachers are by definition endowed with thaumaturgical powers and take pride in describing their miraculous manifestations. In a field interview, a medical doctor living in a small town in Southern Japan candidly revealed that he usually cured his patients more quickly with a laying on of hands than with his professional skills. Another famous Makuya miracle-worker, Mrs. Kimura, related how she was called to the bedside of an 89-year-old lady who had just died of exhaustion. The bereaved relatives beseeched Mrs. Kimura to restore her to life. Mrs. Kimura rapped on her forehead three times, with increasing strength, while at the same time calling her name loudly. At the third blow, the old lady opened her eyes and sat up. She has now lived well into her nineties, and enjoys perfect health.

The miracle is the Makuya movement's most effective instrument of proselytization. Many of the members believe because they or a member of their family were miraculously healed. Statements like the following are quite common among the Makuya believers: "Teshima (or some other *sensei*) laid his hand on my head. At that very moment I felt a flash of powerful light entering my mind and a strong energy running from the head to the tips of my feet. I cried out of happiness. The fever and any other trace of the sickness had disappeared. I was fully healed."

Teacher-disciple relationships are based on the traditional *oyako* principle—the absolute authority of father over son, and corresponding filial devotion of disciple to teacher. The group's religious experience creates deep emotional ties ensuring conformity with the teachings of the leader, and this conformity is further strengthened by a sense of the group's sectarian uniqueness. The Makuya believe that their religion constitutes the last and most perfect stage in the development of Christianity, following the successive failures of Catholicism, Protestantism, and Mukyokai Christianity. They are bonded together by a sense of mission and by constant expressions of the Spirit in their daily lives—miracles, glossolalia, and faith healing. Since they firmly believe that salvation cannot be found outside of their movement, they proselytize constantly. One of their popular rallying cries is, "Let each of us bring five new members to the Original Gospel Movement this year!" The Makuya target is an individual, often a disaffected member of a Church, as a base from which to work on the entire family. It is estimated that some 40 percent of the Makuya members are ex-members of the Christian denominations.

The Bible meeting is the central religious practice of the movement. Groups may vary in size from as few as five or six to as many as three hundred people. Teshima's meeting (so-called even after his death) is considered to be the most compelling within the movement, and several Makuya groups in Tokyo hold their own meetings on a weekday in order to be able to attend it on Sunday. . . .

It is clear that the Makuya movement resembles many of the new religions in Japan, and it performs the same social function of filling the vacuum in the lower strata of society created by the postwar breakdown of the traditional value system. It does this by offering a social relationship based on the paternalistic system which is so comforting to disadvantaged Japanese, and by promising miraculous solutions to the problems of life. What distinguishes the Makuya is its Christianity. Although many Christian elements are found in several of the new religions, particularly in the *Konkokyo* (Golden Light) and *Tenrikyo* (Divine Wisdom), they are so mixed with indigenous elements that none of them can be directly identified with Christianity. The Makuya is the only movement to indigenize Christianity—traditionally an upper-class religion—in the Japanese lower classes. By emphasizing its pentecostal aspects, the Makuya has ingeniously succeeded in fostering the continuity of a Japanese folk-religious tradition dominated by shamanism, magic, and miracles.

CHAPTER NINE

Syncretism in Japanese Religious Life

R eligion in Japan is characterized both by a plurality of religious traditions and by mutual influence among these traditions. With the possible exception of Christianity, all the major religious lines within Japan have intersected to form a distinctive national heritage. This means that although it is possible to distinguish the religions as formal traditions, each tradition is shaped in part by the other. What is more important, in the life of the people there has been no neat pigeonholing of religions. For example, in the selection on page 121, we saw that individuals are more interested in the totality of a ritual or cult than in its historical influences. (For a description of this kind of religious interaction in one village, see p. 221.)

Japanese people have usually experienced religion in terms of an overall worldview and mutually reinforcing acts of worship. Selections in this chapter show how individuals have naturally integrated parts of several traditions into a total philosophy of life. Several authors state specifically that there is no difference between Shinto, Buddhism, and Confucianism. This has been the majority opinion in Japanese history, but some religious leaders and some groups (such as Nichiren Buddhism) have assumed exclusive commitment to one tradition. (For a Buddhist interpretation of interaction in Japanese religion, see p. 50.)

Usually this kind of interaction or "mixing" of religious traditions has been called "syncretism" in the West. However, if we are to continue to use this term, we should avoid any mistaken implications that there are "pure" religions as opposed to syncretistic traditions. Just as there is no pure language, so there is no pure religion. For example, just as Buddhism arose out of Hinduism and still contains many of its elements, so Christianity arose out of Judaism and still includes many of its features. Proponents of a religion, such as Buddhists and Christians, naturally see the distinctiveness of their respective traditions, rather than the composite character. The important contrast to make here (apart from definitions of terms like *syncretism*) is that in the West the overwhelming ideal was to maintain one tradition as distinct as possible, while in Japan the most common ideal was to blend together two or more traditions as smoothly as possible.

34
Religious Life in Medieval Japan

It has long been the practice in Japan to participate simultaneously in several religious traditions with no sense of contradiction. The extracts from the will of a tenth-century nobleman in this selection illustrate this practice. The will offers simple advice to the nobleman's heirs, showing concretely how several religious traditions are interwoven in a person's daily life. According to this will, one should be aware of astrological and calendrical concerns as soon as he arises in the morning. Even a small matter such as washing one's hands has a specific procedure—facing west, the direction of Buddhist paradise. Other restrictions concerning personal cleanliness are in conformity with the calendar. The author of the will recommends chanting the name of Buddha and *kami,* but he feels no need to label the source of these diverse elements—it is enough that they define a total personal worldview.

Advice on personal behavior—especially concerning frugality and filial piety—is indirectly Confucian. On the other hand, daily devotion to a specific divinity is advisable, as is the chanting of Buddhist mantra (formulas). Additionally, just as one cares for his family during life, so should he set aside money for his own memorial services. George Sansom, a noted historian and author of the following extract, points out how Buddhist, Confucian, and even Shinto elements interact freely in this will. Of course, this last testament sets a very high ideal of personal conduct and devotion, which the average person might not attain, but the document is valuable for showing how several traditions are blended in the religious life of an individual.

THE WILL OF A TENTH CENTURY NOBLEMAN

George Sansom

The ascetic motive, the feeling for simplicity, purity, frugality, is as characteristic of Heian taste as is the strong sense of form and colour expressed by contrast in brilliant costume and elaborate ceremonial. It is an integral part of the great aesthetic tradition, which is perhaps rooted in early ideas of ritual purity.

It is certainly an aspect of Japanese social ideals which should not be overlooked, and we may therefore turn for a little while to the circles of high-minded statesmen and severe moralists. Their standards of propriety are set forth in many diaries and injunctions to posterity, notably of the tenth century, some of which have already been cited. It is significant that one of the most important of these is a document known as *Kujo-den no Goyuikai,* the Testamentary Admonitions of Kujo-den, who was none other than the great Fujiwara leader Morosuke, Minister of the Right at his death in 960. Though it is too long for full quotation here, the following extracts will give a fair idea of its quality. It must be read as setting forth a rule of life followed by Morosuke and recommended by him to his heirs and successors.

> Upon arising, first of all repeat seven times in a low voice the name of the star for the year. [There are seven—the seven stars of the Great Bear.] Take up a mirror and look at your face, to scrutinize changes in your appearance. Then look at the calendar and see whether the day is one of good or evil omen. Next use your toothbrush and then, facing West [i.e., in the direction of Paradise], wash your hands. Chant the name of Buddha and invoke those gods and divinities whom we ought always to revere and worship. Next make a record of the events of the previous day. [Throughout the document much stress is laid on the careful use of the calendar for noting engagements and on the accurate recording of the day's business as soon as possible after the event.]
>
> Now break your fast with rice gruel. Comb your hair once every three days, not every day. Cut your fingernails on a day of the Ox, your toenails on a day of the Tiger. If the day is auspicious, now bathe, but only once every fifth day. There are favourable and unfavourable days for bathing.
>
> Now if there is any business upon which you must go abroad, put on your clothes and cap. Do not be sluggish in attending to your duties.
>
> When you meet people do not talk a great deal. And do not discuss your personal affairs. State your opinion, and say what is necessary, but do not repeat what others have said. The disasters of mankind proceed from the mouth. Beware, be on your guard. [Note that most works of this kind emphasize the importance of reserve, of circumspection in speech and gesture.] And when you read documents concerned with state affairs always treat them with discretion.
>
> At the morning and evening meals you must not make a habit of eating and drinking to excess. Nor should you eat except at proper times. [This rule is supported by a slightly garbled quotation from the Odes.]
>
> Careful planning can secure the future. In general as you get on in years and become well-acquainted with affairs, you should read classical

Reprinted from *A History of Japan to 1334,* by George Sansom, with the permission of the publishers, Stanford University Press. © 1958 by the Board of Trustees of the Leland Stanford Junior University. The bracketed remarks are from the original.

literature in the morning, next practise handwriting, and only after this indulge in games or sports. But an excessive addiction to hawking and hunting is positively wrong.

After receiving your manly robes [this refers to the ceremony called "genbuku," the donning of the toga virilis] and before you embark on an official career, conduct yourself in this manner: Early in life select a divinity as the object of your devotion and chant his holy name, after cleansing your hands in a basin of water. One may judge how near a man is to salvation from the frequency with which he recites the mantra [the invocations and spells of the mystic sects].

There are many warning examples close at hand of disaster and calamity overtaking our irreligious colleagues. Thus the Third Regent, the Lord Tadahira [Morosuke's father], has told us: "In the eighth year of Encho (930) when a thunderbolt struck the Pure Cool Hall, the courtiers went pale. I, having taken refuge in the Three Treasures [the Buddhist faith], found in this event nothing to be frightened about. But the Great Counsellor Kiyoyuki and the Vice-Counsellor Mareyo, who had never paid homage to the Law of the Buddha—these two were struck dead." From this we may draw our lesson, that the grace bestowed upon us by our faith in the mantra will save us from misfortune. Moreover, many of the clergy, men of faith, purity, and wisdom, can according to their spiritual power bear witness to similar events. But faith is not of help only in this life, for it will indeed ensure for us the life to come.

If you would learn something of literature, let your attention be devoted especially to the histories and chronicles of our native land.

In all things render always the utmost loyalty and upright service to your Lord. Always devote the fullest degree of filial piety to your parents. Let your deference to your elder brother be like that which you pay to your father, and your love for your younger brother like that which you feel for your child; so that in all things great or small your hearts may be all one, and the aspirations of all [members of the family] so united that they do not differ by a hair's breadth.

Cherish your defenceless sisters with all care. . . .

In general, so long as you are not ill, you should always wait upon your father once every day. Should there be some obstacle, send word and enquire whether it would be suitable to call in the evening. The son and heir of King Wen will serve exceedingly well as a model of filial behaviour. [This is the celebrated Duke of Chou, regarded by Confucius as the paragon of all virtues.] . . .

Let the income of your house as it is received be divided first into ten parts, and let one part be devoted to alms.

Make complete plans beforehand for the conduct of your affairs after your death. . . . When this is not done you invite all manner of inconvenience for your wife, your children, and your servants, who then must ask favours of those from whom they ought not to expect them, or will lose that which they ought not to lose, thus leading to the ruin of your house and to censure by others.

Always put by a portion of your income to provide for the Seven Requiem Masses,[1] for the repose of your spirit, beginning with the cost of the funeral itself. . . .

Do you who come after me reflect fervently on these things, and always devote yourselves to public and private affairs with the utmost diligence.

These cold injunctions to posterity do not sound like the sentiments of a great noble presiding over an extravagant and dissolute aristocracy. They are more akin to the utterances of a prophet deploring the evils of his day. But they are not really moral principles. Rather they are rules for success in life, calling for extreme self-control, and the observances of a very strict code of behaviour exacted by Buddhist faith and Confucian piety. Perhaps their most notable feature is the great weight given to filial duty, together with a disapproval of all social intercourse beyond what is required for the due performance of public obligations. The family is the unit, the means, and the purpose of life. It is self-contained and independent of, if not hostile to, other families. In public what is to be prized is gravity and solemnity. Only in the bosom of the family may one abandon something of the reserve which distinguishes a man of breeding, and relax in an atmosphere of humanity and love.

What seems at first sight surprising is the repeated stress upon frugality and simplicity. It is, of course, in part of Confucian origin, for the Sage must always avoid excess of any kind; but it comes also from a persistent strain in the Japanese character which finds expression in the earliest Shinto ritual and is visible throughout Japanese social history. It is interesting to note that the passage recommending simple clothing and furniture and condemning display is quoted in later literature as a classical dictum on frugality.

35
Unity of Shinto, Confucianism, and Buddhism as the Rationale of the Government

The previous selection illustrates the interaction of religious traditions in the life of the individual; this selection illustrates similar interaction on the level of government. The occasion for this letter from the sixteenth-century Japanese military ruler (civil dictator) Hideyoshi was an earlier letter from the Roman Catholic viceroy of the Indies. The tone of the letter pictures a bold, powerful leader who is proud of his national heritage and not timid about criticizing foreign traditions.

First Hideyoshi outlines his political ambitions, such as ruling China (called here the great Ming nation and the Middle Kingdom). Then he describes the foundation of the Japanese heritage, drawing freely upon Shinto, Confucian, and Buddhist notions. For example, his opening statement, "Ours is the land of the Gods, and

---

1. Requiem masses were always conducted by Buddhist priests.—ED.

God is mind," derives from Shinto—the idea that Japan is the land of the Gods—and from Neo-Confucianism—the more philosophical principle that God is mind. But the document specifies for the foreign reader that this "God" is identical in Japan's three major traditions, and "To know Shinto is to know Buddhism as well as Confucianism."

This official government document demonstrates the strong sense of unified religious worldview as a distinctive Japanese heritage, in clear opposition to foreign "heresies." Especially to be protected is the Confucian ethical and political notion of humanity, which the Catholic priests have allegedly tried to destroy. Christianity is criticized as preaching but one doctrine "to the exclusion of others." Hideyoshi turns the tables on the Christians by offering to send instruction in Japan's "profound philosophy."

LETTER TO THE VICEROY OF THE INDIES

From *Sources of Japanese Tradition*

Reading your message from afar, I can appreciate the immense expanse of water which separates us. As you have noted in your letter, my country, which is comprised of sixty-odd provinces, has known for many years more days of disorder than days of peace; rowdies have been given to fomenting intrigue, and bands of warriors have formed cliques to defy the court's orders. Ever since my youth, I have been constantly concerned over this deplorable situation. I studied the art of self-cultivation and the secret of governing the country. Through profound planning and forethought, and according to the three principles of benevolence, wisdom, and courage, I cared for the warriors on the one hand and looked after the common people on the other; while administering justice, I was able to establish security. Thus, before many years had passed, the unity of the nation was set on a firm foundation, and now foreign nations, far and near, without exception, bring tribute to us. Everyone, everywhere, seeks to obey my orders. . . . Though our own country is now safe and secure, I nevertheless entertain hopes of ruling the great Ming nation. I can reach the Middle Kingdom aboard my palace-ship within a short time. It will be as easy as pointing to the palm of my hand. I shall then use the occasion to visit your country regardless of the distance or the differences between us.

Ours is the land of the Gods, and God is mind. Everything in nature comes into existence because of mind. Without God there can be no spirituality. Without God there can be no way. God rules in times of prosperity as in times of decline. God is positive and negative and unfathomable. Thus, God is the root and source of all existence. This God is spoken of by Buddhism in India,

Reprinted by permission of the publisher from *Sources of Japanese Tradition*, edited by Ryusaku Tsunoda, Wm. Theodore de Bary, and Donald Keene (New York: Columbia University Press, 1958), paperback edition, Vol. I, pp. 316–318.

Confucianism in China, and Shinto in Japan. To know Shinto is to know Buddhism as well as Confucianism.

As long as man lives in this world, Humanity will be a basic principle. Were it not for Humanity and Righteousness, the sovereign would not be a sovereign, nor a minister of state a minister. It is through the practice of Humanity and Righteousness that the foundations of our relationships between sovereign and minister, parent and child, and husband and wife are established. If you are interested in the profound philosophy of God and Buddha, request an explanation and it will be given to you. In your land one doctrine is taught to the exclusion of others, and you are not yet informed of the [Confucian] philosophy of Humanity and Righteousness. Thus there is no respect for God and Buddha and no distinction between sovereign and ministers. Through heresies you intend to destroy the righteous law. Hereafter, do not expound, in ignorance of right and wrong, unreasonable and wanton doctrines. A few years ago the so-called Fathers came to my country seeking to bewitch our men and women, both of the laity and clergy. At that time punishment was administered to them, and it will be repeated if they should return to our domain to propagate their faith. It will not matter what sect or denomination they represent—they shall be destroyed. It will then be too late to repent. If you entertain any desire of establishing amity with this land, the seas have been rid of the pirate menace, and merchants are permitted to come and go. Remember this.

As for the products of the south-land, acknowledgment of their receipt is here made, as itemized. The catalogue of gifts which we tender is presented on a separate paper. The rest will be explained orally by my envoy.
Tensho 19 [1591]: Seventh Month, 25th Day [signed] The Civil Dictator

36
Blending of Religious Traditions in Popular Teaching

As can be seen in the selection on page 158, the Japanese people tended to draw from a number of religions in their daily lives, even though leaders of Shinto and Buddhism tried to maintain the distinctiveness of their respective traditions. In the late Tokugawa period, however, a number of popular teachers attempted to lead the people with a mixture of notions from several traditions.

One teacher who gained great fame was Ninomiya. Ninomiya tried to simplify the doctrines of Shinto, Confucianism, and Buddhism so that they would form a unified practical guide for the common people. Therefore, he relied not so much on abstract argument as on precepts for frugality and virtue in an agrarian setting.

Ninomiya attempted to resolve what he thought were artificial differences between the three great religions of Japan and blended them into one prescription, or "pill." Each ingredient in the pill was effective for a specific area of the Japanese tradition, yet when in the form of a compounded prescription, the several ingredients could

not be distinguished. The thrust of Ninomiya's teaching was that because man is indebted to nature, he should repay this debt with virtue, and in his view, each of the
three traditions supported the repayment of virtue. Ninomiya's basic idea combines the
Shinto sense of gratitude toward nature (in the sense of cosmic rhythm) and the Confucian sense of respect for superiors in a hierarchical society. The following excerpt is
taken from a collection of Ninomiya's teachings handed down by his followers.

THE "PILL" OF THE THREE RELIGIONS

From *Sources of Japanese Tradition*

Old Ninomiya once said, "I have long pondered about Shinto—what it calls
the Way, what are its virtues and what its deficiencies; and about Confucianism—what its teaching consists in, what are its virtues and deficiencies; and
also Buddhism—what do its various sects stand for, and what are their virtues
and deficiencies. And so I wrote a poem:

> The things of this world
> Are like lengths
> Of bamboo rod
> For use in fish nets—
> This one's too long,
> That one too short.

"Such was my dissatisfaction with them. Now let me state the strong and
weak points of each. Shinto is the Way which provides the foundation of the
country; Confucianism is the Way which provides for governing the country;
and Buddhism is the Way which provides for governing one's mind. Caring
no more for lofty speculation than for humble truth, I have tried simply to
extract the essence of each of these teachings. By essence I mean their importance to mankind. Selecting what is important and discarding what is unimportant, I have arrived at the best teaching for mankind, which I call the
teaching of Repaying Virtue. I also call it the 'pill containing the essence of
Shinto, Confucianism and Buddhism.'". . .

Kimigasa Hyodayu asked the proportions of the prescription in this "pill,"
and the old man replied, "One spoon of Shinto, and a half-spoon each of
Confucianism and Buddhism."

Then someone drew a circle, one half of which was marked Shinto and
two quarter-segments labeled Confucianism and Buddhism respectively. "Is it
like this?" he asked. The old man smiled. "You won't find medicine like that
anywhere. In a real pill all the ingredients are thoroughly blended so as to be
indistinguishable. Otherwise it would taste bad in the mouth and feel bad in
the stomach."

Reprinted by permission of the publisher from *Sources of Japanese Tradition*, edited
by Ryusaku Tsunoda, Wm. Theodore de Bary, and Donald Keene (New York:
Columbia University Press, 1958), paperback edition, Vol. 2, pp. 79–80.

PART II

Themes
in Japanese
Religion

CHAPTER TEN

Closeness of Humans, Gods, and Nature

J apanese religion comprises a half dozen different traditions that interact with one another, so that the Japanese people have tended to participate in all these traditions simultaneously. Therefore, in order to understand the sum of these traditions, we need to define the nature of Japanese religion as a whole, or the Japanese religious worldview. One way is to recognize the persistent themes that characterize Japanese religion throughout most of its history, cutting across most of its religious traditions. In Japan at least six persistent themes can be distinguished; Chapters 10 through 15 each discuss one of these themes.

One of the major features of Japanese religious life is the way in which humans, gods, and nature are closely interrelated on the same plane. The term *gods* can mean *kami,* Buddhist divinities, or even venerated human beings and souls of the dead. *Nature* means not an objective and inert collection of substance but the sacred rhythm of the cosmos as a living unity. From the earliest times to the present, the Japanese people have celebrated their closeness to the *kami* and their intimate relationship to nature. (For the notion of *kami* see p. 9.) As seen in Shinto mythology (see p. 13), the *kami* express their sacredness and power through their embodiment in nature, such as the wind, trees, rivers, and mountains. Indeed, in the exceptional case of Matsudaira Sadanobu, he actually worshiped himself as a *kami.* This idea contrasts sharply with the Judaic and Christian traditions, which tend to emphasize the distance between God and man and the inferiority of nature to man.

This triangular relationship of gods, humans, and nature is found in Japanese Buddhism as well as in Shinto; in fact, some of the best examples of this theme are in Zen Buddhism. Zen masters encourage individual enlightenment and the person's identity with the natural world rather than the relationship of the person to God. Even art forms such as landscape painting and the poetry of haiku contain the notion of conformity to nature, which in the Japanese worldview is an important religious orientation. (This is a good illustration of Kishimoto's statement that Japanese religious and artistic values are closely related; see Chapter 1.) Examples from explicitly religious materials appear in other chapters. (For instance, see p. 185 for a discussion of how the dead become *kami* and p. 270 for a description of a foundress who is treated as a "living-*kami*" in her own lifetime.)

37
Matsudaira Sadanobu: Self-Deification

The notion of *kami* is at first difficult for Westerners to grasp because they are more familiar with the concept of God as a singular supreme being above nature and human life. However, in Japanese religion *kami* can appear in either natural or human form. Trees, mountains, and waterfalls, as well as the founders of some New Religions, are seen as *kami*, and some founders of Buddhist sects are viewed as living Buddhas and treated as divinities. The test of a cultural or religious concept such as *kami* is to see how far it can be "stretched." The present selection shows that the idea of *kami* can even be expanded beyond humans as living *kami* to the practice of self-deification, or self-worship.

Matsudaira Sadanobu (1758–1829) was a "charismatic bureaucrat" who was critical of Buddhism, especially of Zen Buddhism for its emphasis on mental exercise and neglect of the body. Instead he was drawn to the discipline of the martial arts and to Neo-Confucian ideas found therein. When he was satisfied that he had perfected himself according to these teachings, he set up an enshrined effigy of himself and proceeded to worship himself. This self-deification is rather complex, not limited just to the ancient notion of *kami* and Shinto, but incorporating Neo-Confucian practices of cultivating virtue, and Matsudaira is an exception rather than a typical case. Yet his example is a good indication of how far the notion of *kami* or divinity can be extended within Japanese religion.

SELF-DEIFICATION

Herman Ooms

In his late fifties, Sadanobu considered that he had achieved his principal life objectives: he had successfully completed his political mission, had conquered evil in himself, and had even held out against death. His belief in a divine state as a human possibility (which he mentioned for the first time in 1787, the year that he became chief councillor in the bakufu) inspired him to express that belief through a cult toward himself. In a shrine in the garden of his mansion where he had retired, before a curtain that hid other deities and spirits, he enshrined in a central position a wooden effigy of himself. There he performed daily a rite to his deified self.

Kato Genchi, a scholar of religion, interprets this unusual practice as a kind of religious schizophrenia, whereby Sadanobu's imperfect self worships his perfect self. This explanation, however, overlooks two important elements: Sadanobu's self-image in his later years and the aspect of himself to which he paid religious respect.

In the years after Sadanobu's retirement as daimyo in 1812 and after some three decades of earnest moral striving, he thought of himself as having attained a state of mind in which his desires had been overcome. In his account of self-training, the *Shugyo roku* (Record of self-training), he traces his spiritual development to a peaceful state of mind of near total self-possession and detachment. The objectified image may thus have been a projection of his perfect self; the worshiper, however, was conscious not of his imperfection but of his quasi-divine state.

Second, the name he had given himself, and which he had also decided upon as his posthumous name, was "Protector of the Country" *(Shukoku myojin)*, in homage to his achievements as a statesman. The name shows Sadanobu's ideal image of himself and what he wanted to mean to posterity. Although during his unexpectedly long life (he died at seventy) Sadanobu developed intellectual interests in many diverse fields of human activity, he saw himself primarily as a successful statesman.

The practice of self-deification needs some further explanation. Usually a victorious confrontation with the ultimate challenge of death produces heroes; and moral perfection is the path to sainthood. Sadanobu was not a hero, but he was more than a saint. The state he had reached was divine, but the halo he had given to himself was clearly political. This particular blend of the profane and the sacred must be understood within the context of Japan's indigenous religious mode of construing reality and human experience.

In Japan's religious tradition, which underlies institutional religions such as Buddhism, Confucianism, or Sectarian and State Shinto, the natural and su-

Reprinted by permission of the publisher from Herman Ooms, *Charismatic Bureaucrat: A Political Biography of Matsudaira Sadanobu 1758–1829* (Chicago: The University of Chicago, 1975). The notes have been deleted.

pernatural are more continuous or overlapping categories than in the Judeo–Christian tradition. It is not unusual for men to become gods and objects of ritual worship after their death. Ieyasu is an example, and Sano Masakoto, the assassin of Tanuma's son, is another. More recently there is emperor Meiji, who has a magnificent shrine in Tokyo. What is even more relevant, though less known, is that the Tokugawa period saw the flourishing of personality cults of people during their lifetime, a practice that persisted until World War II. Kato Genchi collected some eighty-five such instances, half of them from modern times. At least three people personally known to Sadanobu were the object of cults while still living—Hosokawa Shigekata (1715–85), outside lord of the . . . domain of Kumamoto, who belonged to Sadanobu's early circle of friends; Okada Kanzen (1740–1816), a follower of the Ansai school, who was called to Edo in connection with the ban on heterodox doctrines and later served as deputy . . . in a bakufu territory; and Hitotsubashi Narimasa, who in 1787, on Sadanobu's order, filled the latter's place as successor in the Tayasu house. Finally, Sadanobu himself was worshiped in some villages of his domain.

In contrast to China, where the worship of "living gods" was also practiced but with a more mystical slant, in Japan the objects of cultic worship during their own lifetime were all exemplary or beneficent administrators. These cultic expressions of religiosity were of a political mode.

One may argue that being worshiped by others is altogether another matter from worshiping oneself. But even the latter practice was not without precedents in Japan. The oldest mythological example is the deity O-ana-muchi (not unknown to Sadanobu), who enshrined his own spirit in a sanctuary after having pacified the country—the archetype of a work of statecraft. Of more direct significance for Sadanobu was Yamazaki Ansai. In agreement with his teacher Yoshikawa Koretaru (1616–94) Ansai bestowed upon himself the title of *Suika reisha,* shrine of the Suika (Heavenly Blessing and Assistance) spirit, and built a shrine for his cult. There is evidence also that Hoshina Masayuki (1611–72), Ansai's famous patron and disciple and founder of the . . . domain of Aizu, had before his sudden death taken the necessary steps for his own live canonization.

It is difficult to trace precisely the relationship between these two "autola-trists" or self-worshipers and Sadanobu, but they undoubtedly influenced Sadanobu in other areas as well. First, there is a great similarity between Sadanobu's world view and Ansai's teachings. They both unconditionally rejected Buddhism; despised intellectual sophistry; and held to the indistinguishable unity of Heaven and man and to the essentially moral nature of the universe. Sadanobu's theory of the divine ether in man and the techniques to cultivate it seem a further elaboration of Ansai's view of the divine within man, the respect . . . one has to pay to it in oneself, and the obligation . . . one has toward it in others. For both Ansai and Sadanobu, the divine character of man—a basic Shinto concept—was a dynamic force that could always be activated, renewed, and perfected. In the service of politics it could animate men in their commitment to the polity.

38
Religious Sentiment in Ancient Poetry

The *Manyoshu,* compiled in the eighth century, is the oldest collection of Japanese poetry. This work contains thousands of poems of diverse subject matter, and because it is respected as an ancient watershed of Japanese poetic and religious expression, it is still widely read today.

As explained in the modern introduction to the *Manyoshu,* the inspiration for this poetry is usually ascribed to the many spirits (or *kami*) that inhabited the natural world. There was no attempt to distinguish between the forces of nature and the power of the *kami,* they were so closely related. As man participated in and appreciated the beauty of the natural world, he acknowledged the presence of the *kami.* This intuitive and aesthetic (rather than rational) approach to the divine is typical of ancient Japan and Shinto in general.

In the stanzas of this collection, lyric poetry and religious sentiment intertwine, even when the subject matter is rather fanciful. For example, the poem "The Three Hills" retells the age-old account of how two (male) mountains competed for the love of another (female) mountain. Here not only aesthetic and religious but also romantic subjects are blended. For the Japanese audience, it also recalls the landscape of the Yamato plain, the setting for much of early Japanese culture. The poem of Lady Otomo of Sakanoe expresses her earnest prayer in seeking communion with the ancestral *kami.* The final selection shows that already in the eighth century the Japanese possessed their curious sorrow and delight in the evanescence of life. Usually this awareness is described in the idiom of Buddhism, but in this case the essence of life is captured completely with only the image of a boat that passes out of sight.

THE *MANYOSHU:* "COLLECTION
FOR A MYRIAD AGES"

The Manyo man lived in a world peopled by multitudes of gods and spirits, genii and fairies. And it is noteworthy that despite the wide acceptance of Confucianism and Buddhism, almost all the gods whom he sang, or who fed the well-spring of his lyric inspiration, were purely Japanese. They were gods of the indigenous cult which was named Shinto, or the Way of the Gods, in contradistinction to Buddhism.

There is here no need of attempting to explore the whole field of Shinto mythology. So far as the *Manyoshu* is concerned, it suffices that on the one hand there were the spirits, which had survived from the remote past in folklore, and which still affected daily life; and on the other, those whose influ-

Reprinted by permission of the publisher from *The Manyoshu* (New York: Columbia University Press, 1965).

ence was steadily rising as gods of the clan or nation. When analyzed historically, it will be seen that the Manyo idea in this connection was really an admixture and fusion of concepts which had different origins and which were in various stages of development. There were mysterious powers which moved and had their being in nature but which were too vaguely felt to be personified: lands and provinces, mountains and rivers, trees and herbs, and even human acts such as speech, were believed to be endowed with spirits, and as such were made objects of reverence or fear. There were gods possessing full personalities, namely the ancestors of the Imperial House and of various clans, the patrons of arts and industries, the tutelary deities of communities and the spirits of nature. Thus, individual objects of nature in their various capacities, sometimes as mediums through which gods manifested themselves to man, sometimes as gods in themselves, and sometimes as divine property or demesne, occupied their respective places in the religious life of the nation. . . .

Emperor Tenji

The Three Hills

Mount Kagu strove with Mount Miminashi
    For the love of Mount Unebi.
Such is love since the age of the gods:
As it was thus in the early days,
So people strive for spouses even now. . . .

Lady Otomo of Sakanoe

Chanted at a Religious Service to Her Ancestral God

Oh, our heaven-born god,
Descended from the heavenly plains—
With the *sakaki*[1] branch
Fresh from the inmost hill,
Tied with white paper and mulberry cloth,
With a wine-jar set in the purified earth,
With a cord of many bamboo-rings
Hanging from my neck,
With my knees bent like the deer's,
With my maiden's scarf flung over me,—
Thus I entreat thee, our god,
Yet can I not meet him? . . .

---

1. *Sakaki,* an evergreen tree sacred to Shinto and grown around Shinto shrines.

Manzei

To what shall I liken this life?
It is like a boat,
Which, unmoored at morn,
Drops out of sight
And leaves no trace behind.

39
Religious Aspects in Painting

If traditions such as the Shinto *kami* and Zen Buddhism describe the religious content of nature, then the fullest expression of nature in concrete form is through art.
The way in which people relate to nature is seen in their artistic depiction of the natural world. In this selection we encounter yet another form of the Japanese appreciation of nature—a painter's own theory of the nature of painting. The description
of Mitsuoki's theory of art and the translations of his writings provide a fascinating
illustration of the sacredness of nature in traditional art.

The gist of Mitsuoki's theory is that art is poor when it is a bad copy of nature
and even when it is a good copy of nature if it does not go beyond being simply a
copy. To be most successful, to be ranked as a Divine Work, art must capture the
spirit or motion of life. To attain this level artists need more than ordinary human
skill and craftsmanship—they need the gift of heaven. This means that artists, to be
successful, must live in accord with the rhythm of the universe, so that they can express the same rhythmic spirit in their painting.

This theory draws on Chinese precedents, so that it is difficult to label its religious sources. It is as close to Taoistic ideas as it is to those of Shinto and Zen Buddhism. But the historical source of the theory is not as significant as the impact of
the theory in artistic and religious life. The goal of the traditional artist painting a
landscape and the housewife practicing flower arrangement today is the same: to
bring one's own life into conformity to the rhythm of nature in such a way that arti-
ficiality is avoided and a pleasant harmony is attained.

THE ART OF PAINTING

Makoto Ueda

. . . It was not until the last years of the seventeenth century that any effort
was made toward the formulation of a Japanese theory of painting. One of the
earliest who attempted this was a renowned court painter, Tosa Mitsuoki
(1617–91). The title of his book, *The Authoritative Summary of the Rules of
Japanese Painting* ("Honcho Gaho Taiden"), itself suggests his conception of
Japanese painting as independent of Chinese art. . . .

What type of art theory emerges through these sections? Its central thesis seems to be summarized by Mitsuoki in a passage that appears in "The Essentials of the Theory of Painting": "Among works of painting that delineate various kinds of objects, some are mediocre because they are exceedingly lifelike, and others are mediocre because they are not lifelike. If there is a painting which is lifelike and which is good for that reason, that work has followed the laws of life. If there is a painting which is not lifelike and which is good for that reason, that work has followed the laws of painting. Herein lies the essence of my precepts." Mitsuoki is here clarifying the relationship between nature and art in a fourfold argument. Art should imitate nature, but a mere duplication of an object of nature does not necessarily produce a good work of art. The artist must at some point depart from, or even distort, nature. But of course a casual distortion of nature would not bring forth a good work of art, either; such a work, being not lifelike, would be lifeless. All good works of art are lifelike, not so much in the sense that they copy all the outward details of real life, as in the sense that they observe all the inward laws of nature. The painter may omit some external particulars in order to stress a certain invisible law of nature, thereby making his work more lifelike in effect. A superb artist might go even further; his painting may not appear lifelike but has a forceful effect for that very reason. He has gone beyond the laws of life; he has entered a sphere governed solely by the laws of art. According to Mitsuoki, such is the ultimate of the art of painting.

It should be noted that Mitsuoki here conceives the laws of nature and of art not as mutually exclusive or contradictory, but as complementary. The artist must first observe the laws of nature before he comes to cope with the laws of art; otherwise his work would not resemble life but become lifeless. To observe the laws of nature and to follow them faithfully are, in fact, the two most elementary laws of art. Details of an object of nature should never be overlooked. A student in painting should start his training by learning how to depict the way things are in real life. Mitsuoki's advice to beginners is very revealing: "Anyone who wishes to learn the art of painting should first study the way of things in nature. He should then proceed to learn how to use the brush in outline-drawing. Finally he should come to have a good grip of the spirit. On the last point there is a good deal that cannot be said in word." The study of nature comes even before learning how to handle the brush. Without thoroughly knowing how things are in real life, one cannot draw their outlines. A careful observation of objects in actual life is an absolutely necessary preliminary for anyone who wishes to learn drawing, and eventually, the spirit of painting. . . .

Closely following Hsia Wen-yen, Mitsuoki classifies into three categories all the works of painting above the acceptable level: the Competent work, the

Reprinted by permission from *Literary and Art Theories in Japan,* Makoto Ueda
(Cleveland: The Press of Western Reserve University, 1967), copyright
© 1967 by The Press of Western Reserve University.

Marvelous Work, and the Divine Work. On the first of the three Mitsuoki re-marks: "A painting which succeeds in reproducing the original figure and which follows all the technical rules of painting may be called a Competent Work. The painter has well observed the disciplines and mastered an estab-lished style. Such is commonly called a skillful artist. One can reach this stage through training. No ordinary painter can attain the ranks of the Divine Work and the Marvelous Work." In other words, a painter who has learned all the rules and techniques of painting necessary for an exact reproduction of color and shape can produce a Competent Work, which, although itself a fine ac-complishment, still leaves much to be desired.

The next higher in rank is the Marvelous Work. Mitsuoki explains: "A painting in which the brushwork is superb, the coloring is perfect, and the meaning overflows, may be called a Marvelous Work. The painter has tran-scended established styles, for his art is now fully mature; even though he paints independently of the rules, he never breaks the rules. This is because he paints the meaning rather than the shape." The student of painting, as he ad-vances in his training, must try to go beyond the rules after completely mas-tering them. He will go beyond the mere copying of color and shape, beyond a faithful reproduction of the external appearance. If he successfully does this, his work will show a charm not so much through its outward lifelikeness as through its meaning, for the meaning of a painting lies not in the shape or color of the object but in the way in which the painter delineates it. There are therefore cases where the artist departs from ordinary rules and does not copy the exact shape or color. An advanced painter can do this because he, thor-oughly knowing the objective of his work, paints the meaning rather than the shape. . . .

When the painter pursues this principle to the ultimate, he will reach the realm of the Divine Work, the highest of the three ranks. Mitsuoki, again quoting from Hsieh, writes: "This is a work which has 'the spirit's circula-tion—life's motion.' It springs from heavenly nature and surpasses any ordi-nary man's skill. It is therefore called the Divine Work." The painting of the highest order is a product of inborn nature given by heaven, something even a painter of the most meticulous craftsmanship cannot attain. For this reason it cannot be learned by training: there is some superhuman quality accessible only to a limited number of geniuses. Mitsuoki tries to explain this mysterious quality by referring to a well-known Chinese aesthetic term, Hsieh Ho's "the spirit's circulation—life's motion." The term has aroused a great deal of con-troversy as to its precise meaning, and painters and critics in China and Japan have given scores of different interpretations. Mitsuoki felt it imperative to ex-plain the term in his own words and to clarify what he meant by it. This he does in the very first paragraph of the *Summary*. He writes:

> "The spirit's circulation" means that the painter, as he sets out to work, lets the spirit of his soul circulate through his body. When his soul is small and his spirit insufficient, his brushwork will be stunted, feeble, and always unsatisfactory. The painter's brushwork should become gentle and soft upon grief, coarse and strong upon anger, mellow and carefree upon

joy; it is essential that the painter choose the precise emotion. He should first enter into a calm frame of mind, a mind devoid of nervousness or excitement; he should let the spirit expand through his body, with his soul filling up heaven and earth; in such a mindless state he will begin a work of painting. "Life's motion" means that a painting, whether of a god or a devil or a man, whether of a beast or a bird or a tree, contains the spirit of the object and thereby makes the spectator feel as if the object were standing before his eyes. A warrior should show his martial glory, a court lady her elegant charm, a Buddhist priest an appearance of his holy mission. A bird should have the force of soaring and singing, a beast the vigor of howling and scampering. A pine or cypress tree should show the mysteriously venerable shape with which it stands through the snow and frost; a dragon or a tiger should display the force by which it catches the spirit of the wind and the clouds, moving even heaven and earth. Spring flowers, ready to burst open, have the air of warmth and resourcefulness; summer trees, with their cool verdure, have the potentiality of powerful growth; autumn grass, with wilted dryness in the atmosphere, has an appearance of harsh desolation; and winter flowers, with the snow and frost, have the color of withstanding the cold. The foremost principle in the art of painting lies in a successful rendering of the spirit each object has. Particularly important is the case of painting men and human life. Unless the painting successfully transmits the spirit of the object, it will have nothing divine in it, and, if that is the case, the work is like a shrine with no god in it. No ordinary artist can transmit such a spirit into his work; but, unless the student strives with this aim in mind from the first day of his training, how could he expect to attain the ultimate of the art of painting eventually? The same is true of all other paintings. There would be no need for talking about principles of painting, if painting were no more than an art of copying the shape. The ultimate aim of painting is to represent the spirit of the object. In every work of painting, whether it is of human life, a bird, a beast, an insect, or a fish, the spirit of a living object can be represented only by putting eyes into the painting. A portrait, whatever fine complexion or shapely figure it may have, will suffer from the lack of a living spirit if it is dead in the eyes.

Mitsuoki has given the age-old Chinese term an interpretation typical of medieval Japanese aesthetics.

In essence the so-called Divine Work is a further development of the Marvelous Work. The meaning, which was essential to the Marvelous Work, is now replaced by the spirit. But the spirit is really the source of the meaning; each object has its meaning, its *raison d'etre,* because of its spirit given by nature. The spirit is the life-force of the object. It is not an attribute but a potential power. An artist who paints a bird should do it in such a way as not merely to copy all the attributes of a bird but to transmit the "bird-ness" of it; otherwise his bird will neither fly nor sing, it will be devoid of spirit and of life. One who paints the portrait of a man should of course reproduce his complexion and appearance with precision, yet far more important is the making of the eyes, for it is the eyes that reflect the spirit of the man. Without the spirit the portrait is soulless and lifeless; the man is a corpse. That painting, in other words, would have no "life's motion."

How, then, could the artist put life into his work? Through "the spirit's circulation," Mitsuoki would answer. The painter can give spirit to his painting only by growing into the object of the painting himself—that is to say, by identifying his spirit with the spirit of the object in his painting. In order to do this, he would first have to unite himself in one spirit; his whole being, and not his intellect alone or his emotion alone, should be inspired. However, this does not mean that his mind is all in excitement; on the contrary, he will be in a most tranquil state of mind, with no interference of his ego. His body fully pervaded with the spirit, is empty of the spirit; the maximum of fullness is void. The mind of the artist in such a state can fill up the whole of heaven and earth; it can transform itself to any outside object with ease. Himself a bird, the painter can paint a bird that has its true spirit, a bird ready to fly or sing at any moment. Himself liberated from his personal grief, he can paint a grieving man with life and spirit, for the grief he paints is not his own but that of the particular man he is painting. The artist must paint a precise emotion, Mitsuoki has said; in painting an emotion, the artist ought to exclude all emotions of his own. Only then will the painting have an emotion of its own, a life of its own; it will have "life's motion." "The spirit's circulation" is the creative process, and "life's motion" its resulting product.

40
Religious Content in Haiku

Hokku—the "telegraphic," seventeen-syllable form of poetry—was originally the "starting verse" of several linked verses. These short poems are now read separately, and are known by the more recent term *haiku.* Haiku has rapidly become an international art form. Western poets often write haiku in English and other Western languages, and several haiku magazines are printed in America. But it is well to remember that haiku developed first in Japan (where composing the short, disciplined poems is still an important personal experience), and many people who are familiar with this poetry feel that the haiku of Matsuo Basho, a seventeenth-century Japanese poet, have never been surpassed.

In the first selection, the author provides background on the life of Basho and commentary on several of his haiku so that we can better appreciate the poet and his work. The crucial juncture in Basho's life was his practice of Zen, which seemed to add a new dimension to his poetry. Zen emphasizes a sudden enlightenment, one result of which is the realization of the intimate tie between humans and nature. In many haiku, especially those of Basho, the flash of poetic insight is an artistic counterpart to the Zen moment of enlightenment. One of the difficulties Westerners may have in first reading haiku is the extreme compactness and suggestive character of these miniature poems. The author helps us see the utter simplicity yet the vast profundity in such haiku as Basho's "frog" poem, which illustrates the religious character of nature in Japan. Although not all haiku are explicitly religious in content, this poetry generally forms a bridge between artistic and religious activities.

The second selection quotes Basho more broadly on the nature of art as depending on "the creative power of the universe." Thus, for painter and poet alike, as well as the perceptive beholder, the crucial factor is to have "spirit." This teaches us that Basho's poetry was not a pedantic sophistication but rather an insight into the essence of art and even a statement of humans' relation to the universe. In this, Basho is in sympathy with the art theory of Mitsuoki (see p. 179).

THE HAIKU OF BASHO

Harold G. Henderson

. . . Basho was consciously looking for the poetic beauty to be found in things not themselves particularly beautiful. He was still developing both his technique and his poetic insight. Two years later, in 1681, something happened to him. He announced that his life, simple as it was, was "too worldly," and he began the serious study of Zen—the Buddhist sect which gives most attention to contemplation. It was after this, in the last ten years of his life, that nearly all of his finest poetry was written.

Early in 1686 Basho wrote what is probably the best-known haiku in the Japanese language—one which he himself considered as marking the most important turning point in his poetic life. The poem itself is deceptively simple. Literally translated, it is:

> Old pond:
>   frog jump-in
>   water-sound.

Many competent critics have found in this a deep and esoteric meaning; others have considered it too darkly mysterious to understand at all. Perhaps some light may be thrown by the fact that the last two lines were the first to be composed. The circumstances seem well attested. Basho was sitting in the garden of his little house in Edo with some friends and pupils, when suddenly a sound was heard, necessarily during a period of silence. Basho, without premeditation, looked up and said: *"Kawazu tobikomu mizu no oto"* (frog-jump-in water-sound). This was immediately recognized as a possible ending for a haiku, and after the others had made various suggestions, Basho completed it with "old pond" for the first line. If this story is correct, the closest possible English for the poem would seem to be:

> Old pond—
>   and a frog-jump-in
>   water-sound . . .

If this were the only poem that Basho had ever written, one might wonder whether the poet really put into it all the deep meaning that one finds. But the proof is overwhelming that, consciously or unconsciously, Basho did put into most if not all of his later haiku all the meaning that anyone can find, and probably much more. It has been my own experience that the more one reads them, the more one finds depths in each single one, even in those that appear most trivial. One gets a feeling that they are somehow all parts of one whole. Japanese who have had the same experience have explained it by saying that Basho was so imbued with the spirit of Zen that it could not help showing in everything he wrote. This is quite possibly true, but as an explanation it suffers from the fact that nobody has yet been able to define what the "spirit of Zen" actually is. Zen "illumination" *(satori)* is apparently a strong emotional experience for which there are no words. It has been called a "realizing of reality," and some Christian theologians have praised it as being "the highest form of natural mysticism." About all that non-Zen people can do is to observe its effects on Basho and on his poems. Among the qualities which are often considered as indicative of his Zen are a great zest for life; a desire to use every instant to the uttermost; an appreciation of this even in natural objects; a feeling that nothing is alone, nothing unimportant; a wide sympathy; and an acute awareness of relationships of all kinds, including that of one sense to another. Whether or not these qualities are due to Zen, they do exist in Basho's haiku, at least in the originals.

Only comparatively few of Basho's poems are obviously religious, though several seem to be records of semi-mystic experiences. For example, in his *Sarashina Journey* Basho records that while he and his pupil Etsujin were journeying through the mountains of Kiso, they found themselves climbing a steep and dangerous path. On their left was a deep gorge, and at its bottom, thousands of feet below, a rushing river. They took each step in terror, until they came to the fragile ivy-covered rope bridge which spanned the gorge and which they had to cross. Basho gives no details of his feelings, but appends the haiku:

> Around existence twine
> (Oh, bridge that hangs across the gorge!)
>   ropes of twisted vine.

There are also other poems, which would be obviously religious to a Japanese Buddhist of any sect:

> Octopus traps: how soon
> they are to have an end—these dreams
>   beneath the summer moon.

Octopus traps are earthenware pots, set horizontally in shallow water, into which during the nighttime the animal backs as if it were a crevice in the rocks. In the morning it is unable to get out. In the original, which is prefaced with the words: "On board the boat," the effect of *wo* is to make the moon the subject, and suggest that it looks down on the whole sea- and landscape, and all its "ephemeral dreams." Here the religious implications are obvious, even if we do not go into the Buddhist symbolism of the boat and the moon. It is, however, worthy of note that whenever Basho uses the word "dream" he seems also to be thinking of human life; and perhaps it is even more noteworthy that to him the "illusion" of the world does not seem to mean that it is in any sense unreal, but rather, as with St. Thomas Aquinas, that it is far more real than it seems.

The vast majority of Basho's haiku are not obviously religious, whatever the Zen content may be. They are for the most part simple descriptions of actual scenes and events, with just enough detail given to allow the reader to put himself in Basho's place and so share his emotions. . . .

In 1694 Basho died, and died as he would have wished, on one of his beloved wanderings, and surrounded by many of his friends and pupils. During his last illness he was constantly discussing religion and philosophy and poetry (three things that were almost one to Basho), and when it became evident that he was dying his friends asked him to give them a "death poem"— the sum of his philosophy. Basho refused, on the ground that every poem in his last ten years, starting with the "old pond" haiku, had been composed as if it were a death poem. But on the next morning he called them to his bedside, saying that during the night he had dreamed, and that on waking a poem had come to him. And he gave them:

> On a journey, ill,
>   and over fields all withered, dreams
>   go wandering still.

To get the force of *kakemeguru,* "go wandering" should be given its most active sense. For those who wish to go back to the original I must add that the word "still" is used, not only because it seems definitely implied, but also because of Basho's subsequent reference, as reported in the "Oi Nikki," to *nao kakameguru yume,* dreams which run about "still" or "still more." Surely as lovely a farewell as any poet ever gave to the world.

BASHO AND THE POETIC SPIRIT

Makoto Ueda

In truth, the poetic spirit was conceived by Basho on an even grander scale. He believed that this spirit went far beyond the realm of the Haiku, that, indeed, it pervaded all areas of creative arts. Basho says this in his own writing:

> There is a common element permeating Saigyo's lyric poetry, Sogi's linked verse, Sesshu's painting, and Rikyu's tea ceremony. It is the poetic spirit, the spirit that leads one to follow the ways of the universe and to

Reprinted by permission from *Literary and Art Theories in Japan,* Makoto Ueda (Cleveland: The Press of Western Reserve University, 1967), copyright © 1967 by The Press of Western Reserve University.

become a friend with things of the seasons. For a person who has the spirit, everything he sees becomes a flower, and everything he imagines turns into a moon. Those who do not see the flower are no different from barbarians, and those who do not imagine the flower are akin to beasts. Leave barbarians and beasts behind; follow the ways of the universe and return to nature.

Somewhat metaphysically Basho has here conceived a spirit that underlies all creative activities. It is a spirit that produces all works of art, and ultimately it goes back to the creative power of the universe. The universe creates beautiful flowers and the lovely moon, and so does the artist; they are both creative, and appreciative, of things beautiful. The creation and appreciation of beauty is essentially what distinguishes civilized men from barbarians and beasts; it is the prime factor of culture. Thus Basho's poetic spirit comes to assume a form of cultured primitivism; his concluding words are fittingly enough, "return to nature."

CHAPTER ELEVEN

Religious Significance of the Family, Living and Dead

In Europe and America, religious life tends to focus on the church or synagogue, but in Japan, the family is at least as important as the shrines and temples of organized religion. Indeed, George DeVos says that certain types of psychological security found in a relationship to a personal God in the West are found only in relation to the family in Japan.[1] Until modern times Japanese people always participated in religion primarily as families and only secondarily as individuals.

In ancient Japan the head of the clan was both a political and a religious leader, since he had the all-important right and duty of leading the rites for the ancestors. In other words, the clan itself constituted a religious group, with its own objects of veneration, its own rituals, and its own religious leaders. The general outline of the family as a religious institution continued into later history; for example, in the system of main families and branch families, a major characteristic of the main family is its right to house the memorial tablets and to conduct rituals for the ancestral spirits.

In recent times the traditional home would often feature a *kamidana* (*kami-* or god-shelf) for Shinto-style offerings as well as a *butsudan* (Buddhist altar) for commemorating the family dead. The family as a group was affiliated to at least one Shinto

1. Quoted in David W. Plath, "Where the Family of God Is the Family," *American Anthropologist* 66, no. 2 (1964): 300–317.

shrine by its geographical location and to a parish Buddhist temple by the succession of a family tradition. Families participated in shrine life mainly through seasonal festivals and in temple life through annual celebrations and memorials for the family dead. Only when an individual wanted to make a special prayer (for help in crisis or relief from sickness) did he or she make a trip to specific shrines and temples. However, in contemporary Japan, as in most modern industrialized, urbanized countries, the family and its traditional practices are undergoing considerable change.

41
The Family as the Basis for Religious Activities

In traditional Japan, one participated in religion not so much on the basis of individual decision as on the basis of group membership; a person saw him- or herself primarily as a member of a group of interrelated families, and this group set the tone for religious activities.

An important family unit in earlier Japan that still exists in some regions is the *dozoku,* an arrangement of branch families around one main family. The religious character of this social group is borne out by the fact that "in principle each has its own particular shrine and its own cemetery." Members of any *dozoku* are bound together by the obligation of participating in both annual and special ceremonies (such as funerals). In this selection Ichiro Hori describes a *dozoku* and the religious calendar it follows. This yearly round of ceremonial observances throws light on traditional religious life in Japan. For example, professional religious leaders are conspicuously absent because the head of the main household is automatically the family religious leader. His leadership is evident in the facts that the most important memorial tablets are in his home and that he conducts the annual memorial rites. (The dominant role of the two annual festivals of New Year's and Bon is also discussed in the selection on p. 206.)

DOZOKU AND ITS BELIEF SYSTEM

Ichiro Hori

Dozoku is the smallest family unit in contemporary rural Japan and is, so far as we know, the smallest unit in which collective beliefs lie. The term *dozoku* denotes a family grouping of a main family *(hon-ke)* and branch families *(bun-ke)* which are linked by patrilineal kinship. The *dozoku* group which one may find exemplified in several districts at the present time seems to have a historical connection with the clan system of antiquity and the kinship system of the medieval period. The *dozoku* is thought to have been the basic unit of Japanese rural society. One of the oldest and most common Japanese terms for the *dozoku* group is the word *maki* (literally "an enclosure"), which is a group having the same surname. Even today, the main family is called *maki-gashira,* which means "head of the *maki.*"

The *dozoku* is the smallest economic, social, and cultural unit in the village. The religious unity of any given *dozoku* group is shown by the fact that in principle each has its own particular shrine and its own cemetery. The members of the *dozoku* group must take part in the annual festivals and the memorial services for ancestors under the leadership of the head of the main family. The main family, or its head, possesses political, economic, and spiritual authority, and has the responsibility of overseeing the daily life of all the branch families. In turn, members of the branch families are obliged to serve the main family spiritually and materially. . . .

The Saito *dozoku* group in Iwate prefecture offers a typical example of an actual *dozoku* system. It consists of thirty-four families: a main family, five patrilineal branch families, two patrilineal sub-branch families, and twenty-six non-consanguineally related ("fictive") branch families and their sub-branch families promoted from servant status. . . .

The relationship between the main family and the branch families in the Saito *dozoku* group is reflected in mutual aid in daily life. This cooperation is especially apparent on such occasions as the building or thatching of a house, well sinking, and at the times of births, marriages, and deaths. There is also a custom that the members of branch families must periodically greet, or in some way help, the main family as the following calendar shows:

> Thirtieth day of the twelfth month of the lunar year.—*One person from each branch family goes to the main family to help make rice cakes* (mochi), *the most important and sacred food at the New Year and other festival days and ceremonies in Japan. About this time, the main family gives gifts to the branch families, who in turn offer their small, hand-made goods to the main family* (seibo-rei).

> First day of the first month.—*The men of the branch families usually visit the main family to give greetings on the New Year; the host and hostess of the main family give them special food and sake in return. On the next day, the same greetings are performed by the women of the branch families.*

> Fifteenth of the first month.—*Members of the branch families gather at the house of the main family to make rice cakes for the Little New Year* (koshogatsu). *After dinner, there is a mock celebration of rice planting in the garden of the main family's house.*

> Nineteenth of the first month.—*Sacred rice cakes for the New Year are ceremonially distributed. The members of the branch families take pieces of sacred cakes and dine together at the main family's house.*

Reprinted by permission of the author and publisher from Ichiro Hori, *Folk Religion in Japan: Continuity and Change,* edited by Joseph M. Kitagawa and Alan Miller (Chicago: The University of Chicago Press, 1968). Copyright © 1968 by the University of Chicago.

Thirteenth to sixteenth of the seventh month.—*This is the time of the Bon festival (memorial services for the spirits of ancestors and all souls of the dead). Members of branch families clean the ancestors' tombs (usually stone monuments) in the main family's graveyard on the thirteenth day. Early in the morning of the fourteenth day, members of branch families gather at the main family's house in order to celebrate the Bon festival; they clean the house and prepare the ornaments and new altars for the coming spirits or souls from the other world. After this, all members of the* dozoku *group go to the graveyard with offerings and worship at their ancestors' tombs. Breakfast and lunch are served by the host of the main family. On the afternoon of the sixteenth day, members of the branch families again gather with the main family to honor the ancestors' spirits as well as all the souls enshrined in the special altars and to say good-bye to those who are returning to the other world.*

Centering in the New Year and the Bon festival, ceremonial gatherings or visitings at the main family's house take place on the third day of the third month (so-called Hina-matsuri *or Doll festival), on the third day of the fourth month, on the fifth day of the fifth month (so-called* Tango-no-Sekku *or Boys' festival), on the fifteenth day of the eighth month (the Harvest Moon), on the twenty-ninth day of the ninth month (Twenty-ninth Day festival) and on the twentieth day of the tenth month (Twentieth Day festival).*

The customs are not unique to this *dozoku* group, but are universal in *dozoku* groups in Japanese rural society. The ancestral tablets are often in the Buddhist altar of the main family's house, and therefore members of branch families usually gather with the main family to take part in the services. I suppose that underlying these customs are deep-rooted and ancient feelings of ancestor worship which are reflected in the New Year festival, in the ancestor worship at the equinoctial week in spring and autumn, and in the Bon festival.

The spiritual and religious center of the *dozoku* group is symbolized by the *kabu-ko* or *senzo-ko*. *Kabu* is a synonym for *maki* and essentially means *dozoku*. Thus, the *kabu-ko* is the religious association of the *dozoku* group, and the *senzo-ko* is the association governing the ritual meeting for common ancestor worship. One of the significances of these *ko* is that the privilege of joining them is limited to members of the *dozoku* group and never extended to members of families which are related only by marriage. Presumably it reflects the prototype of ancestor worship, basic to the social structure in Japan.

Ancestor worship in *senzo-ko* or *kabu-ko* gradually deteriorated with the rise of the tutelary kami or deities of these *dozoku* which attained social prominence, and these newly emergent kami ultimately became the ordinary village kami *(mura-uji-gami)* of today. The beliefs which evolved from the *dozoku* groups are of basic importance in the structure of contemporary Japanese village society. These beliefs center in the idea that the spirit becomes deified thirty-three years after death, and becomes subject to ancestor worship along with the kami who have some connection with the ancestor of the *dozoku* group.

42

Transformation from Impure Corpse to Purified Ancestor

Just as death is an inescapable fact of life, so is ritual treatment of the dead an inevitable rite of passage in every religion. However, the death rites in any particular tradition hold both distinctive features and common themes. Throughout the world death and the corpse are associated with impurity or defilement, and rites for the dead indicate some kind of transformation of the corpse (or passage of the spirit or soul) and some form of other life or afterlife. This general picture of death rites holds true for Japan, but the details show also a distinctive set of practices and notions.

There are four key features of Japanese death rituals: every dead person eventually becomes an ancestor; becoming an ancestor depends on the actions of the living rather than the character or status of the dead person; the household (at least traditionally) has played a major role in the transformation of the dead into ancestorhood (although Buddhist priests might argue that their role is more important); and the transition is initiated at the time of the funeral, but requires many years and numerous rituals to reach its conclusion. These prominent features of funeral and memorial rites provide only the broad outline of a scenario with many local variations.

For the Westerner, some details such as the ancestral tablet and the household altar may be of particular interest because they are not found in a Western setting. These details are part of a total pattern of caring for the dead. This elaborate concern for the dead with its extensive ritual procedures is clear proof of the family as an important religious institution, and the home as a primary religious site.

CARING FOR THE DEAD

Robert J. Smith

The death of a person sets in motion a series of rites and ceremonies that culminates in the observance of a final memorial service, most commonly on the thirty-third or fiftieth anniversary of death. Between a person's last breath and the final prayers said on his behalf, his spirit is ritually and symbolically purified and elevated; it passes gradually from the stage of immediate association with the corpse, which is thought to be both dangerous and polluting, to the moment when it loses its individual identity and enters the realm of the generalized ancestral spirits, essentially purified and benign. Ooms has described this transformation . . . :

> The ancestor cult creates order in the passing of time as experienced in the household. It gives order to the inevitable fact of death and by the

Reprinted by permission of the publisher from Robert J. Smith, *Ancestor Worship in Contemporary Japan* (Stanford: Stanford University Press, 1974).

same token orders life: everybody is destined to become an ancestor. The order is structured as a process where the stages leading to this final purpose of life are outlined (memorial services, steps on the path to ancestorhood). Everybody finds himself in due time on the appropriate stage. The shift from one stage to the next and the acquisition of this new status are not the result of individual endeavor or personal achievement of the subject himself. The outsiders have a certain power over him, because it is thanks to their loyalty that one can become an ancestor. But their power of intervention is limited; the order is fixed and only when the time is ripe will the change occur almost as the result of a natural growth.

An outstanding feature of the ceremonies for the dead is that from start to finish they are primarily the responsibility of the household and its members, for all of whom, regardless of sex and of age at death, these same devotions will be performed in some degree. Indeed, the longer the time since a person's death, the more likely that only household members will look after his spirit. Many people will attend the funeral; fewer will attend the rites of the forty-ninth day; and the number will dwindle over the years as the memorial services are marked. The priest, too, has less and less to do with rites for the deceased as time passes. It can be said without exaggeration that the household members alone, through their observance of the rites, prevent the ancestors from becoming wandering spirits. . . . Some rites involve all the members of the house, others only the household head and his wife; still others may be performed by any individual who wishes to approach the ancestors.

In this chapter I will set forth in the most general terms a paradigm of the interactive worlds of the living and the dead. For every observance, belief, and practice entered in this paradigm, Japanese folklorists and ethnologists provide a myriad of local variations. Nonetheless, all these variations conform to a general pattern that reflects (with rare exceptions) a commonality of attitude and belief throughout the country. . . . Where the variants occasionally provide a striking illumination of a particular point, or where they appear to offer evidence for a contrary view, they will be discussed for the light they shed on the historical and social contexts of ancestor worship.

Even within the same small district, and sometimes within the same hamlet, different ways of dealing with these concerns have been developed. Although some of this variability can be attributed directly to sectarian Buddhist doctrine, by no means all of it derives from this source. In this connection a priest of the Nichiren sect told me that he had faced an unexpected dilemma while serving an immigrant Japanese population overseas. Like most priests, he had learned to conduct the orthodox funeral rites of his sect, but in arranging funerals with his parishioners he often found that local customs of the regions from which they came had to be accommodated. Early on he protested what he considered to be unorthodox practices, but he gave in as he became more experienced. "I had never dreamed that local customs could be so divergent. Yet here were people telling me that in their village such and such was always done this way or that. They even reminded me that their families had been adherents of Nichiren temples for generations, implying that they were right and I wrong. So now I usually go over the funeral procedures with some older person in the family so that no one will be upset."

The problems of the priest are further complicated by the rather minor role he plays in the funeral—a role that is usually confined to the recitation of sutras whose words no one can understand. . . . The principal actors in the funeral rites are the household members, although the meaning of most of the rituals is unknown to them. . . . It is they who light the incense, carry the memorial tablet in the procession, and gather up the bones and ashes after the cremation. All direct participants in the funeral ceremony are thereby exposed to pollution, whereas the priest, essentially a bystander, is not. Not only are household members central to the funeral rites, they are also the chief officiants at the household altar, where the memorial services are held. In some important senses, then, rites for the dead have never been exclusively the province of the temple and the priesthood. . . .

Whatever the details of custom, the general outline and intent of the practices are clear enough. During the first forty-nine days after death, steps are taken both to separate the spirit of the newly dead from its association with the corpse and to free it from its attachment to the world of the living. To achieve these ends the survivors undertake first to confuse the spirit. The coffin may be carried in a circle around the room of the house where it has rested and only then be borne outside for the funeral procession. The mourners may return from the grave by a route other than that taken by the procession. The path of the cortege may be swept clean in order to obliterate the footprints of the mourners and prevent the spirit from using them to find its way back home. The funeral service itself ends in the symbolic separation of the corpse or ashes and the spirit: a temporary memorial tablet representing the spirit is taken away from the cemetery and serves as the object of veneration during the first forty-nine days.

Now what are we to make of the apparent contradiction that after seeking to make certain that the spirit cannot follow the procession back from the grave, the tablet representing that spirit is carried back to the house from the funeral ceremony? I asked several people about this, and their replies may be grouped roughly into two categories. In the first category, the larger of the two, no contradiction is seen, nor any rationale offered; both things are done and that is all there is to it. The other set of replies also sees no contradiction, but would have it that the efforts to confuse the spirit aim at preventing its returning to the wrong house, which is why the table is carried back from the grave directly to the deceased's household. There the spirit will be sure to be in the place where all the proper observances will be held so that it can rest peacefully.

Whatever the case, a succession of rites is then performed whose chief aim is to transform the spirit of the dead (shirei) to the status of an ancestral spirit (sorei). The temporary tablet is first set on a low table in front of, but not within, the altar, and it is often accompanied by a photograph of the deceased, candles, an incense burner, and a bell or gong. On the forty-ninth day in most instances, but in some cases as late as on the third anniversary of death . . . , the temporary tablet is disposed of and the photograph put away. A permanent tablet, inscribed with the deceased's posthumous name, is placed with the others already in the altar, to be separated from them only once when it is singled out for special treatment at the first bon. On that occasion the tablet will be placed on its own altar in the main room of the house and will be the object of far more elaborate offerings than are made to the other tablets. It is obvious that the special bon altar for the newly dead is constructed "to keep the observance for purified souls of distant ancestors from contamination with mourning for the newly dead." . . . In many areas special boats of straw or paper are made to send off these new buddhas at the end of their first bon. The boats have sails bearing the words "paradise boat" (*gokuraku-maru, jodo-maru*), and sometimes they contain a small altar bearing the mantric inscription *namu amida butsu*, the invocation to the Amida Buddha on behalf of the souls of the dead. . . . With the conclusion of the rites of the first bon, the spirit is thought to have begun the long process of becoming an ancestral spirit. Over the years, on occasions marked by successive memorial rites, the dead person becomes more and more remote and fades from the memories of family members. At length, the final services are held for the individual ancestral spirit, which thereupon passes from the ranks of the household dead into a larger collectivity.

43
The Role of Women in Family Religion

As we saw in earlier selections (pp. 34 and 76), women played a much more prominent role in the early forms of Shinto and Buddhism than they do in the contemporary institutions. Today Shinto priests are in control of both ritual and institution in Shinto shrines (with *miko* as female helpers); Buddhist priests are in charge of both rites and organization in Buddhist temples (with Buddhist nuns a rare exception). In other words, women are largely excluded from positions of performance and power in the two major organized religions in Japan, Shinto and Buddhism.

There are, however, three areas of Japanese religious life where women do play a prominent—in fact, dominant—role. Within New Religions women are conspicuous in many ways—as foundresses, as composing about two thirds of the members, and as forming a core of recruiters and counselors. Within shamanistic practices (see p. 129), women usually are the shamans, or mediums, who come into contact with the other world. Also, within the household it is women who are in charge of most religious activities.

The next reading describes local examples of Shinto and Buddhism before concluding that their "androcentrism" is in sharp contrast to the leadership of women in "nontraditional religions." The author details the domestic religious duties a wife must complete in her role as caretaker of the household ancestors. An irony of this definitive female religious role is that a wife is considered an outsider to the line of her husband's ancestors, yet she is bound by tradition to serve them in elaborate detail.

JAPANESE WOMEN AND RELIGION

Takie Sugiyama Lebra

As the local government plays a mundane role in maintaining Shizumi[1] as a community, so does religion play a symbolic role in doing the same. To be sure, the TV generation is less involved in traditional religions, and local priests—both Shintoist and Buddhist—deplore the decline of faith in gods and buddhas. Nevertheless, one still finds signs of communal solidarity as symbolized by ritual action. Some aspects of the local religion, targeted by the tourist industry as attractions for visitors, are actually being revitalized. The most notable is an annual festival held by each ward according to its schedule, design, and tradition. One of the main attractions is the wild parading of the *mikoshi,* a palanquin shrine containing the god body temporarily removed from the regular ward shrine, through the streets of the ward. The *mikoshi* rests on criss-crossed poles which are supported on the shoulders of as many as thirty or more men jointly, facing in all directions. In consequence, no individual is in control of his movement, rather all the carriers move back and forth or sideways more or less blindly. The *mikoshi's* movement thus can get out of hand. The whole display is a dramatic reminder of a "communitas," . . . where individuals are totally submerged in the unpredictable will of the group (or of the god in the *mikoshi*). An older group of men who have carried the *mikoshi* in the past surround it to control and guide its movement. Further away from the *mikoshi* is a procession of elders who, in formal black kimono with family crests, embody the traditional authority of the community. Among the latter are the representative of the ward shrine members *(ujiko),* ward chairman and councilors, and district officers.

There has been no change in this traditional form of festival, I was told by one of the elders participating in a shrine procession. I did notice, however, a member of the guiding group serving as an automobile traffic controller. It was amazing to see how the cumbersome, potentially destructive shrine was handled amidst the heavy street traffic. Another "innovation" was the placement of the shrine on wheels when it had to go through heavily congested streets. These nontraditional accommodations did not interfere with the participants'

Reprinted by permission of the publisher from Takie Sugiyama Lebra, *Japanese Women: Constraint and Fulfillment* (Honolulu: University of Hawaii Press, 1984). The bracketed remarks are from the original.

---

1. Shizumi is the pseudonym for the Japanese city where this research was conducted.—ED.

enjoyment of the affair however. Contrary to my assumption, the carriers were all volunteers, I was told, and had not been forced into this as a part of a young man's obligation. A leading member of the guiding group said, "Everybody wants to be near the god once in life." He continued to say that, though young men do this sort of thing only once a year, the experience really ties them together. And this solidarity is necessary, he said, for the fire brigade to work effectively since "fire fighting is not a matter of technique but high-spirited cooperation." It now becomes apparent that many of the shrine carriers and guides were also members of the ward fire brigade. It was further learned that these young men all used to be organized into young men's associations *(waka-mono-gumi)*, and required to sleep in the association's dormitories.

The show climaxed when the shrine plunged into the water, drifting out to sea, finally disappearing from view between the waves. The beach was now covered with excited spectators. The majority of the spectators—other than tourists—were women and children. Women and children had no part in this shrine show, and yet practically the whole show was addressed to them as an audience. Women also prepared food and drinks, entertained the male "actors" wherever they stopped to rest, and received visitors from other wards. The children, accompanied by their mothers, participated in pulling the floats, another attraction, which carried performing dancers and drummers under the guidance of adult male "presidents" of children's associations. Everyone seemed affected in one way or another by the two-day festivity. Each household in the ward was solicited to make donations for the event; some people complained but few would refuse. The sound of drums permeated the whole area.

The *mikoshi* belongs to the ward, as does the stationary ward shrine generally called *ujigami*. The *ujigami*, also denoting the lineage god, evolved historically into a communal god or shrine worshipped and sustained by the villagers. The communal activity of the villagers, centering around the *ujigami*, has been the local representation of Shinto.

As Shinto emerged after the Meiji Restoration virtually as a state religion to embrace the "restored" emperorship in its mythology and mysticism, adherence became de facto compulsory. New national shrines were built, and attempts were made to reorganize old local shrines as well in a standardized hierarchy of official ranks and titles, at the apex of which was the Ise Shrine of Amaterasu (the Sun Goddess). The priest of a Shizumi *ujigami* shrine recalls how well off the Shinto priests were under the state's protection before the war, and that even the lowest-ranking local priest received a government-funded salary of sixty yen while the schoolteacher's salary was forty-five yen. Postwar reform abolished this privilege, leaving the shrines and priests impoverished. Nonetheless, *ujigami* shrines in Shizumi continue to provide local foci for residential identities. Those who usually pay no attention to religion become aware of their *ujigami* affiliation at the time of life transition rites, particularly those of weddings and childbearing.

Most Shizumi residents are Buddhist as well, belonging to one of the Buddhist sects and one of the local temples. Even a prominent communist politician is a devout Buddhist who recites sutras every morning. Each family has a

Buddhist affiliation, supposedly handed down from their ancestors. This, of course, is a survival of the compulsory Buddhist registration politically imposed upon every household during the Tokugawa era. The retention of the old parishioner identity is mainly because the family cemetery is in the temple compound and death rites are presided over by the temple priests. In other words, Buddhist identity for Shizumi residents, as for most Japanese, is inseparable from the cult of the dead and ancestors of the family.

The Buddhist affiliation is by the family not by wards as is the *ujigami* membership, and thus could be communally divisive rather than integrative. Nevertheless, in Shizumi there is a rough correspondence between residential areas and affiliated sects as far as the dominant sects (the Nichiren and Soto Zen sects) are concerned. Moreover, there is little evidence of animosity between sects. Mutual tolerance and acceptance are also seen between Buddhism and Shinto. A Shinto priest belongs to a Buddhist temple as a parishioner, and a Buddhist priest acknowledges his membership in one of the *ujigami* shrines. (This flexibility in religious adherence may be attributed to the long history of Shinto-Buddhist syncretism prior to the Meiji Restoration. Locally it was the Buddhist priests who were in charge of the shrines and services of Shinto, while the Shinto gods were regarded as guardians of the Buddhist temples.) Furthermore, as far as Shizumi tradition goes, when death strikes in a family, the whole neighborhood (usually the neighborhood association) is involved in conducting the funeral and hosting the attendants regardless of sectarian differences, although the funeral is *ritually* presided over by Buddhist priests. In sum, both Shinto and Buddhism tend to reinforce communal solidarity.

The promulgation of freedom of religion in the Meiji Constitution brought Christianity to the surface again after more than two centuries underground. But as Japan entered into the chauvinistic era of the 1930s and early 1940s, it again became a victim of political control. Shizumi witnessed its first missionary work—organized by a Scandinavian group in the 1890s—which led to the emergence of local ministers and later to the establishment of a church. After experiencing its share of wartime suppression, local Christianity enjoyed a sudden boom in membership and church attendance, and a proliferation of several denominations including Catholic, Seventh Day Adventist, and Holiness. This pro-Christian enthusiasm turned out, however, to be little more than a postwar fad which reached its peak around 1948–1949. . . . Or the Christian faith, if any, tends to be as superficial as suggested in the caricaturized Japanese religious career: "Born Shintoist, marry Christian, and die Buddhist." To be sure, this is an indication of the tenacity of traditional and nativistic religions, but the failure of Christianity may have much to do with its inflexibility, which is disruptive of the communally based flexibility of the Shinto-Buddhism complex. Most of the households I visited in Shizumi were furnished with both a *kamidana* (god shelf associated with Shinto) and a *butsudan* (ancestral altar symbolic of Buddhist affiliation).

Nonetheless, the traditional religions have not remained immune to the encroachment of "new religions." In Shizumi, along with more than ninety traditional temples and shrines, there are several nontraditional sects including

Tenrikyo, Konkokyo, Reiyukai, Seicho-no-ie, Gedatsukai, and Nichiren Shoshu. While most of these share the nonexclusiveness and flexibility of the traditional religions and thus are regarded as harmless, the exclusive and militant sects like Nichiren Shoshu, more commonly known as Sokagakkai, do upset the adherents of traditional religions. Since sectarian loyalty precedes all other loyalties, some member children do not even bother to attend school, a schoolteacher complained to me, when there is a major sectarian ritual. The strength of Sokagakkai is estimable from the success of the Komei party (the sect's political arm) in gaining three seats (1975) in the thirty-member city assembly.

What is interesting about the nontraditional religions is the role women play in them. Traditional Shinto and Buddhism either relegated women to a secondary position or excluded them from public rituals due to the pollutions ascribed to their sex. This androcentrism is peculiarly lacking in nontraditional religions. Tenrikyo, for example, emerged in the late Tokugawa era under the leadership of a female shaman, Miki Nakayama. Postwar Japan has witnessed a series of "living goddesses" founding new sects. To mention a few conspicuous female leaders: Kimi Kotani of Reiyukai, Toshiko Nagaoka of Jiukyo, and Sayo Kitamura of Tensho-kotai-jingukyo.

A smaller version of female dominance is observed in Shizumi's branches of nontraditional religions. The ward branches of Gedatsukai, when I studied them in 1970–1971 . . . , were headed by elderly women; the local cell of Tenrikyo was established by a woman; Sokagakkai has several female leaders in its local branches; and so on. Among the rank and file, too, female members are much more active and aggressive in these sects than in the traditional ones. It seems that the new sects, unhampered by the traditional sex polarization, harness the energy of women which has been pent up in their mundane lives. These sects also mobilize and use as a resource the women's receptivity for supernatural communication. Indeed, one of the Gedatsukai branch leaders was known as "always talking or listening to gods." . . .

The Domestic Rites for Ancestors

A woman's responsibility as a domestic caretaker extends to the deceased members of the *ie* as identified as *senzo* (ancestors). A secular-minded housewife may become interested in the cult of the dead or obligated to assume the role of a domestic priestess when her old mother-in-law hands this duty over to her together with financial and other domestic power, when death occurs in the household, or when she finds herself getting old. Whether or not they actually conduct rites, my informants concurred in recognizing the importance of "worshipping" or "serving" the ancestors. They learned how to conduct the rites in their childhood by watching their mothers perform.

The domestic rites center upon the household altar *(butsudan)* where the ancestral spirits are enshrined. The rites vary somewhat by sect, but generally involve: candle lighting, incense burning, offering cooked rice and tea, placing fresh flowers, bell ringing, and prayers. This is done every morning, and at night a thanksgiving service may be given. A devotee will further elaborate the rites and chant sutras, whereas a "Western-style breakfast eater" is embarrassed to say that she cannot even offer rice.

The ancestors are symbolized by *ihai* (mortuary tablets). As recognized by Plath . . . , there are two kinds of *ihai*—communal and individual. The communal *ihai* is a single tablet representing all the "generations" of the dead of the *ie* whose individual identities have been lost from the memory of the living generation. The individual *ihai* stands for a recently deceased member who is still remembered, and has his/her *kaimyo* (posthumous name) inscribed on it. Among my local informants, the *ihai* of the latter type usually represent parents-in-law, husband, and/or children. Some *butsudan* contain what Smith[2] calls "unusual *ihai*," particularly the *ihai* of the wife's parents and other natal kin. Such apparent deviation from the patrilineal principle occurs more among neolocal households (in the case of uxorilocal, *mukoyoshi* marriage this is not a deviation), devout members of nontraditional sects, as well as among divorcees. The most unusual collection of *ihai* is in Akiyo's custody: her first husband, his mother, his father's two previous wives (Akiyo lives with her second husband and her ninety-year-old father-in-law by her first marriage). When my informants talked about *senzo,* they meant all or some of these or the recently departed only, without clear discrimination. But if asked whether their *senzo* are of their husbands' side or whether their natal ancestors are also included, their answer was unequivocal in pointing to the husbands' ancestors, thus revealing their conviction in the patrilineal principle. Indeed, their sense of responsibility as a custodian of the *ihai* is intensified by their self-identity as outsiders. Yukie, for example, takes the responsibility of "protecting" the ancestors seriously and is eager to learn, before it's too late, everything necessary to be done for them (e.g., the burning of the individual *ihai* on the thirty-third or fiftieth death anniversary so as to incorporate it into the communal one). Her teacher is her mother-in-law, another outsider. The insiders like her father-in-law and husband are bypassed in this transmission of the domestic culture.

Occasionally, family conflicts surface over the placement of *ihai* as a symbolic target. Mieko, married to a widower, had custody of the *ihai* of his first wife. When this couple moved to join his mother, the latter would not accept that *ihai*. The same trouble was repeated when Mieko's stepson, also widowed, remarried, leaving his first wife's *ihai* in the stepmother's charge. Her mother-in-law insisted that this *ihai* go to the postmarital household of the son's (her grandson) "blood" daughter. This was an outrageous alternative for Mieko, who believes in the *ie* system whereby the daughter, virilocally married, is not permitted to bring her own mother's *ihai* into her husband's household. What really upset Mieko was the old woman's reasoning: "Because they [son's first wife, and grandson's first wife] are strangers." If so, "I am a stranger too,"

---

2. Robert J. Smith, "*Ihai:* Mortuary Tablets, the Household and Kin in Japanese Ancestor Worship," *Transactions of the Asiatic Society of Japan,* 3d ser., 9 (1966): 83–102. See also Smith's treatment of ancestors on page 185.—ED.

exclaimed Mieko. In this case, there was conflict between Mieko and her mother-in-law, ending with the latter's departure. The *ihai* issue was only a symbolic manifestation of this conflict, but it does suggest the psychological weight that an *ihai* tablet carried for the Japanese, particularly for its female custodians.

As an extension of the domestic priestly responsibility, women also inherit the obligation to fulfill the duty of *danka* (parishioner) of a Buddhist temple such as dues payment, making donations, inviting the professional priests to important household rites, arranging memorial rites to be held at the temple. In the course of interaction with temple priests, some women become personally involved, taking them as counselors.

Bound by her roles as a custodian of the *butsudan* and household religion (one of the Buddhist sects) and as a liaison between the household and the temple, a woman tends to be conservative in her religious attitudes. Now and then, she is drawn to another sect or even Christianity, but becoming a member is another matter. Sayo attended Seicho-no-ie meetings for a while and was impressed by its teachings but never thought of joining it as a member "because I would feel guilty toward the ancestors." Those who do join other religions or sects try to be sure that these are compatible with the household religions, as most Japanese religions are. Another alternative seems to be a conversion of the whole family as in the case of Kazuko, a Sokagakkai convert.

CHAPTER TWELVE

Importance of Purifications, Specific Rituals, and Charms

I n comparison with the Christian tradition, the practices of traditional Japanese religion are more similar to the Old Testament than to the New Testament, especially the Japanese emphasis on purification and rituals. The Japanese do not have a pattern of sin and forgiveness, in the sense that sin means disobeying a monotheistic God and forgiveness means that God bestows grace on a repentant person. Rather, in Japanese religion the crucial pair of terms is closer to defilement and purification; defilement means a kind of impurity or unclean condition, and purification means restoring purity by ritual procedures.

The ideal is a cosmic harmony in which humans, the *kami,* and nature all participate in total unity. In early times, sickness, childbearing, blood (especially menstrual blood), death, and ritual mistakes all tended to upset the triangular balance of the sacred. Purification procedures were a very important part of religious life in premodern Japan. For example, in the home there were special procedures at the end of the year for cleaning the house of impurities and purifying it by lighting a new fire. Similar procedures were followed when a death occurred in the family. Many of these traditional practices have fallen into disuse in modern times, but even today the Japanese people are concerned with personal cleanliness, as evidenced by the hot face towel (*o-shibori*) provided in good restaurants and the ubiquitous hot bath.

In the contemporary Western world "religion" is often perceived as individual faith, a highly interiorized attitude; in traditional Japanese religion there is more concern with groups of people engaging in specific rituals for particular purposes. It is not enough for a person to think or feel or believe he or she is clean or pure, a ritual is required to purify the person. Similarly, a ritual is required to exorcise a malevolent spirit or to purify a house. The two selections here introduce a seasonal purification in a Shinto setting, and an exorcism to drive out "malign spirits" possessing an individual.

Closely related to purification and specific rituals are the many charms or amulets people obtain from most Shinto shrines, Buddhist temples, and even New Religions. Most shrines and temples large enough to have attendants or staff present will be selling a wide array of amulets or talismans, ranging from the most popular traffic safety amulet to talismans blessing the home or business. Every New Year millions of people make their "customary" visit to a shrine or temple, and even those who say they are "not religious" or "have no religion" will bring an old amulet or talisman to deposit and then buy a new one to take home, put in their car, or carry with them. Like purification and specific rituals, these amulets and talismans help us appreciate the implicit religious worldview in Japan.

44
Purification in the Ritual Prayers
of Ancient Shinto

Purification is important on many occasions in Japanese religion, but probably the most widespread and most formal occasion is the semiannual ceremony of purification at Shinto shrines. The translation of the ancient *norito* (ritual prayer) that follows is the age-old text of the Shinto ritual for dealing with impurities on a nationwide basis. Of the numerous *norito* that have been handed down, the one for Great Exorcism was performed at midyear and at year's end. On these two days, most local shrines carried out the "great purification," reciting prayers, making offerings, and thereby purifying the surrounding people and land.

The "sins," or impurities, to be purified are described in terms of the ancient mythology rather than as contemporary actions. These mythological allusions are difficult to grasp without a knowledge of the *Kojiki* and *Nihongi*, but we can readily understand the prayers and offerings for purification and the purifying images of wind and water. The precedent for purification is the mythological incident when the great *kami* descended to earth and pacified the land. In accord with this precedent, the deities are invoked to descend once more and with their power to remove impurities from the land. The purifying *kami* are symbolized as the cleansing force in water and wind.

This highly formal rite of purification expresses a main theme of Japanese religion that is echoed in various popular and family practices. The Japanese have always held cleanliness important; the sixteenth-century Jesuit missionaries to Japan commented that Japanese hygienic standards were much higher than those in Europe at that time. Traditionally, every Shinto shrine provided water with which worshipers washed their hands and rinsed their mouths—ritual purification—before approaching the shrine itself. These examples, which could be multiplied endlessly, demonstrate that purification is a crucial ceremonial experience in the religious life of the Japanese.

GREAT EXORCISM OF THE LAST DAY OF THE SIXTH MONTH

Donald L. Philippi, translator

This is the exorcism formula read at the Great Exorcism (Oho-harahe) held twice a year: on the last days of the sixth and twelfth months. Its purpose was, of course, to remove all sins from the entire kingdom; however, it would seem that sin *(tumi)* referred more precisely to what we would call pollutions. The sins of the nobles, courtiers, and palace functionaries were all rubbed off onto "sin-bearers"—the "heavenly narrow pieces of wood" and the "heavenly sedge reeds" which figure in the ritual—which were taken and thrown into the river.

The *norito* was recited in the presence of a great assembly of courtiers and nobles; it was spoken by either a Nakatomi or an Urabe. . . .

Hear me, all of you assembled princes of the blood, princes,
  court nobles, and all officials. Thus I speak.

The various sins perpetrated and committed
  By those who serve in the Emperor's court,
    The scarf-wearing women attendants,
    The sash-wearing men attendants,
    The quiver-bearing guard attendants,
    The sword-bearing guard attendants,
  As well as all those who serve in various offices—
These sins are to be exorcised, are to be purified
  In the great exorcism of the last day of the sixth month
    of this year—
Hear me, all of you. Thus I speak.

Reprinted by permission of the publisher from Donald L. Philippi, translator, *Norito: A New Translation of the Ancient Japanese Ritual Prayers* (Tokyo: Institute for Japanese Culture and Classics, Kokugakuin University, 1959). The bracketed remarks are from the original.

By the command of the sovereign Ancestral Gods and Goddesses,
   Who divinely remain in the High Heavenly Plain,
The eight myriad deities were convoked in a divine convocation,
   Consulted in a divine consultation,
   And spoke these words of entrusting:
         "Our Sovereign Grandchild is to rule
         "The Land of the Plentiful Reed Plains of the Fresh Ears
         of Grain[1]
         "Tranquilly as a peaceful land."

Having thus entrusted the land,
   They inquired with a divine inquiry
   Of the unruly deities in the land,
   And expelled them with a divine expulsion;
They silenced to the last leaf
   The rocks and the stumps of the trees,
   Which had been able to speak,
And caused him to descend from the heavens,
   Leaving the heavenly rock-seat,
   And pushing with an awesome pushing
      Through the myriad layers of heavenly clouds—
Thus they entrusted [the land to him].

The lands of the four quarters thus entrusted,
   Great Yamato, the Land of the Sun-Seen-on-High,
   Was pacified and made a peaceful land;
The palace posts were firmly planted in the bed-rock below,
   The cross-beams soaring high towards the High Heavenly Plain,
   And the noble palace of the Sovereign Grandchild constructed,
      Where, as a heavenly shelter, as a sun-shelter,
         he dwells hidden,
      And rules [the kingdom] tranquilly as a peaceful land.

The various sins perpetrated and committed
   By the heavenly ever-increasing people to come into existence
   In this land which he is to rule tranquilly as a peaceful land:
First, the heavenly sins:
   Breaking down the ridges,
   Covering up the ditches,
   Releasing the irrigation sluices,
   Double planting,
   Setting up stakes,
   Skinning alive, skinning backwards,
   Many sins [such as these] are distinguished and called the
   heavenly sins.

---

1. A poetic reference to Japan.—ED.

The earthly sins:
    Cutting living flesh, cutting dead flesh,
    White leprosy, skin excrescences,
    The sin of violating one's own mother,
    The sin of violating one's own child,
    The sin of violating a mother and her child,
    The sin of violating a child and her mother,
    The sin of transgression with animals,
    Woes from creeping insects,
    Woes from deities of on high,
    Woes from the birds of on high,
    Killing animals, the sin of witchcraft—
    Many sins [such as these] shall appear.

When they thus appear,
By the heavenly shrine usage,
    Let the Great Nakatomi cut off the bottom and cut off the top
        Of heavenly narrow pieces of wood,
    And place them in abundance on a thousand tables;
    Let him cut off the bottom and cut off the top
        Of heavenly sedge reeds
    And cut them into myriad strips;
    And let him pronounce the heavenly ritual, the solemn
    ritual words.
When he thus pronounces them,
    The heavenly deities will push open the heavenly rock door,
    And pushing with an awesome pushing
        Through the myriad layers of heavenly clouds,
    Will hear and receive [these words].
Then the earthly deities will climb up
    To the summits of the high mountains and to the summits of
    the low mountains,
    And pushing aside the mists of the high mountains and the
    mists of the low mountains,
    Will hear and receive [these words].

When they thus hear and receive,
Then, beginning with the court of the Sovereign Grandchild,
    In the lands of the four quarters under the heavens,
    Each and every sin will be gone.
As the gusty wind blows apart the myriad layers of heavenly clouds;
    As the morning mist, the evening mist is blown away by the
    morning wind, the evening wind;
    As the large ship anchored in the spacious port is untied
    at the prow and untied at the stern
        And pushed out into the great ocean;
    As the luxuriant clump of trees on yonder [hill]

Is cut away at the base with a tempered sickle, a sharp sickle—
As a result of the exorcism and the purification,
    There will be no sins left.
They will be taken into the great ocean
        By the goddess called Se-ori-tu-hime,
        Who dwells in the rapids of the rapid-running rivers
            Which fall surging perpendicular
            From the summits of the high mountains and the summits
                of the low mountains.
When she thus takes them,
        They will be swallowed with a gulp
            By the goddess called Haya-aki-tu-hime,
                Who dwells in the wild brine, the myriad currents
                of the brine,
                    In the myriad meeting-place of the brine of
                    the many briny currents.
When she thus swallows them with a gulp,
        The deity called Ibuki-do-nusi,
            Who dwells in the Ibuki-do,
        Will blow them away with his breath to the land of Hades,
        the under-world.
When he thus blows them away,
        The deity called Haya-sasura-hime,
            Who dwells in the land of Hades, the under-world,
        Will wander off with them and lose them.
When she thus loses them,
        Beginning with the many officials serving in the Emperor's court,
        In the four quarters under the heavens,
        Beginning from today,
        Each and every sin will be gone.
Holding the horses
        Which stand listening,
            Pricking up their ears towards the High Heavenly Plain,
Hear me, all of you:
Know that [all the sins] have been exorcised and purified
        In the great exorcism performed in the waning of the evening sun
        On the last day of the sixth month of this year. Thus I speak.

Oh diviners of the four lands,
        Carry them out to the great river
        And cast them away. Thus I speak.

45
A Rite of Possession and Exorcism
in a Heian Novel

A novel is an imaginative work, creating a world that may or may not exist outside the author's mind; a novel may also be a reflective mirror, re-creating the world in which the writer lives. The eleventh-century *Tale of Genji,* written by Murasaki Shikibu, weaves a story of courtly intrigue partly out of her own experience, partly out of her literary talents. We should not overlook the artistic landmark that this novel constitutes: it is often considered the first, and one of the greatest, novels in world history. (See p. 28 for Motoori Norinaga's views on the significance of *The Tale of Genji.*) Our primary interest in this short excerpt is how it presents a rite of possession in earlier times.

Much of this tale centers around the romantic affairs of Prince Genji. At this point in the story the prince is married to Aoi who lives at the mansion called Sanjo, but he has been involved with other women. When his wife Aoi is "in the grip of a malign spirit" for some time, in spite of prayers and the attempt to remove the malign spirit (or spirits) through the help of a medium and exorcists, it is suspected that the ultimate source of the malign spirit is either the spirit of a dead person close to the family, or an agent motivated by the jealousy of another lover, probably the Rokujo lady.

Although the Rokujo lady does not think she could be the source of this vengeful spirit, the fact that she harbors anger against Aoi and dreams of harming her indicates that she probably is. Genji learns that the malign spirit possessing Aoi is indeed the Rokujo lady, because when Aoi is near death during childbirth, she calls out "in the voice of the Rokujo lady." We read also that the Rokujo lady's "robes were permeated with the scent of the poppy seeds burned at exorcisms"—in other words, although she was not physically present at the exorcism of Aoi, she was spiritually present.

The *Tale of Genji,* is a Heian tale. Yet the basic pattern of an evil spirit possessing a person and a rite of exorcism to drive out this spirit is apparent in contemporary Japan, especially within shamanistic practices (see p. 129) and in New Religions (see p. 283).

THE TALE OF GENJI

Murasaki Shikibu
Edward G. Seidensticker, translator

At Sanjo, Genji's wife seemed to be in the grip of a malign spirit. It was no time for nocturnal wanderings. Genji paid only an occasional visit to his own Nijo mansion. His marriage had not been happy, but his wife was important to him and now she was carrying his child. He had prayers read in his Sanjo

Reprinted by permission of the publisher from Edward G. Seidensticker, translator, *The Tale of Genji* (New York: Alfred A. Knopf, 1977). Some notes have been deleted.

rooms. Several malign spirits were transferred to the medium and identified themselves, but there was one which quite refused to move. Though it did not cause great pain, it refused to leave her for so much as an instant. There was something very sinister about a spirit that eluded the powers of the most skilled exorcists. The Sanjo people went over the list of Genji's ladies one by one. Among them all, it came to be whispered, only the Rokujo lady and the lady at Nijo seemed to have been singled out for special attentions, and no doubt they were jealous. The exorcists were asked about the possibility, but they gave no very informative answers. Of the spirits that did announce themselves, none seemed to feel any deep enmity toward the lady. Their behavior seemed random and purposeless. There was the spirit of her dead nurse, for instance, and there were spirits that had been with the family for generations and had taken advantage of her weakness.

The confusion and worry continued. The lady would sometimes weep in loud wailing sobs, and sometimes be tormented by nausea and shortness of breath.

The old emperor sent repeated inquiries and ordered religious services. That the lady should be worthy of these august attentions made the possibility of her death seem even more lamentable. Reports that they quite monopolized the attention of court reached the Rokujo mansion, to further embitter its lady. No one can have guessed that the trivial incident of the carriages had so angered a lady whose sense of rivalry had not until then been strong.

Not at all herself, she left her house to her daughter and moved to one where Buddhist rites would not be out of place.[1] Sorry to hear of the move, Genji bestirred himself to call on her. The neighborhood was a strange one and he was in careful disguise. He explained his negligence in terms likely to make it seem involuntary and to bring her forgiveness, and he told her of Aoi's illness and the worry it was causing him. . . .

The malign spirit was more insistent, and Aoi was in great distress. Unpleasant rumors reached the Rokujo lady, to the effect that it might be her spirit or that of her father, the late minister. Though she had felt sorry enough for herself, she had not wished ill to anyone; and might it be that the soul of one so lost in sad thoughts went wandering off by itself? She had, over the years, known the full range of sorrows, but never before had she felt so utterly miserable. There had been no release from the anger since the other lady had so insulted her, indeed behaved as if she did not exist. More than once she had the same dream: in the beautifully appointed apartments of a lady who seemed to be a rival she would push and shake the lady, and flail at her blindly and savagely. It was too terrible. Sometimes in a daze she would ask herself if her soul had indeed gone wandering off. The world was not given to speaking well of people whose transgressions had been far slighter. She would be notorious. It was common enough for the spirits of the angry dead to linger on in this world. She had thought them hateful, and it was her own lot to set a hateful example while she still lived. She must think no more about the man who had been so cruel to her. But so to think was, after all, to think.

---

1. They were out of place in the house of a Shinto priestess.

The high priestess, her daughter, was to have been presented at court the year before, but complications had required postponement. It was finally decided that in the Ninth Month she would go from court to her temporary shrine. The Rokujo house was thus busy preparing for two lustrations, but its lady, lost in thought, seemed strangely indifferent. A most serious state of affairs—the priestess's attendants ordered prayers. There were no really alarming symptoms. She was vaguely unwell, no more. The days passed. Genji sent repeated inquiries, but there was no relief from his worries about another invalid, a more important one.

It was still too early for Aoi to be delivered of her child. Her women were less than fully alert; and then, suddenly, she was seized with labor pains. More priests were put to more strenuous prayers. The malign spirit refused to move. The most eminent of exorcists found this stubbornness extraordinary, and could not think what to do. Then, after renewed efforts at exorcism, more intense than before, it commenced sobbing as if in pain.

"Stop for a moment, please. I want to speak to General Genji."

It was as they had thought. The women showed Genji to a place at Aoi's curtains. Thinking—for she did seem on the point of death—that Aoi had last words for Genji, her parents withdrew. The effect was grandly solemn as priests read from the Lotus Sutra in hushed voices. Genji drew the curtains back and looked down at his wife. She was heavy with child, and very beautiful. Even a man who was nothing to her would have been saddened to look at her. Long, heavy hair, bound at one side, was set off by white robes, and he thought her lovelier than when she was most carefully dressed and groomed.

He took her hand. "How awful. How awful for you." He could say no more.

Usually so haughty and forbidding, she now gazed up at him with languid eyes that were presently filled with tears. How could he fail to be moved? This violent weeping, he thought, would be for her parents, soon to be left behind, and perhaps, at this last leave-taking, for him too.

"You mustn't fret so. It can't be as bad as you think. And even if the worst comes, we will meet again. And your good mother and father: the bond between parents and children lasts through many lives. You must tell yourself that you will see them again."

"No, no. I was hurting so, I asked them to stop for a while. I had not dreamed that I would come to you like this. It is true: a troubled soul will sometimes go wandering off." The voice was gentle and affectionate.

"Bind the hem of my robe, to keep it within,
The grieving soul that has wandered through the skies."

It was not Aoi's voice, nor was the manner hers. Extraordinary—and then he knew that it was the voice of the Rokujo lady. He was aghast. He had dismissed the talk as vulgar and ignorant fabrication, and here before his eyes he had proof that such things did actually happen. He was horrified and repelled.

"You may say so. But I don't know who you are. Identify yourself."

It was indeed she. "Aghast"—is there no stronger word? He waved the women back.

Thinking that these calmer tones meant a respite from pain, her mother came with medicine; and even as she drank it down she gave birth to a baby boy. Everyone was delighted, save the spirits that had been transferred to mediums. Chagrined at their failure, they were raising a great stir, and all in all it was a noisy and untidy scene. There was still the afterbirth to worry about. Then, perhaps because of all the prayers, it too was delivered. The grand abbot of Hiei and all the other eminent clerics departed, looking rather pleased with themselves as they mopped their foreheads. Sure that the worst was past after all the anxious days, the women allowed themselves a rest.

The prayers went on as noisily as ever, but the house was now caught up in the happy business of ministering to a pretty baby. It hummed with excitement on each of the festive nights. Fine and unusual gifts came from the old emperor and from all the princes and high courtiers. Ceremonies honoring a boy baby are always interesting.

The Rokujo lady received the news with mixed feelings. She had heard that her rival was critically ill, and now the crisis had passed. She was not herself. The strangest thing was that her robes were permeated with the scent of the poppy seeds burned at exorcisms. She changed clothes repeatedly and even washed her hair, but the odor persisted. She was overcome with self-loathing. And what would others be thinking? It was a matter she could discuss with no one. She could only suffer in distraught silence.

Somewhat calmer, Genji was still horrified at the unsolicited remarks he had had from the possessive spirit. He really must get off a note to the Rokujo lady. Or should he have a talk with her? He would find it hard to be civil, and he did not wish to hurt her. In the end he made do with a note. . . .

The Sanjo mansion was almost deserted. Aoi was again seized with a strangling shortness of breath; and very soon after a messenger had been sent to court she was dead. Genji and the others left court, scarcely aware of where their feet were taking them. Appointments and promotions no longer concerned them. Since the crisis had come at about midnight there was no possibility of summoning the grand abbot and his suffragans. Everyone had thought that the worst was over, and now of course everyone was stunned, dazed, wandering aimlessly from room to room, hardly knowing a door from a wall. Messengers crowded in with condolences, but the house was in such confusion that there was no one to receive them. The intensity of the grief was almost frightening. Since malign spirits had more than once attacked the lady, her father ordered the body left as it was for two or three days in hopes that she might revive. The signs of death were more and more pronounced, however, and, in great anguish, the family at length accepted the truth. Genji, who had private distress to add to the general grief, thought he knew as well as anyone ever would what unhappiness love can bring. Condolences even from the people most important to him brought no comfort. The old emperor, himself much grieved, sent a personal message; and so for the minister there was new honor, happiness to temper the sorrow. Yet there was no relief from tears.

Every reasonable suggestion was accepted toward reviving the lady, but, the ravages of death being ever more apparent, there was finally no recourse but to see her to Toribe Moor [for burial].

CHAPTER THIRTEEN

Prominence of Local Festivals and Individual Cults

Neither Shinto shrines nor Buddhist temples observe a weekly day of worship like the sabbath of Jews and Christians. Some devout laypeople—especially housewives—may present daily offerings at a *kamidana* (Shinto altar) or make offerings and recite sutras at a *butsudan* (Buddhist altar). However, what most characterizes the public life of Japanese religion is the yearly round of festivals that enliven family activity and participation in both shrine and temple celebrations. In modern times the government has declared a number of national holidays, but still the typical festival *(matsuri)* is the shrine affair organized and celebrated by the local shrine and nearby residents. The most important annual celebration is New Year's, and a close second is Bon, the late summer festival for the dead.

Another important feature of traditional Japanese worship has been the voluntary organizations for honoring specific *kami* or Buddhist divinities. A regular (usually monthly) meeting of the members is held by rotation in a member's home, and it includes a joint worship service, a meal, and social relaxation. (Such a group, which happens to focus on a Taoist divinity, is seen in the selection on p. 121.)

Some worship in Japanese religion lacks even the structure of these lay groups or voluntary organizations. Individuals may honor a *kami* such as Inari or make offerings to a Buddhist divinity such as Jizo or Fudo, either visiting nearby shrines or temples, or making longer pilgrimages to sacred sites honoring these objects of worship. Typically these people purchase an amulet from the shrine or temple and either carry it on their person or keep it in their home or car. The many people who worship the same *kami* or Buddhist divinity are not necessarily linked by any formal organization; for this reason we can talk about the "cult" of Inari or the "cult" of Jizo, much as we would talk about the "cult" of the Blessed Virgin Mary in Catholicism. The word *cult* has come to have a negative meaning in recent times, as a fanatical or deviant religious movement, but we use the term here to refer to individual or devotional practices directed to particular objects of worship without any necessary formal organization.

Whether in group or individual activities, much of Japanese religious worship is quite different from the weekly congregational services of Jews and Christians in Europe or North America. The two selections in this chapter focus on local festivals: first the annual cycle of festivals, and then the atmosphere or "flavor" of such celebrations.

46
The Annual Cycle of Festivals

One of the most interesting aspects of Japanese religion is the rich panorama of rites and festivals celebrating the stages of life and the sacred events of the year. Previously, we discussed the rites of passage that mark the ritual transition in the life cycle, from "cradle to grave" (see p. 127). The present excerpt, taken from the same work on folk religion, focuses mainly on the annual cycle, from the New Year through a round of festivals to the end of the year. After describing the taboos that apply to many forms of worship, the author discusses the auspicious and inauspicious days of the almanac that determine the times of many of the occasional undertakings such as travel and weddings.

Some rituals found on the almanac, performed on an annual basis, constitute the "yearly round of observances." Fifteen festivals are described, starting with the week of celebrations marking the New Year, and ending with the Festival of the Water Kami in December. Some festivals are celebrated by the solar calendar, held on a specific day of a particular month; others are celebrated by the lunar calendar, depending on the phase of the moon.

These annual festivals should not be seen simply as a sequence of individual, unrelated events. First the author classifies them according to three categories: ancestral festivals, agricultural festivals, and rituals of exorcism and purification. Then he shows that these festivals fall into two symmetrical halves related to the agricultural rhythm of planting and harvesting. Just as rites of passage provide a unified pattern of meaning for the human life cycle, from birth through various stages on to death, so the yearly round of festivals provides a unified pattern of the annual cycle of time.

SURVEY OF PRESENT-DAY
RITES AND PRACTICES

Hitoshi Miyake

Worship and Taboos

Worship in which people make offerings to the *kami* and spirits and communicate with them is by no means limited to the organized religions but constitutes the most fundamental aspect of folk religion rituals. The context in which such worship takes place ranges from the privacy of the home to the inclusiveness of the community festival. More explicitly, worship offered before the family Shinto and Buddhist altars, at the shrines of the household and kinship group, before the stone pillar of the *kami* who guards the entrance to the village (*sai no kami* or *dosojin*), at the community hall, etc., normally takes this form without reference to any institutional religion.

Correlated with worship, particularly with communal festivals, goes a strong belief in taboos. The taboo idea is generally associated with that of purification, causing a man to avoid whatever might render him ritually impure. At festival times this involves suspending the normal activities of daily life, and since death, birth, and menstruation are deemed sources of defilement, anyone associated with them is expected to refrain from participation in the festival.

Taboos are especially emphasized when a festival is to be held, but they influence people at other times as well. Some of the most commonly observed are: the geomantic directional taboos prohibiting the placing of a house entrance or toilet on the northeast corner, the so-called devil's gate *(kimon)* or unlucky quarter; the taboos relating to unlucky days, dictating, for example, that a marriage should not be scheduled on one of the days known as *butsumetsu* ("Buddha's death") or a funeral on one known as *tomobiki* ("bring a friend"); and place taboos, which reduce the price of residential lots located near cemeteries.

The Yearly Round of Observances

During the course of the year, many Japanese people, in planning their activities, still rely on an almanac. The almanac predicts success and failure, good and bad fortune, for all kinds of undertakings, depending on such things as the direction involved and the starting day. In accordance with a time-honored astrological scheme, *kami* of various kinds, bountiful and menacing, propitious and malignant, are believed to make a circuit of the heavens and take

Reprinted by permission of the publisher from Hitoshi Miyake, "Folk Religion," in *Japanese Religion,* edited by Ichiro Hori, *et al.* (Tokyo: Kodansha International, 1972).

turns controlling the points of the compass. If the direction one proposes to travel in, for example, is one then governed by Toshitokujin, the *kami* of the virtue of the year, the prospects are highly favorable, whereas if it is governed by the dread Konjin, the golden *kami,* one ought to reconsider. Again, some days are auspicious and others not. A *dai-an* ("great security") day is full of good promise for weddings, journeys, and the like, while a day designated as *butsumetsu* ("Buddha's death") bodes ill for any enterprise. All told, there are six kinds of days, each with a proclivity toward bane or blessing (which may change at the noon hour), and every day of the year is classified as one of the six. For many people it is still highly important to take these matters of direction and timing into account.

The almanac also lists a number of rituals whose observance has become a matter of custom. These rituals constitute the yearly round of observances *(nenju gyoji)*. Over the centuries some rites have dropped out, some have changed their character, and a few new ones have made their way into the almanac, but of the rituals observed at the present time, those described below are the most important. (The dates of starred items are determined in accordance with the lunar calendar.)

1. New Year *(shogatsu),* approximately one week beginning 1 January. In preparation for the New Year people give their houses a thorough cleaning, decorate the entrance with a braid of straw rope *(shimenawa)* symbolic of the sacred, and toward the end of the year welcome at a specially erected altar the *kami* of each year's harvest of rice *(toshigami)*. During the New Year's season, the family enjoys a festive food known as *zoni,* a stew of vegetables to which cakes of pounded rice have been added; people make their first visit of the year to a Shinto shrine or Buddhist temple; and students call on their teachers, employees on their employers, adult children on their parents, etc., to present their greetings and renew their ties.

★2. The Lesser New Year *(koshogatsu),* approximately one week ending 15 January. According to the old lunar calendar, the new year began on what is now 15 January, and many people observe both New Year's seasons. For the latter, whatever might make one impure is avoided beginning 7 January. On the evening of 14 January, a bonfire is lit in sign of welcome to the *kami* whose munificence provides people with rice each year, and on the following day, people engage in certain ritual activities which may generally be characterized as anticipatory celebrations of the arrival of spring and as ways of divining whether the new year will be a year of plenty or a year of want.

3. The Turn of the Seasons *(setsubun),* 3 February. Though 4 February is considered the first day of spring, the rituals connected with the coming of spring are held on the last day of winter, 3 February. On this day people spend a brief and often happy time, frequently in the early evening with their children joining in, performing the ritual of throwing toasted soybeans from the house into the garden, crying "Oni wa soto" ("Devil, get out!"), and from the garden into the house, calling out "Fuku wa uchi" ("Fortune, come in!").

4. Doll Festival *(hina matsuri),* 3 March. A fete for girls, the Doll Festival involves a tiered display, in the main room of the house, of a set of dolls,

costumed in varying degrees of elaboration depending on the family finances. The dolls represent the nobles and ladies of the ancient imperial court. On this day families celebrate their daughters' growth and advancement by drinking together a toast of sweetened sake. Originally, the dolls, then much simpler, appear to have served as scapegoats to which people transferred their sins and impurities, then casting the dolls into a stream to be carried away.

★5. Spring Veneration of the Tutelary Deity of the Territory *(haru no shanichi).* The day *(nichi)* set aside for veneration of the local tutelary deity *(sha)* in the spring *(haru)* is selected in accordance with the yin-yang cosmological scheme. This school of thought holds that the universe is composed of five basic elements: wood, fire, earth, metal, and water. Moreover, each element has two aspects: the female, associated with darkness, cold, moisture, passivity, etc.; and the male, associated with light, warmth, dryness, movement, etc. In Japanese the yang or male component is called *e,* meaning "elder brother"; the yin or female component is called *to,* meaning "younger brother." The resultant ten classifications are assigned in order to each day of the year. *Haru no shanichi* falls on the "elder brother earth day" *(tsuchi no e)* closest to the vernal equinox, for example on 18 March in 1972. Most people who follow this custom know little of the cosmology, but they maintain the tradition of honoring the tutelary *kami* of their area on this particular earth day with rituals and offerings intended to keep the deity well-disposed.

6. Spring Equinox *(haru no higan),* approximately one week including the day of the equinox, 23 March. *Higan,* one of the words used to designate the equinox, is also a Buddhist term referring to "the other shore." Mindful of this association, people return to their home towns and villages at the equinoctial period and visit the family graves, making offerings of pounded rice cakes, sake, incense, and so on.

7. Flower Festival *(hana matsuri),* 8 April. The festival *(matsuri)* of flowers *(hana)* is a day when those who preserve this custom climb to the top of a nearby hill, there eat and drink together, gather wild flowers, and return home. Originally, the belief appears to have been that the mountain deities *(yama no kami),* who are in the last analysis ancestral *kami,* followed the flowers, thus returning to their homes and becoming rice-field deities *(ta no kami).* Even today 8 April is regarded by many as the day set apart for welcoming the *kami* of the rice fields, and during the month of April, rituals in honor of the kin-group *kami* are held in many parts of the country. This day also commemorates the birth of Gautama and is celebrated by pouring sweetened tea over an image of the Buddha.

8. Boys' Day *(tango no sekku),* 5 May. In earlier years the timing of the Boys' Day festival was a matter of astrological calculation. As mentioned above, every day of the year is still classified by the almanac as belonging to one of the five elements, either in its superior *(e)* or subordinate *(to)* form. But in addition to these ten primary classifications *(jikkan),* it is now necessary to indicate that there are also twelve secondary classifications *(junishi):* mouse, ox, tiger, hare, dragon, snake, horse, ram, monkey, bird, dog, and wild boar. In fact, therefore, the classification process involves combining the *jikkan* and the

junishi. Thus, for example, a day assigned to the element of water *(mizu)* would first of all be an *e* or *to* day, in addition to which it could come under any one of the twelve horary signs. The title *tango no sekku* means the annual festival *(sekku)* held on the day of the horse *(go)* at the beginning *(tan)* of May. With regard to content, this is the day on which families with boys celebrate their sons' growth and advancement with a display of dolls representing armored fighters, a carp streamer flown from a tall pole in the yard, etc. Originally, the purpose of this festival was to pacify the malevolent, vengeful spirits *(goryo)* whose visitations were so catastrophic, and the armed dolls were set up at the gate to ward off spiritual danger, only later making their way into the house as decorations. During April and May, incidentally, a number of ceremonies relating to rice production are observed, such as the Rice-Planting Festival *(ta ue matsuri)*, the Drumming Out of Noxious Insects *(mushi okuri)*, and so on.

9. The June Observances. The first important rite in the month of June is the Festival of the Water Kami *(suijin matsuri)* held on 15 June. This festival seeks to enlist the aid of the water *kami*, the deity who controls all agricultural productivity, in averting disease or other harm that might be inflicted by the *goryo*. The summer festivals held in urban areas, usually toward the end of June according to a lunar calendar calculation, are also typically concerned with the prevention of plagues. On 30 June a special ceremony is held at the shrines of territorial tutelary deities in every corner of Japan. This is the rite known as the Grand Purification *(oharai)*, when people symbolically transfer the sins and defilements accumulated during the preceding half year to a paper doll which they take to the shrine, there leaving it and receiving group exorcism and purification from a priest. Because June is rather heavily loaded with ceremonies that call for avoidance of whatever might make one ritually impure, it is sometimes referred to as "a month of taboos." July marks the beginning of a new period.

★10. Star Festival *(tanabata)*, 7 July. The ideographs used to write *tanabata* mean "the evening of the seventh." Tradition has it that the night of 7 July is the time when two stars, Vega and Altair, personified respectively as a weaver woman and her lover, have a rendezvous in the heavens. In their honor, and with a prayer for self-improvement in arts and crafts requiring manual dexterity (calligraphy, for example), people compose brief poems on gaily colored strips of paper, fasten them to the leaves of a bamboo in the yard, and later float them away in a nearby stream. Originally, it was from this time that people began to observe certain abstentions in preparation for the next major holiday, the *bon* festival.

★11. Feast for the Dead *(bon)*, 13–16 July. The word *bon* means a tray or platter for food, and the *bon* festival is essentially a time when the ancestral spirits are welcomed back to their homes with gifts of food and other offerings. As the *bon* period approaches, families tend the graves of their ancestors, trimming the shrubbery and rinsing the gravestones, erect a special altar inside or outside the house on which to present their offerings, etc. On the evening of 13 July, people build a small fire just outside the gate as a sign of welcome to the returning spirits. Sometime during the next two days, a Buddhist priest may be invited to come to the house and chant a sutra before the altar, while in the evenings, people participate in community folk dances *(bon odori)* intended to gladden the hearts of the deceased and keep them assuaged. On 16 July the offerings are carried to a stream and floated away on the current, and in the evening another small fire is lit at the gate to see the spirits off.

★12. Moonviewing *(tsukimi)*, 15 August. The evening of 15 August, according to the lunar calendar, is a time when people hold parties to enjoy and admire the beauty of the full moon. Originally, this festival, which according to the solar calendar comes in the month of September, was a time when people offered thanks for the first fruits of the rice, presenting in token of their gratitude white, sphere-like rice dumplings *(tsukimi dango)*. Today, these gatherings are for the most part only mildly religious, but a sense of gratitude and appreciation is not entirely absent. The eighth lunar month, it should be added, is the month of typhoons. For this reason it is also the month of ceremonies called Wind Festivals *(kaze matsuri)* intended to propitiate the wind *kami* and stave off damage from storms. From the middle of August to the beginning of November according to the lunar calendar, the dates varying with the locality, a number of rites connected with the harvesting of rice are held, variously called the Reaping Festival *(kariage matsuri)*, the Harvest Festival *(shukaku matsuri)*, the Festival of First Fruits *(niiname sai)*, etc. The day on which such a festival falls is also the day on which the *kami* of the rice fields return to the mountains, and in the same connection autumn festivals in honor of the *kami* of the kinship group are seen everywhere in Japan.

★13. Fall Veneration of the Tutelary Deity of the Territory *(aki no shanichi)*. Like its spring counterpart, this festival is held on the "elder brother earth day" *(tsuchi no e)* closest to the appropriate equinox, consequently on 24 September in 1972. The purpose of this festival is, as before, to keep the territorial guardian *kami (sha)* peaceable and beneficent.

14. Autumnal Equinox *(aki no higan)*, approximately one week including the day of the equinox, 23 September. Sometime during the autumn equinoctial period, people make an effort to visit the family graves and pay their respects to their ancestors on "the other shore" *(higan)* with offerings of incense, flowers, cakes of rice, fruit, and so on.

15. Festival of the Water Kami *(suijin matsuri)*, 1 December. As in the festival of the same name held in June, the purpose of the 1 December festival is to ward off the potentially calamitous thunderbolts of the vindictive *goryo* through appeal to the water *kami*. December, like June, is known as "a month of taboos." From about the middle of the month people go over their houses, cleaning and making necessary repairs, hanging at the entrance the previously mentioned straw rope *(shimenawa)*, suggestive of the sacred, and otherwise start making preparations for the New Year. The last night of the year, sometimes called *joya* ("night of expulsion"), stands in polar relation to the last day of June, being again a time when people rid themselves of the sins and defilements of the preceding half year through the shrine ritual of Grand Purification.

Reflection on the yearly round of observances as presented above suggests that the various rites and ceremonies may be classified under three headings.

At New Year and the Feast for the Dead we have to do with ancestral festivals; at the Lesser New Year with its divinatory elements and anticipation of blessings to come, at the Flower Festival with its symbolic welcoming of the *kami* of the rice fields, at the Rice Planting Festival and again at the Reaping and Harvest Festivals viewed as times when people bid farewell to the rice-field *kami,* we meet with agricultural rituals; while in the Turn of the Seasons Festival, the Doll Festival, Boys' Day, the Festival of the Water Kami, the times of Grand Purification, the Star Festival, the Drumming Out of Noxious Insects, the Wind Festivals, etc., we encounter rituals of exorcism and purification.

Again, when the yearly round of observances is considered in broad perspective, it is interesting to note that it falls into symmetrical halves. While the first half of the year includes such agricultural rites as the welcoming of the rice-field *kami* and the ceremonies in anticipation of harvest blessings, the latter half comprehends the harvest festivals and the seeing off of the rice-field *kami.* In the same way both the New Year's season and the Feast for the Dead are preceded by rituals to expel malignant spirits and by purificatory abstentions or taboos, while the spring ritual to eliminate destructive insects has as its counterpart the autumn ritual to avert typhoon havoc.

47
The Atmosphere and
"Sensation" of Festivals

The preceding selection and the selection "Rites of Passage in the Life Cycle" (p. 127), are straightforward analyses of rites and festivals as celebration of the life cycle and the annual cycle within the worldview of Japanese religion. The following selection begins with a reflection on the ways in which scholars may choose to study and analyze festivals: the *historical, functional,* and *structural* approaches. The historical approach treats the origin and development of a festival; the functional approach shows the relationship between the festival and the particular group (or groups) supporting it; and the structural approach demonstrates the internal unity of the festival, comparable to a literary or dramatic work. Although the author has used each of these approaches, in this work he introduces a different perspective, the "sensation" of festivals.

By focusing on the sensation or "sensory side" of *matsuri* (festival), the author explores the actual experience of participating in a festival, which some have compared to the state of ecstasy. This is in sharp contrast to the other methods of analysis. A sensory approach examines the sights, sounds, smells, tastes, and even the involvement of the body and "sense" of balance in an act like carrying the *mikoshi* (divine palanquin, or portable shrine).

Anyone who has been fortunate enough to observe or participate in a Japanese festival knows how easy it is to get caught up in the excitement and enthusiasm of *matsuri*—whether one experiences or only appreciates the "ecstasy" of the moment.

This excerpt demonstrates that no one approach is adequate for studying festivals, at the same time letting us sample the flavor or atmosphere of festival.

MATSURI: FESTIVAL

Keiichi Yanagawa

Numerous methods are possible for the study of *matsuri,* among them the traditional method of investigating the history of the festival. But some people—and I have been among them—have attempted to approach the study of *matsuri* not merely as a problem of history, but of function, namely the way in which the *matsuri* influences or operates on the people involved. In the sociology or anthropology of religion this method is called functionalism, and when taking this approach, one analyzes the nature of the social group supporting the festival in order to find the role of the festival in the lives of the people. Put bluntly, *matsuri* is viewed for its role in integrating the hearts and minds of the people, or giving them a spiritual sense of unity.

While this kind of general theory can be achieved, one must then address the question—with regard to the concrete role of the festival—what is the nature of the group actually supporting the *matsuri?* Is it the family *(ie),* the kinship group *(dozoku),* the overall village, or some particular group within the village? In the specific context of *matsuri* to talk merely about spiritual integration within society seems to leave something to be desired, or to omit what it is that makes a *matsuri* a *matsuri.* Namely, if it is merely a matter of spiritual integration, then virtually any other ritual or aspect of religion could be said to have the same function.

On the other hand, to speak of *matsuri* without any further definitional strictures may be too broad when referring to the Japanese context. As a result, some people have recently begun using the term *shukusai* as a translation for the English "festival" in order to express the sense of a ritual which mobilizes a large number of people, incorporating frequent ceremonial aspects while simultaneously adding elements of recreation, so that the overall tone becomes one of a kind of celebration or rejoicing.

When *matsuri* is thought of as the ritual defined in this way (and if the honorific *o* is attached as in *o-matsuri,* this kind of feeling of "festivity" may be expressed even more strongly), what kind of methodology should we adopt in order to bring out the essential "matsuri-ness" or fundamental festival nature of such rituals?

Reprinted by permission of the publisher from Keiichi Yanagawa, "The Sensation of Festivals," in *Matsuri: Festival and Rite in Japanese Life,* translated by Norman Havens (Tokyo: Institute for Japanese Culture and Classics, Kokugakuin University, 1988). The notes, Japanese characters, and some Japanese terms have been deleted.

Here, rather than looking for the function of the festival, one focuses on its structure, a methodology which I, too, have attempted. When a festival is viewed in particular as a kind of drama, or performance, we have to ask first what kind of plot, or scenario it depicts, and from there investigate where the essential nature of the festival, its essential characteristics, are revealed.

The fruits of this kind of structural research can be seen in the work of such foreign scholars as Edmond Leach and Victor Turner, and it has appeared in numerous forms within Japanese research as well. . . .

When viewing the structure of a *matsuri* in this way, its characteristics appear to involve two radically divergent elements. One is the element of extreme solemnity and formality, while on the other hand there is also what might be called a coarse, or even obscene, aspect, the element of informality. As a result, a *matsuri* appears to contain both an extremely formally correct, "polite" side together with a side representing impropriety or disruption of order, and the structural methodology thus attempts to find the essence of a *matsuri* in the contrast between these two sides.

Included within this same kind of analysis is the attempt to view the symbolic elements of the participants' world view as reflected within a *matsuri,* such as in the motifs of male versus female, or west versus east, and so forth.

A related point of view would indicate the fact that a festival may begin with an extremely solemn ritual, in the midst of which follows an occurrence which introduces a kind of revelry totally at variance with the initial solemn atmosphere. This kind of analysis would note that a *matsuri* contains an exaggeration of these kinds of polar elements which would be unthinkable in normal everyday life. Or again, such contrasts may be viewed diachronically as part of a process in which formality is emphasized at one point and familiarity at another.

All of these viewpoints deal with the structure of a *matsuri,* and this methodology has produced results of considerable value both in Europe and America as well as in Japan.

There are many things about *matsuri* which can be illuminated by using these methodologies; I would like to use this opportunity, however, not to merely reiterate the results of past research, but to introduce a rather different perspective on the problem. This position is one which I have just begun to consider, with the result that my comments do not represent a fully thought-out methodological stance, but I hope to receive helpful criticisms on whether it seems feasible to use it as another means of studying festivals from a standpoint somewhat at variance from structural and functional theories.

To begin, let me introduce as an example, a brief quotation from one of the works I noted earlier; "When carrying the *mikoshi* with an empty mind, a person enters [a] state akin to a religious ecstasy."

This statement is in relation to the *mikoshi,* the divine palanquin carried during a Japanese festival; if it is the case that this *matsuri* has a great fascination something akin to a religious ecstasy (as someone has noted, the carrying of the *mikoshi* has become quite popular among young people recently)—if this carrying of the *mikoshi* is the way to ecstasy, then in the context of the problem of the structure of *matsuri,* the entry into a state of ecstasy can be treated in a quite conceptual way.

For example, Turner speaks of everyday structure, of our everyday lives, against which the period of *matsuri* would represent a completely different order, one which he calls "antistructure," the emergence of a different world. However, while it is understandable how that other world comes about in the sense of structure—and structuralism can point to the fact that it *does* emerge—the problem of *why* it is that this ecstasy, or antistructure totally disrupting the everyday order emerges in the middle of *matsuri,* or under what conditions that world emerges, is not sufficiently explained.

Even if I am unable, however, to experientially grasp, to intuit this world of *o-matsuri,* I can say that I have felt similar situations. For example, during the university riots the fact that the normal "teacher-student" relationship was at times reversed. Such reversals were evident on such occasions as the mass stuggle sessions and criticism rallies, but in these cases, while it was certainly true that everyday order was overturned and that a kind of antistructure came about—somewhat like men's wearing women's clothes and vice versa during a festival—and that this kind of antistructure or anti-order can be expressed on the level of structure, there is something else involved. When we attempt to narrow down the central aspects of a *matsuri*—and I bring this up since it bears on the title of my presentation today—we must consider the problem of sensation; for example, when we talk about a kind of ecstasy in the context of *matsuri,* how do we treat the problem of the sensations of people who accept or enter into that state?

. . . When the *matsuri* is viewed structurally, it can be seen to involve a dualism, or a situation comprised of opposed elements. . . . In other words, rather than merely a matter of structure, there seems to be a kind of raw experience into which such elements themselves draw not only participants, but observers as well.

I want to tentatively label this phenomenon the "sensation" or "sensory side" of *matsuri.* Here, the definition of sensation becomes problematic, but let us offer the formal definition of "the various concrete conscious experiences occurring as the result of the stimulation of specific sense organs, sense nerves, or the sensing portion of the brain." Though not a specialist in psychology, the first thing that comes to my mind from this definition are what mere common sense would call the "five senses."

Granted this definition, the kinds of things which were noted in the earlier passage I quoted about *matsuri,* namely its color, or sounds, or the pain of bearing the *mikoshi* thus become problems of hearing, or sight, or touch, or again in the case of the foods typically consumed at festivals, the "taste" of *matsuri.* When I have my students write reports of *matsuri,* they often say they recall the odor of acetylene gas, thus bringing in the sense of smell as well. . . .

If we then were to attempt an expression of the concept of the *matsuri* using different words, whether the very simple definition introduced earlier or something else, we might say that a *matsuri* involves taking the conscious states received through the senses, namely sensual experience, and indulging it, or using it to the greatest possible limits, without begrudging or restricting it in any way.

In other words, in the context of the five senses, there is sound—the sounds of music or even the noisy uproar—or color—the red and white of Japanese festivals, or whatever other color forms the basic tones of the festival—and there are aromas. It is thus not impossible to define a festival as a ritual in which these things are, to use a somewhat negative term, "exploited" to the fullest as a kind of instrument or tool.

When viewed in this light, the problem of *matsuri* can be linked to one of the methodological streams which I noted earlier, a stream which considers the problem of our attitudes toward the body, or the "flesh" (although it may sound a bit crude). Among us, and even more within Christianity, there has been a considerably strong sense of dualism. As a result, since *sensation* is a kind of conscious experience which occurs through our bodies, the acceptance of this kind of physical sense impression and the signification which it brought with it, was viewed with considerable suspicion.

In contrast, others would say rather that the body and mind are more closely interrelated, and that there are problems involving the fleshly, physical body which cannot be resolved by the kind of dualistic view which claims merely that the spirit is pure and the body impure. . . .

. . . The problem of the body figures greatly in the subject of *matsuri*. As a result, were I to study festivals in the context of this kind of problem, I would likely use the following kind of classification. Namely, in addition to the normally considered five senses, I would add bodily senses which are—from the standpoint of psychology—other than the normal five. Among them I would include (and there seems to be numerous theories about these) the sense of balance, represented by the organs in the ear which, when damaged, cause the sensation of dizziness or impression of vertigo, together with the motor senses, and internal organ or visceral sensations, all of these being bodily sensations in addition to what are commonly conceived as the "five senses."

Take, for example, the motor organs. In a *matsuri* there are various competitions, parades, dancing, and the bearing of the *mikoshi* as noted earlier. These all involve sensations coming from certain motor activities, although needless to say, motor activities also involve the previously mentioned five senses. With regard to the visceral sensations one might note feelings of hunger or nausea, and here, too, like the feelings which occur during fasting or abstinence from certain foods, or when one eats or drinks too much, these all involve a kind of sensation within the internal organs.

If so, then we have here the "ecstasy" of *matsuri*. . . . But if a *matsuri* is not merely a foolish uproar but a religious activity as well, then within it there must be the feeling that the people have somehow been reborn, or that they have touched something extremely fresh and new. And the conscious experiences that occur here have all occurred as the result of sensations.

. . . In a *matsuri*, people are enabled to reach a kind of state of trance or ecstasy through physiological conditions, a state which, in an extremely deviant form, is also experienced by those in the modern-day drug culture who take hallucinogens. The problem, however, remains: within this kind of religious state, what kind of relationship does our consciousness—the psychological consciousness which occurs within people—have with the sensation of surrounding conditions? I have yet to do any specific research in this area, and a rereading of my several previous essays indicates that I was not then considering the problem of sensation at all. As a result, it seems likely that, lacking some kind of specific methodological program introduced from the beginning, mere reinterpretation of earlier studies will not be fruitful in this area. This, I feel, is another for future investigation.

CHAPTER FOURTEEN

Penetration of Religion into Everyday Life

In traditional Japan, religion tended to be highly involved in everyday life and was somehow related to most occupations. From prehistoric times, religion was directly associated with the home, fertility, and agriculture. The intimate relationship between farming and religion in recent times was seen in Chapter 13, but fishing is another major economic activity blessed by religion. Shrines and temples along the seacoast hold special festivals to protect sailors and to pray for large catches, sometimes using decorated boats in the harbor as part of the celebration.

Religious observances were important in the traditional household, as seen in the regular offerings placed on the *kamidana* (Shinto altar) and before the *butsudan* (Buddhist altar). Traditionally, special Shinto rites of blessing were invoked when building a house, in breaking ground, and in erecting the framework. In the farm household, home and occupation were not clearly separated, and religion easily entered both spheres. To take two examples strange to modern Westerners, there was a divinity or patron saint for the toilet and one for the stable.

Another way in which religion penetrated everyday life was by providing "rites of passage" for the crucial junctures in life, such as birth, marriage, and death. In this fashion religious life was delicately interwoven with every step of an individual's life span. At the same time, religion was inseparable from the seasonal and corporate activities of the social group as a whole. In short, religious life in traditional Japan was practically inseparable from individual, social, and occupational activities.

As traditional Japan increasingly feels the pressures of modernity, these old customs are disappearing. However, religion still enters daily life in such practices as flower arranging and the tea ceremony. These practices are much more sophisticated than some of the rustic customs described in this chapter, but they share common notions, such as the sacredness of nature.

48
Religious Life in Prehistoric Japan

The evidence for religious life in early Japan must be reconstructed from archaeological discoveries. In this selection, the author sums up the religious significance of the archaeological finds from various areas of early Japan. Conspicuous among this evidence are the symbols relating to sexuality and fertility. Stone figurines represent the sacredness of fertility as the power of woman, and stone phalli attest to the generative power of the male. As the last paragraph of the selection points out, these figurines and phalli sometimes formed family altars, apparently invoking religious powers for protection and offspring.

It is difficult to reconstruct the daily life of the early Japanese, but burials present solid evidence of concern for the dead, a persistent theme in Japanese religion. (See also Chapter 11.) It is clear that the people held some notion of an afterlife and that the dead were venerated. Probably other rites of passage were also observed, but they have left no permanent records.

Another interesting find from prehistoric Japan is some stone circles, each with an upright pillar surrounded by horizontal stones arranged like spokes on a wagon wheel. Lack of further evidence hinders our understanding of the stone circles, but they probably indicate an early cult that venerated the sun and thus provided a basis for the mythology surrounding the Sun Goddess (Amaterasu). (See p. 13 for the mythological setting of Amaterasu.)

ARCHAEOLOGICAL EVIDENCE FOR
PREHISTORIC RELIGION

J. E. Kidder, Jr.

The artifacts of the Middle Jomon period are replete with symbols that connote fertility. Not until after this time do the figurines become quite specifically female, but large stone clubs of phallic form, stone phalli, standing pillars in dwellings and other objects, more disguised but similarly symbolic, attest to

Reprinted by permission of the publisher from *Japan Before Buddhism* by J. E. Kidder, Jr., Praeger Publishers, Inc., and Thames & Hudson Ltd. (London, 1966).

the emphasis placed upon the magical powers of the male organ. It may be that in the Middle Jomon a desire for greater permanence in the symbols resulted in the making of these in stone that had before that time been fashioned in soft materials, or it may have been due to the arrival of new ideas among the mountain-dwelling societies whose receptivity responded instinctively and expressed these ideas symbolically. It is, of course, even difficult to demonstrate that these symbols were engendered in the mountain regions, but one centre of production is on the west side where sophistication replaced realism, and it certainly does appear that their diffusion spread from the Tosan both east and west and later into the Tohoku. . . .

The methods of burial were not fully standardized, nor does difference in time seem to be a factor in the variation of procedures. About half were carried out in a flexed position in the majority of which heads were oriented towards the south-east; others may be extended, and pointed in all directions of the compass. Of the former, the great percentage were laid on their backs, legs drawn up, but some were deposited on one side fully flexed. Others lie face down, knees near the chest; or extended on the back, side or face. At the Yoshigo shell-mound one of the skeletons was surrounded by a black organic substance interpreted as a burial mat that must have enveloped the corpse, and two skeletons at Ubayama, and similarly at Tsugumo and Ataka, lay by burnt earth and charcoal remains made by a fire perhaps sacrificial in nature. The bones themselves were unmarked by the fire. Traces of red ochre, particularly on skulls and chest-bones, are to be seen on quite a number of skeletons primarily in North Japan and most frequently on children. This may mean that a secondary burial system was in practice by some groups. Other isolated occurrences are of interest: at the Satohama shell-mound, Miyagi, an elderly man and child were buried in an embrace, both in flexed position, and at Yoshigo bones of an adult and child were found together in a clay jar. Flat circular stones were occasionally placed on the chest of the deceased for protection. . . .

The question of burials arises again in connection with the stone circles of North Japan. Recent efforts have been instrumental in bringing a number to light and elucidating facts on known circles. The count now stands at thirty or more in Tohoku and Hokkaido, and the reported destruction of many even during the lifetime of local residents must mean that this is only a fraction of the original number. The ones that can be dated by associated pottery correspond chiefly to Late Jomon, the most ambitious period in circle construction, and others appear to fit in the Latest period. Many cannot be dated at all satisfactorily because of the absence of related finds, but on the basis of a general similarity it is believed that most either belong to the Neolithic period or represent a perpetuation of Jomon ideas.

The great majority of these circles, especially in Hokkaido, consist of stones that are rarely more than 3 feet in height standing in a circle, most often natural and uncut. . . . The diameter of these circles varies considerably; some are more oval, but when so, the orientation too is variable. Komai's study has tended to show that some were cemeteries in which small stones were frequently laid in great quantities within the outline of menhirs. Human remains, however, have not been found, but this is not surprising considering the extreme humidity of the soil. Others provide no indications of their use or significance, but in a particular group that will be discussed below, there is much likelihood that early manifestations of stone and sun worship are represented. . . .

The *Kojiki* and *Nihon Shoki,* the most ancient records of the Japanese people, put into writing in the eighth century, imply that veneration of the Sun Goddess is of extreme antiquity, and whilst this influence was largely of partisan inspiration, it does seem likely that some solar worship was practised before the Yamato people, the authors of these stories, organized themselves or entered the country. In fact, its origins probably date to the second millennium B.C. And again, the worship of spirits of stones, particularly stones of unusual and suggestive shape, is also a very ancient custom not to be disassociated from these Oyu formations. One is reminded of the Izanagi and Izanami myth. These two gods were most responsible for the creation of the island country; they begat the Eight Islands, and propagated them with gods, though only after a first defective offspring. By way of inception, on an island near present-day Osaka, because of its central location, a Pillar of Heaven was set up; the wedding ritual included circling this pillar, done incorrectly the first time, but later amended so that the results were fruitful. One of the offspring of this pair was the Sun Goddess whose descendants landed in South Japan and eventually made their way to the Yamato Plain, the Osaka-Nara area today. Although the solar myth itself has little philosophical profundity to it, the ideas concerning its origins and subsequent history finally became sharp enough to reach a recorded stage by the eighth century, but the implications concerning its belief are for a long and very ancient tradition.

In addition, with regard to the link between stone worship and phallicism, standing stone clubs of Middle Jomon times have already been mentioned. Of the same period are standing pillars in a group of houses at Yosukeone, Nagano. In the north-west corner of the pit-dwellings was built a stone platform on which stood a slender upright stone; arrayed on the platform and around it were such objects as stone clubs, clay figurines and broken pottery. Quite obviously the platforms and pillars mark the family altar or shrine which brings together concepts of stone worship and protection for the processes of and the benefits derived from procreation.

49
Religious Life in a Rural Village

One of the best illustrations of the presence of religion in the midst of everyday life is the description of life in a specific village. The author provides this illustration from his field work in Satoyamabe-mura, balancing his descriptive account with some wider generalizations. He uses the notions of "little tradition" and "great tradition" to describe the interaction between local and universal traditions. Eventually, local customs such as ancient Japanese practices and universal traditions such as Buddhism became so interrelated that they are now experienced by the people as inseparable. (For other treatments of religious syncretism see Chapter 9.)

In this village of 682 families, there is an amazing array of religious phenomena, all integrated into a total system. In the main Shinto shrine itself are found belief in an ancestral *kami,* concern for spirits of the dead, relationship to a major Buddhist temple, and veneration of a famous emperor. The villagers not only participate in the life of this shrine but also belong to a Buddhist temple and participate in the rites of their extended family.

The other religious phenomena of the village read like an encyclopedia of Japanese religion. There are stone phalli for fertility, stones for the guardian deity of horses, and many other monuments. The many stones may be seen as the heritage of the village as a whole, but special religious associations (*ko*) are also numerous. The syncretistic Koshin-ko (see p. 121) is prominent, but so are Buddhist, Shinto, and popular associations. In addition, each family has its own set of religious practices within the home. Satoyamabe-mura may not be exhaustive of the entire Japanese tradition, and it does not reflect modern urban Japan, but it does contain a cross section of the many interwoven religious elements that characterized daily life in traditional Japan.

SOCIAL STRUCTURE AND FOLK RELIGION

Ichiro Hori

I believe that the essence of Japanese folk religion lies in the interaction of two belief systems: a little tradition, which is based on blood or close community ties; and a great tradition, introduced from without, which is adopted by individual or group choice. The belief patterns found everywhere in Japanese rural society are complex, multilayered, and syncretistic. These patterns are based both on the existence of native religion centering in the worship of ancestors and on the various kinds of religion brought from outside by missionaries or believers who belong to the great traditions or to the more advanced little traditions.

Little tradition here refers to the native or folk religions, including the advanced Shinto, which was shaped by ancient Japanese geographic and cultural circumstances; great tradition refers to Confucianism, religious Taoism, and Buddhism—highly developed religious and philosophical importations.

Reprinted by permission of the author and publisher from Ichiro Hori, *Folk Religion in Japan: Continuity and Change,* edited by Joseph M. Kitagawa and Alan Miller (Chicago: The University of Chicago Press, 1968). Copyright © 1968 by the University of Chicago.

These two systems became intertwined after centuries, and Japanese folk religion developed as an integral whole out of the interaction of many separate elements. . . .

Folk Beliefs in Japanese Rural Society:
The Case of Satoyamabe-mura

The relationship between folk beliefs and everyday life in an average rural community can be illustrated from my field research in Satoyamabe-mura, Nagano prefecture.[1] This village consists of 682 families divided into thirteen *o-aza* (large sub-village units) and thirty-three *ko-aza* (sub-village sections). The central Shinto shrine of this village, which all villagers have the duty and right to serve, is called Susuki-no-miya (literally, "Pampas-grass shrine"), in reference to the tradition of the origin of the local kami, who is supposed to have journeyed down the nearby river from a neighboring mountain on a pampas-grass leaf. The Susuki-no-miya now enshrines two kami: Takemi-nakata-no-kami, the ancestral kami of famous ancient feudal lords and the religiously powerful Suwa family who had presided over the neighboring district of Suwagun, and who were known as the Jin-shi (kami's family) until the end of the Ashikaga shogunate (A.D. 1338–1573); and Gozu-tenno, who was originally believed to be a kami of epidemics but later became known as a guardian against epidemics. The latter is a type of *goryo-shin*.[2] . . .

In addition, there is a Buddhist-style miniature shrine and a Buddhist bodhisattva's statue (Bato-kannon, in Japanese; Hayagriva, in Sanskrit) in the inner shrine. This is a remnant of the commingling of Shinto and Buddhism in the medieval period, and indicates that this shrine has been influenced by beliefs from the Zenko-ji temple in Nagano, one of the most flourishing Buddhist temples, belonging to both the Tendai and Jodo sects. There is also a small branch shrine which enshrines Prince Shotoku, a crown prince of the sixth century who played a decisive role in the introduction of Buddhism into Japan. He is especially honored by the Buddhist Shin sect as well as by carpenters and other craftsmen.

Thus, at least four religious elements are found in this shrine: belief in an ancestral kami of a politically powerful and religious family (a developed little tradition); belief in *goryo-shin* (super-community, but belonging to a little tradition); belief in Zenko-ji temple (great tradition); and belief in Prince Shotoku (great and little traditions).

The main Buddhist temple in Satoyamabe-mura is Tosen-ji. It belongs to the Shingon sect and was originally built to serve the main Shinto shrine (Susuki-no-miya). A large number of families have religious celebrations at this temple during the annual Bon festival, at the anniversary rites for ancestors, and during funeral rites.

---

1. Nagano prefecture is in central Honshu, the main Japanese island.—ED.

2. *Goryo-shin,* unfriendly spirits of the dead.—ED.

Beyond these two central religious affiliations, each family and each person in the village has relationships with many other religious belief systems, the most important of which center in the *iwai-den* or *iwai-jin,* which house the tutelary kami of the extended family. Twenty-eight kinds of Shinto and Buddhist deities are enshrined in ninety-one of these *iwai-den.* Among them the Inari shrine contains the largest number, comprising 46 per cent of the total. . . .

Attention should also be given to the other religious phenomena in this village, such as the many stone shrines, stupas, phalli, monuments, memorial statues, charms, and taboo symbols. There are now about 144 small shrines and stone symbols, among which are forty-two Nembutsu stupas and Amida figures, twenty Koshin stupas, a number of offering stupas for the Lotus Sutra (formally, *Saddharmapundarika-sutra* in Sanskrit), memorial stupas for pilgrimages, Bato-kannon statues (Buddhist guardian deity of horses), Nijusan-ya stupas (for worship on the twenty-third night's moon after the new moon), statues of Doso-jin (kami of the road and travel and of sex), statues of Kodama-gami (kami of silk and the silkworm), and others. Moreover, there are many religious associations *(ko)* in this village.

> Koshin-ko.—*Koshin belief is an amalgamation of Shinto, religious Taoism, and Buddhism. Koshin is believed to have many and various functions in the village. He is, for instance, the agricultural kami, the protector against misfortune, the kami of soil, the kami of craftsmanship and so forth, and one* buraku *has two or three associations for service to this kami. In Fujii* buraku *there are four such Koshin-ko, one association each being organized by the eight Hanaoka families, the fourteen Futatsugi families, the four Fujii families, and the fourteen consisting of Akagi, Nehagi, Sakashita, Yamoto families. These associations often overlap with the* iwai-den *system or combine two or three* iwai-den. *The members of each association must meet six times yearly at the duty house (toya) and, after a small festival, discuss the economic and cooperative matters of the community and the common problems of daily public life. Often the old persons talk about the folk traditions, legends, and history of the village. They feast together and, following the old customary Koshin belief, sit up throughout the night.*
>
> Nembutsu-ko.—*This is composed of the believers in Amida Butsu (Amitabha Buddha). Their main function in the community is to serve the spirits of the dead and sometimes to help during funeral rites. This association often combines with the Koshin-ko and is sometimes called Koshin-nembutsu-ko.*
>
> Ise-ko.—*Members are believers in the mythical ancestral goddess of the imperial family which has been enshrined at Ise shrine. Each member of this association must pay monthly dues. One or two delegates, who are decided upon by lot, worship at the Ise Shrine in Mie prefecture once a year. They distribute the charms and the calendars published by this shrine to each member. This association includes almost all members of the village. Almost the same function is performed by* Akiba-ko.
>
> Akiba-ko.—*This is the association of believers in Akiba-sama, the protector against fire.*

Nijusan-ya-ko.—This association for the worship of the 23rd night's moon after the new moon is a volunteer group of women who meet once a lunar month at the village shrine or the duty house. They remain together throughout the night in order to worship the moon which appears at the next dawn. Nijusanyasama is believed to be the guardian of easy childbirth and good fortune.

Kannon-ko.—This is an association of believers in Bato-kannon, the Buddhist deity of the horse. The members are primarily horse drivers and owners of horses and cattle.

Other ko associations are Yama-no-kami-ko (an association of believers in the mountain deity) and Kinoene-ko (an association of believers in Daikoku, a kami of good luck and good harvest, the festival of which is held each Kinoene Day (Elder Rat Day).

In addition to these complicated religious observances, each family has its own Shinto and Buddhist altars in the living room which serve the spirits of the family ancestors and where the kami are prayed to for good health and good harvest. In the kitchen there are usually altars of Daikoku-sama and Ebisu-sama, both of which are generally believed to be kami of good harvest and good luck. Moreover, there are many Shinto, Onmyo-do (way of Yin-yang), and Buddhist charms and amulets on the pillars and walls, distributed by wandering preachers from some of the larger shrines and temples. The villagers also believe there are many kami—of the well, the fireplace, the privy, the gate, and so forth—in each house.

50
Wedding Rituals in Contemporary Japan

We have already seen a glimpse of marriage as an example of rites of passage (p. 127). In this reading we view some of the variety and actual details of wedding rituals, both religious and not so religious, in contemporary Japan.

An important feature of all weddings is the exchange of cups of *sake* between the bride and groom, and between their parents and others involved in the union. Apart from this common element, an amazing variety of wedding practices is found in Japan today. The most popular style is the Shinto wedding, but some couples (not unlike some Western counterparts) choose a nonreligious setting and prefer to fashion their own nuptial procedures. In the past Buddhist temples have specialized in the final rites of passage, funerals and memorial services, but in modern times also marriages have been conducted in some temples. Often receptions held in special wedding halls are the main public event, rather than the actual wedding ceremony.

The traditional custom of holding the wedding in the home was also observed by the author as part of her field work for this book. If Shinto weddings are "before the *kami*," and Buddhist weddings are "before the Buddhist image," then a home marriage may be characterized as "before the ancestors" because traditionally it was performed in the same room as the *butsudan* holding the family ancestors. It is interesting to note that a wedding can be performed in the home, without any religious clergy, and that in any setting the only necessary ritual for uniting the couple is the exchange of *sake* between the several sets of participants. Holding weddings in Shinto shrines and Buddhist temples, and the use of Shinto prayers *(norito)* and Buddhist sutras, are more recent customs that may be considered less essential than the crucial rite of exchanging *sake*.

THE WEDDING

Joy Hendry

There is a good deal of flexibility in the ways in which weddings can be performed, and these seem to follow certain fashions. In the past it was usual to hold the marriage and celebrations in the home, and, according to informants, many weddings continued for three days. Today, many people hold one grand reception in [an] accommodation designed specially for weddings *(kekkon shikijo),* which also provide[s] hire of clothing, photographic facilities, gifts for guests and several other services, as well as the rooms for the wedding and reception. These places have become thriving business concerns, although each individual one seems to have a limited period of success. A less plush atmosphere is available in some traditional Japanese restaurants *(ryotei)* which have facilities for wedding receptions.

It has also become popular recently to hold a religious service for the actual marriage ceremony, followed by a reception, which probably represents an indirect result of Western influence, since this procedure coincides more closely with Western arrangements than that of more traditional weddings. Most popular is the Shinto wedding *(shinzen*—"before the *kami*"), which has flourished since the Meiji period, and many Shinto shrines have invested in facilities for the reception so that they can provide the complete venue for a wedding. Members of some Buddhist sects prefer to marry in a Buddhist temple *(butsuzen*—"before the Buddhist image"), and recently some Japanese have asked to be married in Christian churches, merely to make their weddings completely Western. No doubt also in a Western vein, some modern couples in cities spurn the religious aspect altogether, perhaps referring to their weddings as *hitomae*—"before people." The manual by Fujisaki suggests a procedure for a wedding based entirely on the new Constitution, and also gives details of a "tea party" wedding as well as of marriages held in the air, on top of a skyscraper, and in an Olympic stadium. There are also still people who prefer to hold the whole procedure in as traditional a manner as possible, in the home. Examples of Shinto, Buddhist and home marriages, as well as their

Reprinted by permission of the publisher from Joy Hendry, *Marriage and Changing Japan* © Joy Hendry (New York: St. Martin's Press, Inc., 1981). The notes have been deleted.

attendant receptions, will be given in the section on "Types of Wedding," but for the sake of clarity certain common elements will be discussed first.

The Elements of the Marriage

The crux of the marriage is almost always a pledge through a sharing of cups between the bride and the groom. This rite is occasionally held in advance of other celebrations in a brief ceremony called a *karishugen* (interim marriage ceremony). Since this isolates the essence of the nuptial rites, it will be described first. The next section will be concerned with another important part of any ceremony, the exchange of cups between the principals and their new in-laws, and it will be seen that this element has some interesting history attached to it. The marriage ceremony is followed by an announcement feast *(hiroen)*. . . .

Types of Wedding

Shinto (*Shinzen*) Since the Shinto marriage seemed to be the most popular during field-work in Yame, this will be described first in detail. I witnessed five such ceremonies, four in three different marriage halls and one in a shrine, and each followed a fairly standard order, varying only in minor details. The following is a synthesis.

The families of the bride and groom gather in separate rooms where they may be served a cup of tea while they are waiting. Some wedding halls have numerous marriages to accommodate on the same day and as one party leaves the Shinto altar room another is waiting outside to enter. When all is ready, the two families file in. At one end of the room is a Shinto altar where offerings are made of all that is necessary to sustain life: rice, water, salt, fruit, vegetables, *sake* and some *surume* and *konbu*. Two *tai* may also have been offered, belly to belly to symbolise fertility or the "flourishing of descendants" *(shison han'i)*. Wedding-rings are also placed here, as are the nest of three *sake* cups and two pourers, distinguished by having one pointed tab for the male and two for the female, as well as by the colours red and pink, even if there are no paper butterflies attached.

To the right of the altar stands the Shinto priest *(kannushi)*, and to the left the *miko,* who are maiden helpers dressed in red and white. Sometimes there is a tape-recording to provide background music at appropriate moments, but on one occasion there was a group of Shinto flute players seated behind the *miko* girls. The service may also include dancers.

The bride and groom sit in the centre with the groom on the right of the bride, the go-between behind them, and the relatives of each in order of proximity and age down each side. . . . There is usually a table in front of each person with a *sake* cup and a small packet containing tiny pieces of *surume* and *konbu* which have first been offered to the deity. Thus all may participate in the ceremony. This is the case in other Shinto rites, a "sacred, symbolic feast" being one of the four main parts of Shinto worship. The other parts are the offerings, already described, purification *(harai)* and prayer *(norito)*. The marriage ceremony shares these with all others.

The priest first greets the assembled company, offers his congratulations, then announces that the ceremony will begin. It starts with the purification rite. During this the priest chants then shakes his paper-decorated staff over the altar, the helpers, the bride and groom, and all present. This is followed by the *norito* prayer which is chanted from a scroll by the priest to summon the appropriate deities, in particular that of Izumo shrine, to pay attention to the couple named. The *san-san-ku-do* ceremony is then announced by the priest, as the *seiin no gi* (rite of the oath drink), for which the *sake* is brought by the *miko* girls to the bride and groom, the go-betweens sometimes moving to either side of the couple to help them if necessary. They made a point in the Shinto ceremonies of pouring the *sake* in three movements, the smallest cup filled with the male pourer, offered first to the groom, then to the bride; the second cup, filled with the female pourer would go in the reverse order; the third cup, a repeat of the first. This order was the same at all the ceremonies, although at one of them only a single pourer was used. The couple then steps forward to the altar, where the groom reads from a scroll a pledge before the gods to the effect that they will spend married life in mutual harmony and respect, sharing pain, pleasure and peaceful living, measuring the way of prosperity for their descendants, unchanging until they die. The bride adds her name at the end. There may then be an exchange of wedding-rings, although this may take place later.

Once the bride and groom have been joined, the *sake* is brought out again to link the two families. First, the cups are taken to the bridegroom's father and, after he has drunk, to the bride, then the bridegroom's mother, and back to the bride. Then the bride's mother and father drink alternately with the groom. This is the *oyako-sakazuki* (parent-child cups). It is usually followed by the serving of each relative with a cup of *sake* which all drink together after standing up and chorusing *kampai* (cheers). This is the *shinseki-sakazuki* (relatives' cups). The *oyako-sakazuki* may be abbreviated to a general *kampai* as all drink together, it is said. The go-betweens seemed most often to drink with the relatives, but in one case they drank after the bride and groom and before the parents.

The final part of the ceremony, after some more chanting by the priest, involves the presentation of small paper-decorated *sakaki* branches *(tamagushi)* to the altar. This was explained by one priest as a thanksgiving to the deity. The branches are usually taken first by the bride and groom, then by the go-betweens, and finally by representatives of the two sets of relatives, usually the two fathers. The presentation of the branches is accompanied by two claps and two bows by each person, and as the fathers bow the other relatives join them. The exchange of rings took place at this point in some ceremonies, accompanied by clapping from the relatives. The introduction of relatives takes place either here, after the priest has left, or in a side room.

The *hiroen* is usually arranged by the catering department of the same hotel, marriage hall or shrine, and it follows on immediately the ceremony is completed. A feast is laid out, sometimes at Western-style tables, sometimes in Japanese style at individual trays or long low tables with cushions on the floor. Details in the procedure vary depending on the preferences of the clients and the institution concerned. Some receptions are quite Western, with a tiered wedding cake, one of which had no less than seven tiers. Typically, the guests are first seated, usually in places assigned to them, and the bride and groom then make an entrance with the go-betweens, often to the accompaniment of records such as Mendelssohn's or Wagner's Wedding March. . . .

Buddhist (*Butsuzen*) Marriages in Buddhist temples are much less common, but one that I witnessed was for members of the Soka Gakkai sect. Otherwise informants expressed the opinion that temples were for funerals and memorial services, not for happy occasions such as weddings. The procedure was similar to other forms of marriage, except that the setting and altar ritual were Buddhist. The participants sat on cushions in much the same order as at the Shinto ceremony, facing the altar during the preliminaries and turning to face each other only for the *sake* rites. There were two priests officiating and the ceremony began as the younger banged a drum. The elder entered, sat down and began chanting sutras, accompanied by the occasional ringing of a bell. After some time, a proclamation was read which announced the purpose of the occasion, and the relatives turned to face each other for the sharing of cups. The younger priest brought the cups and served the *sake,* and this time the complete process . . . was performed. The cups were then taken to the bride's parents who each drank, then returned to the groom, who drank out of the same cup. This was repeated from the groom's parents to the bride. Similarly, they shared cups with each of their new relatives in twos, and finally the go-between and his wife drank together. There was then an exchange of rings and the elder priest read aloud a proclamation of the union which had been initiated and the promise which had been enacted by the couple to live in mutual love and respect, and to share sad and happy times together until they die. There was then further chanting and the [wedding] was over. Guests were invited to attend a *hiroen* similar to that described at a conventional marriage hall, and a *yorokobi* was held later at the groom's house.

Home Marriage It was rather paradoxical that two of the three home marriages which took place between 1975 and 1979 in Kurotsuchi involved people who were actually living away from home, in Kyoto and Osaka, both individuals who had returned to their own area to seek a spouse. It may be, however, that such couples had less need to indicate their independence and equality by holding the marriage ceremony on neutral ground. One such wedding, which will now be described, was that of the second son of the village head.

The marriage itself was held before the *tokonoma* in the *zashiki,* which opened out, by the removal of sliding doors, into the next two rooms to make one large, long room. It is sometimes said of home marriages that they are being held before the ancestors, but in this case the *butsudan* was in a separate room. Traditionally, however, the *tokonoma* had some religious significance. . . . The bride, groom and go-betweens sat at one end of the long room, . . . and the relatives sat along each side of the length of the room. One of the groom's relatives had been designated master of ceremonies for the occasion and he sat at the bottom of the groom's side. Most of the formally seated relatives were men, except for parents, siblings and grandparents; the other women, the aunts, who were helping in the kitchen, occasionally offered advice on the proceedings from the open door. Three local girls, unmarried neighbours and relatives, were acting as *kyujinin* (serving people), and these in particular were directed by the aunts from the kitchen. In front of each place, marked by a cushion, was a cup, two small cakes and a name card.

The proceedings began as usual with an introduction from the master of ceremonies, then the helpers came into the middle of the room to greet the guests. This was followed by the *noshi* presentation by one of the girls and then the cups and *sake* pourers were brought in. The *sakazuki* took place in the same abbreviated form as at the *karishugen* and here too *kageutai* were sung from outside the door. A *sakazuki* for the relatives followed, using one cup down each side. After this, tea was brought in and served to each of the guests. The bride and groom stood up, and the groom read an oath to be bound in marriage to his wife, then gave her a wedding-ring. The master of ceremonies proclaimed the couple married, added a few words of congratulation, then asked the go-between to make his speech. This again included a brief biography of each partner and an expression of hope that the marriage would be long-lasting. Again the two fathers said a few words about the pleasure of the occasion. The next item was announced to be a greeting by the *kominkancho* (head of public meeting hall), apparently of the whole of Yame. He was not present, nor expected to be, according to informants, who explained that there would be too many weddings for him to attend them all. Instead, the master of ceremonies sang an *utai,* but the inclusion of this substitute for his greeting seems to serve the purpose of adding a public note to what would otherwise be a completely private ceremony between two families. After this, the two rows of relatives were introduced individually by the fathers of the bride and groom, and the ceremony was complete. The guests then turned round to relax their legs while trays of food were brought in, and the feast with warmed *sake* followed. During this period there was much informal singing and dancing, and the bride changed her kimono. Photographs were taken of each outfit. After a suitable period, the guests were asked to rise and shout three cheers before the rice and soup were brought out to mark the end of the *hiroen.* Gifts were presented to each person as they left.

51
Social and Aesthetic Expression of Religion: The Art of Tea

Because tea is the national beverage of Japan, it shares some of the features of coffee drinking in the West: it is a common drink of refreshment taken with meals or in a period of relaxation, often in social company. But the ceremonial concern for tea in Japan goes so far beyond this mundane level that it has become a cult, or "art," as the next author describes it. Indeed, the process of preparing and serving tea is so elaborate that there are recognized schools and "masters" in the art. Many people, especially young ladies, take lessons in the tea ceremony as a means of spiritual training and to gain poise.

The author is concerned not with the social or manual aspects of serving tea but with its philosophical and religious meaning in Zen. The total atmosphere for the tea ceremony is one of simplicity and harmony with nature; the tea hut and the person alike are stripped of artificial obstacles. By eliminating the unnecessary from the surroundings and from the actions of the tea ceremony, one is able to participate in the rhythm of nature. As a Western interpreter has put it, "Rustic utensils and surroundings were brought into harmony to remind him of the Buddhahood in a clod of earth, and the withdrawn repose of the cottage and its garden turned his mind to the permanent behind the ephemeral—to the intersection of time and eternity."[1]

The last part of this selection is a translation of a statement on the art of tea by the Zen master Takuan (1573–1645). The art of tea has been practiced in Japan for centuries, and long ago it was realized that this art can be turned all too easily into mere sociability or vain pride. To avoid these pitfalls, Takuan described the simple setting and tools for the proper appreciation of the art of tea. Noteworthy is the concern for the little things, the mood of the seasons, the sound of the boiling kettle. In this context worries are set aside and the mind is refreshed. When we view the tea ceremony, it is difficult to decide whether religion has penetrated an everyday activity or whether this mundane activity has been elevated to the position of a cult.

ZEN AND THE ART OF TEA

Daisetz T. Suzuki

What is common to Zen and the art of tea is the constant attempt both make at simplification. The elimination of the unnecessary is achieved by Zen in its intuitive grasp of final reality; by the art of tea, in the way of living typified by serving tea in the tearoom. The art of tea is the aestheticism of primitive simplicity. Its ideal, to come closer to Nature, is realized by sheltering oneself under a thatched roof in a room which is hardly ten feet square but which must be artistically constructed and furnished. Zen also aims at stripping off all the artificial wrappings humanity has devised, supposedly for its own solemnization. Zen first of all combats the intellect; for, in spite of its practical usefulness, the intellect goes against our effort to delve into the depths of

Reprinted by permission of the publisher from *Zen and Japanese Culture,* by Daisetz T. Suzuki, Bollingen Series LXIV (Princeton: Princeton University Press 1959), pp. 271–272, 276–278.

1. Edward G. Seidensticker, in Yasunari Kawabata, *Thousand Cranes,* translated by Edward G. Seidensticker (New York: Berkley Publishing Corporation, 1965), p. v. In this novel Kawabata, the first Japanese winner of the Nobel Prize for literature (in 1968), has woven a fascinating tale into the context and mood of the tea ceremony.

being. Philosophy may propose all kinds of questions for intellectual solution, but it never claims to give us the spiritual satisfaction which must be accessible to every one of us, however intellectually undeveloped he may be. Philosophy is accessible only to those who are intellectually equipped, and thus it cannot be a discipline of universal appreciation. Zen—or, more broadly speaking, religion—is to cast off all one thinks he possesses, even life, and to get back to the ultimate state of being, the "Original Abode," one's own father or mother. This can be done by every one of us, for we are what we are because of it or him or her, and without it or him or her we are nothing. This is to be called the last stage of simplification, since things cannot be reduced to any simpler terms. The art of tea symbolizes simplification, first of all, by an inconspicuous, solitary, thatched hut erected, perhaps, under an old pine tree, as if the hut were part of nature and not specially constructed by human hands. When form is thus once for all symbolized it allows itself to be artistically treated. It goes without saying that the principle of treatment is to be in perfect conformity with the original idea which prompted it, that is, the elimination of unnecessaries. . . .

Takuan on the Art of Tea *(Cha-No-Yu)*

The principle of *cha-no-yu* is the spirit of harmonious blending of Heaven and Earth and provides the means for establishing universal peace. People of the present time have turned it into a mere occasion for meeting friends, talking of worldly affairs, and indulging in palatable food and drink; besides, they are proud of their elegantly furnished tearooms, where, surrounded by rare objects of art, they would serve tea in a most accomplished manner, and deride those who are not so skillful as themselves. This is, however, far from being the original intention of *cha-no-yu.*

Let us then construct a small room in a bamboo grove or under trees, arrange streams and rocks and plant trees and bushes, while [inside the room] let us pile up charcoal, set a kettle, arrange flowers, and arrange in order the necessary tea utensils. And let all this be carried out in accordance with the idea that in this room we can enjoy the streams and rocks as we do the rivers and mountains in Nature, and appreciate the various moods and sentiments suggested by the snow, the moon, and the trees and flowers, as they go through the transformation of seasons, appearing and disappearing, blooming and withering. As visitors are greeted here with due reverence, we listen quietly to the boiling water in the kettle, which sounds like a breeze passing through the pine needles, and become oblivious of all worldly woes and worries; we then pour out a dipperful of water from the kettle, reminding us of the mountain stream, and thereby our mental dust is wiped off. This is truly a world of recluses, saints on earth.

The principle of propriety is reverence, which in practical life functions as harmonious relationship. This is the statement made by Confucius when he defines the use of propriety, and is also the mental attitude one should cultivate as *cha-no-yu.* For instance, when a man is associated with persons of high social rank his conduct is simple and natural, and there is no cringing self-depreciation on his part. When he sits in the company of people socially below him he retains a respectful attitude toward them, being entirely free from the feeling of self-importance. This is due to the presence of something pervading the entire tearoom, which results in the harmonious relationship of all who come here. However long the association, there is always the persisting sense of reverence. The spirit of the smiling Kasyapa and the nodding Tseng-tzu must be said to be moving here; this spirit, in words, is the mysterious Suchness that is beyond all comprehension.

For this reason, the principle animating the tearoom, from its first construction down to the choice of the tea utensils, the technique of service, the cooking of food, wearing apparel, etc., is to be sought in the avoidance of complicated ritual and mere ostentation. The implements may be old, but the mind can be invigorated therewith so that it is ever fresh and ready to respond to the changing seasons and the varying views resulting therefrom; it never curries favor, it is never covetous, never inclined to extravagance, but always watchful and considerate for others. The owner of such a mind is naturally gentle-mannered and always sincere—this is *cha-no-yu*.

The way of *cha-no-yu*, therefore, is to appreciate the spirit of a naturally harmonious blending of Heaven and Earth, to see the pervading presence of the five elements *(wu-hsing)* by one's fireside, where the mountains, rivers, rocks, and trees are found as they are in Nature, to draw the refreshing water from the well of Nature, to taste with one's own mouth the flavor supplied by Nature. How grand this enjoyment of the harmonious blending of Heaven and Earth!

CHAPTER FIFTEEN

Natural Bond Between Religion and State

A combination of factors in Japanese history has resulted in a peculiarly intimate bond between religion and the state, and this bond forms a persistent theme in the religious life of the Japanese people. The Japanese have long possessed a sense of national identity and common destiny, as an island country with a distinctive tradition in ancient times and a continuing sociopolitical unity today. The mythology of antiquity lays the foundation for the notion of Japan as a divinely created country led by the imperial line in descent from the Sun Goddess. With this ancient heritage as a foundation, it is not surprising that the overwhelming majority of religious institutions in Japanese history have assumed a position of subservience to the state, or have at least supported the Japanese nation.

This bond between religion and state runs throughout Japanese history, yet it undergoes various changes. For example, the idea of religion serving the state in Shotoku's Constitution, excerpted next, is not the same as the ideological support for modern nationalism in *Cardinal Principles of the National Entity* (see p. 238). The use—or, one might say, the abuse—of a tradition does not always bring out its essential values. To take an example from Western history, the use of Christianity as motivation for the medieval Crusades does not mean that the essence of Christianity is the crusading spirit. Japanese religion by nature tends to support the cultural and political order of which it is a part. This was assumed in traditional Japan, and was planned in modern Japan. For example, the Imperial Rescript on Education used religious or semireligious loyalty to emperor and state to unify the people into a modern nation-state. But most Japanese feel that the *Cardinal Principles of the National Entity,* whose use in the educational system helped inculcate the unswerving patriotism expressed in Japan's wars with China and Russia and later in World War II, was an abuse of the Japanese notion.

52
Shotoku's Constitution: Religion and State in Ancient Japan

One of the earliest Japanese documents expressing the intimate relationship between state and religion is the so-called Seventeen Article Constitution of Prince Shotoku. According to tradition, Prince Shotoku wrote this document in the early seventh century, and although his authorship may never be proven, the Japanese estimation of Prince Shotoku is very high: he is revered as one of the great early statesmen in Japanese history and as a founding father of Japanese Buddhism. (See p. 50 for the elevation of Prince Shotoku to semidivine status.) This so-called constitution is more a rationale for political action than an actual constitution, but the first three items show the special role of religion in this rationale.

The author presupposes the universal reverence for *kami* and weaves this into support for Confucian and Buddhist values as a means of reinforcing the state. The first article of the Constitution, quoted below, emphasizes the Confucian virtue of social harmony, which is the basis for political stability. The second article pays homage to Buddhism as the way in which humans will be preserved from evil. The third article combines the Japanese idea of the divinity of the emperor with Chinese cosmic notions of the harmony necessary between Heaven and Earth. In later times, the particular formulation of the state-religion relationship varied, but religion usually supported the state, while the state patronized religion.

SHOTOKU'S CONSTITUTION

W. G. Aston, translator

Summer, 4th month, 3rd day. The Prince Imperial in person prepared for the first time laws. There were seventeen clauses, as follows:—

I. Harmony is to be valued, and an avoidance of wanton opposition to be honoured. All men are influenced by class-feelings, and there are few who are

Reprinted by permission of the publisher from W. G. Aston, translator, *Nihongi: Chronicles of Japan from the Earliest Times to A.D. 697* (London: George Allen & Unwin Ltd., 1956).

intelligent. Hence there are some who disobey their lords and fathers, or who maintain feuds with the neighbouring villages. But when those above are harmonious and those below are friendly, and there is concord in the discussion of business, right views of things spontaneously gain acceptance. Then what is there which cannot be accomplished!

II. Sincerely reverence the three treasures. The three treasures, viz. Buddha, the Law and the Priesthood, are the final refuge of the four generated beings, and are the supreme objects of faith in all countries. What man in what age can fail to reverence this law? Few men are utterly bad. They may be taught to follow it. But if they do not betake them to the three treasures, wherewithal shall their crookedness be made straight?

III. When you receive the Imperial commands, fail not scrupulously to obey them. The lord is Heaven, the vassal is Earth. Heaven overspreads, and Earth upbears. When this is so, the four seasons follow their due course, and the powers of Nature obtain their efficacy. If the Earth attempted to overspread, Heaven would simply fall in ruin. Therefore is it that when the lord speaks, the vassal listens; when the superior acts, the inferior yields compliance. Consequently when you receive the Imperial commands, fail not to carry them out scrupulously. Let there be a want of care in this matter, and ruin is the natural consequence.

53
The Imperial Rescript on Education: Religious Support for Modern Nationalism

The Imperial Rescript on Education has greater historical significance than its brief length suggests, for it summed up the nationalistic fervor that stemmed from the Meiji Restoration, and it served as the training guide for absolute commitment to the state until 1945. Powerful symbols such as the emperor and hierarchical patterns of loyalty were invoked to support a nationwide school system, which was developed in the Meiji period (1868–1912). The rescript and a portrait of the emperor were hung in every school, and pupils were required to bow before them much as American pupils pledge allegiance to the flag. Religious undertones may be seen even in the American practice, but the religious character of the Japanese ceremony is more direct. The emperor, often known as a "manifest *kami*," was venerated as a descendant of the *kami*, the living symbol of their spiritual tradition as well as their ethnic and national unity. In short, veneration of the emperor was used to train the people to hold absolute loyalty toward the state.

The content of the rescript, although formally stated, is rather simple: the source of education is the realization that Japan is a sacred empire handed down by the imperial line and to which all are loyal and obedient. The emperor is the visible symbol of the state to which all must (out of sense of obligation) give themselves totally: "Should emergency arise, offer yourselves courageously to the State" in order to protect the imperial throne. Respect for the constitution is mentioned, but the Japanese constitution was handed down from authorities above, not demanded by a grass-roots movement of the people. However, this document succeeded—not because it invoked a new principle but because it reflected and elaborated a central aspect of Japanese tradition. In this sense, the Imperial Rescript on Education did not create the notion of loyalty to the emperor, but it did embody this tradition. At present, one lively discussion among Japanese intellectuals is how Japan can retain her distinctiveness as a national tradition and yet participate in international affairs.

IMPERIAL RESCRIPT ON EDUCATION

Know ye, Our subjects:

Our Imperial Ancestors have founded Our Empire on a basis broad and everlasting, and have deeply and firmly implanted virtue; Our subjects ever united in loyalty and filial piety have from generation to generation illustrated the beauty thereof. This is the glory of the fundamental character of Our Empire, and herein also lies the source of Our education. Ye, Our subjects, be filial to your parents, affectionate to your brothers and sisters; as husbands and wives be harmonious, as friends true; bear yourselves in modesty and moderation; extend your benevolence to all; pursue learning and cultivate arts, and thereby develop intellectual faculties and perfect moral powers; furthermore, advance public good and promote common interests; always respect the Constitution and observe the laws; should emergency arise, offer yourselves courageously to the State; and thus guard and maintain the prosperity of Our Imperial Throne coeval with heaven and earth. So shall ye not only be Our good and faithful subjects, but render illustrious the best traditions of your forefathers.

The Way here set forth is indeed the teaching bequeathed by Our Imperial Ancestors, to be observed alike by Their Descendants and the subjects, infallible for all ages and true in all places. It is Our wish to lay it to heart in all reverence, in common with you, Our subjects, that we may all attain the same virtue.

The 30th day of the 10th month of the 23rd year of Meiji.
(The 30th of October, 1890).

(Imperial Sign Manual. Imperial Seal).

Reprinted by permission of the publisher from Dairoku Kikuchi, *Japanese Education* (London: John Murray Publishers, 1909).

54
Religion as Ideology

The international scene changed significantly from the time of the Imperial Rescript on Education in 1890 to the time of the 1937 publication of *Kokutai no Hongi,* or *Cardinal Principles of the National Entity of Japan.* In less than fifty years, Japan passed beyond the threat of colonial intervention on her own soil and herself became a kind of colonial power. Japan was successful militarily in two wars, the Sino-Japanese War of 1894–1895 and the Russo-Japanese War of 1904–1905, and she profited financially from World War I. Japan controlled Formosa (Taiwan) and Korea as well as parts of continental China, and nationalism and militarism were inflated by this success.

Whereas the Rescript on Education was aimed at unifying the people within a newly formed nation-state, the government's *Cardinal Principles of the National Entity* was intended to gain unqualified support for the military goals of a state that constituted a world power. Excerpts from the latter document reveal a consistent twofold argument. First, the *problems* of Japan are caused by neglect of the native tradition and adoption of Western values. Western thought is contrary to Japanese culture because it does not realize the unique heritage of Japan, and it encourages an individualism that destroys Japanese social ethics. Second, the *solution* to the problems of Japan is rejection of Western thought and recovery of the ancient Japanese heritage, for Japan is a sacred land founded by the *kami* and ruled by the emperor, and every citizen will express filial piety to his parents and absolute loyalty to the emperor. This loyalty, especially for the warrior, means giving his life for his country.

In short, this document of unqualified patriotism, not unlike documents from other countries, calls for support of political and military activities, whatever they might be. Most Japanese agree that this was a use of the native tradition to support an unfortunate war (and this opinion of the war leads many Japanese to oppose the use of Japan as a base for United States military operations). In addition, many Japanese feel that religion and war are incompatible, and they actively support peace movements. The *Kokutai no Hongi* was prohibited by the Allied occupation forces in the so-called "Directive for the Disestablishment of State Shinto" of late 1945, and it is no longer used in Japanese education. (This directive is cited in full on pp. 38–44; for mention of *Kokutai no Hongi,* see provision I.i.)

This document criticizes "foreign ideologies," "individualistic ideologies," and "Occidental ideologies" as threats to Japan's "unique national entity." However, historical hindsight enables us to see that just as Confucianism (or Neo-Confucianism) in the Tokugawa era served as a set of ideas, or ideology, to support the government and the social order, so also was *Cardinal Principles of the National Entity of Japan* an ideology in the 1930s and early 1940s to support the government and militarism. This selection raises two very important questions: how should we properly use the term *ideology,* and how do we critically assess the utilization of religion as ideology?

CARDINAL PRINCIPLES OF THE
NATIONAL ENTITY OF JAPAN

John Owen Gauntlett, translator

The various ideological and social evils of present-day Japan are the fruits of ignoring the fundamentals and of running into the trivial, of lack in sound judgment, and of failure to digest things thoroughly; and this is due to the fact that since the days of Meiji so many aspects of European and American culture, systems, and learning, have been imported, and that, too rapidly. As a matter of fact, foreign ideologies imported into our country are in the main the ideologies of enlightenment that have come down since the eighteenth century, or their extensions. The views of the world and of life that form the basis of these ideologies are a rationalism and a positivism, lacking in historical views, which on the one hand lay the highest value on, and assert the liberty and equality of, individuals, and on the other hand lay value on a world by nature abstract, transcending nations and races. Consequently, importance is laid upon human beings and their gatherings, who have become isolated from historical entireties, abstract and independent of each other. It is political, social, moral, and pedagogical theories based on such views of the world and of life, that have on the one hand made contributions to the various reforms seen in our country, and on the other have had deep and wide influence on our nation's primary ideology and culture. . . .

Paradoxical and extreme conceptions, such as socialism, anarchism, and communism, are all based in the final analyses on individualism which is the root of modern Occidental ideologies, and are no more than varied forms of their expressions. In the Occident, too, where individualism forms the basis of their ideas, they have, when it comes to communism, been unable to adopt it; so that now they are about to do away with their traditional individualism, which has led to the rise of totalitarianism and nationalism and incidentally to the upspringing of Fascism and Nazism. That is, it can be said that both in the Occident and in our country the deadlock of individualism has led alike to a season of ideological and social confusion and crisis. We shall leave aside for a while the question of finding a way out of the present deadlock, for, as far as it concerns our country, we must return to the standpoint peculiar to our country, clarify our immortal national entity, sweep aside everything in the way of adulation, bring into being our original condition, and at the same

Reprinted by permission of the publishers from pp. 52, 54–55, 80, 81–82, 87–88, 144–145, 175, 178 of *Kokutai no Hongi: Cardinal Principles of the National Entity of Japan,* translated by John Owen Gauntlett and edited by Robert King Hall. Cambridge, Mass.: Harvard University Press, Copyright, 1949, by the President and Fellows of Harvard College. The bracketed remarks are from the original.

time rid ourselves of bigotry, and strive all the more to take in and sublimate Occidental culture; for we should give to basic things their proper place, giving due weight to minor things, and should build up a sagacious and worthy Japan. This means that the present conflict seen in our people's ideas, the unrest in their modes of life, the confused state of civilization, can be put right only by a thorough investigation by us of the intrinsic nature of Occidental ideologies and by grasping the true meaning of our national entity. Then, too, this should be done not only for the sake of our nation but for the sake of the entire human race which is struggling to find a way out of the deadlock with which individualism is faced. Herein lies our grave cosmopolitan mission. It is for this reason that we have compiled the *Cardinal Principles of the National Entity of Japan,* to trace clearly the genesis of the nation's foundation, to define its great spirit, to set forth clearly at the same time the features the national entity has manifested in history, and to provide the present generation with an elucidation of the matter, and thus to awaken the people's consciousness and their efforts. . . .

Our country is established with the Emperor, who is a descendant of Amaterasu Ohmikami, as her center, and our ancestors as well as we ourselves constantly behold in the Emperor the fountainhead of her life and activities. For this reason, to serve the Emperor and to receive the Emperor's great august Will as one's own is the rationale of making our historical "life" live in the present; and on this is based the morality of the people.

Loyalty means to reverence the Emperor as [our] pivot and to follow him implicitly. By implicit obedience is meant casting ourselves aside and serving the Emperor intently. To walk this Way of loyalty is the sole Way in which we subjects may "live," and the fountainhead of all energy. Hence, offering our lives for the sake of the Emperor does not mean so-called self-sacrifice, but the casting aside of our little selves to live under his august grace and the enhancing of the genuine life of the people of a State. The relationship between the Emperor and the subjects is not an artificial relationship [which means] bowing down to authority, nor a relationship such as [exists] between master and servant as is seen in feudal morals. . . . The ideology which interprets the relationship between the Emperor and his subjects as being a reciprocal relationship such as merely [involves] obedience to authority or rights and duties, rests on individualistic ideologies, and is a rationalistic way of thinking that looks on everything as being in equal personal relationships. An individual is an existence belonging to a State and her history which form the basis of his origin, and is fundamentally one body with it. . . .

In our country, the two Augustnesses, Izanagi no Mikoto and Izanami no Mikoto, are ancestral deities of nature and the deities, and the Emperor is the divine offspring of the Imperial Ancestor who was born of the two Augustnesses. The Imperial Ancestor and the Emperor are in the relationship of parent and child, and the relationship between the Emperor and his subjects is, in its righteousness, that of sovereign and subject and, in its sympathies, that of father and child. This relationship is an "essential" relationship that is far more fundamental than the rational, obligatory relationships, and herein are the grounds that give birth to the Way of loyalty. From the point of individualistic personal relationships, the relationship between sovereign and subject in our country may [perhaps] be looked upon as that between non-personalities. However, this is nothing but an error arising from treating the individual as supreme, from the notion that has individual thoughts for its nucleus, and from abstract consciousness. Our relationship between sovereign and subject is by no means a shallow, lateral relationship such as [means] the correlation between ruler and citizen, but is a relationship springing from a basis transcending this correlation, and is that of self-effacement and a return to [the] "one," in which this basis is not lost. This is a thing that can never be understood from an individualistic way of thinking. In our country, this great Way has seen a natural development since the founding of the nation, and the most basic thing that has manifested itself as regards the subjects is in short this Way of loyalty. Herein exists the profound meaning and lofty value of loyalty. Of late years, through the influence of the Occidental individualistic ideology, a way of thinking which has for its basis the individual has become lively. Consequently, this and the true aim of our Way of loyalty which is "essentially" different from it are not necessarily [mutually] consistent. That is, those in our country who at the present time expound loyalty and patriotism are apt to lose [sight of] its true significance, being influenced by Occidental individualism and rationalism. We must sweep aside the corruption of the spirit and the clouding of knowledge that arises from setting up one's "self" and from being taken up with one's "self" and return to a pure and clear state of mind that belongs intrinsically to us as subjects, and thereby fathom the great principle of loyalty. . . .

In our country filial piety is a Way of the highest importance. Filial piety originates with one's family as its basis, and in its larger sense has the nation for its foundation. Filial piety directly has for its object one's parents, but in its relationship toward the Emperor finds a place within loyalty.

The basis of the nation's livelihood is, as in the Occident, neither the individual nor husband and wife. It is the home. . . .

The life of a family in our country is not confined to the present life of a household of parents and children, but beginning with the distant ancestors, is carried on eternally by the descendants. The present life of a family is a link between the past and the future, and while it carries over and develops the objectives of the ancestors, it hands them over to its descendants. Herein also lies the reason why since of old a family name has been esteemed in our country. A family name is an honor to a household built up by one's ancestors, so that to stain this may be looked upon not only as a personal disgrace but as a disgrace to a family that has come down in one line linking the past, present, and future. Accordingly, the announcing of one's real name by a knight who has gone out to the battlefield was in the nature of an oath to fight bravely by speaking of one's ancestors and their achievements, so as not to cast a slur on the name of an esteemed family. . . .

Bushido may be cited as showing an outstanding characteristic of our national morality. In the world of warriors one sees inherited the totalitarian structure and spirit of the ancient clans peculiar to our nation. Hence, though the teachings of Confucianism and Buddhism have been followed, these have been transcended. That is to say, though a sense of indebtedness binds master and servant, this has developed into a spirit of self-effacement and of meeting death with a perfect calmness. In this, it was not that death was made light of so much as that man tempered himself to death and in a true sense regarded it with esteem. In effect, man tried to fulfill true life by way of death. This means that rather than lose the whole by being taken up with and setting up oneself, one puts self to death in order to give full play to the whole by fulfilling the whole. Life and death are basically one, and the monistic truth is found where life and death are transcended. Through this is life, and through this is death. However, to treat life and death as two opposites and to hate death and to seek life is to be taken up with one's own interests, and is a thing of which warriors are ashamed. To fulfill the Way of loyalty, counting life and death as one, is *Bushido.* . . .

We have inquired into the fundamental principles of our national entity and the ways in which it has been manifested in our national history. What kind of resolve and attitude should we subjects of the Japanese Empire now take toward the various problems of the day? It seems to us that our first duty is the task of creating a new Japanese culture by sublimating and assimilating foreign cultures which are at the source of the various problems in keeping with the fundamental principles of our national entity.

Every type of foreign ideology that has been imported into our country may have been quite natural in China, India, Europe, or America, in that it has sprung from their racial or historical characteristics; but in our country, which has a unique national entity, it is necessary as a preliminary step to put these types to rigid judgment and scrutiny so as to see if they are suitable to our national traits. That is to say, the creation of a new culture which has characteristics peculiar to our nation can be looked forward to only through this consciousness and the sublimation and assimilation of foreign cultures that accompanies it. . . .

To put it in a nutshell, while the strong points of Occidental learning and concepts lie in their analytical and intellectual qualities, the characteristics of Oriental learning and concepts lie in their intuitive and ascetic qualities. These are natural tendencies that arise through racial and historical differences; and when we compare them with our national spirit, concepts, or mode of living, we cannot help recognizing further great and fundamental differences. Our nation has in the past imported, assimilated, and sublimated Chinese and Indian ideologies, and has therewith supported the Imperial Way, making possible the establishment of an original culture based on her national entity. Following the Meiji Restoration Occidental cultures poured in with a rush, and contributed immensely toward our national prosperity; but their individualistic qualities brought about various difficulties in all the phases of the lives of our people, causing their thoughts to fluctuate. However, now is the time for us to sublimate and assimilate these Occidental ideologies in keeping with our national entity, to set up a vast new Japanese culture, and, by taking advantage of these things, to bring about a great national development.

PART III

Religion in Recent and Modern Japan

CHAPTER SIXTEEN

The Dilemma
of Organized Religion
in Modern Japan

Every religious tradition undergoes minor changes with the passage of time, but religion in recent Japan (starting with the Meiji era in 1868) and in modern Japan (from the end of World War II in 1945) has undergone major changes in a relatively short span. The cumulative effect of more than a century of rapid social and religious transformation presents Japanese religion today with a more serious dilemma than the slight, gradual modifications that inevitably occur. What is at stake is whether Shinto and Buddhism, the major organized religions in Japan, will continue to hold the attention of a majority of the population. The dilemma is complicated because it arises not only out of factors internal to the two religions but also out of external factors such as Japan's shift from a predominantly agricultural socioeconomic orientation to an urban-industrial orientation.

Although the reasons are complex, it seems safe to conclude that internal factors in Buddhism and Shinto helped bring about a tendency toward formalism and a loss of vitality in their respective traditions. Buddhism's attachment to feudal values and the institutions of the Tokugawa period and Shinto's tie with narrowly nationalistic values and programs after the Tokugawa period were especially responsible for the lack of vitality in the postwar period. Additionally, the reformers within each tradition have been unable to renovate the traditions as a whole.

Religious life continues, however, and one major avenue for religious expression is the many New Religions discussed in the next chapter. However, another indication of the state of religious life in the modern period is the rather widespread disinterest in organized religion. Increasingly, particularly in the cities, people either have no Shinto altar *(kamidana)* in their homes or else they make very few offerings; if there are more Buddhist altars *(butsudan),* they are kept more out of respect for the ancestors than out of sympathy with Buddhism. A minority opinion in modern Japan, as represented in the novel *The Pornographers,* is disdain or sacrilegious scorn for all organized religion.

Questions about the vitality and viability of organized religion in the modern world are by no means limited to Japan—similar queries have been raised in Europe and North America, as well as in places closer to Japan such as China. By exploring some aspects of the dilemma of organized religion in Japan we may become more aware of current problems for religion throughout the world.

55
Formalism in Buddhism

Although Buddhism in Japan was the repository of profound philosophy and the developer of dynamic sects, its dominant characteristics from Tokugawa times to the present have been formalism and lack of vitality. In this selection a famous Buddhist scholar uses the term *formalized Buddhism* to describe this situation, and he is openly critical of the manner in which the situation arose. Singled out for criticism are the subservience of Buddhist temples to feudal lords and the neglect of Buddhism's religious mission to serve the political rulers. The result was that funeral masses became the main religious function of Buddhism, a "formality" that could be carried out whether or not priests and people found religious fulfillment in Buddhism.

The extreme conservatism of Buddhist sects and family religion worked together to support feudal values even after the end of the feudal age simply because they had been part of the status quo. The result was that Buddhism in the modern age is still waiting for reform.

Buddhism's weakness in the modern nationalistic period meant that it was powerless to oppose militarism and imperialism, and Buddhism's early support of state and emperor was extended in the 1930s and early 1940s into positive, unqualified support of World War II. The author outlines the details of Buddhist support for the war, concluding with the severe indictment that "it is not to the honor of the Japanese Buddhist order that no Buddhists sacrificed themselves to an antiwar movement during the long aggressive war in China." His indictment even casts light on the contemporary scene, since he characterizes much of Buddhism today as feudal and "reactionary." He challenges the institution of Buddhist temples to reexamine the nature of their role as transmitters of the Buddha's message, and he asks individual Buddhists to reconsider what it means to be committed to the Buddha's way.

JAPANESE BUDDHISM IN THE
TWENTIETH CENTURY

Zenryu Tsukamoto

. . . Not only the Church of Chinese Buddhism but also of Japanese Buddhism were formalized and lost their vitality in the course of the nineteenth century; they no longer held sway in their guidance of society. The political leaders of these two countries, impressed by the advances of European and American countries in the wake of Western Civilization, lost interest in "old Buddhism," despised it, thought it useless, and suppressed and persecuted it. Yet, religion in general resuscitated its original spirit throughout this suppression and persecution, took the chance to recover from the previous decline, and undergoes at present a revolutionary progress.

The modern Buddhist world in China and Japan, on account of government suppression and persecution, accomplished a transformation and managed reforms which were not evident in other Buddhist Asiatic countries. Let us first make a perusory survey of twentieth century Japanese Buddhism.

Many schools of Japanese Buddhism had served the feudalistic lords during the feudal age (Tokugawa; use of the word feudal is quite loose, since the system was in reality absolutism, absolute power in the hands of the *shogun*), which lasted for two hundred and sixty years or more previous to the Meiji period. These schools secured their position and prosperity by cooperating with the feudal lords in their maintenance of the feudal social order; at the same time they fixed their position in the feudal system. The Tokugawa family lords obliged all the people to belong to some temple, called *danka,* in their efforts to suppress Christianity. This meant that all Japanese families, under the leadership of a family head, were, at least nominally, Buddhist believers. Every temple became a branch temple of the *honzan,* or head temple of the school. The abbot of the head temple of every school supervised the high priests of the branch temples and, in turn, was subordinate to the lord or *shogun*. The high priest of every temple not only performed the ancestor rituals and funerals required by those families in his *danka* but also acted as a sort of inspector-guardian of the peace, reporting to the feudal lord both those who professed

Reprinted from Zenryu Tsukamoto, "Japanese and Chinese Buddhism in the Twentieth Century," *Journal of World History,* Volume VI-3, 1960. Reproduced with permission of UNESCO.

belief in heretical teachings and those who planned treacherous action against the social system. Thus, the Tokugawa lords made the temple clergy cooperate in maintaining the feudal society, employing the priests literally as inspectors of the people through the *danka* system. Politically forced to be "believers," there were surely some among them who were sincere believers, but the function of the Buddhist temple in the Tokugawa age was confined to the performance of rituals for the dead. Even the rituals for the dead of the *danka* families were magical in nature, completely incomprehensible to the Japanese people, because they were read in the Chinese style of pronunciation. Eventually, the life of the priests became so stable that the priests themselves became lazy, lost interest in their mission as priests and in their study of Buddhist Truth. Under the stability of this feudal system, Japanese human reason was impotent, and Buddhism became what I term "formalized Buddhism."

Meanwhile, the lords of the Tokugawa family hailed Confucianism, in particular the school of Chu Hsi, as the guide for government, and ordered the political underlings to study Chu Hsi and to propagate his teaching as an example for both politics and morals. The Chu Hsi school, as already well known, protested vigorously against Buddhism, more so than other schools, and they insisted that Buddhism was not only useless but also harmful to a real social life guided by Confucian principles. The Tokugawa intelligentsia, generally called *shitaifu,* who were thoroughly educated in Confucianism, gradually became separated from all Buddhist affairs and despised the Buddhist religion. Even the monks themselves neglected their religious mission, which should be an endeavor to solve the problems of current social life and personal suffering. Instead they indulged in fixed dogmatic study of the doctrines respective to their school, recited the sutras for the deceased, and left aside entirely the religious problems connected with the actual society.

Just as the lords in their castles governed the people by a stratified feudal system, the abbot of each Buddhist school governed the clergy by a hierarchical system. The schools clung to traditional dogma and merely endeavored to maintain and follow the tradition. It was only natural that this "formalized Buddhism," the Buddhist order fixed in its *status quo,* lost all vitality and was unable to meet the rapid social changes which were to occur during the nineteenth century. Professional priests who only preached resignation to the people of the lower classes could only serve one purpose, the maintenance of the *status quo.* The force of Europe and America, which made its assault in the late nineteenth century, awakened the human reason of the Japanese which had been imprisoned and lay dormant inside the walls of this feudal system. The Meiji Emperor system succeeded in establishing itself in 1868, when the *shogun* and lords were defeated by the centralized power of the *samurai* of the lower classes. The leaders of the Meiji era endorsed Shinto as the state religion in order to give a strong backing to the Emperor system, and they separated the Shinto gods from the Buddhist temples where they had for so long a time coexisted with the Buddhist deities. Buddhist priests were obliged to believe in Shinto, and the rulers both despised and denigrated Buddhism. . . .

Although the numbers of educated people in Buddhist orders were small at this time, they tried, in spite of much suffering, to make suggestions for reform of the old system of the orders. They also mapped out plans to fight against not only the new Shinto assertion but also the new system of the Christian missionaries. . . .

Under these circumstances the scientific study of Buddhism which was prevalent in Europe, especially philological and historical studies, was introduced to Japan, and gave a revolutionary light to the Buddhist world in Japan. . . .

The philological and historical free study of Buddhism in Japan advanced with remarkable results; yet, in spite of this advancement, the feudalistic system of the Buddhist schools and their dogmatic study did not make any headway. Each school, which had continued for so long a time under the relation of *honzan* and branch, and under the *danka* system, was naturally shaken by the introduction of democratic thoughts during the Meiji Restoration, and all the schools were eventually ruled by the Conference of Buddhist Priests in imitation of the Diet system. Just as the process of democratization was never completed under the divinization and strengthening of the Emperor, the Buddhist schools remained in the same way an association in imitation of the Emperor-system state, and even exerted themselves to maintain a feudal order rather than tend towards modernization. . . .

In the course of Japan's rapid modernization since the Meiji Restoration these new Buddhist Movements, that had organized the Buddhist priests and laity who were aware of the value of human reason, enthusiastically inspired the Japanese Buddhist Church. However, to the disadvantage of the Church as a whole, these Movements functioned outside the various Buddhist schools, which were composed of temples and priests still entrenched in the conventional propagation of the faith; on the contrary, the various schools did not welcome these Movements and were rather inclined to sneer at them.

The Meiji Restoration had been successful with the slogan "protect the Imperial family and attack our foreign enemies." The "attack our foreign enemies" gradually changed into the opening of the Japanese nation; and Japan not only introduced the nationalism of European countries but also proceeded to establish a Race State in which the Emperor occupied the center. Japanese Buddhism, ever since Buddhism's introduction into Japan, had always had an intimate relation with the Emperor system (*tenno* system), aided the Imperial family, was aided in turn by them, and developed largely along these lines. The Buddhist orders, that had been previously harassed by the new political leaders who were protecting the Emperor system, had now become enthusiastic cooperators with the *tenno* system, in sharp contrast to the servitor status under the *shogun* of the Tokugawa period. The leaders of the Buddhist orders outwardly tried to revive the force of their own schools, and inwardly tried to strengthen and maintain the feudalistic system. . . .

Although no reformation suitable to modern life took place, new education, social services, publications, etc., as commemorative works accelerated an adaptation to modern society. . . .

The family system, in which rituals for ancestors are important functions, still exists in Japanese society and tends to maintain the feudal system, even in the cities. The farmer society, where peasants, lovers of the soil, industrious workers without cares about their poverty-stricken simple lives, have continually supported the Japanese state, has also clung to rampant feudalistic customs. . . . The priests preached "resignation" as a Buddhist doctrine, a doctrine of the distorted Buddhism inherited from the Tokugawa period. No attempt was made to preach about modern life, or that the future will result from the present deeds of life and society, nor was any attempt made to preach any doctrine of awakening or advancement. Passive and distorted theories of Buddhism were the talk of the day: no dissatisfaction with the present actual situation (which is a result of past deeds), let us simply work hard and be content with things as they are.

We do not deny that Buddhism offered spiritual food and enriched the spiritual life of the farming people and many others who form the base of Japan. On the other hand, we cannot help but acknowledge that Buddhism acted as an opium in delaying the awakening of the masses, strongly conservative that they may be in character, and served to maintain the feudal system rather than advance the modernization of Japan.

After the Sino-Japanese War (1894), the war with Russia, and participation in World War I, Japanese militarism and the Emperor system were strengthened, and the Buddhist Church began to cooperate closely with the Emperor system. For example, in 1916 the *Bukkyo gokokudan* (Buddhist Association for the protection of the State), an organ of all Buddhist schools, declared that their aim was to encourage and weld the spirit of nationalism, to protect the Imperial family and State, and to do their utmost to save the world and benefit the people. They thus exhibited themselves as the Buddhism of the Imperial State. In 1937 Japanese imperialism reached a peak by aggression in China: the Japanese government called this aggressive war a sacred war aiming at the punishment of anti-Japan Chinese or coprotection against communism. Along with this plan of aggressive war by the Japanese government, the "Buddhist Movement of the Imperial Way" became very strong within the Buddhist Church. Many slogans, such as "serve the State through Buddhism" *(bukkyo hokoku)* and "make prosperous the force of the State" *(kokuisenyo),* were loudly proclaimed; prayers for the health and long life of the soldiers were made. Sympathy for the army, ceremonies for the dead soldiers, and other religious functions in support of the aggressive war were carried on in great display; these religious functions did not stem from any doctrine of any of the schools, but were performed purely in line with the government policy of war. . . .

At the beginning of Japanese participation in World War II (1941) cooperation between Church and State was reinforced, and all Buddhist churches, including Tendai, Shingon and Jodo, transformed their order into a society for the protection of the State, both literally and figuratively, and renewed their vows of allegiance to the Emperor and the State. Slogans, such as "help and support the Great Policy" *(taisei yoku-san)* and "act as loyal subjects" *(shindo jis-sen),* were pasted on the walls of Buddhist temples. Rites for the protection of the State and welfare of the soldiers were performed; the fighting spirit was encouraged, and the defeats of the United States and Great Britain were hailed before the altar. The Buddhist Association which had been only an organiza-tion of the Buddhist schools was now replaced by the Great Japan Buddhist Association, an instrument for propagating the war policy. Orders from the government were transmitted through this Great Japan Buddhist Association to the Buddhist schools. According to these orders the abbot (chief priest) himself of every school travelled and preached in all parts of Japan, aroused loyalty as Emperor's subjects from his audiences, and reiterated belief in cer-tain victory. Organized groups of preachers continuously performed such functions with catch-word phrases like "complete the sacred war" and "help and support the Emperor." In the midst of these active campaigns the priests were unable to locate any such principles in their own doctrine, so they sought such principles on the outside.

Whether Japanese Buddhists should cooperate in an aggressive war or not was never discussed among the Buddhist orders. To be a follower of the Em-peror's sacred will was regarded as the greatest honor. It is strange that some Buddhist movements in defiance of the Emperor's orders did not appear among the Buddhist schools; the Buddhist schools instead took the standpoint of cooperation between Buddhism and the "law of the Emperor," even em-phasized more the law of the Emperor than the law of the Buddha. No prin-ciple which negated the policy of the Emperor was to be found in Japanese Buddhist doctrine, so no one criticized the "help and support the Great Pol-icy" and the "act as loyal subjects." In fact, to criticize was to be ostracized from one's own Buddhist school. Yet two attitudes could be found: i) com-plete submission to military orders and the Emperor's orders as the greatest of honors, and ii) although complying with the Emperor's law, a considerably sceptic and passive attitude towards the orders of the Emperor. . . .

It is not to the honor of the Japanese Buddhist order that no Buddhists sacrificed themselves to an anti-war movement during the long aggressive war in China. Is it even true Buddhist doctrine that yesterday we performed rites for the protection of the State and today perform rites for peace? After the war the new democratic constitution of Japan forbid the Buddhist order to re-tain the "law of the ruler" *(obo),* on which the order had depended for more than a thousand years. However, now in order to bolster the Buddhist order there are some movements to revive the "law of the ruler"; moreover, the feu-dal system which still prevails on certain levels of Japanese society offers many opportunities to the advantage of these reactionary endeavors within the Bud-dhist order.

Japanese Buddhist followers themselves share the responsibility and decide whether or not they will realize the dignity of the individual self or merely exist under the dignity of an Emperor who is only one person in the world. The vicissitudes of Japanese Buddhism in the latter half of the twentieth cen-tury will depend directly on this question.

56
Formalism in Shinto

Two of the important ideals leading up to the Meiji Restoration were the restoration of the emperor as the head of state and the restoration of Shinto as the religious support of the state. However, after the Restoration, Japanese leaders discovered that these ideals were difficult to actualize: it was even difficult to specify the nature of the ideal, and implementation of the ideal was complicated by the presence of conflicting models. This selection notes especially the problems of establishing a clear policy for the role of religion in relation to the state.

At first, there was a tendency to continue the ban on Christianity and to deemphasize or persecute Buddhism. Establishment of the Department of Shinto in 1868 was an expression of the early Meiji enthusiasm for the centrality of Shinto in the state; this paralleled the state order for Shinto priests to purify themselves from Buddhist practices. Another highly significant state act was the removal of shrines from control by traditional Shinto "sects" and the placement of them under the control of the Department of Shinto. This trend toward unification of worship and government was the official policy until 1945.

Despite the trend toward unification, the government's attempts to make Shinto a state religion were aborted. Officials finally saw no alternative but to make Shinto a nonreligious part of the state. There had been no clear plans for Shinto as a state religion, and both Buddhism—which had revived under persecution—and Christianity had resisted the move to establish Shinto. About the same time, Western countries demanded the lifting of the ban on Christianity. These pressures practically forced the state to grant freedom of religion, but to preserve Shinto's favored status as the norm of Japanese self-identity, it was officially incorporated into the state.

Buddhism lost much of its vitality in the Tokugawa period (1600–1867), when it was made an arm of the government, and under different circumstances Shinto lost much of its vitality after the Meiji Restoration (1868), when it was made part of the national ideology. On the local level, particularly in the rural shrines, Shinto maintained its contact with the people and preserved its religious heritage of local festivals and annual celebrations. On the national level, however, the institutional life of Shinto was controlled by and for the government, and the religious life and identity of Shinto became overshadowed by political concerns. This diminished vitality and sense of identity as a religious tradition were further weakened when Shinto faced disestablishment in 1945 (see p. 38) and was forced to reconstitute itself as religion outside the state on an equal basis with other religions.

SHINTO IN THE MEIJI ERA

Ichiro Hori and Yoshio Toda

Shinto during the first years of the Meiji era permeated the whole society, not simply as a religion, but as the central principle of national life: its politics, state religion, ethics, and education. Shinto gradually lost most of its influence. First ritual, then politics, then finally the idea of a state religion itself disappeared. During the middle years of Meiji, government policy toward religion changed and two distinct types of Shinto emerged as a result. One, Sect Shinto, consisted of a number of folk religions which were generally Shinto in nature. The other, State Shinto, was nothing more than an ethical cult based on ancestor worship. This essay deals mainly with the second type. The interpretation of Shinto as a cult was intimately associated with the upsurge of nationalism which began in 1897. Thereafter, the government, while paying lip service to religious freedom as guaranteed by the Constitution of 1889, accorded State Shinto special protection as the national cult. Reforms at the end of World War II resolved this contradiction.

In retrospect, many of the post-Restoration government policies appear ill-advised. The attempt to make Shinto into the national religion was one of them. Another was the abandonment of certain wise policies which the Tokugawa had instituted during its last days.

But the Restoration Shintoists were not able to recognize that these were shortcomings. Their only aim was to return the Emperor to direct rule. The only way to accomplish this was to overthrow the existing government. They had no concrete plans for what they would do once they had fulfilled their aim. . . .

. . . They were unable to substitute another theory of government for Confucianism and Buddhism.

Reverence for the Emperor was the strongest ideal of the Restoration. The most important single element contributing to this ideal was the Shinto theory of the National School. Because of the part the scholars of the National School played in the Restoration, Shinto emerged both as the national political theory and as a popular code of ethics. Both of these, of course, were in addition to its religious elements.

From the first, Restoration Shinto was intolerant of other religions. The reason generally given for this was that neither Confucianism, Buddhism, nor Christianity was genuinely Japanese. All were "contemptible" foreign religions. The members of Restoration Shinto considered Shinto, as they idealized it, to be superior to any other religion. The *Kojiki*, Japan's oldest traditional history, described the characteristics of Shinto that they idealized.

Reprinted by permission of the publisher from Ichiro Hori and Yoshio Toda, "Shinto," in *Japanese Religion in the Meiji Era,* edited by Hideo Kishimoto, translated by John F. Howes (Tokyo: The Toyo Bunko [Oriental Library], 1956).

Motoori Norinaga and Hirata Atsutane rejected everything which did not conform to the pure Shinto they found in the *Kojiki*. Among the elements they rejected were the popular religious groups which later come to be called "Sect Shinto." After the government-sponsored form of Shinto became the national cult, these sects were granted the status of separate religions. Norinaga and Atsutane called them "vulgar," even though they were manifestations of Shinto. With similar narrow-mindedness, these two men rejected all other faiths outside of Shinto.

The Restoration School continued to dominate Shinto throughout Meiji. It did not depart from the outmoded ideas of Norinaga and Atsutane. It contributed nothing towards helping the new Japan adjust to changing conditions. . . .

One chapter in the Meiji Reformation ended in 1867. On November 9, Tokugawa Keiki, the last Tokugawa Shogun, requested permission to restore the actual powers of government to the Emperor. This permission was granted on the following day. The Restoration Rescript, which officially announced the beginning of Meiji, followed within two months.

This Rescript stated that the Restoration of Imperial Rule meant a return, in fact, to the government used at the time of Jimmu Tenno, the founder of Japan and first Emperor of the Japanese people. The government planned to carry out this program practically by re-establishing the Department of Shinto as it had existed in early Japan. . . .

The actual proposal to re-establish the Department of Shinto was delivered to the court in December, 1867. . . . Many leaders of Restoration Shinto enjoyed important government positions as officials in the Department of Shinto.

On April 22, 1869, the Emperor dispatched one of his officials to venerate the grave of the Emperor Jimmu in Nara Prefecture. Three days later, the Emperor himself led a procession of court nobles and daimyo to the Hall of Ceremonies where they performed a worship service before all the gods of the Shinto pantheon and swore allegiance to the Charter Oath, a general statement of the new government's aims. The Emperor then interpreted the Charter Oath and expressed his desire to continue the Imperial tradition of concern for the people's welfare. By these actions, the Emperor Meiji personally demonstrated the meaning of the unity between worship and government.

Three days later, Shinto priests who had been at the same time Buddhist priests were ordered to let their hair grow long as proof that they had renounced their affiliation with Buddhism. The following day, all of the Shinto priests came directly under the control of the Department of Shinto. This ended the system whereby shrines had been licensed by one of the two large sects, the Yoshida and the Shirakawa, or had had to depend directly on court nobles for favors. The Yoshida and the Shirakawa sects, though they had arisen as a result of theological differences, had become financially and politically powerful, so powerful that they dominated most of Shinto. Shrines not connected with them had been obliged to go directly to the nobility to find other means of financial assistance. This order by the Department of Shinto brought all shrines directly under government control.

In June, 1871, the government took the first step in making Shinto the national religion by issuing the following proclamation:

> The function of shrines is to provide a place of worship for all the people of Japan. They are not the sole property of any individual or family. Some shrines still obtain priests in accordance with ancient procedures, but in most cases the daimyo who originally established the shrine has continued to appoint its priests. Often where ownership of the land has changed several times, the connection with the daimyo who established the shrines has ceased, and they have become laws unto themselves. Even in small villages, the priests have made the succession of the priesthood hereditary and use the shrine revenues for their own income; they consider themselves independent. Priests have become a class apart; this is exactly opposed to unifying worship and government, and has many harmful effects. . . . From now on, the government will appoint the priests for all shrines, from the very largest at Ise to the very smallest throughout the country. . . .

Meiji religious policy had tried to substitute Shinto for other religions. This Shinto contained many of the elements necessary to an advanced religion. Its theology included a faith in the end of the world as well as salvation from sin and repentance by means of sacred charms and ceremonies of lustration. On these points Shinto could not avoid conflict with Buddhism and Christianity. When the government tried to force this faith upon the people, therefore, it violated their freedom. This attempt at coercion resulted from confusion over the functions of government and religion. Therefore, the leaders of the other religions naturally attacked this policy. The self-confident champions of democratic rights, represented among those who had received a European education, joined these religious leaders. Their demand for religious freedom received its stimulus from Europe.

Not all those who demanded religious freedom were reflecting Western thinking, however. Many Japanese, particularly Buddhists, based a claim for religious freedom on their Japanese tradition. One priest of the Shin Sect, Fukuda Gyokai, said:

> I have known nothing but the traditional Buddhist chant of *nembutsu*. Now that I am in my seventies, I cannot suddenly change, no matter what the government orders, to tell you that worship of the Shinto gods and patriotism are enough, and that you need give no concern to the future life. Since there has not as yet been an Imperial Rescript urging you to stop saying *nembutsu* and to stop thinking about nirvana, I must urge you to continue your prayers, to encourage them in others, and to go to paradise together. I can do nothing more than to implore you to strengthen your will, to remember the prayers which have been handed down to you, and to decide that you must attain nirvana. . . .

The desire for religious freedom gradually increased in spite of government attempts to make Shinto the national religion. Article 28 of the Constitution of 1889, promulgated on February 11, 1889, said:

Japanese subjects shall, within limits not prejudicial to peace and order and not an-
tagonistic to their duties as subjects, enjoy freedom of religious belief. . . .

Shinto at the beginning of Meiji was more than a body of religious thought
or a group of religious ceremonies. It was the basis of a revolution which over-
threw the old society. After the Restoration, it became the complex guiding
principle in the new Japanese society. It brought together government, ceremonies, and education. But the Restoration made it imperative that Japan do
more than return to the past. It had to modernize speedily. The slogan, "cultural enlightenment," which followed a few years after the Restoration, indicated this need.

Two divergent tendencies in the Meiji Restoration determined the course
of future Japanese history. First, the Restoration resurrected the ancient and
pure folk-vitality of Shinto, and second, it applied the old customs to conditions of the modern world. The first led to suppressing ways of thought other
than Shinto, an attitude which came out of Shinto's basic character. Just as a
spring when released jumps to more than normal length, so anything which is
oppressed clamors for freedom. The Western theories of religious freedom
and separation of religion from government encouraged the Japanese instinct
to clamor for freedom. Cultural enlightenment and intercourse with foreign
countries resulted in the importation of these theories and their use as a basis
for individualism. The conservatism of Shinto and the progressiveness of the
Western ideas inevitably clashed.

57
Religious Life in Postwar Japan

The two previous selections are interpretations of the historical processes by which
Shinto and Buddhism gave way to formalism. This selection describes the effects of
this formalism in the attitudes and behavior of people living in one ward (Shitayama-
cho) of Tokyo in the post–World War II era of the 1950s. The excerpts on religion
are taken from a book reporting the extensive interviews and surveys conducted in
this ward.

Traditionally, the regional shrine is directly responsible for the spiritual welfare of
its parishioners *(ujiko),* and the parishioners are vitally concerned with this spiritual
home. In the following reading, the author shows how this ideal falls short in postwar Shitayama-cho. Support for the shrine is complicated by the fact that the Allied
occupation established the law that religious affairs must be strictly separated from
public affairs such as the ward association. (For the order disestablishing Shinto, see
p. 38.) It is more difficult to gain voluntary contributions for rebuilding the burnt-out
shrine, and people donate without enthusiasm, out of a sense of social duty. About
half the households in this ward have a *kamidana* (Shinto altar), but the sense of
religious dependence on both the household *kamidana* and the ward shrine is
rather weak.

Buddhism seems to fare better in this survey, since a rather high percentage of
established families maintain the *butsudan,* the Buddhist memorial altar. The writer

concludes "that conformity to traditional religious practices centring round the *bu-tsudan* and the *ihai* (memorial tablets) is much greater than conformity to those centering round Shinto shrines and the *kamidana*." However, mere numbers and traditional conformity are ambiguous—on one hand, they point to a continued veneration for family ancestors; on the other hand, they provide the foil for the joke that Buddhist priests are nothing but undertakers. This is borne out by the fact that the overwhelming majority of visits to Buddhist temples by ward residents were in connection with memorial masses.

In critically assessing the religious situation in postwar Japan, it would be a mistake to expect the same kind of religious behavior that is held to be the ideal in the West—a conscious decision or exclusive affiliation to one religious group and regular attendance at periodic worship services. By contrast, Japanese religion has always operated within an implicit religious worldview embracing several traditions. To the extent that this worldview is meaningful for the Japanese people, it continues in the spirit of the earlier religious heritage. What the survey points out, however, is that the traditional worldview itself is being questioned, as reflected in the expressions of the people. Both Shinto and Buddhist shrines and temples survive, along with their customary formalities; however, it is apparent that great changes are occurring in the minds of the people, changes that seriously question the vitality and viability of these two traditions.

RELIGION IN A WARD OF TOKYO

R. P. Dore

The ward as such was officially concerned with the *uji-gami*, the Soga shrine to whose parish it belonged. Shitayama-cho had been included in its parish because it formed part of an estate stretching towards the shrine. The latter was twenty minutes' walk away, and unlike three closer shrines did not lie on the natural lines of communication out of the ward. For this reason relations between the shrine and the ward have always been somewhat less intimate than is usual for the district. Nevertheless, like the other twenty-two wards which made up the parish of the Soga shrine, Shitayama-cho contributed to the shrine's upkeep; its residents, by virtue of their residence, were all "children of the god-family" of the shrine; and the ward as a whole participated in the shrine's annual festival.

Before the war the shrine was managed by a council consisting of representatives *(ujiko-soodai)* appointed by the ward association of each of the twenty-three wards in the parish. Contributions for the shrine were collected

Reprinted from R. P. Dore, *City Life in Japan: A Study of a Tokyo Ward*, 1973; originally published by the University of California Press; reprinted by permission of The Regents of the University of California and Routledge & Kegan Paul Ltd. The bracketed remarks are from the original.

and the shrine's *fuda* (amuletic paper or wooden tablets bearing the name of the *kami* of the shrine) were distributed through these representatives, the ward association, and the neighbour groups, all the subtle pressures which the use of these channels offered being utilized to secure a full collection of contributions. Information concerning the activities of the shrine was conveyed through these representatives to the ward association, from the ward association to each neighbourhood unit, and thence, by circulating noticeboard to each household.

In obedience to S.C.A.P.[1] directive, this system of shrine administration and upkeep was abolished. In its place, a new body was formed called the "Worshippers' Association" *(Suukeikai)*. It is a small body of prominent men in each of the twenty-three wards who are, as the priest of the local shrine put it, "sort of" representatives of the wards. Not all the twenty-three wards had revived their ward association since the war, but where such an association existed, the priest had approached its leaders and asked them to appoint a member of the Worshippers' Association. Where there was no ward association the priest had directly contacted prominent men *(yuuryokusha)* and asked them to join. There was now no longer a fixed number of these "unofficial" representatives per ward. Advantage had been taken of the flexibility of the new organization to recruit as many wealthy men as possible. Thus, as well as preserving the substance of the old, some advantage was derived from the form of the new.

Some idea of the way in which this informal organization operates may be given by describing how contributions were collected for the rebuilding of the Soga shrine. The shrine was burned down during the war, and in 1951 the broad steps, flanked by an imposing concrete balustrade and the guardian "Chinese lions" led only to a small wooden temporary altar which stood forlornly in the middle of a broad concrete base. Plans to rebuild the shrine had long been complete, but with rising costs the original estimate of 2 million *yen* (£2,000) had increased to 3 million *yen* and in mid-1951 only one million had been subscribed. For fifty yards along either side of the approach to the shrine a slatted wooden framework about ten feet high had been erected. It was divided into twenty-three sections and over each section was written the name of one of the wards which were part of the parish of the shrine under the old dispensation. For every contribution received a wooden board was hung in the appropriate section and on it written the name of the donor and the amount.

In mid-1951 some sections were well-filled—mostly those devoted to wards very close to the shrine. The Shitayama-cho section bore only one board recording a donation of 30,000 *yen*. . . .

Another official of the Ward Association, Kataoka, was also a member of the Worshippers' Association and by contrast conscientious, if not enthusiastic. Kataoka, with his obvious delight in occupying positions of authority and his committee-man skill, was nevertheless barred from higher positions of authority

---

1. S.C.A.P., Supreme Commander for the Allied Powers.—ED.

by his limited means combined with a tendency to arouse resentment by a slightly overbearing and pompous manner. Nevertheless he was doing his best, by taking an active part in the Worshippers' Association, the P.T.A., the C.P.T.C.A., and the Ward Association, to develop his connections against the day when his means should make a wider scale of activities possible.

At a meeting of the officials of the ward association, Kataoka reported the decisions of a recent meeting of the Worshippers' Association. So far only a third of the money had been collected, and there was a noticeable absence of contributions from Shitayama-cho. Each ward had been allocated a target on the basis of the number of households contained in it. Shitayama-cho's target was 90,000 *yen* or 300 *yen* (6s.) per household. The discussion ran somewhat as follows:

Okazaki: "Have we really got to pay up?"

Kataoka: "Well, I don't know. That's our apportionment, and when so many of the other wards have contributed we can hardly hold our heads up if we don't *(katami ga semai)*."

Nakazawa: "Sakura [the ward president] has given us a good start anyway. [Hear, Hear!'s.] But it's no good going round asking other people to contribute until T is settled. . . . [the richest man in the ward] Once we get him to pay out we can go to S [a hotelier] and K [a fairly affluent wholesaler]. Then we can start generally."

Okazaki: "How is it best to collect the money, though?"

Izumi: "I don't see what's wrong with K going round and collecting it as *ujiko-soodai*." [Representative of the children of the god-family, i.e. the title of the ward association representative under the old system.]

Kataoka (*apparently embarrassed, perhaps by the writer's presence*): "Well, there aren't any *ujiko-soodai* any longer. There's only a Worshippers' Association. Of course there's talk that there will soon be a new law to make it possible again, but I don't know."

Sakura: "Yes, I think it's best to keep the ward association out of it for the time being at any rate. It would be best for someone from the shrine to come down collecting. One of us officials could go round introducing him, of course. I shouldn't think anyone would grumble about that. If the worst comes to the worst and the money doesn't come in, I suppose we shall have to take it out of ward funds a bit at a time, so much a month."

The general feeling of the meeting seemed to be unanimous. No one felt any enthusiasm for the rebuilding of the shrine, and there was no suggestion that it was a worthy object. In most cases this was the result of a general lack of interest in any matters connected with shrines and the *kami*. In one or two cases it was the result, not of a lack of interest in all shrines but of the lack of any interest in this particular Soga shrine. One of those present, Izumi, was a member of the council of one of the shrines nearer to Shitayama-cho and a conscientious visitor for what appeared to be genuinely religious reasons.

But, though lacking in enthusiasm, all appeared to accept the duty of making contributions to the shrine. "Have we really got to pay up?" was the nearest approach to a note of protest. No one suggested that religious faith was a private matter and should be left to individuals. It is doubtful if "religious faith" entered anyone's head as a relevant factor in the situation; contributing to the upkeep of the local shrine has long been accepted as part of the duty of a good citizen on much the same level as paying taxes. Nor did anyone suggest that the ward as a whole should transfer its allegiance to a more convenient shrine and one to which more residents would be likely to pay spontaneous visits; only an emergency would ever justify such an unfriendly act towards the Soga shrine. In other words, long years of association had created what was called earlier a *giri*-relation[2] between the ward on the one hand and the priest and the *kami* of the local shrine on the other. To break off that relation or neglect the duties which that relation involved would be to lay the ward open to the charge of "not knowing *giri*.". . .

There was, indeed, little evidence of any belief in a special relationship between the people of Shitayama-cho and the *ujigami* of the Soga shrine. Fifty-three percent of households in Shitayama-cho had *kamidana*—the "god-shelves," plain wooden boxes with ritual decoration which contain the *fuda*[3] of the shrines for which they act as substitutes—and eighty percent of these *kamidana* did contain the *fuda* of the Soga shrine. Most parents took newly-born children for a *miya-mairi* ceremony, a registration rite at which the *ujigami* is asked to take note of the baby's arrival and extend it his future protection, but most went to one of the nearer shrines rather than the Soga shrine for the child's next ceremony at the age of three. But here, again, "local patriotism" was the operative notion; there was no suggestion that anything was actually lost by not going to the *ujigami* supposed to be responsible for protecting her particular district.

What such protection used to mean is well described by the ethnographer Yanagita Kunio in his description of the village in which he grew up.

> It would sometimes happen in the summer evenings that children would go out to play and get lost and fail to come home. Then there would be great consternation, but generally the child would come back. The first thing the people of the village would think of then was the *"ujigami-sama."*[4] People would say that it was the *ujigami-sama* who saw that he came back; there would even be plausible-sounding stories going round that the child had met an old man with white hair who had told him that everybody at home was anxious and that he ought to go back. There was this idea that the *ujigama-sama* was the ruler of the village, a sort of hidden protector of the villagers . . .
>
> It would be difficult for people living in Tokyo today to imagine the importance the *ujigami-sama* had for the people of my native village.

---

2. *Giri* is the sense of social obligation that one person or group feels toward another person or group.—ED.

3. *Fuda*, paper charms or talismans.—ED.

4. *Ujigami-sama*, the patron deity of local Shinto shrines.—ED.

This idea is not entirely dead in Tokyo. One woman who said that she had made one visit to the Soga shrine in the past year added as an explanation: "After all, it is thanks to the *ujigami-sama* that we are able thus to live peacefully in this district." But this was a rare instance; the only other piece of evidence of any such belief concerning the relation between the *ujigami-sama* and the community came, not from Shitayama-cho but from a neighbouring ward. The shrine of this parish had been destroyed during a fire raid while surrounding streets had been left untouched. It was considered that the *kami* had taken all the fire bombs on to itself in order to spare the local inhabitants, its children, and it was said to be for that reason that the general level of contributions to the rebuilding fund was so high; the shrine building had been almost completed by the summer of 1951. Perhaps the Soga shrine was too far away for it to be thought to have performed the same function for Shitayama-cho.

The *ujigami,* in theory, not only provides general protection for its *ujiko,* but may also be the object of personal prayers by any one of them. However, as far as individual visits to the shrine were concerned, the Soga priest knew of only one resident of Shitayama-cho, a middle-aged widow, who came regularly to pray at the shrine on the traditional shrine-visiting days, the 1st, 15th, and 28th of each month. And of all the shrine visits which a hundred respondents said they remembered having made in the past year (averaging less than ten per person even including the 365 visits of one individual) only 11% were to the Soga shrine. . . .

The wife of the priest of the Soga shrine was apt to complain of the financial embarrassment which the apathy of post-war parishioners brought to her family. On one occasion she remarked wryly, that the Buddhist temples had less to complain about; "They look after the *hotoke-sama.*" The implication that it is their stake in the *hotoke-sama* (the spirits of the dead) which keeps the temples on their feet is probably a just one. The religious rites and beliefs with which the Buddhist temples are chiefly concerned are those which centre around the worship of the spirits of the dead. They are, that is, rites in which either the family is the worshipping unit, or, at least, consciousness of membership of the family is an important constituent of the worshippers' attitudes.

The Buddhist rites in the home centre around *butsudan,* the "Altar of the Buddhas," which may be a simple wooden box or an elaborate lacquer-and-gilt altar, six feet high and of careful and expensive workmanship. This contains the *ihai,* tablets bearing the posthumous names of former members of the family. Sometimes there are their photographs as well, and occasionally family heirlooms. One man in Shitayama-cho kept in the *butsudan* the swords which were the symbols of his family's former samurai status; another had a history of his native district. There were also genealogical scrolls, and "registers of the past" *(kakochoo)* recording the death-days of former members of the family. (One family also kept its money in the *butsudan* under the ancestors' care.)

In addition to all these *family* symbols, some *butsudan* contain the symbols of the Buddhist faith, scroll paintings or brass images of Kannon, Amida and other Buddhas and Bodhisattvas; photographs, often of a very high quality, of famous Buddha statues in Nara or Kyooto, brought back from a sight-seeing tour; sometimes the amuletic *fuda* of some famous temple. (And, in one case, the similar *fuda* of a Shinto shrine. Another woman had a photograph of Christ—"The priest knows about it and he says it's all right.") Whereas every *butsudan* had *ihai* of the family dead, however, only a very little over a half had any of these symbols of the Buddhist faith proper.

In ordinary speech no distinction is made between the spirits of the dead and the Buddhas and Bodhisattvas of the Buddhist faith. They are both called *hotoke (—sama)*. There is evidence, though, that the two are differently conceptualized, and it will be convenient to distinguish the two as *hotoke* and *Hotoke* respectively. A further distinction can be made among the *hotoke*, between Grandpa, Father, or brother Jiroo on the one hand, and "the ancestors" *(senzo)*—all the *hotoke* who have been dead for so long that no surviving member of the family has personal memories of them—on the other. These will be distinguished as "close-relative *hotoke*" and "ancestor *hotoke*." The distinction is reflected in the *ihai* kept in the Altar of the Buddhas. After a certain length of time (in theory, after the fiftieth year, though there is great variation in this respect) the *hooji* rites[5] on the anniversaries of the death-days of particular ancestors cease to be held. Thereafter the individual *ihai* is removed and the ancestor is subsumed under the one general *ihai* bearing the legend, "Ancestors of the various generations of the—family" and thus become the object only of the general rites for the ancestors at the equinoxes and at the summer Bon festival.

Not every household necessarily has a *butsudan*. The governing principle is that all dead spirits must have their *ihai* kept in some *butsudan*, preferably that of their most direct descendants, rather than that all households must have a *butsudan* at which they can worship their forebears. Where family consciousness is strong, however, younger sons who set up house away from the main family may take duplicates of the *ihai* (generally those of parents or equally close relatives) in the main family altar. But of the 45% of younger sons in Shitayama-cho who did have altars, only a few had them for this reason. Most of them installed altars on the death of a child or a wife.

Of those families in Shitayama-cho which have been established for more than one generation (and must, therefore, have at least one direct ancestor) 80% had a *butsudan*. The remaining 20% (twenty-four families) did not have one for a variety of reasons. A few were Christians. There were also a small number of families who were "out-and-out" Shintoists, who that is to say, follow Shinto, rather than Buddhist, funeral and ancestor rites. Shinto rites are essentially similar in nature to Buddhist rites and clearly modelled on them, but the memorial tablets are kept in an elaborated *kamidana* (a *soreisha*) instead of in a *butsudan*.

Sometimes, again, an eldest son who has left his rural home and allowed a younger brother to succeed to the *de facto* headship of his parental family has left the ancestral tablets to be cared for by him, too. But there were other families which had no such "excuse." Families which were bombed out during the war and lost their *butsudan* as a consequence, have not always replaced

---

5. *Hooji* rites, Buddhist memorial services.—ED.

them in their new homes. Some had simply had new *ihai* made and kept them on a temporary wooden shelf. One man gave as his reason the fact that there was a "superstition" (his word) that if a *butsudan* was bought on any other occasion than on that of a death in the family it would be likely itself to cause someone to die. Others had no explanation to offer. "Since we've moved here we haven't bothered to get a new *butsudan* or new *ihai* or anything," said the owner of a small cosmetics factory, adding, "I'm ashamed to say."

As this implies, a certain amount of apathy there may be, but positive rejection of the duty to look after and pay respect to the ancestors' *ihai* is rarely met with. The only expression of such an attitude in over two hundred households, was the remark of one woman that her husband "has strong objections to people worshipping before *butsudan* and *kamidana,*" and that for that reason the family's *butsudan* was being looked after by his sister in the country. This man, interestingly enough, a lawyer and one of the few professional men in the ward, was also marked out from his neighbors by the strong antipathy which he displayed towards all forms of ward community activities.

There were, however, few such instances. It is a fairly safe generalization that conformity to traditional religious practices centring round the *butsudan* and the *ihai* is much greater than conformity to those centring round Shinto shrines and the *kamidana*.

The worship of the spirits of ancestors, though in all its forms much influenced by the Buddhist religion and by Confucian ideas partly absorbed via that religion, can exist independently of Buddhist institutions. The Emperor's ancestors, to whom essentially similar rites are addressed by the Imperial family, are not *hotoke* but *kami* and they are enshrined in Shinto shrines. Ieyasu, the founder of the last house of Shogun, was also a *kami* to whom several shrines were devoted, so was an even more recent national hero, General Nogi, and, indeed, all those who died in battle are enshrined as *kami* in the Yasukuni shrine. Apart from these national associations some ordinary families, for a variety of reasons, follow Shinto burial and ancestor-worshipping practices. Nevertheless, in the vast majority of families, these rites are associated with the Buddhist religion, and it is necessary for their full performance to have some connection with a Buddhist temple.

From this family temple the priest comes to perform funeral ceremonies and the rites held in front of the family *butsudan* on the anniversaries of ancestors' death-days. Alternatively, these latter ceremonies are held actually at the family temple. In some sects a part of the ashes are deposited at the family temple. In others an *ihai,* a duplicate of that in the family *butsudan,* is also left at the family temple. It is from the fees for such services that the priest derives his income. It is one of Japan's perennial jokes that a priest is a man who does business in funerals. In a somewhat merciless humorous monologue, a favourite of Tokyo music-hall audiences, one priest says to another, "If this goes on much longer I shall have forgotten the taste of decent wine. I haven't had a funeral for weeks. I must say, though, that I admire your enterprise, going around and finding out where people are ill. Here, what about a quick one, just a sort of advance celebration like?"

The business, if not highly paid, at least guarantees a living. At some of the Tokyo temples with a large number of parishioners it is quite efficiently organized with an advance booking system and waiting rooms in which the latest magazines are provided for families waiting their turn for an anniversary ceremony.

Most Buddhist temples are almost exclusively concerned with death and the family cult, and few people in Shitayama-cho ever go to a temple for any other reason. Thus, when a family migrates from the country to Tokyo it normally only seeks a new family temple nearby when a death in the family makes it necessary. Many families in Shitayama-cho gave as their "family temple" that of their parents in a distant part of the country. Ninety-four people out of a hundred acknowledged that they had such a family temple. (Of the others, two were Christians, two Shinto, and two just said they had nothing to do with that sort of thing.) Of these, however, sixteen did not know the name of their temple and seven did not know which of the many Buddhist sects it belonged to. In theory, a loyalty to a sect persists through the generations, so that a migrating branch family will pick a family temple of the same sect as that of the main family, but so blurred are sectarian distinctions and so irrelevant are they to the actual purpose of family temples as a part of the family cult, that several cases were found in Shitayama-cho where the sect had been changed for reasons of convenience.

Of these ninety-four people, fifty-three said that they had visited their family temple in the previous year. They estimated that they had made 241 visits between them. Of these 206 were in connection with anniversary ceremonies. The other thirty-five visits, shared by nine people, were on the occasions of temple services (four people), casual visits "when I happened to be passing" (four people) and "a sight-seeing visit as guide to some business acquaintances up from the provinces."

58
Secularism: From Ritual to Pornography in a Modern Novel

The previous selection indicated that a few people in one Tokyo ward were indifferent to organized religion and at least one man, according to his wife, had "strong objections to people worshipping before *butsudan* and *kamidana*." Such people seem to be in the minority, however, and this should be kept in mind while reading the next selection. This excerpt from a translated Japanese novel does not attempt to present the typical picture of life in Japan; rather, it focuses on the unusual and extreme case of the life of several pornographers. This is *not typical,* but novels often present a creative, inside view of a culture, a view not easily attained by a sociological survey.

This novel, which takes place in postwar Osaka, is filled with characters who have not the slightest attachment to Japan's traditional religious life. Osaka is the financial center of Japan, and in the first episode these pornographers are busy making money from their trade, which at the moment involves the production and distribution of "blue movies." For the moment, Subuyan is the leader of the group. Having run through all the stereotyped plots and scenes, they hit upon the brilliant idea of shooting their pornographic film in a Shinto shrine. This brief sketch is full of ironies, the most dramatic of which is the interruption of filming by the appearance of a devout old lady. Cocky, the assistant Shinto priest who is part of the shady film company and who has suggested the shrine film, almost automatically intones the ancient benediction. This fictional account captures one of the poignant dichotomies of modern Japan: innocent devotion to traditional values by some, particularly the old, offset by complete disregard for traditional values by others, especially the young.

The second episode describes the events surrounding the wake for Subuyan's common-law wife, Oharu. The four pornographers have no use for a Buddhist priest and the usual religious memorial service, but as the evening wears on and they discuss the horrors of death, they feel the need to somehow commemorate this death. A suggestion is made: "So instead of a sutra, let's show a pornographic film." For these men, there are no sacred models to appeal to, so they invoke the only symbolic system they know. Replacement of a sutra by a pornographic film is a complete reversal of traditional religious life. The fictional episode mirrors an increasing sense of estrangement from traditional values and a quest for meaning without the aid of organized religion.

THE PORNOGRAPHERS

Akiyuki Nozaka

The shrine where the film was to be made was dedicated to the Emperor Ojin and stood in a grove of trees, just across the lotus pond from Cocky's shed.

In Subuyan's youth his father would take him to the Shrine of Kusonoki for the traditional prayers in the early morning of every New Year's Day, just after the temple bells had sounded. So now, his scruples still not quieted, he stood with his palms pressed together reverently before doing anything else. But what could he pray for? There seemed to be no common ground between the world of Ojin and that of pornographic films. Cocky, in the meantime, fully at home, had gone into the inner shrine and was bustling about as he noisily chanted one of his favorite blessings.

"Here's a light plug over here. We're lucky. Nowadays even the Sacred Candle is electric," he said, brushing away the dust as he set the stage in order.

Excerpts from *The Pornographers*, by Akiyuki Nozaka, translated by Michael Gallagher. Copyright © 1968 by Alfred A. Knopf, Inc. Reprinted by permission of the publisher and Martin Secker and Warburg, Ltd.

Banteki[1] presented a memorably exotic sight. As if the Shinto priest's robes were not enough by themselves, an electric cord dangled from beneath the pleated skirt. This was a remote-control device; for Banteki, with a true artist's passion, insisted on doing the camera work himself.

According to the plot, a schoolgirl was to come to pray for something or other; and the priest, after smoothly enticing her into the inner shrine and chanting a prayer over her, vigorously goes at her. The girl's role would be played by the model who had caught that unhappy infection while starring in the first movie. This would be her second appearance.

"Well, how about it? Let's get going," said Banteki, who, camouflaged with glasses and mustache, proceeded forthwith to plunge boldly into the action, wholly undaunted by the glaring lights. Subuyan too gradually felt his spirits rising; and he hustled about, now urging this camera angle, now that. Still, in the midst of all this—was it the white stripes at the neck of the middy blouse or was it the pleated skirt that provoked the association?—he found himself all at once superimposing the image of Keiko[2] upon that of the figure pinned squirming to the mat; and he felt himself suddenly choke up at the sight of bared legs and general disarray.

But then at the height of the action, the hollow sound of the shrine bell suddenly obtruded itself, to the horror of all participants. A devout old lady had come to offer worship at the outer shrine. Subuyan pressed his forefinger to his lips, softly hissing for silence; Banteki and the woman froze at an extremely awkward juncture; and Cocky, presumably with the intention of reassuring the old lady outside, began to give forth with the benediction, which was his forte: "Lo, in ages past, ye gods who descended to our mountain peaks, august Sumemutsu, sovereign Kamuromi, thou who shaped the world . . ." And the old lady, her innocent faith wholly unscathed, pulled the bell cord once more and, after its hollow toll had subsided, turned and went the way she had come.

"Hey, let's work that in!" said Banteki, whose genius it was to capitalize even upon misfortune. A worshipper, in other words, would come just at the crucial moment, and the camera would cut back and forth between the figure wrapped in tranquil prayer and the scene of wild lust being enacted just a door's width away.

"Just get out there and pray, that's all," ordered Banteki as he and Subuyan thrust Cocky through the door. And so the camera caught Cocky piously tolling the bell with the lights turned up a bit to give the impression of sunset.

This film was called *The Bulging Pillar*, and it was to achieve the reputation of a genre classic. . . .

Later Subuyan's wife, Oharu, dies, and Subuyan is aided by his fellow pornographers in arranging the wake for Oharu.

---

1. Banteki, a photographer who was one of the group of pornographers.—ED.

2. Keiko, the daughter of Subuyan's common-law wife.—ED.

"How about a priest? Was she registered at any temple?" Cocky asked.

But Oharu had been a woman who instead of worrying much about the afterlife had flung herself whole-heartedly into this one. After she and Subuyan had become more intimate, she even had gone so far as to put away the altar with the traditional picture of her dead husband in front of it. Nor was Keiko any more concerned about religion. But finally, since it was something that was always done, Subuyan decided to call in the seedy priest from the broken-down neighborhood temple to chant a sutra or two.

As the night wore on, Keiko, still weary from watching beside her mother's deathbed, began to nod sleepily. The alert Banteki noticed this, and she was sent to bed on the second floor. Now the four men were left to themselves, and, as might be expected, the prevailing tone of the wake became less reserved.

"Well, whatever you want to say, if somebody dies and gets laid out like this, they're pretty fortunate," said Subuyan. "My mom died from the fire bombs. It was just like she had been in a pressure cooker or something. They wrapped her up in a mat and threw her on a truck with a bunch of other dead bodies. Right there on the banks of the Yodo, they piled them all up, poured gas over them, and whoom!—up they went, and that was that."

Subuyan had struck a rich vein. Everyone had something to contribute.

"Ah, that was terrible, wasn't it? People burning to death. Their bodies would shrivel up like a ball, so that they'd end up just like a baby inside its mother."

"Did you ever see any who got caught in the wind blast from the bombs? The air would go shooting into them from every hole, and they'd blow up like a rubber ball and die."

"It was kind of nice, the way they'd die in slit trenches. Their faces would always be pale."

"A lot of them died, all right. After a raid it was like a sort of exhibition of ways to die. They'd be there, their bodies all twisted, the upper and lower parts together, and some of them weren't quite dead. All twisted and looking right at their own knees—I wonder what a guy would think?"

"I saw this kid laying there, holding on to his ankles, and his feet were torn off."

"The thing I won't forget was this schoolyard where they brought all the bodies. They'd be covered with mats with only their heads sticking out. It would always rain after the fire raids and these burned-black bodies would soak it up and swell up like monsters. Sometimes the skin was burned so much it would crack, and there you could see the flesh beneath, all red."

"You know, when I think of it, this is the first time I've seen anybody dead since the air raids," said Subuyan.

"What are you talking about? Didn't we bury your baby?" remonstrated Cocky.

"Oh yeah. That was a human being, too, I guess."

"Some get buried at sea. Some get burned up. Some have nice wakes like this. But they're all human beings."

"Once you die, that's the end."

"Say, Banteki, did you bring any films along?"

"Films? This is no time for business, Subuyan!"

"Who said anything about business? This is Oharu's wake, isn't it? And she was my wife. The wife of Subuyan the pornographer. So instead of a sutra, let's show a pornographic film."

"Hey, now you're talking. Here, I'll help," said Cocky, as he and Hack sprang to their feet, brimming with enthusiasm, and pushed the altar aside.

They hung the screen above Oharu's coffin and extinguished the holy candles. After a short pause the beam from the projector pierced the darkness, and one of the early masterpieces, The Bulging Pillar, flashed on the screen.

"Subuyan, this'll be a lot better than a sutra."

"Hey, Subuyan, how about being the benshi?"[3]

"Good enough," answered Subuyan, standing up. "Here we see a young virgin who has come to offer a prayer to God. What does she ask? "Oh, dear God, won't you please send me a handsome boy to love me?' " But as Subuyan carried out his role, in his heart he was thinking of something quite different. Oharu, you went for it, too, didn't you, Oharu? Even right from the beginning. I was just thinking now that it was you that started things off between us. You woke me up. You had a stomach cramp, you said, and I could feel your breasts pressing against my back. Of course I was eager enough. Why wouldn't I be? You were in your prime then, and there was plenty of reason for me to be eager. I guess I'll never hold you again."

The altar was put back in its proper place, and everyone had a pleased, contented look.

---

3. *Benshi*, narrator.—ED.

CHAPTER SEVENTEEN

The New Religions

Organized religion in the modern period falls into two sharply contrasting categories: on one hand are the older institutions of Shinto and Buddhism, on the other hand are the new religious movements known as New Religions. Shinto and Buddhism, the two major religious institutions throughout Japanese history, share both an advantage and disadvantage of being in the mainline of the religious tradition. Their advantage is the prestige of embodying the central religious content of Japanese culture; their disadvantage is the burden of bearing images of a past not so relevant and attractive in today's rapidly changing world. Magnificent Shinto shrines and Buddhist temples are monuments to Japan's long and glorious history, and they are visited regularly by students on school trips and tourists. "It is the custom," as many Japanese phrase it, to be married in a Shinto shrine and be buried and memorialized in a Buddhist temple, and to visit shrines and temples on occasions such as during the New Year season.

New Religions share with Shinto and Buddhism the same general worldview of Japanese religion, yet they present a different picture. New Religions have their own set of advantages and disadvantages as the newcomers. Their "youth" can be a disadvantage. Being relatively new they lack the prestige of the older traditions (although they often insist that they are the authentic contemporary forms of classic Japanese religion), and, in fact, the general population has usually been suspicious or critical of New Religions, especially because of their image of aggressive proselytizing activities. Conversely, their youth or novelty is also a great advantage because they are not restricted by the traditional organizational patterns of Shinto shrines and Buddhist temples, which enables them to attract and mobilize large numbers of followers.

Japanese New Religions and their members are conspicuous both by their behavior and their organizational structure. The first few generations of members are full of enthusiasm, actively recruiting other members and eagerly participating in the meetings at branches and regional or national headquarters. Perhaps the single most important feature of New Religions, especially when contrasted with the traditional religions of Shinto and Buddhism, is their development as voluntary organizations: members, at least in the first generation, *voluntarily* make a decision to join. A person must be convinced by the message or rituals of the New Religion, usually related to the shared experiences in small group meetings, before he or she actually joins.

All religious organizations, in Japan and throughout the world, are mixtures of old and new, and are combinations of both informal patterns and formal structures. If we compare Buddhism and Shinto with the New Religions, the former are characterized more by formalism and lack of vitality, while the latter demonstrate renewal (new forms) and greater enthusiasm. The New Religions are highly active voluntary organizations, and their members actively participate both in their respective New Religions and in other social and cultural activities.

It is worth noting that not all New Religions succeed. If the founding figure and his or her message is lacking, or if the initial enthusiasm is insufficient and the new socioreligous forms are unstable, the New Religion may well collapse, as has happened in many cases. Additionally, if the New Religion becomes highly institutionalized—which is inevitable if it is to maintain its form through time—it in turn becomes an "established religion" and inherits all the problems of maintaining an ongoing tradition, often at the expense of enthusiastic participation.

An initial stimulus for such movements is the inspiration of popular leaders, who establish their own scriptures and liturgies. The movements are kept alive by emphasis on lay leadership and lay participation in all aspects of the movement. Of the hundreds, perhaps thousands, of New Religions that have arisen since the early 1800s, several dozen have gained large memberships and have developed comprehensive organizations.

In this chapter we look at five New Religions: Tenrikyo, Soka Gakkai, Kurozumikyo, Gedatsu-kai, and Mahikari. Tenrikyo, founded by a "living *kami*" in 1838, is one of the earliest of the new religious movements, and it formed a kind of precedent that was important in the formation of subsequent movements. Soka Gakkai, founded a century later, developed more around the sacred power of the *Lotus Sutra* than around a charismatic personality, and it also displays a "rational," highly efficient organization. Kurozumikyo, like Tenrikyo, arose in the early nineteenth century, and is very closely related to its Shinto and Confucian heritage. Gedatsu-kai was founded in the twentieth century out of a broad base of Shinto, Buddhist, and Confucian elements. Mahikari's background in this century is complex, including influence from previous New Religions and spiritualism.

The documents representing Tenrikyo and Soka Gakkai are official statements of these two New Religions: for Tenrikyo, this organization's own sacred account of the life of its foundress; for Soka Gakkai, this movement's own publication of its teachings and recommendations for practice. The three other New Religions are represented by a different kind of document: rather than official statements by the headquarters officials, these are the voices of ordinary members recorded as life histories (in English translation). The advantage of a life history is the concreteness of an individual's own words telling how he or she confronted problems and resolved them through the help of a New Religion. These materials (as well as the selection on a Christian New Religion, p. 152) illustrate the remarkable diversity within these movements.

59
Tenrikyo: The Inspiration
of a Living-God

This selection provides insight into a foundress's original inspiration and the institutional formation of a religious movement around this charismatic leader. The opening quotation of the selection is the voice of God, who has entered the body of Mrs. Miki Nakayama and has claimed her as his "living Temple." The document then fills in the background for this remarkable revelation, centering around the rites of exorcism to drive out the evil spirits causing sickness in the foundress's son. Such rites of exorcism, with the medium experiencing temporary possession, were not uncommon in nineteenth-century Japan (see p. 129). What is unusual in this case is the fact that the god did not leave the medium's body at the end of the rite; this constituted the divine revelation that founded Tenrikyo.

    From this time, Miki, as she is commonly known, was seen as a divine figure. Her fame as a religious resource spread first because of her ability to give women easy childbirth, and gradually missionaries propagated faith in Miki and the divinity revealed to her. Because Miki had the status of a living-*kami,* everything she said or did had divine significance. In addition to the sacred scripture, *Ofudesaki,* she also created the Tenrikyo religious service, with a hymn called *Mikagura-uta* and ritual gestures to act out the hymn.

Miki's message can be summed up briefly as follows: since creation, God the Parent has wanted people to live a joyous life, but they are lost in greed and selfishness, thus covering up their true divine nature. Religious awakening occurs when each of us realizes, like Miki, that we are the creation of the gods, that our bodies are "loaned" to us. This helps us overcome the greed and selfishness that makes us miserable and at the same time leads us to the "joyous life" of religious celebration (in Tenrikyo rituals) and service to others.

Tenrikyo was one of the thirteen officially recognized branches of Sect Shinto. The official system of Sect Shinto was abolished after World War II, and the proclamation of religious freedom allowed Tenrikyo to lead a more independent career. Tenrikyo seems to have served as a prototype for other New Religions because it laid down a precedent: it was the first such movement to succeed in developing from a charismatic leadership to a full-scale organized religion.

THE LIFE OF THE FOUNDRESS

"I am the Creator, the true and real God. I have the preordination for this Residence. At this time I have appeared in this world in person to save all mankind. I ask you to let Me have your Miki as My living Temple."

Quite unprepared for such a revelation, her husband Zenbei was much surprised to hear it, and so were all those present, his family, relatives, and the exorcist Ichibei who was at prayer. Needless to say, they had never heard of such a god as "the true and real God," so that they could not give a ready consent to the demand to offer Miki as the Temple God. While at a loss what to do, Zenbei remembered a series of quite strange happenings which occurred one after another during the last year. It started on October 26, 1837, when the eldest son Shuji, who was then seventeen years old, was sowing barley as usual in the field with his mother. Meanwhile, he suddenly began to suffer from a severe pain in the left leg, so severe that he wished to return and barely managed to get home. . . . Of course, Shuji, who was the dearest son to his parents, was at once put under medical treatment, but it did not seem to have any effect upon him. Being advised to send for an exorcist and to have him pray, they sent a servant to the exorcist Ichibei in Nagataki village and asked him to exorcise the pain of Shuji. Then miraculously the pain left him, but the next day it began to attack him again. Again they sent a servant to Ichibei to have him exorcise Shuji and then the pain stopped again. But on the next day it was the same again. On the third day the pain left him at last, and he

Reprinted by permission of the publisher from *A Short History of Tenrikyo,* 4th ed. (Tenri, Japan: Tenrikyo Kyokai Honbu, 1967).

was well for about twenty days, when again his leg began to ache severely. Now Zenbei went in person to Ichibei in Nagataki village, and was given the advice to hold a ritual of exorcism called *yosekaji* at home. So coming back, Zenbei, calling in Ichibei and Soyo[1] of the Magata village, held the ritual in the household. Ichibei offered an earnest prayer and tried to practise a curing with Soyo as the medium, who stood still, in her hands two sacred staffs from which cut-paper was hanging. Then the pain in the leg suddenly left Shuji. But in about half a year, he began to suffer from the pain once more. So he held the ritual of *yosekaji,* and he got well. However, he felt the pain again. Thus he repeated it as many as nine times a year.

Meanwhile, the ninth year of Tempo came, and it was at ten in the evening of the 23rd of October, when the three of the family began to have a severe pain respectively, Shuji in the leg, Miki in the loins, and Zenbei in the eyes. They at once sent for Ichibei, who was found to have been at the house of a family named Inuri in the same village on that day. Ichibei came and was surprised to find things quite serious. He was asked to offer incantations and prayers as soon as possible, but unfortunately he was not prepared for it. So that night he went back and early the next morning he came again to perform incantations, and sent for Soyo who was to become the medium, but she was out and nobody knew where she was. There was no other way but to have Miki stand with the sacred staffs in her hands and to offer prayers and incantations through her. Now Ichibei offered his prayers in earnest. Zenbei, reflecting back upon the outline of the happenings in that way, could not but feel that there was something behind it all.

However, they could in no way give a ready consent to the demand put under the name of the original God, so he made up his mind to reject the demand, saying that there were many children to be brought up, and that he was so busy as a village official that he could not afford to offer Miki as the Temple of God, and that if he was a god who would save people in the world, he was requested to descend elsewhere, because there were many other good places as well.

At that time Miki was forty-one years old, and Zenbei fifty-one, both of whom were in the prime of life as householders. The eldest son Suji was eighteen, the eldest daughter Masa fourteen, the third daughter Haru eight, the youngest Kokan was yet no more than two, counting in the Japanese way.

Rejected thus, the pains of Miki became even greater, and the original God would not draw back. In such a situation praying being compelled to stop, he consulted with the relatives who were staying at the house, and the relatives and friends who were called together that day, but no one would persuade him to accede to the demand.

So Zenbei came near Miki who was sitting at the ritual place, and refused compliance with the demand on the grounds that his children were all too young, and that Miki was a householder who could not be spared. At the

---

1. Soyo, a woman who served as medium for Ichibei.—ED.

reply, however, Miki assumed the more solemn attitude, saying rather sooth-
ingly and persuadingly, "It is no wonder that you fear so much, but the day
will come in twenty or thirty years when you would all be convinced of the
justice of My demand." But Zenbei and the others repeated the rejection, saying that they could never wait for so long as twenty or thirty years, so they
wished Him to draw back at once. At the reply, Miki began to assume a wild
appearance, the sacred staffs in her hands flung up, and the paper on the staffs
was torn. So, putting their heads together about what they should do, they refused again and again, but the original God would not draw back. They were
compelled to keep consulting day and night for three days, during which they
refused repeatedly, and then the voice of the original God said, "If you should
refuse, this house shall be destroyed."

At his sharp and harsh words, Zenbei and the other people were frightened into deep silence once more, while Miki who from the beginning had
taken no meal, sitting upright and solemn with the sacred staffs in her hands,
urged the people to accede to the demand. If it should continue like this, what
would become of her? Zenbei began to be anxious about her fearing for the
worst, and at the same time to feel the possibility of being convinced. For
however troubled he might be, he could not but find in the words of God
wishing to save the world some truth convincing enough to him.

So Zenbei made up his mind to act upon his resolution, and gave his answer with a firm determination, to offer Miki willingly as the Temple of God.
It was 8 o'clock in the morning of October 26, the ninth year of Tempo.

As soon as the reply was made, Miki became pacified, and at the same time
Miki Nakayama became the Temple of *Tsuki-Hi,* God the Parent. The mind
of God the Parent entered the body of Miki, and She came to establish the ultimate teaching of saving the people of the world.

As we are taught in the Ofudesaki:

> "What I think now is spoken through Her mouth. Human is the mouth
> that speaks, but Divine is the mind that thinks within.
>   Listen attentively to Me! It is because I have borrowed Her mouth,
> while I have lent My mind to Her,". . . .

The mouth of the Foundress is not different from that of an ordinary person,
but the words spoken through the lips are those of God the Parent, and it is
God the Parent Himself that is speaking through the mouth of the Foundress.
Her outward appearance is quite similar to that of an ordinary person, but it is
the mind of *Tsuki-Hi,* God the Parent that dwells in Her body. Therefore the
teachings which were later given through the lips, through the pen, through
action, and through wonderful salvation, are the very ones directly given by
God the Parent. . . .

The Foundress first urged the family that they should be reduced to
poverty. The Foundress not only taught the family the need of being reduced
to poverty, but She Herself set an example by giving away Her property which
She had brought to the family when She married, and then clothes of family
members and food.

When we part with things, and wipe out our worldly desires, we shall have our mind brightened, and then the path to the life of *yokigurashi* will be opened up. But that was not all the Foundress urged, She went so far as to urge the family to take down the main house. . . .

In this way the Foundress went through a hard time for as long as fifteen years. Fifteen years after the opening of the way of faith, that is, on February 22, in the sixth year of Kaei, Her husband Zenbei passed away, at the age of sixty-six, the Foundress was then fifty-six. Though in this deep sorrow, just as God the Parent ordains, the youngest daughter Kokan who was seventeen years old, went to Osaka to promulgate the holy name of Tenri-O-no-Mikoto to the world. Miss Kokan walked to Osaka accompanied by several attendants, and taking up their lodgings in an inn near the Dotonbori street, she promulgated the holy name of God the Parent, chanting, "*Namu,* Tenri-O-no-Mikoto" in the crowded streets beating wooden clappers. It was the first mission of our religion to the world. Soon after the main house of the Nakayama family found a buyer in a village to the north from Shoyashiki. When the house was taken down, the Foundress served to the helpers *sake* and some food, saying, "I want to set about My task of building a new world. I wish you to celebrate My enterprise with me." The helpers were all deeply impressed with Her cheerful attitude of mind, saying, "It is natural to feel sad when one takes down one's house. We have never seen or heard of such a cheery taking down of a house." . . .

While she was passing through such a narrow path of faithful life with bright spirit, filled with the parental affection of whole-hearted saving of mankind, She came to be famous first as the god of easy delivery, as is often said, "*obiya* (the grant of easy delivery) and *hoso* (the smallpox healing) are the opening of universal salvation." It began with the easy delivery granted to the third daughter Haru, when she had been staying with the Foundress to give birth to her first baby. Among the villagers, a woman named Yuki Shimizu was the first to be given the grant.

As the rumor of wonderful easy delivery was spread all over Yamato Province, there began to appear in the country a large number of worshippers, who crowded about Her with such devotion as to call Her a living deity of delivery. . . .

Soon after, the Foundress taught the words and gesture of the *"tsutome"* or service for the first time;

"Sweep away all evils and save us, O, Parent, Tenri-O-no-Mikoto." It was on this occasion that the gesture was first adopted in the service. For up to that time, the service had been performed by repeating the name of God the Parent, "*Namu,* Tenri-O-no-Mikoto; *Namu,* Tenri-O-no-Mikoto," clapping the wooden clappers. "*Namu*" means *Tsuki-Hi,* the Parent.

Since then the form of service was brought to perfection, that is, in the third year of Meiji, the Foundress taught the second and fourth sections of the Mikagura-uta, and in the eighth year of Meiji, the accompanying words and gesture of *kagura teodori* were almost completed, and then the eleven kinds of gesture were taught, and at last in the fifteenth year of Meiji, the present words of the service were completed.

60
The Teachings of Soka Gakkai

Soka Gakkai (or Sokagakkai) first arose in the 1930s as an educational society with a religious foundation in Nichiren Buddhism. Its slow growth was cut short by government persecution during World War II, but from the early 1950s it experienced a fantastic expansion of membership. This movement has upheld absolute faith in the *Lotus Sutra* and Nichiren, objecting to any compromise or mixture of this faith. As it was rapidly expanding, Soka Gakkai emphasized its role as a lay movement of the Buddhist sect Nichiren Shoshu (and in the United States was known as Nichiren Shoshu of America), rejecting the label of "New Religion." However, tensions between the priestly leadership of Nichiren Shoshu and the lay movement of Soka Gakkai led to a rupture between the two in 1991, when Soka Gakkai became an independent religious movement.

The following excerpts are from one of the early English translations published by Soka Gakkai (while it was still affiliated with Nichiren Shoshu) for dissemination abroad, translations especially designed to attract and guide non-Japanese members. These excerpts illustrate the kind of religious life found in the largest and most active New Religion: resolution of everyday problems, dynamic faith, and active missionary work. "The Objective of the Sokagakkai" is to worship the *gohonzon,* a symbol of the *Lotus Sutra,* so that all people may eliminate suffering and attain happiness. Subsequent sections portray the ideal religious life as including daily worship *(gongyo),* conversion of others *(shakubuku),* and discussion meetings *(zadankai).* These discussion meetings are a powerful means of attracting and holding members, particularly among the religiously unaffiliated people of the cities.

According to the document, every member should study the doctrine of Buddhism, and go on a pilgrimage to Taisekiji, the head temple. The document's statement that 6 million members, out of a population of about 100 million, would visit this temple in 1970 indicates the size of the movement. Soka Gakkai has also been closely involved in Japanese politics, and it claims members in one hundred countries, where formerly it was known as Nichiren Shoshu.

SOKAGAKKAI AS THE TRUE BUDDHISM

The Objective of the Sokagakkai

The objective of the Sokagakkai lies, first of all, in teaching the individual how to redevelop his character and enjoy a happy life, and in showing all mankind how eternal peace can be established, through the supreme Buddhism, the religion of mercy and pacifism. Through this supreme religion, a

Reprinted by permission of the publisher from *The Nichiren Shoshu Sokagakkai* (Tokyo: The Seikyo Press, 1966). This work, now out of print, has been corrected at the request of Mr. Tomiya Akayama, Chief, Foreign Relations Bureau, Information Centre, The Sokagakkai; these official corrections are indicated in footnotes.

person can escape[1] from poverty and live a prosperous life, if only he works in earnest; a man troubled with domestic discord will find his home serene and happy; and a man suffering from disease will completely recover his health and be able to resume his work. Through the power of the Gohonzon, a mother worried with her delinquent son will see him reform, and a husband who is plagued with a neurotic wife can have her return to normalcy. We often hear of a man whose business is failing and who, after being converted to Nichiren Shoshu, has a brilliant idea, or makes a contact with an unexpected customer and begins to prosper again.

Most people are afflicted with various problems—either spiritual, physical or material, but everyone who believes in the Gohonzon (the object of worship in Nichiren Shoshu) can solve any problem and achieve a happy life. Men who are timid or irritable can gradually become normal before they become aware of the change in their character.

The true intention of the Daishonin[2] is to save the whole world through the attainment of each individual's happiness in life. Consequently, members of the Sokagakkai are actively trying to make, first of all, the Japanese people realize this great Buddhism as soon as possible. But there is no nationality in religion. Nichiren Daishonin made a wonderful prediction about seven hundred years ago to the effect, "As the Buddhism of Sakyamuni found its way to Japan from India by way of China, conversely, Our Buddhism will return from Japan to India by way of China."

Without a doubt, the Buddhism of the Daishonin will spread all over the East in the near future,[3] and finally throughout the whole world. World peace as well as the welfare of individual nations can be achieved only when the true religion is made the basic thought. If you take this Buddhism as the guiding principle of your daily lives, the happiness of the individual will be closely reflected in the prosperity of the society in which you live.

Each country can achieve prosperity without any harm to, or discord with, any other country. This is the spirit of Kosen-rufu (propagation of Nichiren Daishonin's teachings) and the Nichiren Shoshu Sokagakkai is positively striving to achieve this sublime purpose. . . .

Members' Daily Activities

The Sokagakkai's objective is to make all people happy. To achieve this, the members themselves enjoy happiness through their practice of Buddhism and at the same time introduce the immense blessings of the Gohonzon to others. The Sokagakkai promotes various activities so that each individual member can deepen his faith and also help the unhappy.

Gakkai members' most fundamental activities are Gongyo, daily prayer, and Shakubuku, introducing the True Buddhism to non-believers.

---

1. "Escape from" has been corrected to read "overcome."—ED.

2. Daishonin, literally "great saint," a title which in this case means Nichiren.—ED.

3. "Over the East in the near future" has been corrected to read "over the East in the future."—ED.

The practice of Gongyo is indispensable for all Gakkai members. Neglecting it would be the same as living without eating! At the same time, the practice of Shakubuku for agonized and troubled people is also indispensable. Thus, Gongyo and Shakubuku are the fundamental practices for believers and at the same time the source of the unfathomable blessings of the Gohonzon.

Another important Gakkai activity for general members is the *Zadankai,* discussion meetings, where they talk freely with other members and with non-believers who attend the meetings for the first time.[4] This helps the members to enrich their knowledge of the True Buddhism.

The study of Buddhism is also encouraged, as well as *Tozankai,* pilgrimage to Taisekiji,[5] which is also an important activity for members.

Members can enjoy the immense delight of having faith in Nichiren Shoshu through these various activities.

Gongyo, Daily Worship

The most important of all the activities of the Sokagakkai members is practicing Gongyo in the morning and evening. [Sokagakkai] President Ikeda spoke of the importance of Gongyo as follows:

"Suppose a man has an excellent TV set. He cannot enjoy interesting programs unless he turns it on. No matter how precious a book a man may have, he cannot gain any knowledge from it unless he opens it.

"In a like manner, you cannot gain any blessings from the Dai-Gohonzon unless you practice Gongyo. Earnest prayer to the Gohonzon is the only true source of all your acts in life, the origin of the vital life-force, the root of your study in Buddhism, and the mainspring of your blessed life."

In the early stages of faith, every member is apt to neglect Gongyo for he feels the time required is too long, or often he stops Gongyo when he has a visitor because he feels embarrassed to be seen at prayer. As every member has joined the Sokagakkai to gain happiness, he should keep his faith untiringly and never be swayed by external hindrances or difficulties which may try to disturb[6] his faith.

Shakubuku, Introduction to True Buddhism

Shakubuku literally means to correct one's evil mind and to convert it to good. It results from the delight of believing in Nichiren Daishonin's Buddhism and from the heartfelt wish for helping the unhappy through Buddhism.

Shakubuku is rooted in humanity, and by practicing Shakubuku, one can enjoy the great blessings of the Gohonzon. The most conspicuous blessings one can receive by practicing Shakubuku are lively spirit and vigorous life-force. Shakubuku is the source of the Gohonzon's blessings and strong vitality.

---

4. "Attend the meetings for the first time" has been corrected to read "attend the meetings."—ED.

5. "Taisekiji" has been corrected to read "Daisekiji."—ED.

6. "Which may try to disturb" has been corrected to read "which may disturb."—ED.

Shakubuku should be carried out for the purpose of helping people from misery and misfortune.

There are many who are not helped by politics, money or the arts. Such people, whether or not they are conscious of it, are seeking the Gohonzon to change their karma.[7] This is the revelation of the Buddhist mercy which comes from earnest practice. It is natural for believers to devote themselves to the salvation of all mankind, if they but realize the unfathomable mercy of the True Buddha.

It is desirable for members to practice Shakubuku for people who, being ignorant of the True Buddhism, are simply opposed to having faith in it. When one looks back upon the days before he was converted to Nichiren Shoshu, he will realize that he also had been more or less opposed to it. After being converted to this religion, however, he found his view of life to be false, and was awakened to the need to march forward on the highway to happiness. This fact well testifies to the necessity of Shakubuku for nonbelievers.

Zadankai, Discussion Meeting

Zadankai, discussion meetings, are held daily wherever the Sokagakkai members live. Meetings are held every day[8] with 20–30 members or sometimes even more than 50 attending. They talk about the True Buddhism and encourage one another so that all attendants deepen their faith. To the nonbelievers who attend the meeting, members try to explain fully how True Buddhism can improve human life. Naturally, the discussion meeting is filled with a cheerful atmosphere and hope for constructing a brighter future.

Discussion meetings, a traditional activity of the Sokagakkai, have been conducted since the days of first president Tsunesaburo Makiguchi. In those days, his home was the meeting place. In the days of second president Josei Toda, also, it was through discussion meetings that he embarked on the reconstruction of the Sokagakkai.

President Ikeda promoted all his Gakkai activities around the traditional *Zadankai*. He also made it a rule to read the Gosho (the collection of Nichiren Daishonin's works) for those present. Thus the foundation for the Sokagakkai's development into its present position was established by the three successive presidents with the discussion meetings as its foundation.

Some might think it easier to promote the propagation of a religion through propaganda—for example, by holding large-scale meetings rather than *Zadankai* which are attended by only a limited number of persons. In reality, however, the small discussion meetings are the best and the surest way for propagating the True Buddhism. One will clearly understand this if he considers that the fantastic advance of the Sokagakkai stemmed from the *Zadankai*.

---

7. Karma, meaning here their destiny or life.—ED.

8. "Every day" has been corrected to read "once every other week."—ED.

61

A Couple's Experience of Counseling in Kurozumikyo

Kurozumikyo has a rich religious life, much of which centers around daily worship of the sun as a deity. In this selection we see only the power of Kurozumikyo's counseling technique in the context of a Kurozumikyo meeting place, which is called a "church." The author disagrees with interpretations of New Religions that view their activities and members as concerned only with the "quick fix" of healing or a particular problem; the author shows that Kurozumikyo not only handles particular problems, such as a difficult pregnancy, but also counsels individuals, couples, and their family members in order to "restructure their way of life." This restructuring or reorienting brings the individual (the self) "into harmony with the body, the family, society, and the cosmos."

The case of the couple named Abe came up accidentally when the researcher was recording the blessing of the safe delivery of triplets. What came out in the presence of the husband and wife who are the leaders of this Kurozumikyo church was the drinking problem of the husband and general disharmony in their married life. Although we get only a glimpse of the two-hour counseling session, the gist is that faith in Kurozumikyo will not only help the husband give up excessive drinking but also restore conjugal harmony.

The conclusion of the author is that such counseling is quite different from the one-time, quick-fix techniques of occultists *(ogamiya)*. The Kurozumikyo leaders see the husband's drinking as a symptom rather than the problem itself, and go behind the drinking to see that he and his wife are out of tune with the cosmos. The solution of this disharmony is to "rise above egotism" and see that their marriage and family are based on union brought about by Kurozumikyo's deity. This demonstrates that Kurozumikyo goes far beyond "this-worldly-benefits" to restructure a person's life as a whole.

BLESSINGS IN THIS LIFE

Helen Hardacre

When asked why they keep coming back to the Oi Church, the followers report that they have received many blessings, *okage,* through the church and that they return to express gratitude. These blessings take the form of healing, of solving a problem in human relations, or of escaping a disaster. Virtually any adult Kurozumikyo follower can describe numerous larger and smaller

Reprinted by permission of the publisher from Helen Hardacre, *Kurozumikyo and the New Religions of Japan* (Princeton: Princeton University Press, 1986). The notes and Japanese characters have been deleted.

blessings received. They are eager to recount these vivid experiences and point to them as proof of the truth of Kurozumikyo's doctrine and the spiritual power of its ministers.

Scholars of the new religions, however, have seen in these blessings the distinguishing mark of the new religions (sometimes of modern religious consciousness as a whole) and have implied that this orientation is superficial by comparison with the "established" religions. Employing such slogans as "Coca-cola consciousness," some have relegated the new religions to the ephemera of mass culture. On this view, an individual comes to one of the new religions when sick or in trouble, receives a cure or advice, and then leaves, terminating the relationship. Since little of this scholarship is based on fieldwork, its authors seldom have had the opportunity to observe the process of reorientation of life set in motion by the cure or counseling. It is also important to distinguish religionists of the *ogamiya,* [or] "occultist," variety from the new religions.

In contemporary Japan the number of *ogamiya* is legion. These are individuals or small groups who practice prayer healing, fortune telling, horoscopy, grave geomancy, palm reading, astrology, and other arts of the occult. They receive clients for a fee and perform a ritual to heal sickness, change or predict fate, divine the future, contact spirits or ancestors and divine their will, or diagnose a family problem as due to a mistaken arrangement of the family plot.

Much as a patient consults a doctor and pays for treatment, an untold number of people consult *ogamiya* on the same "cash on the barrelhead" basis. If they do not care for the result, they are free to go elsewhere, just as a dissatisfied patient may find another doctor. In neither case is the practitioner purveying a comprehensive doctrine or guidelines on how to live. What the client does after the transaction is of no concern to him, and he is entirely uninterested in the ethical or moral dimension of the client's life. This commercial mode of interaction is different from the new religions in general and from Kurozumikyo in particular.

Blessings are the starting point, the "doorway," as the followers express it, to the religious life, which for them is a process of reorientation of life around Kurozumikyo doctrine. That not all go beyond this stage does not alter the fact that the blessing is only a single moment in a longer process in which the ministers support the followers in their attempt to restructure their way of life.

The first stage comes in the form of a problem followers have, sickness or some difficulty in personal relationships, which they bring to the church. The ministers counsel them with advice and sermons. Generally they tell them to pray the Great Purification Prayer as often as possible, to pray at the church daily, and to believe they can return to the original state of joy and happiness. There may be several consultations at this point.

The second stage is entered when clients begin to reorient their life around praying and going to the church. This is the beginning of the change of heart without which blessings cannot be received. It is the ideal of a change of heart that is most crucial in distinguishing the religious consciousness of Kurozumikyo from the *ogamiya* type. In Kurozumikyo, though, the real blessing is this change of heart *(kokoro naoshi),* not the actual benefit received in the form of healing or reconciliation.

The third stage is the blessing: a healing or breakthrough in a personal problem. The fourth stage commences when followers return to the church to express gratitude; this visit is called *orei mairi.* The ministers congratulate them on their faith and encourage them. From the ministers' point of view, the purpose of the entire transaction is to change the heart, to take joy in life, to be thankful, and to develop sincerity. These stages, with variations, are characteristic of the new religions as a whole. This reorientation is the meaning of *kokoro naoshi* and constitutes the major goal of self-cultivation. It can be assumed that self is being brought into harmony with the body, the family, society, and the cosmos through this reorientation. These stages in the reorientation of life can be clarified by a case study of counseling.

The Case of the Abes

The Abes (the name is fictitious) are a family that have been Kurozumikyo *kyoto*[1] since 1833. . . .

The oldest person in this four-generation household is Sanae, mother of Yoshio. She has been a firm believer since childhood, as has her son, who is a mason. His wife Reiko manages a small factory producing women's clothing and employing six persons. Reiko and Yoshio adopted Kazuo as their son because they had no children of their own. Machiko, Kazuo's wife, gave birth to triplets ten years ago.

This pregnancy was the occasion of a consultation at the Oi Church. Reiko and Machiko had been informed that three babies were on the way and were considering whether to abort. Hiroe, however, urged them not to do so, and eventually Machiko had a safe delivery. The birth represented three distinct blessings besides the triplets themselves. First, the fact that the birth was a safe one; second, the birth of three sons assured the family of an heir for the next generation; and third, their births broke the family's long history of having to adopt sons.

Reiko and Machiko paid a visit to the Oi Church on June 8, 1981, ostensibly for the purpose of having this researcher record the story of the blessing their family received in the birth of the triplets. But just as the interview was completed and tape recorder stowed away, the real story came out. Recently Kazuo had been drinking heavily and staying out nights. Both Hiroe and Katsue [the husband and wife leaders of this church] began to counsel the two:

Hiroe: *(to Machiko)* How are you two getting along? [no answer]

Hiroe: He may be an alcoholic. You should pray for him to be cured.

Katsue: You should talk things over with him.

Reiko: He won't stop, or if he does, it will only last a week or two.

---

1. *Kyoto,* individuals or households who habitually have ancestral and funeral rites performed by Kurozumikyo ministers.—ED.

Hiroe: Does he have a lover?

Machiko: No.

Katsue: Are you sure?

Machiko: I think he doesn't.

Katsue: Drinking can turn into a bad habit. How is the atmosphere at home?

Reiko: It could be that's the problem.

Hiroe: Where does he drink?

Reiko: In his car, sometimes in bars. We don't really know. The doctor told him he's got a liver problem and that he won't get well if he doesn't stop drinking.

Hiroe: Have you thought of hospitalizing him?

Katsue: Don't do that.

Machiko: I've heard that there are medicines to stop it.

Katsue: There must be a problem between you and your husband.

Hiroe: *(to Machiko)* You should ask him what's wrong.

Reiko: If she does, he'll hit her.

Hiroe: *(to Reiko)* Do you give him money to drink?

Reiko: No, there would be no end to it. He skips work, and we don't know where he is.

Hiroe: If he is playing around with women, there will be a bad influence on the children. It will be hard to cure him unless he will listen to and heed our sermons. *(to Machiko)* Get him to come to the church. You've got to pray for him. *(to Reiko)* Do you fuss at him?

Reiko: No, not unless he's really awful. The children ask him why he doesn't come home.

Hiroe: Don't let the children look down on their father. They have to respect him. *(to Reiko)* Do you pray for him? [no answer] *(to Machiko)* How about you?

Machiko: No.

Hiroe: You have to pray for him to be a good father to his children.

Katsue: You mustn't will yourself to unhappiness. You should go forward with confidence that the situation will improve. You must have faith. This is a trial sent to test you. Didn't he start drinking outside the home because he felt he couldn't drink at home? Doesn't that mean that all of you are responsible for this? You've got to return to the time when you first fell in love, and the way to do that is worship. Don't just clap your hands before the altar; really put your heart into it. Look for his good points. What he really wants is the love of the family. You have to pray for him to return to his original spirit as a child of God. Don't just pray for him to stop drinking. You can't do it without religion.

After this part of the consultation, it came out that Kazuo's real mother died of uterine cancer and that he had been raised by a very harsh and unloving stepmother before the Abes adopted him. This information suggested to the ministers that Kazuo's real problem was lack of love from an early age. This consultation lasted two hours and ended with Katsue and Hiroe encouraging the two to believe that they can bring Kazuo back to his senses, through faith in Kurozumikyo.

62
A Young Man's Healing and Rediscovery of His Work Ethic in Gedatsu-kai

Gedatsu-kai, founded in the 1930s on a broad base of Shinto, Buddhist, and Confucian features, contrasts with the nineteenth-century origins of Kurozumikyo and its combination of Shinto and Confucian elements. But Gedatsu-kai and Kurozumikyo share a similar worldview of harmony with society and the cosmos that is expressed in self-reflection and a strong personal ethic. In this article the author stresses the Buddhist aspect of Gedatsu-kai as power to dramatically change human lives.

The case of Mr. Abe (unrelated to the couple in the previous selection) is translated from a youth magazine published by Gedatsu-kai for its young members. This testimony tells of Mr. Abe's employment and lack of enthusiasm for having to work over the New Year. During the first week of the New Year he participated in Gedatsu- kai's coming-of-age ceremony and vowed to be a responsible adult. Shortly thereafter when he had a problem with his leg that did not respond to medical treatment, his parents told him to recite a Buddhist scripture. This helped heal his leg and also taught him that his physical problem was actually a warning from the spirit of Gedatsu-kai's late founder.

As was seen in the counseling of the Kurozumikyo couple, resolving a particular physical problem is incidental to diagnosing the entire human condition and restoring harmony both with fellow human beings and with the world at large. The author uses this story to illustrate four kinds of Buddhist power in a New Religion: the power to cultivate, heal, unite, and transform.

SICKNESS CAUSED BY
INSUFFICIENT DISCIPLINE

H. Byron Earhart

Buddhism as Power

The main purpose of this paper is to view the Japanese new religions as, in part, an expression of Buddhism—but using an approach somewhat different than the usual approach to Buddhism as an elite tradition of cultural objects. . . .

The central thesis here is that Japanese new religions contain a unified world view which is, in part, an expression of Buddhism; this world view can be found within the lives and personal statements of the members of the new religions; one way of generalizing the Buddhist dimension of this world view is to see Buddhism as power. In the broadest sense, the power of Buddhism is its ability to provide order, meaning, and direction in a person's life. The overall structure of this order, meaning, and direction can be called a world view, in other words, a world of order and meaning. From a personal viewpoint, the power of Buddhism provides a center of life, an "orientation" to the world, by means of which one gains a sense of direction to one's career.

Buddhist power may not be a physical object, or a concept as traditionally defined within Buddhism, but neither is it something nebulous. Buddhist power can be identified in more specific categories, and it can be documented in the lives of actual people. One way of identifying this power is to indicate the source of the power. Buddhist elements within Japanese new religions illustrate the source of this power. Japanese new religions, like Japanese Buddhism generally, attribute the power of Buddhism as much to Buddhist divinities and Buddhist leaders as to the Buddha himself. Generally the power of the Buddha is seen as the power of enlightenment, in the sense of dramatically changing or enhancing one's personal life. The new religions tend to identify this power in very concrete terms, especially in family ancestors and in particular scriptures (most notably the *Lotus Sutra*) and in particular practices (such as repentance).

At least four kinds of Buddhist power can be distinguished: to transform, to cultivate, to heal, and to unite. Probably the most general Buddhist influence on Japanese new religions is the power to transform. A basic notion of Buddhism that carries over into Japanese new religions is that human beings are subject to suffering, but a life of suffering may be transformed through

Reprinted by permission of the publisher from H. Byron Earhart, "Japanese Buddhism and the New Religions: Religion as Power," in *Japanese Buddhism: Its Tradition, New Religions and Interaction with Christianity,* edited by Miroru Kiyota et al. (Tokyo: Buddhist Books International, 1985). (This testimony was later published in *Gedatsu-kai and Religion in Contemporary Japan.*)

proper realization to make possible an enlightened life. The other three kinds of power are more specific kinds of transformation.

The power to cultivate is a second kind of Buddhist power, in effect personal transformation; Japanese new religions emphasize the development or cultivation of personal character, purity, virtue, especially through the rubrics of filial piety and patriotism (shared with the traditions of Shinto and Neo-Confucianism). Chanting Buddhist scriptures or parts thereof are standard Buddhist practices within Japanese new religions for the cultivation of personal character.

The power to heal is one of the most popular, and well-known of new religions' use of Buddhist power for transformation of physical or personal defects. Both physical illness and personal defects can be interpreted within Japanese new religions as being caused by violation of Buddhist power; similarly, they can be diagnosed through use of Buddhist power and healed through appropriation of Buddhist power. Most Japanese new religions practice forms of healing that draw on Buddhist techniques (even though they usually claim that this is less important than personal and ethical transformation).

The power to unite is Buddhism's power to transform social relationships, not only bringing the living into harmony with family ancestors (and other spirits of the dead), but also providing harmony among family members and within other groups (such as work situations). Just as the testimony of new religions is full of accounts of physical and personal healing, so too there are many stories of dramatic improvement of social relationships.

The Power of Buddhism in Individual Lives

The presence of Buddhist power within Japanese new religions can easily be documented, as has already been indicated. For example, the *Lotus Sutra* is extremely important in all new religions deriving from Reiyukai, as well as some other groups. Other Buddhist scriptures such as the *Hannya Shingyo-sutra* (commonly referred to as the *Heart Sutra*) also play an important role in new religions. Ancestors are central to the teaching of the *Lotus Sutra* line of new religions, but generally are significant throughout all new religions. With important variations from group to group, Buddhist divinities have played key roles in the foundation, and to some extent, in the continued life, of new religions. Some concepts such as *karma* are prominent in many new religions, while the implicit influence of other Buddhist notions such as transformation (in the sense of enlightenment) may be less obvious.

The four kinds of Buddhist power are also conspicuous in new religions generally, and could be documented in various movements, but a more interesting way of illustrating the kinds of Buddhist power is to locate them in the specific lives of individual members. I am most familiar with the new religion Gedatsu-kai, and would like to turn to a printed testimony of a young member of Gedatsu-kai because it is a convenient example of Buddhist power in the life of one person. Here is the testimony *(taiken)* of a young member of Gedatsu-kai, Mr. Abe, which appeared in their monthly journal *Yangu*

Gedatsu (Young Gedatsu).[1] It is quoted here, in English translation, as it was printed in this journal; some explanatory phrases are indicated by brackets.

When I graduated from high school I thought I would become a cook, because it seemed to me that the ordinary salary man was dissatisfied. I went to a special school, and when I finished this special school for cooks I entered a restaurant at Asakusa [a popular entertainment district in Tokyo], through the introduction of my teacher. I thought that it was an ordinary restaurant, but then I learned that this restaurant was actually controlled by Toshiba (a major Japanese company), and that probably in March of the next year I would be transferred to the Toshiba factory— that's why I was hired.

I asked my employer to let me think about it. I went home and discussed it with my father, and since it seemed to be a good thing, I worked at that restaurant. As planned, after the first few months I worked there, and then later I was transferred to the Toshiba company club.

This is what happened toward the end of that year, December 28. Suddenly my body felt weary, and I had a fever—I thought it was because of all the work with year-end parties. And my body just couldn't regain its strength completely. But at New Year's my supervisor said that the Asakusa restaurant would be very busy the first few days of the New Year with all the customers making their traditional first visit of the year to Asakusa, and told me to go help at the Asakusa restaurant for three days. And I wondered why I should have to work through the New Year. [Usually employees are given time off at New Year's.]

This was the year I participated in the coming-of-age ceremony. I gladly received the Gedatsu-kai coming-of-age ceremony at the Sacred Land on the eighth day of the New Year, at the Sacred Land Practice Hall with the North Kanto Block Youth Organization. From now on, I vowed to be self-conscious that I was an adult, and that I must act responsibly.

The Gedatsu-kai coming-of-age ceremony ended without incident, but the next day when I awoke I noticed something strange about my left leg. The muscle behind my knee was stretched, and I couldn't bend it. It didn't hurt, but I had to take off from work. I just rested, but the second day when I woke up it hurt so much I could hardly bear it. The second and third day the calf of my leg hurt so bad that I went to a doctor to have it examined. It hurt so bad that I couldn't stand. But the doctor couldn't diagnose the problem, and had me use an electric massage.

My parents worried about me very much. They said that if it didn't get better after so long, then it must not be only an external cause. They asked me if there was something lacking in my work. My discipline must be lacking, so wasn't there some aspect of my work where I had been lazy. Even if I stayed home and rested, this would not get better. I should recite the *Hannya Shingyo sutra* thirty times before going to sleep.

---

1. Vol. 20, no. 11 (1979): 48–49.—ED.

That night I tried to bear the pain, but then I recited ten times, and thirty times, and while doing so the pain eased up. Then while reciting the *Hannya Shingyo* after five days, a week, ten days—I gradually was able to stand and then to walk. Now I know that my discipline was insufficient, and that I was lazy. This surely was a warning from Kongo sama [the founder], I know without a doubt. So this caused my parents and all of my fellow workers to worry greatly about me, and I really want to apologize to them.

This testimony *(taiken)* has been translated exactly as it was published in the monthly magazine of Gedatsu-kai, in order to preserve the flavor of the story. My thesis in interpreting this story is that it illustrates all four kinds of Buddhist power previously mentioned: power to transform, cultivate, heal, and unite. The power to transform comes in both a "before" and "after" version. The "before" version is when Mr. Abe participated in the coming-of-age ceremony at the headquarters of Gedatsu-kai, and as he says, "From now on, I vowed to be self-conscious that I was an adult, and that I must act responsibly." In other words, coming into contact with the power of Gedatsu-kai enabled him to pass from childhood into adulthood: this is in effect a rite of passage. Some of the power of Gedatsu-kai is Buddhist, in fact the term "Gedatsu" itself means "liberation" or "release," (*vimukti* in Sanskrit), similar to enlightenment. The "after" transformation is following the resolution of his sickness when he also changes his lazy work pattern and becomes a responsible worker and filial son.

The power to cultivate is demonstrated in the recitation of the *Hannya Shingyo* thirty times before going to sleep. His parents suggest that his discipline must be lacking, and yet he is not aware of the root cause of his sickness. Gradually, as he recites the sutra and gets better, he comes to a realization: "Now I know that my discipline was insufficient, and that I was lazy." He has cultivated insight into his lack of discipline, and this in fact is preparation for his transformation into a responsible worker and filial son.

The power to heal is obvious in the diagnosis and cure of a physical ailment, but more importantly, in the correction of the lack of discipline that was the cause behind the physical ailment. The parents of Mr. Abe helped with the diagnosis, suggesting that "if it didn't get better after so long, then it must not be only an external cause," and suspected a lack of discipline. The assumption here is that if it were only an external cause, simply a physical ailment, then a doctor would have been able to cure it quickly; since this was not the case, both the cause and the cure must be internal. Therefore, the parents encouraged recitation of the *Hannya Shingyo* to help their son see the cause of his problem, enabling him to correct his lack of discipline and be healed.

The power to unite is interwoven with the other aspects of power in this tale. Mr. Abe's lack of discipline caused not only a physical ailment, but also a breach of unity with his parents and with his fellow workers. Mr. Abe discussed his offer of a restaurant job with his father, so the father is involved in the son's commitment to work hard; and implicitly the notion is that by being lazy at work the son has let down his parents. His laziness also has created a breach between him and his fellow workers. The correction of his lack of discipline and the healing of his physical ailment also enabled him to restore a harmonious relationship with parents and fellow workers. It is noteworthy that this new relationship is not created automatically by the self-reflection and physical healing: it is brought about by his apology to parents and fellow workers. This apology is a form of repentance.

63
A Single Woman's Experience of Possession and Healing in Mahikari

Mahikari was founded in the 1960s. It is more similar to Makuya—a New Religion considered to be a Japanese form of Christianity (see p. 152)—than to the other New Religions we have studied because it has a much greater emphasis on healing and miracles. Mahikari practices a form of "purification and healing," or *okiyome.* Other New Religions also utilize such purification (and some, such as Gedatsu-kai, even use the term *okiyome*), but Mahikari has its own distinctive practice. The main deity of Mahikari is Su-god, and the practice hall, or *dojo,* is where worship, purification, and healing are carried out.

The case of Miss Nakata is one of a number of life histories collected by the author in a study of Mahikari. He describes the many problems she has had as a young woman and her attempt to succeed in life, including her goal of finding a husband. Although she attended a Protestant church and still considers herself a Christian, not until she entered Mahikari did she fully understand that evil spirits possessing her were the cause of her problems. Finally through purification both her body and the evil spirits were cleaned up and her seizures stopped.

The author provides psychological explanations for these spirit experiences, which "seem to be reflections of the traumata of the single woman." Miss Nakata found a substitute family in the practice hall of Mahikari, but her life is not a model that recommends itself to other single Japanese women.

AN "OLD MISS"

Winston Bradley Davis

Let us look at the story of what the Japanese call an "Old Miss" or "High Miss," that is, a woman who has never married. Hers, after all, is the fate that every young Japanese woman fears most.

Nakata Michiko is a diminutive, rather plump lady of fifty-four who lives by herself in a small room on the first floor of the dojo. Every day she can be

Reprinted by permission of the publisher from Winston Bradley Davis, *Dojo: Magic and Exorcism in Modern Japan* (Stanford: Stanford University Press, 1980).

seen bustling about the dojo in strange floor-length dresses of indeterminate shape. Miss Nakata was born and raised in Seoul, Korea, where she was graduated from a Japanese high school. According to her mother (who also became a member of Mahikari), Michiko never did very well in school and used to fall asleep under her teacher's nose. After the family returned to Japan, Michiko (then twenty-three) tried to maintain herself in various ways. Unlike her elder sisters—one of whom became a physician in Tokyo, and the other, the owner of a button shop—she never was able to hold her own. When she joined Mahikari she was working in a camera shop and living on the edge of poverty. Hearing this, Yoshida Sensei decided to give her about $30.00 a month to give okiyome to people who dropped into the dojo during the day. On Wednesdays, when the building is closed, she goes about the city selling cosmetics.

Before one of her sisters introduced her to Mahikari, Miss Nakata used to go to a Protestant church. Although she thinks that the Savior, Okada, was greater than Jesus Christ, she continues to regard herself as a Christian. She likes to point out that when Jesus cast out evil spirits in the country of the Gerasenes (Luke 8:26–33), the spirits entered a herd of swine that went berserk and drowned themselves. Okada, on the other hand, was able to save not only demoniacs, but the demons themselves. She had always been impressed by Jesus's saying, "There is nothing outside a man which by going into him can defile him; but the things which come out of a man are what defile him" (Mark 7:15). It was only after she entered Mahikari that she began to understand what these internal defilements really are: evil spirits.

The day after she completed the intermediate training course, Miss Nakata had a spirit seizure that recurred each time she received okiyome during the next two weeks. The evil spirit possessing her was that of an older sister in a previous life. Bedridden with tuberculosis from the age of eighteen, this woman had died when she was only twenty-eight. Just before she passed away, she married a man who was willing to take her family name and thereby preserve her family's identity. Because of her unfortunate death, she became a malevolent ghost, possessing and killing off her own family, so that finally she had no one left to care for her own memorial tablet. As a result of her murderous career, she was demoted by Su-god and transformed into various animal spirits. Originally these animal spirits, which also possessed Miss Nakata, were "as big as elephants." Gradually, as she got cleaned up, they became smaller and smaller, until finally they seemed "no bigger than dragonflies." After two weeks of okiyome, her sister's spirit once again took on human shape, confessed all of her evil doings, and wept bitterly.

Before Miss Nakata joined Mahikari, she had always been sickly. "Once my abdomen became filled with water so that I looked pregnant," she said, stretching out her hands in front of her stomach. Finally, she had to go to her sister's clinic in Tokyo for an operation. She also had been afflicted with a serious cough. For years, wherever she was, whether on a streetcar or in the bathtub, once she started coughing she was unable to stop. After her elder sister's spirit apologized to Su-god, the cough disappeared. "It was this evil spirit who, because she could not be healthy and happily married herself, became jealous and caused me to be sick." The spirit also had caused her to remain single. "When I was younger I had some suitors. But either they grew tired of me or I of them. Sometimes a third party came into the picture. If only I had met Su-god two years earlier, I could have found a husband," she sighs to her friends.

Miss Nakata has had several other interesting spirit experiences. The spirit of a young man who broke his neck in a motorcycle accident has appeared to her several times. She has also been possessed by the spirits of aborted infants. Sometimes she has been possessed by as many as twenty animals at the same time, miserable creatures that perished in fires and earthquakes.

One year, on the day after the Obon (All Souls) Festival in midsummer, the ghost of Miss Nakata's grandmother appeared to her to complain that she was hungry. This surprised Miss Nakata, since Obon is a festival for worshiping and feeding the souls of all the departed. "Grandmother should be full," she thought to herself. Nevertheless, she sent a postcard to her mother to suggest that special offerings be placed before her grandmother's memorial tablet. "In spite of this, her ghost continued to appear every day. Finally, I decided to go home to see what was wrong. There I discovered that a member of our family who had converted to Soka Gakkai had wrapped grandmother's tablet in white cloth and put it away for storage. In its place stood a new tablet. Grandmother's spirit obviously had not moved into the new tablet. No wonder she was hungry!" Miss Nakata put the two tablets side by side to induce her grandmother to move from one to the other. At last the spirit received her offerings and "went away rejoicing."

In the summer of 1975, the seizures finally stopped. "The evil spirits were cleaned up the same way I was, through okiyome," she explained. In December of that year, she was made a member of the dojo's auxiliary cabinet (*junkanbu*) and vice-chairperson of the Helpers' Society.

Miss Nakata's spirit experiences at the dojo seem to be reflections of the traumata of the single woman. Although one can only guess the unconscious origins of these spirits, it would seem that possession by the spirits of aborted children—and a disease that made her look pregnant—might be symptomatic of her own frustrated desire to marry and bear children. It is not impossible that the spirit of the young man killed on a motorcycle was a would-be intended. But this is mere speculation. What is certain is that the appearance of an "elder sister" from a previous existence was a case of homeopathic possession. Possession by this spirit also explained why Miss Nakata was sick and never married (etiology), and removed all personal responsibility or guilt for her failure to find a husband (exoneration). It is curious that this "elder sister" married an "adopted husband." Miss Nakata's real elder sister actually did take an "adopted husband" in order to continue their family line.

Happily, the dojo has become both a home and an ersatz family for Miss Nakata. By giving okiyome to hundreds of people who visit the dojo every month, she feels that she is raising her own spirit level, so that in future lives she will avoid the same diseases and frustrations. Although she has come to terms with her fate through her religious experiences, her life is obviously no model the single young Japanese woman would want to emulate.

CHAPTER EIGHTEEN

The History and Future of Japanese Religion

This final chapter turns from the past and the present to the uncharted future of Japanese religion. Although no one can foresee exactly the course of subsequent events, scholars who risk predictions of the future usually do so by pointing out the major outlines of a tradition, indicating its strengths as well as the serious problems it faces, and alternative solutions to these problems. The selections in this concluding chapter provide a glimpse into the future by reflecting on the conditions and problems of religion in recent history, and by considering the prospects for Japanese culture and religion.

Probably the safest generalization to draw from these readings is that the current ambiguous state of religion in Japan will continue for some time. The strength of Japanese religion is that it possesses a distinctive religious heritage that will no doubt extend into the future; it will undergo change but will not lose its Japanese character. The organized religions will strive to reform and reshape themselves as the New Religions try to consolidate their gains.

One of the extensive problems facing Japanese religion is the rapidly changing scene in Japan. Many of these changes began after the Meiji Restoration of 1868, when Japan shifted from an agricultural and rural country to an industrial and urban nation. In this dramatic shift, social patterns changed, and the role of religious life became unclear. More changes occurred after the end of World War II in 1945, when

Japan underwent what Westerners call the "economic miracle"—not only recovering from extensive wartime destruction, but also moving rapidly from the status of a less-developed country to the position of one of the strongest industrial and commercial nations in the world. Once considered by outsiders as an Asian island country, apart from Europe and North America, Japanese culture has now become as international as any in the West. The Japanese musicians who are members and conductors in many Western symphonies are but one (usually unacknowledged) example.

As Japan becomes more international, absorbing both rock music and classical music, as well as many other aspects of non-Japanese culture, how can its ancient, distinctive culture be preserved? And what will be the result of the interaction of Japanese culture and religion with non-Japanese heritage? Two general responses to this question seem obvious: first, this is a process that has been continuing from the beginning of the Japanese heritage several thousand years ago; second, Japan is not only a receiver, but a giver in this pattern of cultural interaction. To mention just one instance of Japan's contribution to the rest of the world, many of the animated cartoons and video games in America—some of the "new mythology" of young people in America and other countries—originate in Japan. This means that while Japan is redefining its tradition, other countries such as the United States are redefining their traditions in response to Japanese influence.

In the past Japan has had a distinctive tradition that enabled the Japanese to understand and live out their lives. The selections in this chapter look at the ways Japanese people in recent times have utilized this tradition to understand themselves within their world situation. Just as there never was one fixed Japanese tradition in the past, so there never will be one in the future; problems such as changing conditions and the need for reformulation are never completely resolved, and no tradition ever completes or ends the process of its own transformation.

64
The Search for Identity
by Modern Japanese

Harp of Burma was published after World War II as a story for Japanese children, but it soon became popular among adults. The novel is set in Burma during and shortly after the war, when the Japanese soldiers were prisoners of war awaiting return to Japan. It is an unusual war story in that it focuses not so much on military affairs as on the morale of the soldiers.

This brief excerpt is from a discussion of the Japanese prisoners in their intern-
ment camp. With time on their hands they are reflecting on the differences
between Burmese life and Japanese life. For example, is the compulsory military
training of Japan better than the compulsory religious training of Burma? This in
turn raises the question of the contrast between traditional Japan and modern
Japan.

Debates of these surface contrasts lead to more basic issues, such as the definition of humanity, a person's relationship to nature and technology, and what constitutes civilization in the modern world. In the discussion, we view the Japanese
prisoners trying to hold on to their traditional roots while eliminating undesirable
elements: they want to preserve their distinctive heritage, yet they want to avoid
war and remain at peace with the Burmese; nature is to be valued, yet technology
is inevitable; civilization is a high ideal, but it is difficult to attain in an atomic age.
These debates, framed imaginatively in the context of a novel, dramatize the contemporary Japanese in their quest for identity in the modern world.

JAPANESE PRISONERS OF WAR IN BURMA

Michio Takeyama

The Burmese are so religious that every man spends part of his youth as a
monk, devoting himself to ascetic practices. For that reason we saw many
young monks of about our own age.

What a difference! In Japan all the young men wore soldiers' uniforms,
but in Burma they put on priestly robes. We often argued about this. Compulsory military training or compulsory religious training—which was better?
Which was more advanced? As a nation, as human beings, which should we
choose?

It was a queer kind of argument that always ended in a stalemate. Briefly,
the difference between the two ways of life seemed to be that in a country
where young men wear military uniforms the youths of today will doubtless
become the efficient, hard-working adults of tomorrow. If work is to be done,
uniforms are necessary. On the other hand, priestly robes are meant for a life
of quiet worship, not for strenuous work, least of all for war. If a man wears
such garments during his youth, he will probably develop a gentle soul in harmony with nature and his fellow man, and will not be inclined to fight and
overcome obstacles by his own strength.

In former times we Japanese wore clothes that were like clerical robes, but
nowadays we usually wear uniform-like Western clothes. And that is only to
be expected, since we have now become one of the most active and efficient

Reprinted from *Harp of Burma* by Michio Takeyama, with permission of the
publisher, Charles E. Tuttle Co., Inc.

nations in the world and our old peaceful, harmonious life is a thing of the past. The basic difference lies in the attitude of a people; whether, like the Burmese, to accept the world as it is, or to try to change it according to one's own designs. Everything hinges on this.

The Burmese, including those who live in cities, still do not wear Western clothes. They wear their traditional loose-fitting robes. Even statesmen active in world politics dress in their native Burmese costume, to avoid losing popularity at home. That is because the Burmese, unlike the Japanese, have remained unchanged. Instead of wishing to master everything through strength or intellect, they aim for salvation through humility and reliance on a power greater than themselves. Thus they distrust people who wear Western clothes, and whose mental attitude is different from their own.

Our argument tended to boil down to this: it depends on how people choose to live—to try to control nature by their own efforts, or yield to it and merge into a broader, deeper order of being. But which of these attitudes, of these ways of life, is better for the world and for humanity? Which should we choose?

One of the men who scorned the Burmese said: "I've never seen such a weak, lazy people. Everything they have, from electric lights to railroad trains, was manufactured for them by some foreign country. They ought to modern-'ize, take off their *longyi*[1] and put on their pants. Even the schools here are only for dramatics or music; there aren't any business or technical schools. They say the level of education is high, but that's compared to the rest of Southeast Asia—all it amounts to are priests teaching the sutras[2] in their temple schools. At this rate the country will go to rack and ruin. No wonder it's a British colony."

Someone objected, saying that exchanging *longyi* for pants wouldn't necessarily bring happiness. "Look at Japan!" he said. "And not only Japan—the whole world is in a mess. When people get conceited and try to impose their will on everything, they're lost. Even if they have a few successes, it's worse in the long run."

"Are you saying it's all right to go on forever being uncivilized, like the Burmese?"

"Uncivilized? Sometimes I think we're not as civilized as they are."

"You're crazy. Do you mean to tell me we're not as civilized as the people of this filthy, backward place, who don't even try to work and educate themselves to stand on their own feet?"

"That's right. We have tools for civilization, but at heart we're still savages who don't know how to use them. What did we do with these tools but wage a gigantic war, and even come all the way here to invade Burma and cause terrible suffering to its people? Yet they accept it and go on living quietly and peacefully. The Burmese never seem to have committed our stupid blunder of

---

1. *Longyi,* loose Burmese pants.—Ed.

2. Sutras, Buddhist scriptures.—Ed.

attacking others. You say they're uneducated, but they believe in Buddhism and govern their whole lives by it. They spend part of their youth as monks, and the way of the Buddha becomes second nature to them. That's why their hearts are serene, why they live at peace. Isn't that a far nobler kind of education?"

"But what about the low standard of living? It isn't fit for a human being. In the first place, their kind of Buddhism doesn't make sense. Abandon the world. Put up with your miseries. Don't worry about whether things are getting better or worse, just concentrate on saving your soul—and salvation comes only after you leave the world and enter a new life as a monk. That's what comes of taking Buddha's words literally, I understand. You get this Hinayana Buddhism[3] in Burma. They all became monks. They're not concerned about the real world. Life on earth seems so insignificant they have no desire to invent new things, and it never occurs to them to try to improve their conditions. They still haven't developed a system that lets everybody live in freedom. Can you call that happiness? At this rate there'll never be any progress."

65
Religion and the State in Modern Japan

The "modern century" the author of the next selection is reflecting on is the hundred years after the Meiji Restoration, from 1868 into the 1970s. In his analysis of this modern period of Japanese history the author is critical of attempts by the state to control and dominate government; he traces the events and policies illustrating these attempts.

In this brief excerpt he focuses on the restoration of the emperor system seen in incidents of the late 1960s and 1970s. By noting the social, economic, and political conditions of these decades he identifies the national and international problems faced by the people and religions in Japan at this time. As a critic of the imperial system and the imperial state, he objects to the movement to renew State Shinto reflected in public actions by members of the imperial family, which in effect speak for the former imperial state. As a critic of state religion, he objects to the "reactionary politics" of legislation "to consider the Yasukuni Shrine as a nonreligious special foundation."

Also reviewed are legislative actions and legal cases that the author claims are instances of "infringement on the principle of the separation of state and religion." These examples may be too brief to enable a reader to reach a clear decision about the relative merits of each case, but at least they afford a good look at some of the legal issues regarding religion and state that will be prominent for some time to come.[1]

---

3. Hinayana Buddhism, the term that Mahayana Buddhists (dominant in Japan) use to describe the monastic Buddhism common to southern Asia.—ED.

1. For an interesting recent description and interpretation of some of these issues, see Norma Fields, *In the Realm of a Dying Emperor* (New York: Vintage Books, 1993).

RELIGION IN JAPAN TODAY

Shigeyoshi Murakami

In the decade or so from the mid-1960s, Japanese society experienced major social change. Japanese capitalism continued to grow at a rapid rate and penetrated the markets of Southeast Asia and then throughout the world. Eventually, the high quality and low prices of Japanese products threatened European and American industries. However, in the 1970s the successive oil crises rocked the economic world, the growth of the Japanese economy suddenly stagnated, and society as a whole suffered from inflation. Japan entered a period of slow economic growth, and a new international environment emerged with the aggravation of relations between China and the Soviet Union, the conclusion of the Vietnam War, and the Japanese and American restoration of relations with China. To cope with this situation, Japan strengthened military and economic ties with South Korea and the United States, and within Japan the trend toward reactionary politics has continued.

The Revival of the Emperor System

The various religions of Japan reflected these changing internal and external conditions and intensified their social and political activities. In October, 1968, the government sponsored the Meiji Centennial celebration honoring the one hundredth anniversary of the Meiji Restoration of 1868. This was analogous to directly linking the contemporary Japanese state of popular sovereignty with the former Japanese empire of imperial sovereignty, and served to strengthen the move to reinstate the earlier imperial state and excuse its aggressive wars. Taking advantage of this opportunity, the movement to restore State Shinto displayed an unprecedented upsurge.

In 1973, the ritual rebuilding of Ise Shrine took place, and Princess Takatsukasa Kazuko, the third daughter of the emperor, served as the temporary chief priestess of Ise. The next year, the emperor and empress made a pilgrimage to Ise Shrine and on that occasion they revived the ritual of *kenji doza*. This is a ritual performed on the occasion of the emperor's travels, when two of the three sacred regalia of the imperial throne, the sword and jewel, accompanied the emperor; this ritual had been abolished after World War II.

In November, 1976, ceremonies honoring the fiftieth anniversary of the emperor's rule were conducted on a grand scale, and the movement to restore the imperial system reached a new stage. In August, 1977, at a summer resort in Nasu, Tochigi Prefecture, the emperor made a public statement in which he denied that in 1946 he had actually disclaimed his divine character and proclaimed his human character. On February 11, 1978, National Foundation Day, for the first time the government encouraged popular celebration rites,

Reprinted by permission of the publisher from Shigeyoshi Murakami, *Japanese Religion in the Modern Century* (Tokyo: University of Tokyo Press, 1980).

and once more made clear its position on commemorating the origin of the imperial state. The same year conservative forces sought legislation on the tradition of maintaining an era name for the duration of an emperor's reign. This problem of era names became the focus of much political conflict.

During this period the movement for state administration of Yasukuni Shrine intensified. In June, 1969, the Liberal Democratic Party presented the Yasukuni Shrine Bill to the Diet. This bill, whose import was to consider the Yasukuni Shrine as a nonreligious special foundation and to place it under the jurisdiction of the prime minister, was an open violation of the Constitution. The driving force behind the movement, religious groups, such as the Association of Shinto Shrines, Seicho no Ie, and Bussho Gonenkai, and also the Survivors' Association, the Goyu Remmei, and right-wing groups, participated in an active nationwide movement for the bill. In opposition to this, peace movements within various religions—Christians; within the new religions, Rissho Koseikai, Perfect Liberty, and Myochikai; and within established Buddhist sects, the Jodo Shinshu Honganji sect and the Shinshu Otani sect—were a broad democratic force which developed into a deep-rooted opposition movement. They held that state administration of Yasukuni Shrine would be a revival of State Shinto and would open the door to the reemergence of Japanese militarism. This bill was presented to the Diet six times before June, 1974, and during this period faced such opposition from citizens at all levels that the bill failed.

In February, 1975, the Liberal Democratic Party made public the concept of the so-called Memorial Respect Proposal and immediately expressed its intention of legislating formal visits to Yasukuni Shrine by such figures as the emperor and prime minister. Formal visits by the emperor and prime minister would mean that Yasukuni Shrine, which is a religious juridical person, is considered to have a national or public status. This constituted a frontal attack on the basic principle of separation of religion and state as determined by the Constitution. In the same year on August 15th, the anniversary of Japan's surrender in World War II, Prime Minister Miki Takeo visited Yasukuni Shrine, the first postwar visit for a prime minister; thereafter it became customary for these de facto official visits by the prime minister to be made. In June, 1976, an association was formed in honor of the souls of the war dead, with the purpose of developing a nationwide people's movement for legislation on official visits to Yasukuni Shrine, and many conservative religious leaders lent their names in support of this cause.

In 1965, in the city of Tsu, Mie Prefecture, city officials used public funds to perform a Shrine Shinto form of ritual called *jichin* (invoking *kami* to bless a building site). A communist member of the Tsu city council brought suit, charging that this was a violation of the Constitution. In court the argument was whether a Shrine Shinto form of *jichin* ritual was a religious act or a common custom. In 1971, the Nagoya High Court ruled that the use of Tsu public funds was a violation of the Constitution. The city of Tsu appealed, and in July, 1977, the Supreme Court laid down its decision that the city of Tsu's action had been constitutional, thus supporting the theory of the nonreligious character of shrines, which in turn was the basis for the argument to restore State Shinto.

The movement to restore State Shinto is based on the religious conscious-ness of the majority of citizens, who accept Shrine Shinto as a public religion, as they did in prewar times. In opposition to this infringement on the princi-ple of the separation of state and religion a counter-movement has developed momentum. This opposition movement has exposed the close connection be-tween shrines and regional public organizations as well as citizens' groups throughout the country.

In 1973, the widow of an official of the Self-Defense Force, who had died while on duty in an automobile accident, sued the state for enshrining her husband in a *gokoku jinja* of Yamaguchi Prefecture. Her litigation claimed that this was a violation of freedom of religion by the state (that is, the Self-De-fense Force), because it was an infringement on the basis principle of the sep-aration of state and religion. In the trial the militaristic character of the *gokoku jinja* and Yasukuni Shrine (which were strong supporters of State Shinto) be-came evident, and the unconstitutional character of state administration of Ya-sukuni Shrine became patently clear.

66
Religious Values in a White-Collar Workplace

In any country, at any historical point, the activities of religion are not confined to the official times, places, and persons of organized religion. Religious activities and religious values may also be present in the lives of laypersons in their homes and daily occupations. In this selection the author describes the ideology, worldview, and ceremonies of a modern Japanese bank (called here Uedagin); such actions and values are either directly or indirectly religious.

In an earlier selection (see p. 73) Japanese Buddhism was viewed as patterned after the family system; in the present selection, the bank Uedagin is considered as a kind of larger family with its own value system based upon Japanese values in gen-eral. "One of the richest ceremonial events" of this bank is the ceremony of joining the company; when joining the bank the new recruits chant Confucian-style values and become "adult members of society." In other words, this entrance ceremony is like a rite of passage. The bank president promises the parents of the new employ-ees that he will take responsibility for these recent additions to the bank family.

This bank has a yearly round of ceremonies, including a memorial service for de-ceased members. The ideology (a set of "ideas and ideals") of this bank family is spelled out explicitly in this anthropologist's analysis and interpretation. The fact that Uedagin does not make such an explicit and logical statement of its ideology is prob-ably due to the fact that its values of strength and harmony are assumed by the peo-ple joining it. The sacrifice of individual preferences for group unity in a hierarchical organism is the heart of this ideology. The author concludes that harmony, or *wa,* is typical of most Japanese companies: "*Wa* is undoubtedly the single most popular component in the mottos and names of companies across Japan."

Obviously this ideology is given here in its ideal form, and the Western reader may be skeptical of the use (or abuse) of religious values by managers to encourage more work out of subordinates, but the argument here is that the analogies and metaphors of this ideology derive from the daily life of such entities as families and schools. This is a good example of how philosophical, ethical, and religious values and ceremonies have been employed in a commercial setting.[1]

SONGS, CEREMONIES, AND THE UEDAGIN IDEOLOGY

Thomas P. Rohlen

Japanese companies of all sizes and activities pay considerable attention to the philosophy that serves as the official explanation of their enterprise. No one in Japanese business would be so naive as to deny the centrality of economic goals and motives, but this does not detract from the significance of official ideals and interpretations within each organization. In Uedagin, not only is there a general requirement for common direction and meaning, many informants indicate that the bank's philosophy is useful because it enhances the satisfaction of work by establishing a sense of joint effort and shared value. To these ends company leaders expend considerable effort to enunciate a world view that is acceptable, inspiring, and a bit unique.

By the term ideology is meant the public, official expression of the ideas and ideals that define Uedagin as a social enterprise, provide its goals, explain the relationship of its personnel to the bank, and define the relationship of the bank to the rest of society. The major responsibility for the maintenance of this ideology rests with the top leaders, the staff of the training institute, those in charge of the company magazine, and the people who arrange company ceremonial meetings. There is no paucity of material of an ideological nature available, but most of it is scattered, fragmentary, and coded in both verbal and nonverbal form. Our task, therefore, is to seek the composite, underlying structure of its message.

Reprinted by permission of the publisher from Thomas P. Rohlen, *For Harmony and Strength: Japanese White-Collar Organization in Anthropological Perspective* (Berkeley: University of California Press, 1979). The notes have been deleted.

1. For a popular presentation of *wa* in the context of Japanese baseball, see Robert Whiting, *You Gotta Have Wa* (New York: Macmillan, 1989).

The Ceremony of Joining the Company

Let us begin by considering in detail one of the richest ceremonial events, the *nyukoshiki* (literally "entering-bank-ceremony") in which new recruits are officially recognized as members. There are two of these each year, one for women and one for men. It is the latter which we will follow point by point. Without exception all new men who are accepted as members have just graduated from high school or university, and at the time of the ceremony they are in the process of undergoing a rigorous three-month introductory training.

Three groups of participants are involved: the top officers of the bank, the new recruits together with their instructors, and as many parents of the recruits as can attend. The first group, some fifteen or twenty senior men, sit on the stage of the company's large auditorium. The new men, 120 of them in 1969, sit in the front rows of the audience. The parents, well over one hundred in number, sit behind their sons toward the rear of the auditorium. All the men wear dark business suits, and the mothers are dressed quite formally in either kimono or Western attire. Most of the new recruits have fresh haircuts.

As the time for the ceremony approaches everyone has taken his assigned seat except the president, whose conspicuously more comfortable chair at the front of the stage remains empty. Hanging above the stage are the company and Japanese flags and a large banner of congratulations. The president's arrival is the signal that the event may begin. Over to one side, the chief of the personnel section states the name of the ceremony and the year and then announces the company song. Everyone stands and new and old members sing [the company song, praising the bank and its "productive people"]. . . .

They remain standing to recite in unison the "Uedagin Principles" (*Uedagin koryo*) . . . :

> Possessing a spirit of love for Uedagin, we pledge to plan for the prosperity of the bank and for the public welfare and to make the bank the greatest in Japan.

And finally, before sitting down, a second catechism is recited, this one known as the "President's Teachings" (*shachokun*).

> Harmony (*wa*). The bank is our lifelong place of work, let us make it a pleasant place, starting with our greetings to each other each morning.
>
> Sincerity (*seijitsu*). Sincerity is the foundation of trust, let us deal with our customers with a serious and earnest attitude.
>
> Kindness (*shinsetsu*). Have a warm heart. Be scrupulously kind.
>
> Spirit (*tamashii*). Putting our heart and soul into it, let us work with all our strength.
>
> Unity (*danketsu*). Strong unity is the source of energy for our business.
>
> Responsibility (*sekinin*). Responsibility makes rights possible; first let us develop responsibility.
>
> Originality (*soi*). In addition, let us think creatively and advance making each day a new day.

Purity *(seiketsu)*. Have a noble character and proper behavior.

Health *(kenko)*. With ever growing pride let us fulfill the Uedagin dream. . . .

[Various people give speeches.] The president is the next to speak. Representing the rest of the bank, he expresses gratitude that such a fine group of young people are joining the organization. He thanks the parents in the audience for raising such excellent young people. (Many of the parents bow silently in their seats as he says this.) Then in a rambling manner, since he has no prepared speech, the president discusses the history of the bank, the difficulties of contemporary competition, and the problems facing the nation. The stage is set for his direct admonition to the new members.

They are now *shakaijin,* "adult members of society," he says. This means they have heavy responsibilities to serve the society and thus to repay it and their parents for the nurture and sacrifice of raising them from infancy. His tone grows more impassioned as he proceeds to outline the seriousness of working for the bank.

In contrast to life as a student, working in society brings us face to face with reality each day. That reality is, first, the necessity to work, and, second, the fact that no one is going to care for us. We must care for ourselves. Therefore our decision must be to make the steady progress of our work one of our great lifelong values.

As a shakaijin working in this organization you are expected to fulfill your individual responsibilities as well as you can, for the prosperity of each of us depends on the prosperity of the bank. . . .

Finally, addressing the parents, he promises to take responsibility for their children, to educate and care for them, that they may continue to grow as shakaijin.

The president makes speeches of this sort frequently and the themes become repetitious after the third or fourth hearing, yet the man's involvement in what he is saying and his deep personal commitment to the success of the bank remain fresh and at times truly inspiring. He is a large man of impressive posture and energy, yet delivering this speech he has grown so emotional that his voice has broken off and tears have streamed down his face.

The master of ceremonies next calls on the representative of the parents, who walks to the platform and stands before the president. He first expresses the parents' pleasure with the company their children are joining and offers their good wishes for its success. The parents from now on will support the bank's business whenever possible. He requests that the bank discipline and guide their offspring, who are "yet immature and naive." The parents have brought them this far, he says, it is now the bank which must continue their upbringing. During this brief address the president is also standing, a sign of respect.

When the parents' representative has returned to his seat, the master of ceremonies calls the roll of new members, reading their names and the school from which they have just graduated. As his name is called, each stands and bows with great formality. The president and other leaders nod in response. The list is ordered not alphabetically nor by region, but rather by the status of the schools—national university graduates are first and distant high schools last.

The president again stands to listen to the address by the representative of the new men. . . .

> We regard the bank as our life and our career. We are committed to battle with all our strength under the banner and spirit of "harmony and strength." We will trust and aid each other as we face the difficulties before us. We will take our responsibilities seriously, and feel joy in the bank's good name. We are young and as yet spiritually and technically underdeveloped. We ask our seniors to lead and educate us, for we know it is imperative that we become hardy and brave Uedagin men, possessing a spirit of devotion and a capacity for sharp, effective action. . . .

[Everyone sits down and begins eating.] Polite conversation ensues. As people are finishing up, the president moves to the microphone to offer his congratulations. He then concludes the program by leading everyone (now standing) in three hearty banzai cheers for the long life and success of Uedagin.

Comment on Uedagin Ceremonies

The bank has numerous such ceremonies throughout the year, and most of them take place in its plush auditorium—perhaps the finest in the city—which holds about four hundred people. The following is a list of the major regularly scheduled ceremonies:

1. New Year's Ceremony (January)
2. Entrance Ceremony for New Women (April)
3. Branch Chiefs' Conference (April)
4. Award Ceremonies (April and November)
5. Entrance Ceremony for New Men (May)
6. Memorial Service for Deceased Members (June)
7. Graduation Ceremony for Class of Entering Men (July)
8. Summer Camp Out (August)
9. Boost Deposits Conference (August)
10. Retired Members' Association Meeting (October)
11. Brief End of Year Ceremony (December)
12. Uedagin Beauty Circle General Meetings (quarterly)
13. Uedagin Junior General Meetings (quarterly) . . .

The Ideology Summarized

It is necessary for us as outsiders to Japan and to Uedagin to make the structure underlying all of this explicit. The interpretation that follows is mine, based on the numerous fragments collected, such as the above entrance ceremony.

> The way work is organized is the same as the organization of the body. A variety of people with different functions are put together as an interdependent whole. If everyone does his job well the organization begins to operate successfully and this allows each person to improve his ability even more. In school, where grades were an individual matter, you could get out of doing your work without causing trouble for others, but in banking, if one person is slow or lazy it causes everyone else inconvenience and their work declines as a result. Work is a living thing. Behind the superficial appearances of simplicity lies the living reality of society.

Taking a cue from this explanation offered to new members by a director of the bank, we may summarize the various themes of the Uedagin ideology as forming a conception of the bank and of Japanese society as integrated and hierarchical organisms with all constituent parts (individuals and institutions) interrelated and interdependent. The story of the kingdom lost for want of a nail expresses the same view, for it too presents a picture of a functionally unified system containing levels of ascending integration. Instead of the nails in the shoe of the horse of the knight, the Uedagin view of society begins with individuals, who are workers, related directly to institutions such as Uedagin, which are, in turn, part of the larger society. If the workers are married men, their families are also included. Starting from the bottom we find families dependent on workers who themselves are dependent for jobs on some company. These relationships are hierarchical, but they are also reciprocal, for the worker depends on his family, and the company depends on the worker. Relationships at the higher level of institutional integration are also matters of interdependence. The company succeeds only if the national system succeeds, and the nation depends on the contribution of companies. As long as each constituent element fulfills its tasks, the entire scheme can be expected to operate smoothly. Production is efficiently organized upwards, and this provides sustenance that flows downward to the worker and family levels.

Competition is between companies, rather than individuals, and international competition is clearly recognized as threatening the total Japanese system.

This simple and not unusual conception of society lies at the heart of the entire Uedagin world view. It is in the Confucian tradition (a point we will take up shortly), except in its lack of emphasis on the family. Instead, it elevates the company's importance as the key organizational focus between individuals and the national polity. Let us note a number of logical extensions based on this assumption of organic unity. First, there is no conflict of interest between levels of the system. Individual interests are inextricably interrelated with institutional and national interests, and only institutions are in direct competition. Second, because the hierarchy is reciprocal and levels are interdependent, there is no reason to assume that it is inherently tyrannical or exploitative. Third, institutions have an implied responsibility for the welfare of their workers, just as the government has a responsibility for the welfare of constituent institutions. Finally role fulfillment is a moral duty of individuals and institutions alike. . . .

Statements of the ideology are never so explicit or logical as the foregoing account. To be effective, that is, to be reasonably acceptable and hopefully even inspirational, the presentation of the ideology must depend on a set of images more tangible and closer to the important moral sentiments of daily Japanese life. Thus, most messages of an ideological nature revolve around analogies and metaphors that derive not from bank work, but from the daily life of families, schools, and the like.

Uedagin is at times referred to as "one great family" *(daikazoku)*. The implications of this image are extensive. First, the bank, like the ideal Japanese family, is an entity in which the interests of members are secondary to the interests of the family as a whole. It is everyone's duty to work for the well-being and reputation of the family, and in return the family exists for the benefit of all its members. The same relationship holds, by implication, between workers and the bank. . . .

Closely related is the highly valued quality of social concord, most often expressed by the term *wa*. The bank's motto is *wa to chikara* ("harmony and strength"), and the assignment of *wa* to the "President's Teachings" illustrates its preeminent position in a list of values. The term is also to be found in descriptions of the pleasures of company recreational outings, and the New Year's greetings from some offices (which the company magazine publishes) show individual pictures of the staff grouped around the character *wa* written large in the center of the design. Nor is Uedagin at all unusual in this emphasis. *Wa* is undoubtedly the single most popular component in the mottos and names of companies across Japan.

67
Religious Values in a
Blue-Collar Workplace

Religious values and activities are present at blue-collar workplaces as well as white-collar ones such as a bank. The following author describes workers in a brewery and in a confectionery who use religious values to understand their work. Although in the West factory work is often seen as a dehumanizing situation of alienation, these workers view themselves not only in harmony with fellow workers but also in harmony with their machines: "machines were extensions of themselves as spiritual beings, as creators of things, things of high quality."

The Japanese "penchant for humanizing the machine" may be related to the fact that in Japan *kami* may inhabit both animate and inanimate objects. When a new piece of machinery is installed, such as the boiler for the confectionery factory, a Shinto ritual of purification readied the new boiler. At New Year's, this boiler is honored with offerings, the same way that traditional artisans give thanks or gratitude to their tools.

The author's conclusion is that tools and machinery are not inevitably forerunners of alienation because they can also be used in the artistic act of creating. A Westerner may be suspicious of the use of these religious values in the workplace, but obviously they can only be effective if they mirror some values and activities in the society at large. In fact, Japanese ritual may even sanctify borrowing from the West. In a scene that is typical of modern Japan, the author recalls a film in which the opening ceremony for a Kentucky Fried Chicken franchise is conducted by a Shinto priest who purifies the shop before the first customers enter. Whether in a white-collar or blue-collar setting, or in the service industry of fast food, purification and ceremony are equally appropriate.

WORK: ARTISANS AND MACHINES

Dorinne K. Kondo

The artisanal idiom of work depends on the interconnectedness of persons and the material world. Artisans gracefully transform nature, and there can be a relationship of respect, a kind of cooperation, among human beings, their materials, and their tools. For example, Tanoue-san, the woodworker, used to talk of the *kosei,* the unique characteristics, of each piece of wood. "Traditional" artisans like Tanoue-san worked with simple, hand-held tools and a mechanical lathe, creating objects of great simplicity and beauty, objects we have come to associate with a distinctively Japanese aesthetic. In this setting, perhaps it is not surprising to find a relationship of respect and mutuality among artisans, their tools, and their materials.

Yet even in more "industrial" workplaces I found similar discourses. Another neighbor, Mr. Fukuzawa, was a *puresuyasan,* the maker of plastic accessories, including Snoopy and Hello Kitty. His small, dark workplace and the incessant clanking of the press hardly seemed the stuff of enthusiasm or romance. On the contrary, however, he spoke animatedly about the pleasures of his work. He was always trying to work *with the machine,* to do his work more quickly, more cleanly. What seemed to me like drudgery represented to Fukuzawa-san a testament to his ingenuity and creativity. And again, the machine was not an instrument of alienation, but something with which he could cooperate in the production of a fine object.

This mutual affinity between human being and machine can be seen in even more apparently atomized, industrial contexts. Lest readers think this

Reprinted by permission of the publisher from Dorinne K. Kondo, *Crafting Selves: Power, Gender, and Discourses of Identity in a Japanese Workplace* (Chicago: University of Chicago Press, 1990). The notes have been deleted.

affinity is a function only of the size of the workplace, I quote extensively from the unpublished field notes of Matthews Hamabata, who, in his research on large family enterprises, *dozoku gaisha,* visited a brewery that manufactured a well-known variety of Japanese liquor. This particular factory was viewed as a model for all other breweries owned by the company; from conception and design to management techniques, it was the most efficient and productive in the chain. Even here, or perhaps especially here, there is a close relationship between men—the gendered term is used intentionally—and their machines, for the machines are considered extensions of human beings. The factory drew upon its symbolic fund of "traditional craftsmanship," displaying on the walls, above the metallic glint of the machines, artisanal tools from various historical periods. Again, they consciously invoked the legacy of the craftsman, seen as creating himself in his products, as a direct precursor of the present-day artisans. The invocation seemed to work.

> The odd thing is: all three managers felt that there was a special spiritual presence in all of their machines; and they stressed over and over again that their major concern was the maintenance of their machines. . . . But it wasn't a love of machinery as machinery, but of machinery as some kind of spiritual extension of themselves: *kikai o migakeba, kokoro mo migakimasu* (if you polish the machines, you're also polishing your heart). . . . For them, machines were extensions of themselves as spiritual beings, as creators of things, things of high quality. Quality was their main goal, . . . quality over speed and productivity. At any rate, there is a connectedness between men and machines, not only between men and men; there is a constant transcending of the self to create a beautiful product, a community product. . . .

The penchant for humanizing the machine implies that human beings and machines partake of the same world, and that people are intimately identified with the process of production, for the very machines they use in creating their products—even if the product is made on an assembly line—can be thought of as parts of themselves. The quality of the product reflects on its maker. The worker has many avenues, then, for identifying with the product: through his skill, through the machine that helped produce it, and through the product itself, as a creation of both a particular individual and a larger company community. Thus machines both partake of the human world and, through their use in the work process, provide one of the ways human beings reaffirm their connectedness to one another. By cooperating in the creation of a product, the artisans Hamabata describes can reaffirm their social identities. Far from contributing to alienation, artisans like these at the brewery and Ohara-san in the confectionery factory can find satisfaction in their connectedness to nature, tools, and machines.

This notion may seem less difficult to accept when placed within a particular religious and cultural context. In Japan, Shinto spirits, *kami,* may inhabit both what we would call animate and inanimate objects. Trees, rocks, waterfalls, and other natural formations can be imbued with *kami* and are sometimes worshipped as sacred. *Kami* may also reside in the workplace and in tools that workers use. Perhaps this close interrelationship was most evident in the factory on ritual occasions. During the dedication of the new Sato factory, a Shinto ritual of purification readied the *kama*, or boiler, for its new home—for workplaces and homes are always purified by Shinto priests before business begins as usual. One of the most interesting examples occurs in the film "The Colonel Comes to Japan," by John Nathan. In one of the scenes at the opening ceremony for a new Kentucky Fried Chicken franchise, a Shinto priest in full regalia brandishes his sacred staff, purifying the shop, before the ribbon is cut and the expectant crowds pour in. The New Year provides occasion for more ritual acknowledgement of cooperation among human beings, tools, and machines. At the confectionery, the center of the factory was the *kama*, or boiler. Here one could find the New Year's display of *omochi* (rice cakes) topped by a *mikan* (mandarin orange). Artisans like Tanoue-san also make a New Year's display in their workrooms, to indicate their gratitude to their tools. Artisans give thanks to the machines for aid in the previous year, and make requests for the same benevolence in the coming year: the same New Year's greeting they would give to their bosses, their friends, and their customers. Tools and machines can, then, participate in the human domain; they can even be invested with a certain spirituality or life force.

Becoming a full-fledged artisan and a full-fledged human being at the workplace means engaging with the world in a particular way, cultivating a close relationship between men—again, I use the gendered term intentionally—and the material and natural worlds. Solidarity is created between men and the world, and between men and men: those who share this engagement with tools, materials, and the seasons.

Clearly, we cannot dismiss the evident enthusiasm of the artisans as mere sham, bad faith, or false consciousness. Though we (specialists in "mental" work, accustomed to thinking of machines as instruments of drudgery and alienation) may find a combination of aesthetics, spirituality, and industrial work odd, it may not be so in every culture. Machines and tools are not necessarily harbingers of alienation, for they can also be instruments of artistic creation. The enthusiasm and poetry animating these tales demand to be taken seriously as integral components of a mature artisanal identity.

Yet locating these romantic tales in the contexts of their telling should begin to arouse our suspicions. Ohara-san was talking to a foreign researcher and a woman at that, trying to convince me of the value of his work and displaying his artisanal/masculine prowess. The brewery managers were in a similar position as representatives of an exemplary factory. Surely under these circumstances they, too, would accentuate their romantic connections to work, and their invocations of an artisanal ethos through the display of artisanal tools was certainly a reinvention and appropriation of tradition. Such stories also lead us to another series of questions: How are idioms of romantic connectedness and participation implicated in relations of power in particular situations? Do all workers share this same vision of work? And what of the potential ambiguities in even a single tale? Does even Ohara-san feel connected and fulfilled in his work all of the time?

68
Christmas: A Modern Japanese Festival

Americans may be surprised to find Christmas used as an example of a modern festival in Japan. The surprise is twofold: first, we know that fewer than 1 percent of the Japanese population belongs to institutional Christianity; second, Christmas is not usually seen as an example of modernity and democracy. One point that the writer makes is that the Japanese celebration of Christmas is a symbolic form borrowed from the West to express her modernity. Toward the end of this selection, the writer argues that the Japanese, like other "modern" people, are no longer sure what constitutes their tradition. In this uncertain atmosphere, Christmas has been accepted along with other modern importations, such as decorated cakes.

A Westerner may object that what has been borrowed is only the external form of Christmas—above all, the commercial trappings. This should remind us that the commercial, musical, and familial aspects of Christmas cannot be so easily divorced from specifically religious meanings. Christmas is modern partly because it is tied up with the consumer world of department stores and seasonal sales. Christmas is democratic partly because Christmas parties allow men and women to celebrate together, something they could not do in the ordinary Japanese seasonal parties. It also seems significant that most of the Christmas lore is borrowed from America, not Europe—more evidence of America's world influence.

This scholar emphasizes that traditions are not just passive agents but are active forces that help a people restate themselves, and "the American popular Christmas is one such self-restatement." It is also worth noting that the form of restatement is that of a festival—festivals have always been an important part of Japanese religious life. (For other examples of festivals see Chapter 13.)

CHRISTMAS IN JAPAN

David W. Plath

Many peoples today are scanning Western cultures in search not only of ways to become modern, but also of ways to cope with living in a modern milieu. They seek not only the institutional forms of modernity; they seek as well those symbolic forms that can make modernity a meaningful way of life. American popular culture has generated a number of such symbolic forms: one need only instance the global popularity of cowboy movies, jazz, or Disneyland. Likewise the American popular Christmas—the cult of Santa Claus, trees, reindeer, presents, and so on—which emerged under modern condi-

Reprinted by permission of the author and publisher from David W. Plath,
"The Japanese Popular Christmas: Coping with Modernity," *Journal of American Folklore* 76 (1963): 309–317.

tions, and which is being widely adopted outside the United States as part of the modern style. To judge from newspaper reports and from the evidence assembled by James Barnett, scarcely a nation today fails to contain at least a few citizens who celebrate the annual visit of Santa. The Japanese have been doing so, with growing enthusiasm, for nine decades; and the popular observance of Christmas has come to be a Japanese commonplace. . . .

Today Christmas is celebrated throughout the Japanese islands. In some urban shopping centers the decorations are up by mid-November; and news commentators quip about "instant Christians" who flock to the Ginza bars on Christmas Eve. In the rural areas as well there are youth-group parties and household gift-exchanges. A survey I conducted in central Nagano prefecture in 1960 found that (1) approximately half of the households in the sample, rural as well as urban, have a home Christmas celebration, and that (2) Christmas is the only holiday in a list of more than two dozen that has gained a significant number of adherents since the war.

In describing the present-day celebration I will focus upon the Anchiku region of central Nagano prefecture, with glances to the wider national scene. My materials derive from fieldwork in Anchiku in 1959–60.

Christmas Day is not a legal holiday in Japan, as it is in the United States. Work and school-work are not vacated on its account, at least not in Anchiku, although I have heard of Tokyo schools that begin their "New Year's vacation" in time for Christmas. In other words, Christmas activities take place after the day's work is done.

Interestingly enough, though, recent proposals for doubling the number of national holidays include a new holiday for December 25th. It would be known as "International Goodwill Day"—an inspiration that prompted several newspapers to wonder whether such a gesture would be regarded as international goodwill by people in Islamic and Buddhist nations. Again, Christmas usually is listed in calendars issued by Shinto and Buddhist organizations in Japan, which apparently do not interpret it as a religious threat.

Note that the date is December 25th. This is, of course, Anglo-American usage, in contrast to other usages such as the Dutch Christmas on December 5th. Christmas thus falls within the traditional Japanese year-end holiday season, and it is bracketed by the winter solstice on the one side and by New Year's Eve on the other. Historically there has been no major Japanese holiday on the 25th. . . .

Christmas comes early enough so that it does not interfere in a crippling way with household preparations for the New Year. The only persons seriously bothered are storekeepers and their salespeople, who by mid-December are embroiled in year-end bargain sales. Christmas also comes close on the heels of the solstice observance, and most Anchiku households still honor the day, usually by preparing a dish of "solstice squash" *(toji no kabocha)*.

In the downtown stores and streets of Tokyo or Osaka the decorative trees, Santas, angels, and candy canes are every bit as gigantic as in Chicago or San Francisco. Not only that; in Tokyo I have seen them torn down on December 26th and at once replaced by equally gigantic decorations heralding the remaining few days of the year-end sale. In Anchiku, however, decor is more restrained. Supermarkets, bakeries, department stores, and such display a small evergreen and perhaps a few paper streamers with "Merry Christmas" blazoned upon them in Roman letters and in Japanese syllabary. But street decor is limited to the year-end bargains.

The dramas and readings that are a familiar part of the American popular celebration—Dickens, Menotti, Clement Moore—are rarely heard in Japan. But the topic of Santa Claus is frequently encountered on children's radio and TV programs in December, and Christmas music is inescapable. Choral societies offer Christmas concerts. And the shopping arcades, the department stores, the commercial broadcasters, all pour out floods of recorded carols. One missionary reports that Japanese Christians carol in the streets, although I did not encounter this in Anchiku. But for many families, playing recorded carols on the phonograph is a regular part of the family Christmas gathering. To my informants, the loan-word carol *(karoru)* includes such ecclesiastical songs as "White Christmas," "Jingle Bells," and "Rudolph the Red-Nosed Reindeer."

Christmas cards are used, but only sparingly, by American standards. School children often exchange them. They are of course appropriate to send to one's Western friends and acquaintances, but they are felt to be rather frivolous for ordinary adult intercourse; they cannot, for example, take the place of the New Year postcards. The latter are exchanged much the same as Christmas cards are exchanged in the U.S., and most families devote a good deal of time, money, and thought to them.

The Christmas tree also has a New Year's competitor. This is the "gate-pine" *(kadomatsu)* seen before nearly every Anchiku house from late December until mid-January. Gate-pine decor varies over a wide range; some families put up elaborate clusters of 10-foot firs and 25-foot bamboos, others merely paste on the doorpost a sheet of paper with a pine tree printed upon it. By contrast, Christmas trees usually are set up inside, and are sparsely decorated. The tree has fared somewhat better in competition than the card, and many families set up pine decor both for Christmas and separately for New Year's (a doubly unproductive use of precious timber which becomes a handy target for the complaints of literal-minded conservationists).

Christmas parties are held both by instrumental and by expressive social groups. These parties are a syncretism with "closing-the-year parties" *(bonenkai)* long customary in December. But a *bonenkai* tends to be a man's affair, with *sake,* group singing, and displays of masculine affection. Only professional women are allowed in the room: waitresses, geisha, entertainers. The Christmas party, on the other hand, provides a role for "proper" women. There is social dancing in place of the music of samisens, and often port wine is served rather than *sake.* Understandably enough, the Christmas party tends to be more favored than the *bonenkai* in heterosexual groups such as office staffs, or the employees of a department store, or village youth clubs, This is one reason why some Japanese see Christmas as democratic.

Democracy also is read into the exchange of Christmas gifts. In many households, Christmas gifts are distributed even though New Year's gifts (*toshidama,* literally "year-jewel") are given to the same persons a week later. Because of the duplication, some families have elected to give only on one of the two occasions. New Year's gifts go unilaterally from the head of a household to its junior members: children of course, but also servants and apprentices if any. In many Anchiku households, Christmas presents follow the same channels. However, some families are aware of the American conception of an "exchange" of presents from every individual to every individual, and in these households gifts are given multilaterally. This kind of attention to the individual also seems democratic to some. . . .

Family Christmas foregatherings do not center around dinner, as in the American ideal, but rather upon mutual partaking of a Christmas cake. Many Anchiku housewives do indeed prepare "something different" *(kawatta mono)* for the Christmas meal, but this is just as likely to be raw fish or a rice curry as it is to be a Western dish. A few white-collar wives bake a chicken, but turkey is not available in Anchiku.

The Christmas cake also is called a "decoration cake" (*dekoreshon keki,* a loan word), emphasizing its ridges and waves of thick frosting. The cake almost always is purchased, and in the cities some bakeries prepare a supply of cakes early in December and quick-freeze them until the sales demand mounts. In the Anchiku village where I lived, a local confectioner—who prepared only Japanese-style sweets—served as agent for an urban baker, and distributed mimeographed order blanks early in December. Decorated cake is not an item in the usual American popular Christmas, although we do have our fruitcakes and cookies of various derivations. So perhaps the precedent here is European, although none of the European forms I know of seems to correspond exactly with the Japanese form.

Parents, peers, teachers, and the mass media collaborate to inform the young about Santa Claus and his visit. The stockings can not be hung by a fireplace in the typical Japanese house, so most parents place the presents by the children's pillows during the night. Some of the more literal-minded transfer Clement Moore's chimney motif to its closest Japanese counterpart, the pipe for the bathtub stove. And the stockings are hung by the bathtub with care. (The Japanese word *entotsu* is a generic for many forms of waste-gas conveying tube that are distinguished in English as chimney, smokestack, stovepipe, and so on.)

The Japanese Santa Claus robes himself in the familiar red-and-white garment attributed to the nineteenth century American illustrator Thomas Nast. Thus arrayed, he appears in advertisements or is impersonated in the streets, either standing by Salvation Army kettles or carrying placards announcing the opening of a new pinball parlor.

. . . Milton Singer epitomizes our present-day awareness of the active as well as the passive side of tradition. Traditions, he says, "are, ordinarily, the things that we take for granted, the unquestioned assumptions and the handed-down ways of our ancestors. But it has become a commonplace of modern history that even the most traditional societies are no longer sure of what it is they can take for granted. Confronted by swift currents of internal and external change, they have been compelled to restate themselves to themselves in order to discover what they have been and what it is they are to become." The American popular Christmas is one such self-restatement. Like any expressive form it defies reduction to formulae. Like any dramatic form it defies easy verbal explanation, for it deals with conditions in which (to borrow Suzanne Langer's dictum) apprehension outruns comprehension. And yet, although some of its components hold long pedigrees in Western lore, they have been creatively reassembled under modern conditions. Although some of its themes are pan-human, their configuration seems peculiarly apt in the modern milieu. One could scarcely argue otherwise in the face of massive evidence for the growing popularity of the event not only here where it was developed, but also among many peoples overseas. . . .

Overseas the spread of a popular Christmas celebration to so many peoples such as the Japanese can scarcely be explained away by once-prevalent notions of non-western imitativeness (an attribute once especially projected upon the Japanese). The popular Christmas seems to offer to many peoples one means, however small, for making sense of life in a modern milieu. And if the Japanese are somewhat more captivated by the Santa Claus cult than other non-western peoples, this would seem no more than correlate with the recognized extent of Japan's modernity.

The modern milieu differs for different peoples, and in this regard, American and Japanese justifications of the popular Christmas stress different aspects of it. Japanese tend to see its democratic tenor; Americans tend to see its implications of material well-being. (This in the context of many aspects stressed by both peoples: the happy family gathering, doing nice things for children, and so on.)